The Two Great Mysteries of the Cheyennes

SWEET MEDICINE

THE CIVILIZATION OF THE AMERICAN INDIAN SERIES

PETER J. POWELL

SWEET MEDICINE

The Continuing Role of the Sacred
Arrows, the Sun Dance, and the
Sacred Buffalo Hat in Northern
Cheyenne History Volume One

UNIVERSITY OF OKLAHOMA PRESS : NORMAN

THE FRONTISPIECE

The Two Great Mysteries of the Cheyennes

This painting by Dick West, Southern Cheyenne, is in the author's collection.

The charge of the Sacred Arrows and the Buffalo Hat against the enemy. A Kit Fox warrior, bearing Mahuts tied to one of the society's bow lances, leads the way. An elk Society scalp short owner wears Is'siwun. The tip of the horn of a pronghorn antelope hangs around the neck of his pony. This "horse medicine" gave the pony power for speed and endurance and protected the horse from stepping into a prairie dog hole or stumbling in battle. This charge of the two Great Mysteries rendered the enemy blinded and helpless.

ISBN 0-8061-3028-8

3   4   5   6   7   8   9   10   11   12

Contents

Part I

The Two Great Mysteries and Northern Cheyenne
History, 1830–1880

Part II

New Battles to be Fought: Episodes from the
1880–1965 Era

Illustrations

SWEET MEDICINE

RETURN TO THE SACRED MOUNTAIN

MAP

Acknowledgments

Mari Sandoz first encouraged me to write this book. She introduced me to the Northern Cheyennes. Then she approached various foundations on my behalf. She was unfailingly generous in opening up new sources of research material for me—including her own files. I never cease to thank her for giving me both the vision and the means whereby this book became a reality.

At Mari Sandoz's death, Caroline Sandoz Pifer, her sister, became executrix of her estate. I am grateful to Mrs. Pifer for many courtesies involving the use of Mari's notes and letters.

To Alice Marriott and Carol Rachlin, I owe more thanks than the most eloquent words could express. They introduced me to

Mary Inkanish, as well as to the Pawnees. Their wisdom and encouragement have sustained me all along the way. Their house is the place of warmth, laughter, and knowledge that is "home" in Oklahoma City.

The Pawnee people were more than open-hearted. I owe a special debt of gratitude to Blanche Matlock, the late Lucy Tilden, Bessie Matlock Horsechief, Mr. and Mrs. Adam Pratt, and Dolly Moore.

A Rockefeller Foundation grant for field work and a Bollingen Foundation Fellowship for recording the sacred ceremonies financed most of my reservation research. Both foundations supplied the means for studying archival materials. Phelps-Stokes Fund, through Arrow, Inc., supplied money for early field research. Professor Fred Eggan, Department of Anthropology, University of Chicago, dipped into his own funds to see me through a crucial summer of field work in 1959.

Savoie Lottinville joined Alice Marriott and Mari Sandoz in sponsoring me in my applications to the foundations. His faith in this book and his graciousness in telling me of it carried me through many a frustrating period of writing.

My ordinary, Right Reverend Gerald Francis Burrill, D.D., bishop of Chicago, and the late Right Reverend Charles L. Street, Ph.D., bishop suffragan of Chicago, kindly granted permission for the extended weeks of field work that took me away from my cure.

In Chicago, Colton Storm, former curator of Special Collections and curator of the Ayer Collection of Newberry Library, went far out of his way to be of assistance. Matt Lowman II, the present curator, has carried on that tradition. So have Charles Eubanks, Michael Kaplan, and John Aubrey, past and present members of the Newberry staff.

Margaret Blaker, archivist, National Anthropological Archives, Smithsonian Institution, sacrificed many spare hours locating photographic and manuscript material for me. The same was true of Rella Looney, archivist of the Indian Archives Division of the Oklahoma Historical Society, assisted by Dorothy

Williams, former librarian of the same organization. Julio Perez, Carmelita Ryan, and Roy Wilgus of the National Archives were equally kind. Marvin Kivett and Donald Danker were of great assistance while I worked at the Nebraska Historical Society. Vance E. Nelson, curator of the Fort Robinson Museum, was most helpful in locating information concerning the Cheyenne imprisonment there. Richard Williams, interpretive specialist at Bear Butte State Park, was an invaluable source of knowledge concerning Cheyenne visits to the Sacred Mountain. The late George E. Hyde supplied numerous details relating to his correspondence with George Bent.

Maurice Frink, former director of the Colorado State Historical Society, has been my constant mentor, both in writing and research. Elizabeth Lochrie, Montana's noted artist of Indian life, added her encouragement and introduced me to the Cheyennes' neighboring tribes. Thomas and Marva Belden of Bethesda, Maryland, generously opened their home to me throughout many a long Washington visit. Fred Rosenstock of Denver and Wright and Zoe Howes of Chicago acquired numerous manuscripts and volumes relating to the Cheyennes for me.

Harry Anderson, director of the Milwaukee Historical Society; Donald Collier, chief curator, Department of Anthropology, Field Museum of Natural History; John Gray, chairman, Department of Physiology, Northwestern University Medical School; Don Russell, author of many books on Western history; Sol Tax, professor of anthropology, University of Chicago; James Van Stone, associate curator of North American Archaeology and Ethnology at the Field Museum; all have been extremely helpful in reading sections of the manuscript or in discussing it with me.

Almost the entire community of Big Horn, Wyoming, had some hand in this book. Ken and Emmie Mygatt opened their hearts and their home to me, beginning with my first summer at Lame Deer and continuing to this day. Harry and Margaret Fulmer, Carlo and Beatrice Beuf, Dean and Alida Sage, Wendell, Wyla, Marion Loomis, the Victor Garber family—all left their latch strings out so that this book might be written both summer and winter. When I was not off with my Cheyenne relatives, Randall and Louise Alexander of Lame Deer made me one of their family.

Back in Chicago, Father Lucien Lindsey and the entire staff of St. Augustine's Center carried on with faithfulness and rare good humor while I was off to Sun Dance or away reading in some distant archives. I am proud to be their director; and I hope that they believe it was worth all the effort.

Doreen Mimura Lin, of our own household, spent many a day and night typing the manuscript. Then, as if that was not enough, she made possible the reproduction of most of the photos in these volumes. Her mother, Jeanne Nakamura Mimura, generously shared in the expenses of doing so.

Lee and Dorothy Raisch uncomplainingly cared for my immediate clan when I was in the field. It is part of the constant joy of being their son-in-law to know that they, too, believed this book should be written.

Virginia Lee, Kathy, Christine, John, and Posh—my wife, daughters and sons—have loved and encouraged me in spite of being constantly neglected while I traveled and wrote. They have done so because they are unselfish to begin with; and because they, too, have seen the beauty that is the heart of the Cheyenne Way.

And there is my mother, Helena, who, years ago, first encouraged her son in his dream of serving Maheo's people as a priest.

This is, at best, a limited list when compared to all those persons who have made some special contribution of knowledge, encouragement, or assistance during the writing of these volumes. My warmest thanks to all of you whose kindnesses have carried me through all these years.

The Cheyennes
Who Made This Book Possible

My warmest gratitude and affection to all the Cheyennes, both Northern and Southern, who have guided and assisted me throughout the years. At best, the following is an incomplete list of the people, both Tsistsistas and Suhtaio, who made this book possible. Those whose names appear below have been major sources of knowledge.

Little Face, Southern Cheyenne. Born ca. 1864; died ca. 1961. Father, Roman Nose; mother, Belly Woman or Big Body. Little Face, who was reared by Chief Hill, insisted that he was twelve years old at the time of the Custer fight. The 1894 Southern Cheyenne census gives his age as seventeen and his birth date as

1877. However, the compilers of the census rolls often were highly inaccurate in estimating Indian ages.

Charles Sitting Man (Wolf Necklace), Northern Suhtai. Born, 1866; died, 1961. Father, Holy or Medicine or Doll Man, a Crazy Dog chief. Sitting Man was an Elk, and a Sun Dance instructor.

Baldwin Twins (Scabby), Southern Cheyenne. Born ca. 1874; died 1964. Father, Yellow Calfskin Shirt. Twins was Keeper of the Arrows from 1936 to 1956.

Henry Little Coyote, Northern Suhtai. Born, 1875; died, 1969. Father, White Frog or Eagle Feather Horse, a Suhtai; Mother, Comes Together, Suhtai, a niece of Coal Bear. Little Coyote is a Kit Fox, and he was Keeper of Is'siwun from 1959 to 1965.

Frank Waters, Northern Cheyenne. Born, 1875; died, 1962. Father, Braided Locks. Waters was Sweet Medicine Chief of the Northern Cheyennes from 1940 until his death. He also was keeper of the Sun Dance bundle with its sacred doll.

Charles Whistling Elk, Northern Cheyenne. Born, 1876; died, 1958. Father, Brady or Braided Hair. Whistling Elk was a Crazy Dog leader. He was noted as the instructor of the men who fasted on the Sacred Mountain and those who sacrificed themselves in the hills.

Mary Little Bear Inkanish, Southern Cheyenne. Born, 1877; died, 1965. Her brother had pledged the Sun Dance, and her mother had been the Sacred Woman in the Southern Sun Dance ceremonies. At the time of her death, she was the most noted beadworker among the Southern Cheyennes.

John Fire Wolf, Northern Suhtai. Born, 1877; died, 1966. Father, Chief Black Wolf; mother, Yellow Woman or White Buffalo Calf Woman. Fire Wolf was the most highly respected of the Northern Buffalo priests during the last years of his life. He was also a Sun Dance instructor and painter. He was an Elk Society man.

Ben Woods (Feather Hair Ornament), Southern Cheyenne. Born ca. 1879. Father, Starving Coyote (half Cheyenne, half Arapaho); mother, Little Woman. Woods is a priest of the Sacred Arrow lodge.

George Brady (Buffalo Wallow or *Corn Planted on Good Level Ground*, a name associated with the old woman in the spring who gave the people the corn and the buffalo), Northern Cheyenne. Born, 1881; died, 1968. Father, Brady; mother, Plains Woman. George Brady was a Crazy Dog. Like his brother Whistling Elk, he has instructed some of the men who have sacrificed their bodies in the hills.

Jay Black Kettle (Gentle Horse), Southern Cheyenne. Born, 1881; died, 1969. Father, Black Dog or Wolf (later he is said to have assumed the name of his brother, Black Kettle); mother, Ghost Woman. Jay Black Kettle was Keeper of the Arrows from 1957 to 1962.

John Stands in Timber, Northern Cheyenne. Born, 1882; died, 1967. Father, Stands Different; mother, White Buffalo Cow. John Stands in Timber was the formal historian for the Northern Cheyennes. At the time of his death, he was a member of the Chiefs' Society. Prior to that, he had been Doorkeeper for the Kit Foxes.

Ralph White Tail (Black Turkey), Southern Cheyenne. Born ca. 1884; died 1961. Father, White Tail. Ralph White Tail had been a member of the Kit Foxes. Later he became a Dog Society man. In 1947, the Southern Arapahoes made him one of their Chiefs. He was a noted Sun Dance instructor and Arrow Lodge priest, who had been trained by Mower, a former Keeper of Mahuts.

Davis Wounded Eye (Small Blanket), Northern Suhtai. Born, 1885; died, 1961. Father, Wounded Eye, Keeper of Is'siwun.

Willis Medicine Bull (Screeching Bald Eagle), Northern Cheyenne. Born, 1887. Father, Medicine Bull or Buffalo Medicine. Willis Medicine Bull has been a member of the Contrary Lodge. He has twice been Instructor in the Medicine Lodge (1967), and has danced in the Sun Dance seven times. He has instructed fasters on the Sacred Mountain, and he kept the Chiefs' bundle for a time after Frank Waters's death.

Rufus Wallowing (Egg), Northern Cheyenne. Born, 1887; died, 1965. Father, Bull Wallowing, a Contrary who fought Fetterman and Custer; mother, Sioux Woman. Paternal grandfather, High Wolf.
Cora Young Bear (Bear Woman), Northern Cheyenne, Born, 1888; died ca. 1961. Step-daughter of Black Bird, Keeper of Is'siwun.

Fred Last Bull, Northern Cheyenne. Born ca. 1888; died ca. 1961. Father, Last Bull, Chief of the Kit Foxes. Fred Last Bull was Keeper of the Arrows during their stay in the north. He was also a Sun Dance and Buffalo priest.

William Red Robe, Northern Cheyenne. Born ca. 1893; died, 1969. Father, Fred Red Robe; mother, Nora Red Robe or Plume Feather Ornament. Red Robe has danced in the Sun Dance, carrying Box Elder's Ox'zem bundle during the final day.

Wesley Little White Man (Broken Bow or Black Bear), Northern Cheyenne. Born, 1897. Father, Little White Man or Aaron White Man (?); mother, Porcupine Dress.

John Hill (Beaver Heart), Southern Cheyenne. Born, 1896; died, 1969. Father, Joseph Hill or Black War Bonnet; mother, Flying Woman. Maternal grandfather, Whirlwind, Southern Chief killed when the Southern Cheyennes missed a shot at the Pawnee man figure tied to the Sun Dance pole. Hill was a respected Southern Sun Dance priest and an Arrow Lodge man.

Alex Brady (Little Swift Hawk), Northern Cheyenne. Born, 1898. Father, Brady; mother, Frog Woman. Alex Brady is a Crazy Dog Society man. He also is a Sun Dance instructor and a painter of the Swift Hawk and Deer paints. He fasted on the Sacred Mountain in 1965.

William Hollowbrest, Northern Cheyenne. Born, 1900. Father, Hubert Hollowbrest (Roached Hair or Pompadour), Suhtai; mother, Buffalo Woman, Tsistsistas. Paternal grandfather, Wrapped Hair; maternal grandfather, White Mustache, Tsistsistas. William Hollowbrest has danced in the Medicine Lodge four times. As of 1964, he had painted in the Sun Dance three times. He has both the Eagle and Grasshopper paints.

Josephine Head Swift Limpy (Stands by the Fire), Northern Suhtai. Born, 1900. Father, Head Swift, Keeper of Is'siwun. Josie Limpy guarded the Sacred Hat from 1952 until January, 1958. In July, 1969, Is'siwun again was placed in her care.

Albert Tall Bull, Northern Cheyenne. Born, 1906; died ca. 1972. Father, Jacob Tall Bull (adopted); mother, Medicine Rock. Albert Tall Bull was a respected Northern Sun Dance instructor.

James Medicine Elk (Blind Wolf), Northern Cheyenne. Born, 1907; died, 1974. Father, Medicine Elk, Northern Cheyenne; mother, Mary Bird Bear. James Medicine Elk participated in the last Massaum ceremony in the south. He was Keeper of the Arrows from 1962 until 1971. Succeeded by Ed Red Hat.

Elmore Brady (Whistling Elk), Northern Cheyenne. Born, 1907; died 1970. Father, George Brady. Elmore Brady is a noted Northern Crazy Dog and Sun Dance painter.

James Medicine Bird (Walks with the Wind), Northern Cheyenne. Born, 1914. Father, Nelson Medicine Bird; mother, Yellow Woman (Ribbed Woman), daughter of One Eyed White Man. His grandfather was the brother of White Bull or Ice. Medicine

Bird is an Elk Society member, and for many years kept the Elk Society bundle.

Henry Tall Bull, (Standing Twenty), Northern Cheyenne. Born, 1917; died, 1973. Father, Charles Tall Bull (Little Wolf or Little Kit Fox); mother, Mary Brady, daughter of Brady. Henry Tall Bull's great-grandfather was Tall Bull, Chief of the Dog Soldiers.

William Tall Bull, (Wolf Feathers), Northern Cheyenne. Born, 1921. Father, Charles Tall Bull; mother, Mary Brady. William Tall Bull has offered the sacrifice of his body in the hills. He is the brother of Henry Tall Bull.

Roy Bull Coming (Starving Wolf or *Hungry Wolf)*, Southern Cheyenne. Born, 1914. He is Keeper of the Badge bundle during the Sacred Arrow ceremonies. He also is a painter of the Lizard paint in the Sun Dance.

Edward Red Hat (Fan Man), Southern Cheyenne. Born, 1898. Father, Red Hat; mother, Walks in the Middle. He and his brother Roger are makers of the Blue Sky for the Sacred Arrow ceremonies. He became Keeper of Mahuts in 1971.

Roger Red Hat (Crow Hollering), Southern Cheyenne. Born, 1903. Father, Red Hat; mother, Walks in the Middle.

Charles Crazy Mule, Northern Cheyenne. Born, 1917. Father, William White Horse; mother, Liz Spotted Hog. Charles Crazy Mule has been Crier in the Sun Dance ceremonies seven times (1965). He is also a Sun Dance instructor.

Aaron White Man, Northern Cheyenne. Born, 1923. Father, Stanley Little White Man; mother, Grace Walking Bear. Aaron White Man has danced in the Sun Dance eleven times (1965) on the Cheyenne Paint side. He has been Lodge Maker four times, and the Earth Maker four times (1965). He has been a Sun Dance instructor twice (1965).

XVI

Introduction: Last Bull Asks a Question

When I, a priest, first stood be-
fore the Sacred Arrow lodge, the beauty of the Cheyenne north
country had disappeared, replaced by a faded blue sky and a
prairie of burned-out browns and yellows. The year was 1957,
and the land blistered beneath the early August sun. The air
was dry and clear; for on the high plains there is little atmosphere
to halt the power of the sun's rays. Dust was everywhere, scuffed
up by children's running feet, the tires of ancient cars, or the
hooves of the horses moving slowly in the distance. Evening
would bring the cooling prairie breezes, bearing the sweet, fresh
smell of white sage, the "man sage" of the Cheyenne sacred ceremonies. At the moment, however, there was only the blazing

sun and the feeble hope that rain would fall soon, bringing new life to the withered lands.

I looked around for the shining white tipi that should be rising above Mahuts, those four Arrows which remain the most treasured of Cheyenne sacred possessions. Maheo, the All Father, the Supreme Deity Himself, first gave them to Sweet Medicine, the Cheyenne culture hero. The gift was bestowed inside a cave within the Sacred Mountain, the place better known as Bear Butte, near Sturgis, South Dakota.

Ever since the time Sweet Medicine bore Mahuts from the holy mount, the four red-and-black-painted Arrows had given the Cheyennes dominance over other men and dominance over the animals as well. The very name Mahuts is derived from the name of Maheo, the All Father. The Arrows are uniquely sacred objects which share the supreme power of the Creator Himself. They are the channel through which Maheo's supernatural life flows into Cheyenne lives. Mahuts remain the continuing means by which the Cheyennes are united with the All Father. The Arrows also unite the Cheyennes as Votostataneo—the People— the particular singled-out ones from among the other people of the earth.[1]

On this August day, however, a wood and tarpaper shack stood before me, supplanting the new tipi that traditionally marked the Arrows' home. A padlock held the flimsy door shut, affording poor physical protection for the supremely holy objects that were hanging within.

At this time in 1957, the Northern Cheyennes were just commencing to wage their own war against poverty on the reservation. Many of the people were living in log houses. A number of such houses sprawled on either side of the temporary Arrow lodge, their color blending with the shades of the burned-out

---

[1] "Votostataneo, the top, surface people, human beings. Some Cheyennes claim that this is the specific name for their people and would mean 'the particular, singled-out people' . . . . Other Cheyennes insist that the name refers to human beings as distinguished from the 'above beings' and 'under beings' (i.e., the Maiyun who live above and beneath the earth)." Rodolphe Petter, *English-Cheyenne Dictionary*, s.v. "people," 806.

land surrounding them. Eighty-one years before, Northern Cheyenne homes had been made of finely tanned buffalo hides. Within these tipis, beautifully painted skin linings protected the people from drifting snow, driving rain, and the shifting prairie winds. Brilliantly colored warriors and horses darted in battle across the faces of the linings. These battle scenes were so vividly portrayed that even hardened cavalrymen were struck by their beauty as the soldiers were burning the villages of Black Kettle, White Antelope, Old Bear, and Morning Star. Only prairie soil insulated the Cheyenne homes around me now, the heat-baked mud unequal to the task of holding back the wind and dust that filtered between the uneven edges of split logs or boards.

A few hundred feet away, sleek, newly painted government school buildings rose above the Indian houses. Their cool brightness contrasted with the heat and dust that surrounded the Cheyennes who dwelt there, in Busby, Montana. History had been lived all around the place where I stood. In 1876, Long Hair Custer camped nearby, his horses pointed toward the Little Big Horn and death. A few miles down the Rosebud, the Cheyennes and their Sioux allies had thrown back Crook and his men. Within sight of where I was standing, White Bull, the old-time Cheyenne holy man, had been buried alive. He was placed in a pit, and a great rock was rolled over the hole, sealing White Bull inside. That stone sat unmoved as the holy man escaped, and the Cheyennes say that the Sacred Powers aided him, preserving his life.

Rufus Wallowing, a respected friend and a past president of the Northern Cheyenne Tribal Council, had told me that I would find the Arrows at Busby. His father, Bull Wallowing, fought the troopers of Fetterman, Crook, and Custer before he died an agency policeman. Rufus Wallowing explained to me that it had been many years since Mahuts had been in the north country. Five months after the Cheyenne victory at the Little Big Horn, the whites finally struck back in force. It was in November, 1876, that General Ranald Mackenzie's men surprised and destroyed Morning Star's village in the Big Horns. Black Hairy Dog, the Sacred Arrow Keeper, had escaped with Mahuts then; and he had borne the Arrows to safety in the south. Ever since that time, Mahuts had remained among the Southern Cheyennes in what is now western Oklahoma.

Recently, however, the Arrows had been carried north by Baldwin Twins, their present Keeper. This time they were borne in a swiftly moving automobile rather than on the slowly moving horses the old-time Arrow Keepers rode. Because of a series of circumstances described elsewhere in this book, Twins had decided to leave Mahuts in the custody of a Northern Cheyenne priest.

I had come from Chicago to Busby, seeking the Ark of the Cheyenne people, as some Cheyennes now describe the Sacred Arrows. In the free days, when Mahuts were being carried against an enemy, every Cheyenne man, woman, and child followed—just as the Israelites had marched behind the Ark of the Covenant. Now the sacred palladium was hanging in this temporary lodge before me, this lumber and tarpaper shed beside a wooden cabin.

Even the Arrow Keeper was temporary. Fred Last Bull was guarding Mahuts at this time. However, controversy was raging over the legality of bringing the sacred objects north without the consent of the Southern Cheyenne Arrow priests, Chiefs, and military society leaders. Fred was the son of Last Bull, who, years before, had been deposed as chief of the Kit Fox Society. Traditionally, the Kit Foxes and Dog Society men were the special protectors of the Arrows. Yet old Last Bull's arrogance had enabled Mackenzie's soldiers to destroy Morning Star's village. There, Northern Cheyenne wealth and material beauty had disappeared in the fires set by the soldiers' torches.

The younger Last Bull was some sixty-eight years old at this time—a thin-faced, short-haired, tubercular man. His shirt was open when he stepped from his cabin to greet me. White scars were exposed, reminders of the piercing of his chest with skewers during the 1945 Sun Dance, the first occasion on which such a sacrifice had been made publicly since the 1890's.[2]

We stood together there in the heat and dust enveloping this latest lodge of the Sacred Arrows. In polite Cheyenne fashion, Last Bull listened to my questions. Then he asked some questions of his own:

> Why do you, a white man and a priest, want to see our Sacred Arrows that Maheo gave Sweet Medicine for the blessing of the Cheyennes?
> Why do you care about our old sacred ways?

For the Cheyennes who have made me one with them and in doing so have made this book a reality, I long since have answered Last Bull's query. However, there may well be others who ask the same question as they begin these pages.

To you, as to that old Cheyenne priest who now lies buried near Busby, an explanation is in order.

From earliest youth, I have studied the history and the ceremonies of the Plains Indians. The Plains tribes were, and are, people who believed their culture to be well worth living and dying for. There are profound spiritual depths in the older sacred ceremonies, with their constant theme that man's vocation is to live in harmony with the Creator and with creation as a whole. Traditionally, the men who conducted the ceremonies and guarded the sacred bundles were persons of real strength: men who sometimes were priests, lawgivers, and warriors simultaneously. They possessed the awareness that worship must permeate and give meaning to every phase of life.

The Cheyennes long have been people whose entire existence was guided by the sacred ceremonies. They acknowledged, and continue to acknowledge, one Supreme Being. He is Maheo or Maxemaheo, the All Father. Under Maheo, the Cheyennes ven-

[2] Last Bull told the author that he did this in 1945, as a sacrifice for victory in World War II. However, cf. Maurice Frink, "A Little Gift for Last Bull," *Montana*, Vol. VIII, No. 2 (April, 1958).

erate the Maheyuno, the four Sacred Persons who dwell at the cardinal points of the universe. Grandmother Earth is invoked and respected as a living, supernatural being. So are the Above and Below Persons called upon for blessings: the Sun, Thunder, Moon, Morning Star and Stars, the Whirlwind, Badger, and the lesser Sacred Powers who assume the forms of animals, birds, and natural phenomena when they appear to men. For the Cheyennes, all creation is alive; all creation is infused with supernatural power. Cheyenne life was, and still is, lived in the knowledge that man must seek continual harmony with Maheo, the Maheyuno, and the Maiyun, as the lesser Powers are known collectively.

What we know of Cheyenne history begins in Minnesota. Then, in a series of moves, the people traveled westward across the Missouri, past the shadows of the Sacred Mountain and the Black Hills, and out onto the high plains. Older tribesmen recall traditions of their ancestors' making this journey with their faces turned straight ahead, as one must do in obeying a supernatural command. Behind them lay the cornfields and earth lodges that bordered the banks of the Red and Cheyenne rivers. Some of the agricultural ceremonies were left behind too, sacred rites in which women played important roles as the renewers of the earth and fields.

Finally the Cheyennes reached the prairies where the rippling blanket of buffalo grass was cut by the swiftly flowing waters of the Yellowstone, the Tongue, and the Platte rivers. Ahead lay the apparently endless sweep of the plains country, its color changing with the shifting rays of the sun. Here, except for the pine hills and low-lying buttes, there were few places where a man could fast and pray. Thus the heights of the Sacred Mountain remained all the more deeply embedded in Cheyenne tribal memory. Mahuts, the Sacred Arrows, and Is'siwun, the Sacred Buffalo Hat, now provided the supernatural power by which life could be lived in this beautiful but harsh new home, this prairie world where hunting and war would become dominant over the older agricultural ways.

The Sacred Arrows not only bound the entire tribe to Maheo, the All Father. They were, and for conservative Cheyennes still are, the supreme symbols and sources of male power. Through Mahuts, the All Father gives the Cheyenne men power over other men as well as power over the animals.

Is'siwun, the Sacred Buffalo Hat, is the great symbol and source of female renewing power. Therefore, throughout this book, I refer to the Sacred Hat as "She." Is'siwun's power renewed the buffalo herds of the past, as well as the cattle herds of the present. It was through the Buffalo Hat that the Sun Dance first came to the Suhtai people, and when the Suhtaio merged with the Cheyenne proper, they brought the Sun Dance with them.[3] It is in the Sun Dance that a Sacred Woman, as well as the male Pledger, offers the sacrifice of her body. Thus, in the Sun Dance, woman joins with man in bringing about the renewal of the Cheyennes and their world. Through the supernatural power of the Arrows and Buffalo Hat, the male and female relationships in Cheyenne life are blessed, ensuring continual strength, harmony, and new life for the People and their world.

I write of these Cheyenne sacred ways as an Anglo Catholic priest who possesses profound respect for both history and ethnology. One of the fundamental precepts of the undivided Catholic Church is that Christ came as the Perfector, the Fulfiller, of all the world's cultures and traditions. The Church holds that the finest in the pre-Christian religions reflected the eternal truth and beauty of God. Thus, these religions were, in their way, preparations for God's revelation of Himself in human

---

[3] It is of interest that recently Alice Marriott and Carol Rachlin, both distinguished anthropologists and authors, happened to mention the name of Is'siwun to an aged Sac Woman of Oklahoma. The woman was Lucy Griggs, a lady now in her late seventies. She had been raised in both the Medicine Lodge and Drum religion of the Sac and Fox tribe. When Lucy Griggs heard Is'siwun's name, she remarked that this was a very old Sac and Fox name, meaning "Something Coming Out of the Ground." She recalled an aged Sac woman, older than her own grandmother, who had borne the name Is'siwun. "It is a woman's name," Lucy Griggs observed. Here, in the Suhtai name for the Sacred Buffalo Hat, we may well have an extremely old basic Algonquian word for female renewing power.

flesh as Jesus Christ. The Hebrew patriarchs and prophets are obvious representatives of men who pointed the way to the appearance of our Lord. However, there are others. Plato's figure stood beside the ikons of the Old Testament saints in some ancient Eastern Orthodox churches. In these days of what Pope John XXIII named *aggiornaménto,* we priests are rediscovering and reinterpreting the Church's traditional respect for the holy men of other religions—Buddhism, Hinduism, Confucianism, and Islam, to name a few.

Moreover, even closer analogies may be drawn between certain Plains Indian traditions and those of Christianity. There is the Teton Lakota account of the appearance of the White Buffalo Maiden, who visited the Sans Arc band at the will of Wakan Tanka, the Great Mystery. She gave the Sans Arcs the Sacred Calf Pipe and the seven holy ceremonies that went with it: Purification, the Vision Seeking, the Sun Dance, the Ball Throwing, Making a Buffalo Woman, Making as Brothers, and Owning a Ghost.[4]

The White Buffalo Maiden may be interpreted as the prefiguring of that Virgin who bore in her womb the eternal Son of God. That Son gives His power to man through seven sacraments. The seven ancient Teton ceremonies are the prefiguring of those sacraments, I believe, and must be venerated as such.

I could cite other examples of Plains Indian concepts and ceremonies that can be viewed as prefiguring the Church's life and faith. The Kiowa traditions and ceremonies concerning the Ten Grandmother bundles and the Northern Arapaho rites of opening the Sacred Flat Pipe are such.[5]

Finally, there is one further concept that runs through much of Plains Indian worship. It is most profoundly expressed in the

[4] Royal B. Hassrick, *The Sioux,* 217–20. Cf. John Epes Brown, *The Sacred Pipe,* 3–10; J. L. Smith, "A Short History of the Sacred Calf Pipe of the Teton Dakota," *Museum News,* W. H. Over Dakota Museum, Vol. XXVIII, Nos. 7–8.

[5] Details on these ceremonies will be found in Alice Marriott, *Ten Grandmothers;* James Mooney, *Calendar History of the Kiowa Indians;* J. G. Carter, "The Northern Arapaho Flat Pipe and the Ceremony of Covering the Pipe," B.A.E. *Bulletin,* Vol. CXIX (1938), 69–102.

pledging of the Sun Dance ceremonies among the Cheyennes and the Teton Lakotas. This is the belief that a man, through the sacrifice of himself and his body, brings blessing and renewal to his tribe and to all creation. Traditionally, the Cheyennes and Tetons have considered such a sacrifice, as offered in the Medicine Lodge, to be the highest means whereby new life may be brought to the tribe and to the world.

These Cheyenne and Sioux concepts may be construed as the closest of analogies to the great central fact of the Church's life and worship. For it was the offering of one man, Jesus Christ, that brought blessing, peace, and new life, first to his own people, the Jews, and then to all the world. The sacrifice of the Sun Dance usually is offered once a year. The Sacrifice of Christ is re-petitioned day by day in the Mass. Both Eucharist and Sun Dance possess in common the belief that new life begins with the sacrifice of one man. Thus, the pledging of the Sun Dance may be viewed as the earlier form of sacred revelation to the Cheyennes and Tetons, and the self-oblation of Jesus on the Cross as the perfecting of that sacrifice which is still offered in the Medicine Lodge.

It has seemed to me that, of all the Plains tribes, the Cheyennes most completely centered their lives upon the sacred ceremonies. According to their beliefs, supernatural power permeated every phase of Cheyenne being: peace, war, hunting, courtship, art, and music. To this day, such seemingly ordinary items as beaded tipi decorations are properly made only after certain ceremonies have been performed. The decorations themselves carry spiritual blessings for those who live or camp in the tipi. Ideally, such beadwork is made only by women of fine character as well as beadworking skill. As they labor on the tipi decorations, the women are blessed by the power emanating from one of the four sacred bundles that belong to their Beadworkers' Guild.

In earlier days, representations of the Maheyuno, the four Sacred Persons, were painted upon warrior shields. These shields were formed from the heat-shrunken neck hide of a buffalo bull.

In battle, they could turn aside an arrow or even a smoothbore rifle ball. However, the Cheyennes believed that it was the Maheyuno's blessing upon the shield that gave it its real protective power.

The decorations on a man's war or ceremonial clothing often came to him during his fasting or vision quest. Thus, each painted, beaded, and feathered ornament worn by a Cheyenne warrior usually possessed supernatural power and significance to him.

An oath taken upon the Sacred Arrows, before the Buffalo Hat, or on her symbol, the buffalo skull, could never be broken. To do so would bring down the wrath of Maheo and the Sacred Persons. When Custer lay dead in the dust and heat of that June day on the Little Big Horn, to the Cheyennes there was a supernatural reason for his defeat, for they recalled how he had lied as he smoked with Stone Forehead, the Arrow Keeper, beneath the Sacred Arrows themselves in the spring of 1869.

After studying what others had written, I went to the Northern Cheyennes themselves in 1956. I went able to say to them that I believed their sacred ways to have come from God Himself. I continue to believe, with the Cheyennes, in the supernatural power that flows from their sacred bundles and sacred ceremonies. I have gone among them as an Anglo Catholic priest, but equally as a brother to those Cheyenne priests whom Maheo has sent to the People throughout their history.

For fourteen summers now, and for some winter visits as well, I have returned to the Cheyennes. I have lived with the Sacred Arrow and Sun Dance priests and pledgers, and I have assisted in the ceremonies themselves. In 1959, I was present when the Sacred Hat was exposed for the first time since General Hugh Scott's visit in 1930. On five occasions, I have participated in the Sun Dance ceremonies. Four of these occasions were in Montana, the fifth in Oklahoma. Four is the Cheyenne sacred number. A man is not qualified to be a Sun Dance Instructor until he has offered the Medicine Lodge ceremonies four times.

Therefore, on four occasions—1960, 1961, 1962, and 1964—I remained with the Cheyenne priests throughout the entire Sun Dance. I assisted in both the Lone Tipi and the Medicine Lodge itself. This included driving the Sacred Hat and her Keeper to and from the Sun Dance camp, as well as assisting the Chiefs in cutting down the center pole.

In the south, John Stands in Timber and I assisted in the 1960 Sacred Arrow ceremonies. With the permission and blessing of the Arrow Keeper and priests, the ceremony was recorded in its entirety. Later, I traveled to Pawnee country to see those Arrows captured by the Skidi in 1830. The Pawnee people extended kindnesses to me comparable only to the graciousness of my own Cheyenne relatives. However, the Skidi politely informed me that the captured Mahuts were Pawnee Arrows now, and that they intended to keep them that way!

The chapters concerning the Sacred Arrow and Sun Dance ceremonies have been carried back to Montana and to Oklahoma. There they were read to the Sacred Arrow and Sun Dance priests. What you read here bears the approval of the Arrow Keeper and former Keeper of Is'siwun, as well as the other priests, both Northern and Southern.

From 1956 through 1967, John Stands in Timber, the formal historian for the Northern Cheyennes, was my interpreter, one of my chief informants, and my brother-friend. It was he who encouraged me to see tribal history through as many Cheyenne eyes as possible, rather than through his eyes alone. Together we recorded the recollections of the more than thirty-five Cheyennes who have made this book a reality. Often, as we talked together, John Stands in Timber would say: "That reminds me of something else . . . ." Then he would be off, recounting details that he had not recalled while he was dictating his own book. You will find many of these details in the chapters concerning the wars with the soldiers. Before he died in 1967, John Stands in Timber asked that I be the executor of his estate. Then, in his will, he bequeathed me his papers, diaries, notes, and photographs—the results of a lifetime spent in recording the history of the Northern Cheyennes. I never cease to miss him, his warm affection, his quiet strength, and his endless quest for further knowledge about his people. His family are my family now.

And I miss the others who, before this book was completed, joined John Stands in Timber in climbing the Milky Way trail to Se'han. Over the years, many of my informants became my relatives, Cheyenne-fashion. Anyone who knows the Cheyennes will understand the affection and respect that we held for each other as relatives. I long to see them again, and I long to hear the quiet pride in their voices as they speak of the greatness of being "all Cheyenne."

Among the Southern Cheyennes, Ralph White Tail (Black Turkey) adopted me as his son. Prior to his death in 1961 he was a leader in both the Sacred Arrow and Sun Dance lodges as well as an active member in the Native American Church. Ralph White Tail, with the permission of the old-time Keeper's descendants, gave me the name Hohonai'viuhk' Tanuhk—Stone Forehead. The Cheyennes still recall that it was Stone Forehead's power that brought about Custer's defeat and death at the Little Big Horn.

In July, 1962, the Northern Cheyenne Chiefs' Society invited John Stands in Timber, John Woodenlegs, the late Verne Dusenberry, and me to membership in their lodge. "The Chiefs can go in anywhere. They can go into any ceremony," the people say. During the period between the death of Frank Waters, the former Sweet Medicine Chief, and the choosing of Willis Medicine Bull as his successor, I was given custody of the Chiefs' bundle. This is the bundle Little Wolf carried, the bundle that Sweet Medicine himself left to the men who continue to represent his presence in the Council of the Forty.

I have participated in decisions concerning the care and custody of many of the Cheyenne sacred bundles. Among them are Box Elder's Ox'zem, or Sacred Wheel Lance, as well as his straight pipe and Sacred Arrow bundle. Also, the Northern Massaum bundle, with its great yellow wolf hide; the Elk Society bundle with its sacred snake carved from horn; and the

Northern Sun Dance bundle with its sacred doll. The ceremonial notebooks of Ralph White Tail and three of the Northern Cheyenne Sun Dance Instructors are in my keeping.

Mahuts, the Sacred Arrows, are back in Oklahoma. There they still hang in their own tipi, guarded by Edward Red Hat, the present Keeper. He succeeded James Medicine Elk as Keeper in 1971.

Thus, throughout these years I have been privileged to know and to share the name and role of the Sacred Arrow Keeper as well as the power and blessings that flow from the sacred bundles. I have been privileged to know the Cheyenne priests as brother priests. We have offered the ceremonies together, worked together, and prayed together. We also have laughed together, for even in the midst of holy work quiet laughter with a friend is permissible. This is partly because what is done in the sacred ceremonies is more important than what is said; but quiet laughter is also a sign of the affection and unity that Sweet Medicine first admonished the priests that they must have if the holy rites are to be brought to a blessed conclusion.

These are the holy ways of the people who are Maheo's people and my own.

Most of my time has been spent with the Cheyennes when they were at their spiritual best. During the Arrow ceremonies and at Sun Dance time, the people in camp were hard at work living the holiness and harmony implicit in these two most sacred ceremonies. Thus it is the Cheyenne "best side" that is reflected throughout the pages of this book.

Obviously, not all the Cheyennes are holy men and women. The people are much too human for that! Like most of the rest of humanity, some of them fall short of the spirituality taught in the sacred traditions and ceremonies. This book will tell of the conflict between the Elks and the Kit Foxes, a conflict that ended in tragedy for the entire Northern Cheyenne tribe. Even today, there are still disagreements between priests, for the holiness of their vocation does not completely eliminate the hard reality that they are also men. However, even in the midst of arguments, the Cheyennes realize that persons who bring disharmony into the sacred ceremonies violate the spiritual heart of what it means to be Cheyenne.

Some reader is bound to ask, "But what of the role of the Sacred Woman in the ceremonies?" Obviously, it is her position that is hardest to interpret to non-Cheyennes. Contemporary Cheyennes are themselves divided on the holiness of her role. Some argue that no Woman ever was used in the Arrow ceremonies, and the Arrows are Maheo's supremely sacred gift to the people. These Cheyennes hold that the Woman's use in the Suhtai-originated ceremonies is actually a departure from the standards of purity Tsistsistas men and women have maintained through the power of Mahuts.

Here, I would offer the observation that it is the intention that makes an act basically sacred or profane. The Sun Dance priests constantly stress the holiness of the Woman's role. She aids in the renewing of creation through her sacrifice. The tribe also is renewed through the Sacred Woman's role—both symbolically and actually. Finally, her offering of herself in the Sun Dance is meant to be a living prayer for the continuing chastity of all Cheyenne womanhood. Her giving of her body to the Instructor is her sharing in the sacrifice that her husband (or ceremonial husband) is offering. I can only add that not one of these intentions is, in itself, base. In fact, quite the opposite.

Throughout this book I shall use the word "sacred" in exactly the same sense that the Cheyennes themselves use it. "Sacred" will mean holy power coming from Maheo, the Maheyuno, and the lesser Sacred Powers. The word also will refer to those ceremonies, objects, and bundles used in worship by the Cheyenne people.

Nowadays the entire tribe no longer gathers when the Sacred Arrow ceremonies are offered. Distance, jobs, and time all prevent them from doing so. Some of them, however, continue to pitch their lodges in the form of the old-time crescent moon. At Sun Dance time, it is only on the fourth day, the final day when sacred power is at its height, that people pack the outer edges of the Medicine Lodge. It can be argued that at least part of this spiritual deterioration springs from the latent fear that what happened once—the loss of the Sacred Arrows and the violation of the Sacred Buffalo Hat—may happen again. Such a loss would sever the supernaturally blessed male-female relationship that has made it possible for the Cheyenne tribe to survive so many years of conflict. Without Mahuts and Is'siwun the Cheyennes would no longer exist as the People.

Yet, for some Cheyennes at least, the old-time sacred ceremonies remain the wellspring of tribal unity and identity. For them, the Sacred Arrows, the Sacred Buffalo Hat, and the Sun Dance still offer the power by which the Cheyennes experience the living reality of what it means to be Maheo's People.

This is their book and this is their story.

Note to the Second Printing

These volumes were written and published with the blessing and approval of Jay Black Kettle and James Medicine Elk, successive Keepers of the Sacred Arrows; and of Henry Little Coyote and Josie Head Swift Limpy, successive Keepers of the Sacred Buffalo Hat, during the 1959–1969 era. In addition, the Chiefs and headmen of the Northern and Southern Cheyennes, with the priests and pledgers of the holy ceremonies, gave me permission to record the sacred rites pictured and described on the following pages.

These are the holiest ceremonies of the people who are Maheo's Own chosen, called-out People. In honor and respect of that fact, I have distributed all my author's royalties among the Northern and Southern Cheyennes, particularly among those Old Ones whose wisdom helped to make these volumes become a reality. To this day, the Keepers of the Sacred Arrows and the Sacred Buffalo Hat receive regular funds from these royalties, to support them in their most holy offices.

The same will be true of the author's royalties from this Second Printing. All those funds either will be distributed among Old

Ones of the Northern and Southern Cheyenne people, including the Keepers of the Sacred Arrows and the Sacred Buffalo Hat; or that money will be used to fund a project (or projects) designated by them as being of blessing and benefit to the People themselves.

PETER JOHN POWELL

Chicago Illinois
15 April, 1979

Note to the Third Printing

The spellings used in the following new orthography are those of Josephine Stands in Timber Glenmore, Wayne Leman, and their Cheyenne associates in *Cheyenne Topical Dictionary*, Cheyenne Translation Project, Busby, Montana 59016, 1984.

In *Sweet Medicine* I followed some of my Cheyenne mentors, with Dr. Rodolphe Petter, in translating Maheo (Ma'heo'o) as "All-Father Creator." However, the intensive linguistic research of Josephine Stands in Timber Glenmore, Wayne Leman, and their Cheyenne collaborators substantiates that "All-Father Creator" is inaccurate. For a discussion of Ma'heo'o see *Cheyenne Topical Dictionary*, pp. 182–83, and also Rodolphe Petter, *English-Cheyenne Dictionary*, p. 512, "God."

Since publication of *Sweet Medicine* and *People of the Sacred Mountain* I have been able to devote more intensive study to the Cheyenne language. I am now convinced that the most accurate translation of Ma'heo'o is "The Great Sacred Power." He is also called Mamanstomaneheo, "All Creator," and Maxematasooma, "Great Spirit," that is, "He who is superior to all other Spirits." These translations are substantiated by my oldest Cheyenne mentors and by Ma'heo'o's position in Cheyenne theology, where He is described as the ultimate source of all power and life. Among my mentors are Jay Black Kettle and Henry Little Coyote, former Keepers of Maahõtse and Esevone respectively, as well as those Sacred Arrow, Sun Dance, and Buffalo priests identified at the beginning of *Sweet Medicine*. The translations of Ma'heo'o above agree substantially with those of Josephine Stands in Timber

Glenmore, Wayne Leman, and their Cheyenne associates, all of whom have contributed richly to our knowledge of the Cheyenne language. I would call attention also to the important studies concerning the Cheyenne language being carried on by Connie Hart Yellowman and her associates among the Southern Cheyenne People.

I have retained those names of the Four Sacred Persons used earlier, as they were verified by the oldest of my Cheyenne priestly mentors.

Old Spelling	Meaning	Page	New orthography
Votostataneo	The People, the particular singled-out ones	XVIII	Voto'ėstataneo'o
Maheo	The Great Sacred Power	XVIII	Ma'heo'o
Mahuts	The Sacred Arrows	XVIII	Maahõtse
Is'siwun	The Sacred Buffalo Hat	XXIII	Esevone
Maheyuno	The Sacred Powers. The same term is sometimes used for the Four Sacred Persons.	XXV	Ma'heono
Se'han	The Place of the Dead	XXVIII	Séãno
Hohonai'viuhk' tanuhk	Stone Forehead	XXVIII	Ho'honaeve'óhtanéhe
Tsistsistas	The Cheyenne proper	XXX	Tsitsistas or Tsétsėhéståhese
Suhtai	A person of the So'taeo'o band or tribe	4	So'taa'e
Suhtaio	A small Algonkian-speaking tribe which affiliated with the Cheyenne proper in the Missouri River country, eventually becoming a band within the Cheyenne People.	4	Só'taeo'o

Old Spelling	Meaning	Page	New orthography
Nimhoyoh	"The Turner." A part of the Sacred Hat bundle and lodge.	15	Nimhoyo'o or Nemȯheo'o
Ox'zem	The Sacred Wheel Lance	16	Oxohtsemo ?
Nowah'wus	The Sacred Mountain	18	Noavose
Hotoanamos	An aged priest	20	Hotoanamosestse (Left Hand Bull or Bull Left Hand)
Enanoe-she	"The Planting Moon"	20	Ẽnano'éeše'he
E'omita'i	The Missouri River	22	E'ome'tãã'e
Maiyun	A Spirit or Spirits, i.e. the Sacred Powers (see p. 434, fn. 4)	40	Maheo (sing.) or Ma'heono (pl.)
Issio me'taniu	The Ridge People or Hill band	54	Hese'omeetaneo'o
Ivistsinih'pah	The Aorta band	57	Heveškėsenėhpȧhese
Ho'ko	The younger wife of Broken Dish	78	Ho'ko (same spelling)
Mochi	The warrior woman sent in chains to Ft. Marion	86	Mochii or Mókéé'e (Little Woman)
Me-o-tzi (Monasetah)	Captured by Custer's men at the Washita. Said by some Cheyennes to have born him a son.	122	Meoohtse'e
Veho or Wihio	A White man	299	Vé'ho'e
Vonhaom	The Buffalo sweat lodge	324	Vonȧhéome
Emaon	The ordinary sweat lodge	324	emaome
Hohnuhk'e	A Contrary	331	Hohnohka. Hȯ'nohkao'o, pl.

Old Spelling	Meaning	Page	New orthography
Haseoveo	Wife of "George Enemy Capture."	343	Háse'hoveóó'e
Mosa	Calf	343	Mó'êsá'e or Mo'esa'e
Vohokass	Light or Eugene Standing Elk	347	Vo'ho'kase
Massaum	The Crazy Lodge	352	Masaome or Måsêháome.
Hineh ha!	"That's all."	386	Hena'haanehe
Esh piveh	"That's good."	411	Eešepeva'e
Nivstanivoo	The Sacred Four Directions; also the Four Sacred Persons dwelling there.	434	Névêstanevoo'o
Meheyuno	The Sacred Powers	434	Ma'heono
Essenetah'he	Sacred Person of the Southeast	436	Essenetah'he
Sovota	Sacred Person of the Southwest	436	Sovota
Onxsovon	Sacred Person of the Northwest	436	Onxsovon
Notamota	Sacred Person of the Northeast	436	Notamota
Esceheman	"Our Grandmother" the Earth	437	Escheman or Estšemane
Niesehaman	"Our Sun"	437	Neeše'hamane
Hetanehao	The Sun emblem or Man Power design	438	Hetanehao [Petter sp.]
Nemevonam	"Our Thunder"	438	Nemevonan or Nemevonane

Old Spelling	Meaning	Page	New orthography
Mistai	Ghosts	439	Méstaeo'o
Hevsevama'tasooma	Evil spirits	440	Mestaeò havêseve-måhta' soomaho or Haveseve-mahta'soomaho
Ma'tasooma	The soul	441	Måhta'sooma
Seozemeo	"The Road of the Departed." Literally, departed spirit road.	441	Seotse-meo'o
Hekozeemeo	"The Road of the Hanged Ones."	441	E'kotsee-meo'o
Se'han	The Place of the Dead.	441	Séãno
Sexameo	Fork of the Milky Way leading directly to Sehan	441	Sexameo'o
Mut'si'i-u'iv	Sweet Medicine the Prophet	460	Motsé'eoeve
Nizhevoss	Eagle's Nest, former name of Sweet Medicine	460	Netsévôhe'so or Netsefo'so.
Tomsivsi	Erect Horns	467	Tomôsévêséhe or Tomosevsehe
Hoimaha	Winter Man or Cold Person or Old Man Winter	481	Hóoema'hahe
Oxheheom	The Sun Dance Lodge	614	Hoxéheome

PART ONE

The Two Great Mysteries
and Northern Cheyenne History,
1830–1880

1. The Restless Time

Great sorrow comes to great people. The Cheyennes have experienced more than their share of sorrow. However, in the life of the Cheyenne tribe two disasters assumed such supernatural proportions that they cast their shadow upon all subsequent tribal history. These tragedies affected Cheyenne continuity as Votostataneo—the People, the particular, singled-out ones from among all other people. Even today, conservative Cheyennes recall and speak of the twin misfortunes: the capture of the Sacred Arrows by the Skidi Pawnees and the mutilation of the Sacred Buffalo Hat by the Keeper's own wife.

The Sacred Arrows fell into Pawnee hands about 1830, causing the worst spiritual catastrophe ever experienced by the tribe. Mahuts, the four Arrows, are the supremely sacred objects uniting the Cheyennes to Maheo, the All Father Himself. Maheo pours his life into the lives of the people through the Arrows. The Arrows unite the Cheyennes to the All Father and to each other. Without the Arrows, there can be no Cheyenne tribe, no People in any supernatural sense.

Mahuts are also the divinely-given symbols of male power. No female dares look at them when they are exposed for veneration. Even today, a devout woman excuses herself from the presence of men who are speaking about the Arrows. Mahuts give the Cheyenne males spiritual dominance over the men of other tribes and also give them power over the animals that the people must have for sustenance.

When the Pawnees captured Mahuts the Cheyennes were faced with a tremendous spiritual dilemma. They had to regain the Arrows or they would lose their identity as a people. Two Arrows were regained, and two substitutes later were made by supernatural command and guidance. Maheo had not entirely forsaken his people. Male power was regained. However, for the Cheyennes, life was never quite the same again after that Skidi victory.

Then, about 1874 Is'siwun, the Sacred Buffalo Hat, suffered desecration. No enemies were involved this time. Instead it was a Suhtai woman, the Keeper's own wife, who, in anger and spite, ripped a horn from the Sacred Hat.

Again, disaster was foretold for the Cheyennes. Erect Horns, the Suhtai culture hero, had received the Hat from the All Father at a sacred mountain to the north. The people had been starving, but when Erect Horns returned to camp wearing the Sacred Hat the buffalo herds followed, and the Suhtaio never starved again.

The word "is'siwun" (esevon) means a herd of buffalo. However, in the context of the Sacred Hat the term also means a group of female bison. The Buffalo Hat is formed from the horned scalp of a female buffalo, and traditionally Is'siwun's power guaranteed a plentiful supply of buffalo for the people.

4

In this power to renew the herds the Hat is linked to the Sun Dance and to the Buffalo ceremony. A woman, usually the wife of the pledger of the ceremony, played a vital part in both these ceremonies, for she offered herself in the role of the symbolic reproducer of the tribe, the family, the buffalo, and of creation as a whole.

Consequently, the Sacred Hat is the animate symbol of female renewing power.[1] If the Buffalo Hat is desecrated, there is danger that woman's power will be broken or destroyed. When this happens there can be no new Cheyennes nor any new animals or plants upon which the people can subsist and increase. In traditional Cheyenne thought, the capture of the Arrows and the desecration of the Hat involved the tribe in a two-fold disaster. First, the violation of these two Great Mysteries disrupted the unity between the tribe, its Creator, and the Sacred Powers. Secondly, the violations ruptured the harmonious male and female relationship that must exist if the tribe and creation are to survive.

The results were the sorrows that have followed the tribe since that day in 1830 when a crippled Pawnee wrenched the Arrows from Cheyenne hands. Some forty-two years later, the final wars with the whites followed hard upon the violation of the Buffalo Hat. Even after the fighting ended, the Cheyenne sacred ceremonies were threatened by the government and by white missionaries. Thus George Bird Grinnell could write in 1910: "Almost all the Cheyenne troubles are believed to have followed close on the loss of the medicine arrows and the desecration of the sacred hat."[2]

Today there remains, among conservative Cheyennes, a haunting fear of the ultimate loss of these two sacred tribal bundles,

[1] Grinnell implies this when he says, "The arrows were medicine for the men alone—women might not look at them. The hat was chiefly for women. Both were strong war medicines." Grinnell, "The Great Mysteries of the Cheyenne," *American Anthropologist*, N.S., XII, No. 4 (October–December, 1910), 567.

Grinnell was reticent to discuss the woman's role in the Cheyenne ceremonies, although it is fairly certain that he was aware of it. Cf. the chapter, "Fighting for the Sun Dance" in this book.

[2] *Ibid.*, 567.

either through theft or through indifference on the part of the younger Cheyennes. If this should happen, it would be the end of Cheyenne identity as the People. The loss of the Arrows or the Buffalo Hat would mark the final scattering of the tribe, an event long ago prophesied by Sweet Medicine himself.

In 1959, this old and deep-seated fear broke out anew in Lame Deer, Montana.

From the Custer battlefield, it is some forty-four miles to the Northern Cheyenne tribal office at Lame Deer. There are great stretches of sage-covered prairie along the way, broken by the rolling, pine-clad hills so characteristic of the Cheyenne lands in Montana. In late afternoon the hills are enveloped in violet as the shadows of their pine trees lengthen against the yellow-green land. Highway 212 climbs one last pine-covered ridge, then the road plunges into the valley of the Lame Deer.

Nearby, in May of 1877, White Bull saved General Miles's life during a skirmish with the Sioux chief whose name is borne by both the stream and the town. Seven years later, in 1884, the Northern Cheyennes finally were given a reservation of their own. Here, at the foot of the pine hills near Lame Deer Creek, Tongue River Agency was established. Here the wandering bands of Two Moon, Little Wolf, Black Wolf, White Bull, and Little Chief finally reached home. Over these pine-shadowed hills Head Chief and Heart Mule rode to their deaths in 1890—the last of the suicide warriors to fall fighting the whites. Here, too, on a sun-scorched slope beyond the Mennonite mission, many of the great warriors lie buried, Little Wolf and Morning Star among them.

Roads from the four directions cross at Lame Deer, and the town is divided into two sections, government and non-government. Miles City, site of old Fort Keogh, lies to the northeast. It was here that Two Moon's band surrendered in 1877, and White Bull became the first of General Miles's Cheyenne scouts.

Tongue River flows twenty-one miles east of Lame Deer, its waters forming the eastern boundary of the Northern Cheyenne reservation. Land twenty by forty miles, some 460,000 acres, is all that remains of the beloved Cheyenne North Country. Near Sturgis, South Dakota, almost 170 miles to the southeast, Bear Butte, the Sacred Mountain, still casts its long shadow across the prairies.

The Northern Cheyenne tribal office is located a few yards north of the east-west highway. A modest, white-painted building, it sits on the edge of one of the few patches of green lawn within many miles. Here the elected representatives of each Cheyenne district gather, serving as the liaisons between the tribe and the federal government. Across the road, farther north, stands what was once the hospital. It is an imposing, well-kept building which now houses the representatives of Washington, the superintendent of the reservation and the other Indian Bureau and United States Public Health Service personnel. The tribal court is in the basement.

The Petter Memorial Mennonite Church is on the northern edge of town. Doctor Rodolphe Petter, the noted linguist and missionary, was the pastor here for many years. His bright-eyed, snowy-haired widow was still living in the parsonage beside the church in 1959. Within the mission many a spiritual battle was waged between the followers of the old sacred ways and those embracing the newer Christianity.

Lame Deer's "business section" lies to the south of the east-west road. Here are the Alexander family's Lame Deer Hotel, Mr. Cady's store and trading post, the laundromat, pool hall, garage, new grade school, the Mercantile Company, and the Mormon and Capuchin missions. These and other lesser buildings stand out against the background of the pine hills. In the heat and dust of a northern summer all appear much the same color as the land around them.

Until 1965, many of the Cheyenne homes rose beyond these buildings. In order to reach the houses near Lame Deer Creek, one drove along rutted trails so deep that the underside of the car often scraped the ground. One such road ended near the earlier homes of John Stands in Timber and George Brady, whose knowledge and recollections are scattered throughout this book.

7

Many of the houses lining the trail were of 1930 vintage—built during the days of the New Deal, the Indian Reorganization Act, and the Civilian Conservation Corps. During those times, these shingled dwellings were the latest in Indian housing. During the 1930's many Cheyennes moved into them, leaving behind their allotments along the Rosebud, Muddy, and Tongue rivers. In many cases, white ranchers leased the Indian grazing lands, while a number of the Cheyenne men worked for the CCC. Until the advent of the War on Poverty and the Northern Cheyenne tribal housing program in 1965, these log and shingle houses were the lodges of the still proud, still devout, and still independent Northern Cheyennes, the Morning Star People. Today, most of these homes have been replaced by the new multicolored prefabs that line the road to Birney. However, like the old-time tipis, most of these new houses front toward the east, the direction of the Sun rising and the Sacred Mountain.

At evening in Lame Deer the cloudless sky of a sun-filled day merges into a blanket of silver-flecked brightness, a sparkling dome shaped like the turtle, whose form was that of the old-time Cheyenne world. The harsher outlines of the day dissolve into the softly reflected brilliance of the moon and stars, and the heat and dust disappear in the coolness of the Montana night. Dogs bark and howl, just as they did in the days when scouts could locate a camp by the sound of canine voices.

Then, as the night deepens, even those noises disappear. A breeze arises, sometimes bearing the clear but distant music of a flute, the sound flowing from the direction of Grover Wolf Voice's house. Older Cheyennes say that such music carries a blessing with it.

Henry Tall Bull was not concentrating on blessings as he moved about the tribal office on April 8, 1959. A great-grandson of the famous Dog Soldier chief, he was now vice-president of the Northern Cheyenne Tribal Council.[3] Henry was a stocky,

[3] Chief Tall Bull was killed in the battle with General Eugene A. Carr's troops at Summit Springs, 1869.

8

sturdy man in his early forties. He possessed a broad, good-natured face that belied his abilities as a fighter in the Dog Soldier tradition. Accelerated sales of Indian lands characterized federal "termination" policies during the 1950's. For the first time in years, the Cheyennes again were facing land losses. Henry Tall Bull, John Woodenlegs—the tribal president—and the Tribal Council had been outspoken in their united determination to see that the northern lands remained in the possession of the Cheyennes.

Suddenly the door opened. Members of the Chiefs' Society moved into the room, long-haired older men who wasted little time in coming to the point. Ernest American Horse, Keeper of the Sacred Buffalo Hat, had left for Sheridan, Wyoming. He was carrying Is'siwun in her buffalo hide container. The Chiefs had not authorized the trip.[4]

Tall Bull hurried across the road to the Indian Bureau offices. There, he gave the news to Superintendent Don Jensen. The superintendent, in turn, telephoned Frederick "Buck" Brien, Lame Deer's strapping chief of police. Buck wasted no time in calling the Sheridan sheriff and describing to him the approaching auto and its contents.

Henry Tall Bull later recalled:

> I knew right then that the Sheridan police would ask what was in the bundle. I was afraid that the Sheridan police wouldn't know the significance of the Sacred Hat. It was just another bundle to them.
>
> I called Neckyoke.[5] He is pretty well versed in Cheyenne history. I explained the situation. He said he would call Sheriff Willard Marshall and explain what the Hat was.
>
> They (the sheriff and his men) were waiting for Ernest when he got there. Buck Brien was with Willy Rising Sun. Willy came

[4] Except where otherwise noted, the account of the theft of the Sacred Hat is written from field interviews with Henry Tall Bull, July and August, 1959. I have kept this narrative, and all other narratives in this book, as close as possible to the verbatim accounts.

[5] Neckyoke is F. H. Sinclair, the well-known Wyoming columnist, who wrote under the pen-name of Neckyoke Jones. Mr. Sinclair died in August, 1968. He was the founder of All American Indian Days at Sheridan, Wyoming.

by the American Horse house when Ernest was loading the Hat, and he reported it to the Chiefs.

Next day, the *Sheridan Press* covered the excitement under the headline:

PRICELESS CHEYENNE INDIAN MEDICINE BAG
IS INTERCEPTED HERE

A priceless and sacred medicine bag was on its way back to the Northern Cheyenne Indian tribe at Busby, Mont., late yesterday—at least that was the agreement.

Yesterday afternoon reports reached Sheridan, and local law officials were alerted to be on the watch for Ernest American Horse. It was reported from the reservation by Henry Tall Bull, vice president of the Northern Cheyenne Indian Tribal Council, that American Horse had left with the medicine bag.

Later, Indian police stopped American Horse and his wife just north of Sheridan. Sheriff Willard Marshall was called and went to the scene.

According to Marshall, American Horse agreed to return to Busby with the medicine bag, and agreed not to remove it again without written permission from the tribe.

According to Tall Bull, American Horse has been the caretaker of the highly valued medicine bag. The tribe was considering a change in custodian.

The bag is kept in a special tepee and had not been opened for 55 years. It contained a medicine hat, which is considered an invaluable good luck piece, two pipes and scalps.

When stopped here, it was reported the bag was unwrapped.[6]

For over a year Is'siwun's tipi had stood behind Ernest American Horse's house at Busby, near Rosebud Creek, seventeen miles west of Lame Deer. A few miles away, beside the same stream, the Cheyennes and Sioux had thrown back General Crook, thus ending his attempted juncture with Custer. It was at Busby, too, that Fred Last Bull had kept the Sacred Arrows during their 1956–57 stay in Montana. On January 11, 1958, the Cheyenne

[6] *Sheridan Press*, Sheridan, Wyoming, April 9, 1959.

Chiefs, the priests, and the military societies had accompanied the Sacred Hat there, also.

Before his passing, Erect Horns had directed that only a Suhtai could be Keeper of the Sacred Hat. The Suhtaio always had been a small band within the Cheyenne tribe, and with the passing years it had become increasingly difficult to follow Erect Horn's instruction. American Horse met the Suhtai blood requirement. He was a comparatively young man for such a holy position. However, he was well instructed in the Sun Dance ceremonies; in 1937 Sand Crane, then the Keeper of the Hat, had instructed him in the Suhtai version of the Medicine Lodge rites.

Head Swift, Sand Crane's brother, had succeeded him as Keeper of Is'siwun. After Head Swift's death, his daughter Josephine watched over the Sacred Hat lodge for about five years. Then, in 1957, Whistling Elk, one of the Crazy Dog leaders, summoned the Kit Foxes and the members of his own society. They decided to call a general meeting, one that would include the Chiefs and Elk Society men. But before the meeting could be held, Ernest American Horse sent word to Charles White Dirt, the Elk Society head man, that he wished to be Keeper of Is'siwun. The Chiefs and leaders of the military societies acceded to his request.

Now American Horse had been stopped outside Sheridan. He swiftly set up the Sacred Hat bundle on a tripod and sat down to smoke by Is'siwun, defying all comers to take him. Buck Brien finally persuaded him to place the Hat inside the paddy wagon and ride back to the reservation. American Horse protested his innocence. "I didn't steal it. I was never supposed to leave it alone, so I took it with me. They [the tribe] paid me to watch it," he insisted to the chief of police.[7] However, several miles farther along the road back to the reservation the Keeper

[7] Frederick Brien, former chief of police at Lame Deer, to the author, 1959. Chief Brien also noted that Laverne Kills on Top drove American Horse to Sheridan. Kills on Top's brother later died in an auto accident. Many of the Cheyennes believed that this death was the result of Laverne's sacrilege in assisting American Horse to abscond with the Sacred Hat.

changed his mind and was allowed to get out and hitchhike home.

While Buck Brien was apprehending the Keeper, things were moving in Lame Deer. The Chiefs were taking no chances. They appointed three men to ride with Henry Tall Bull in pursuit of both the Keeper and the chief of police. These men were Marion King, an aged Buffalo, Contrary Lodge, and Sun Dance priest; Charles White Dirt, head man of the Elks; and Alex Spotted Elk, one of the Kit Fox Society leaders. After speeding along the road to Sheridan, they arrived only to discover that Buck Brien had intercepted both Hat and Keeper. The chief of police was already racing up the road back to Lame Deer, his Winchester rifle hanging behind his head in the long, black sheriff's car that once had been a hearse.

When sheriff and passenger arrived back at the agency, there were further complications. Only the Buffalo priests were supposed to touch the sacred bundle, and no Buffalo priests were present. Finally the chief of police and the reservation superintendent, Don Jensen, escorted Is'siwun downstairs to the basement of the tribal office.

Tall Bull was back in the office next morning.[8] He was told that Is'siwun had been placed below for safekeeping. When word of this development spread, the Cheyennes kept away from headquarters. Some of them were murmuring that the tribal office was Is'siwun's tipi now.

The custodian of the tribal office had some news of his own, too. The night before, he had gone downstairs to switch off the basement lights. In a moment he was returning, charging up the steps taking four at a time. "That thing's alive down there! It's moving down there!" he had reported.

However, by one o'clock in the afternoon, things seemed to be quieting down. Tall Bull, the tribal treasurer, and the commodity clerk, were beginning to relax a bit. Henry Tall Bull recalls:

There was nobody around. It was really peaceful, really quiet.

[8] This section from Henry Tall Bull.

12

Then we started hearing noise downstairs. We kept hearing knocking on the walls—first on one wall; then on the other. All the doors were locked and nobody was around. We heard something moving down there.

The Treasurer was really scared. She wouldn't stay in the office by herself.

I said, "Let's take the day off and go home! That thing wants out! It wants a permanent home someplace!"[9]

While Is'siwun was restlessly moving at Tribal headquarters, there was also motion elsewhere. A meeting had been held at the home of Albert Tall Bull, Henry's stepfather, one of the most respected Sun Dance Instructors among the Northern Cheyennes. Decisions were made. Now the Chiefs and military society leaders were again heading for the tribal office.

"On our way out of the office, we met them coming down," Tall Bull recalled. "I told them to make up their minds right away and to get it out of the office!"

Fortunately, Davis Wounded Eye was present. The son of a former Hat Keeper, he had often assisted in the sacred tipi. He knew how to carry Is'siwun in the manner Erect Horns first taught the Suhtaio. While the usual occupants of the tribal office watched from a safe distance across the road (looking through the windows of the Treasurer's house), Wounded Eye entered the temporary Hat lodge. Elmore Brady, a Crazy Dog Society member, accompanied him.

In a while they appeared in the doorway. Wounded Eye was bearing Is'siwun on his back, the buffalo hide sack held in place by a strap encircling his neck. Outside, a station wagon was waiting. The Hat bearer climbed into its back seat, and the car bore them to Albert Tall Bull's home. A tipi was standing there, and Is'siwun was hung in it while the leaders considered the selection of a new Keeper. When his name was finally announced, the choice was Henry Little Coyote.[10]

[9] Henry Tall Bull.
[10] Details of the moving of Is'siwun to the home of Little Coyote are from field interviews with Davis Wounded Eye, 1959. Geographical details are from the author's personal observation.

Again the Sacred Hat was on the move. This time a pickup truck replaced the horses that had borne the older Keepers. Wounded Eye again carried Is'siwun, with Red Woman, another priest, accompanying him. Before they drove away, Wounded Eye gave some final instructions: the Buffalo Hat always moves before the people, so the other priests, the Chiefs, and the military men were to follow in other automobiles.

The Cheyennes say, "The pipe never fails." Nothing sacred begins without the offering of the pipe to the Sacred Persons who dwell at the four directions of the universe, to Maheo, and to Grandmother Earth. For this reason Red Woman carried a pipe as he took his place beside Wounded Eye, the Hat bearer, on the seat of the pickup. The procession of cars moved slowly out onto the highway, heading east, the direction of Ashland and the Tongue River. Red Woman was singing the sacred songs belonging to the Buffalo Hat, the songs sung on horseback as Is'siwun was borne ahead of earlier Cheyenne processions. Slowly, respectfully, the procession rolled along the blacktop road. Across the pine-capped divide, past the turnoff to Crazy Head Springs they traveled. Finally they began rolling down toward the tree-filled valley of the Tongue. Soon they turned off on a rutted dirt road meandering close to the river, the road which cuts back toward Birney village, the most isolated of the Cheyenne communities.

Along this road the procession continued, pausing for a moment while one of the military society members opened the wire gate of White Frog's old allotment. Here the old-time Suhtai priest-warrior had settled about 1900. The last white ranchers left the district then, allowing the Cheyennes clear title to this land along the west bank of the Tongue near Ashland.

Henry Little Coyote, White Frog's eighty-four-year-old son, lived here now. A slender, white-braided man, he was a former Chief and a Kit Fox Society leader. His wife, Weasel Woman, was with him. Although aged and wrinkled now, her classic features still hinted at her beauty as a girl. Then she had been married to Porcupine, the priest who carried the Ghost Dance to the Northern Cheyennes. Years later, after Porcupine's death, Henry Little Coyote had married her. Now they lived on White Frog's old allotment, with the house of Eugene Little Coyote, Little Coyote's son, standing nearby. Below both homes meandered the wooded valley of the Tongue.

Traditionally, the Elk Society men are the special guardians of the Sacred Hat, the Kit Foxes the guardians of the Arrows. Now, however, it was the Foxes who moved down the slope to the bottom land beside the river. Here the grass was long, merging into the cottonwoods that grew nearer the water. The peeled poles and canvas cover of Is'siwun's lodge were carried to an open spot in the middle of this grassy bottom land. The Foxes erected the three-pole tripod. Then they completed the circle of poles forming the framework of the lodge. The cover was lashed to a single pole, which was rested against the others. Finally, the plain white canvas cover was stretched taut over the framework. The building of Is'siwun's lodge was completed.

While the lodge was rising, one of the Kit Foxes had dug a hole some distance east of the tipi doorway. A forked pole was inserted in the hole. One of the military carried a red-painted disk of rawhide, trimmed with buffalo tails, from one of the waiting automobiles. This disk was Nimhoyoh, "The Turner," so-named because this sacred object can turn both sickness and death away from the Cheyenne people. Within the Sacred Hat lodge, Is'siwun rests against the Turner, as both hang suspended from a tripod near the head of the Keeper's bed. Nimhoyoh was hung temporarily upon the forked pole before the sacred lodge. The Keeper's backrest of peeled and red-painted willow poles was borne into the tipi. Then, after making the purifying motions first given by Sweet Medicine, one of the military society men carried the Turner into the Sacred Hat lodge.

Erect Horn's instructions to his successors have been preserved in Suhtai oral tradition. Among them was this admonition:

The Keeper of the Sacred Hat is always praying in his mind.

15

He does not do anything quickly. He does it slowly and well. Then everything will be good, and the game will be plentiful.[11]

While work on the lodge had progressed, the pickup truck and its sacred cargo had remained parked above the bottom land upon which the tipi rose. Now Wounded Eye carefully climbed from the vehicle, bearing the Buffalo Hat in her skin sack. Following Erect Horn's admonition, he slowly moved down the slope to the doorway of the lodge. Stooping, he entered, moving on across the earth floor to the southwest side of the tipi. Close to the west side, the place of honor, the Turner already had been hung upon the tripod of peeled wood. First making the four sacred motions, Wounded Eye rested the Hat bundle against Nimhoyoh, looping the carrying strap over the three intersecting poles.

Red Woman entered the lodge now, bearing the filled pipe in his hand. Little Coyote, Weasel Woman, the Chiefs and the military society members followed in single file, the men first removing their hats out of respect for Is'siwun's presence. The military society leaders took their seats along the north side of the lodge.

Little Coyote was silent as he took the Keeper's place by the Sacred Hat. He had been unaware that he had been chosen Keeper. Yet his family had been strong in the Suhtai sacred ways. White Frog, his father, was an instructor in both the Sun Dance and Massaum ceremonies. His mother, Comes Together, was the niece of Coal Bear, Is'siwun's Keeper during the final days of Cheyenne freedom. Little Coyote himself had danced in the Sun Dance carrying Ox'zem, Box Elder's Sacred Wheel Lance, during the ceremonies of the fourth day in the Medicine Lodge. He knew that the Hat Keeper's sacred responsibilities must be pondered before they were accepted or refused.

All was quiet within the lodge for a time. Then Weasel Woman softly addressed her husband. "Let us accept it, even though we do not know how to carry on all the ceremonies of the tipi."

[11] This quotation and the remainder of this narrative are from Henry Little Coyote to the author, 1959.

16

Little Coyote remained thoughtful for a while after that. Then he quietly spoke to the others sitting in a circle around him:

I am an old man. I will go as far as I can with it. But I want every one of you, and I want all the members of the tribe, to make a new start. We must all together make peace in a good way. Anything out of the way: we must put it from us.

Not only must this be true for the people of the Cheyennes. We have White people who treat us as relatives. We must all go together, with more understanding on both sides. Our Creator knows what happened today. If we do what is right, Maheo will bless us in the future.

Red Woman handed the pipe to Little Coyote, who lighted it. Then the new Keeper offered the pipe to the Sacred Persons who dwell at the four directions, to Maheo, and to Grandmother Earth. Finally, he offered the pipe to the Sacred Buffalo Hat. After this restless time, Is'siwun hung quietly at last.

2. Before We Came to the Buffalo

The mountain rises above the prairie, resembling a great, solitary grizzly bear. Surveying it through the bright clear air of the high plains, the Teton Sioux named it Bear Butte. To the Cheyennes, however, it is the Sacred Mountain, Nowah'wus, "The Hill Where the People Are Taught."[1]

[1] George Bird Grinnell, *The Cheyenne Indians, Their History and Ways of Life,* I, 201.

The Sacred Mountain is also called Pipe Mountain. George Bent to George E. Hyde, December 20, 1915, Coe Collection, Yale University Library.

This description of the Sacred Mountain was written when the author climbed Bear Butte with Richard Williams of Sturgis, South Dakota, in July, 1962. The older Cheyenne sites nearby were noted to the author by Willis Medicine Bull,

As fasters pause on its heights they hear the ceaseless wind moaning through stunted ponderosa pines with remnants of sacred offering cloths flapping from their lower branches. Rising and falling like the echoes of a great waterfall, the noise of the wind recedes into the infinity stretching beyond the four directions where the Sacred Persons dwell. Turquoise pools of water splash the yellows, greens, and browns of the prairie in good summers. In bad times the land lies flat, scorched, lifeless.

Today, Cheyenne pilgrims climbing Nowah'wus see the marks of the past all around them. Circles of rocks form the tipi rings of older camp sites. An eagle-catching pit is near. High on the butte itself, that great bird so close to Thunder still nests. Circling above the stone heights he watches the fasters down below. A spring marks the place from which the people gathered blue clay to make the sky color used in decorating the rawhide parfleches. And to the southwest lies the spot where the Buffalo People themselves first gave the Suhtaio the Sacred Medicine Lodge, the Sun Dance.

This is the heart of the Cheyenne sacred places and sacred ways. This is where the All Father and the Sacred Powers themselves gave Sweet Medicine the four Sacred Arrows. Here is where the story of the sacred ceremonies should begin.

But Cheyenne life has not always centered around the Sacred Mountain and the buffalo. Even after the wars with the whites, some people remained who could recall the woodland traditions, remnants of the sacred ways practiced when the people lived far to the east. In the time of the ceremonies focusing upon Nowah'wus and the buffalo herds, there were still in the tribe some persons who venerated earlier days and ways.

As an elderly priest recalled, the Peoples' history was divided into four parts. There was the ancient time, when the Cheyennes were happy. Then a terrible disease arose, decimating the tribe, leaving the people as orphans. The "time of the dogs" followed

John Stands in Timber, and Albert Tall Bull—all of whom have made pilgrimages to the Sacred Mountain.

this catastrophe, the days when dogs were used as beasts of burden. Next, the Cheyennes moved out beyond the Missouri. "The time of the buffalo" had arrived, ultimately followed by "the time of the horse."[2]

As late as the early 1900's, a few older persons recalled the songs in which the lakes, fish, and waterfowl were praised, "before we came to the buffalo." One elderly woman remembered her grandmother's knowledge of songs praising the old times "when they lived on fishes and fowls, and had not to eat 'this nauseating buffalo meat.' "[3]

Hotoanamos, an aged priest who was born about 1794, declared, "My great-grandfather knew nothing of the religious sweat lodge, Sun Dance, and other ceremonies we have now, which change over the years."[4]

Once, an elderly lady recalled in 1911, the people lived near lakes and ate fish all year round. Springtime brought the opportunity of supplementing this diet with young birds and birds' eggs. Fish bones were pounded and boiled by the women in order to get the rich, clear white oil from them. Canoes were made from tree trunks. The centers of the trunks were burned out, and the residue then hacked away to form the boat. Willow snares were made in which to catch fish. In the fall, the Cheyennes hunted skunks, because these animals were fat at that season. Dogs were the pack animals—large, strong beasts that howled at the approach of morning like their relatives the wolves.[5]

Dwellings were simple. Poles were stuck into the ground to form a framework which was covered with mats constructed from rushes, bark, and slough grass tied in bundles. An opening in the top allowed smoke to escape. The doors made from grass or rushes were so low that the Cheyennes had to crawl on hands

---

[2] Petter, *Dictionary*, s.v. "Cheyenne," 229.

[3] *Ibid.*

[4] Rodolphe Petter, *Reminiscences of Past Years in Mission Service Among the Cheyenne*, 29.

[5] George Bent to Hyde, August 12, 1911, and August 22, 1911, Coe Collection.

and knees to enter or leave. These early lodges were built near the lakes, where fish and fowl would be readily available. Not until they came to the Missouri did the people make earth lodges similar to those of the Mandans and Arikaras. The Cheyennes were poor in those early times, possessing little more than the belongings men and women could pack on their backs.[6]

Timber was scarce, so bunches of grass were used for fuel. Tied in bundles, the grass would burn slowly when lighted. Robes were fashioned from the skins of skunks, raccoons, and minks.

In fact, they used most any kind of skins to make robes to keep warm, as it was very cold where they lived in olden times.[7]

These are random memories of life in the valley of the Minnesota river in southwestern Minnesota, life in the land where forests were beginning to merge into prairie.[8]

However, even in these early times the Cheyennes were beginning to feel the power of the white man. Hudson's Bay Company was organized in 1670. Its chain of trading posts extended across the territory of the Cree tribe. Prior to 1679, the Assiniboins allied with the Crees, who had already obtained guns from the English. To the east, the French had been supplying the Chippewas with firearms. Thus, from both east and northeast these armed tribes began to press upon the surrounding tribes— especially the Sioux.

At that period the Cheyennes were dwelling in the valley of the Minnesota. They had learned to cultivate the soil and had built a village near Lac-qui-Parle. Remote from both French and British, the people possessed few, if any, firearms. Under the mounting pressure from Crees, Assiniboins and Chippewas,

[6] George Bent to Hyde, March 5, 1914, Coe Collection.

[7] George Bent to Hyde, August 22, 1911, Coe Collection.

[8] Cf. Donald J. Berthrong, *The Southern Cheyennes*, "Early Migrations of the Cheyennes," 3–26. Professor Berthrong gives the fullest available account of Cheyenne movements west.

the Cheyennes and Sioux were steadily pressed nearer and nearer to the Missouri River.[9]

Moving westward, the people came to the valley of the Red River of the North. Here they occupied at least one village at the great bend of the Sheyenne River.[10] They had acquired horses sometime after 1750, but they also continued the practice of agriculture. If they owned any firearms at all, they were exceedingly few.[11] The Chippewas, long since armed with guns, burned this Cheyenne village about 1780. Again the people were forced further west.[12]

Of the crossing of the Missouri River, only fragments of tradition remain. Black Moccasin, long regarded as their most reliable historian, stated that some Cheyennes reached the river about 1676.[13] Another account says that when they first came to the river many recently drowned bison lay along the banks. They then named the Missouri, E'omita'i—"It gives us, the people, fat"—in remembrance of this welcome food supply.[14]

The Cheyennes were still a poor people, possessing no buffalo skin lodges or lodge poles.[15] The Mandans and Arikaras transported them across the river in buffalo rawhide bullboats.[16] This crossing appears to have taken place above the Arikara, and below the Mandan, villages. On the west side of the Missouri, the Cheyennes built their own fortified earth-lodge village above

[9] James Mooney, *The Cheyenne Indians. Memoirs of the American Anthropological Association*, I, 364.

[10] G. F. Will and G. E. Hyde, *Corn Among the Indians of the Upper Missouri*, 44f.

William D. Strong, "From History to Prehistory in the Northern Great Plains," *Smithsonian Miscellaneous Collections*, Vol. C, 359ff.

[11] Strong, *ibid.*

[12] Will and Hyde, *op. cit.*, 44f.; Berthrong, *op. cit.*, 8.

[13] George Bird Grinnell, *The Fighting Cheyennes*, 3.

[14] Grinnell, "Cheyenne Stream Names," AA, N.S., Vol. VIII, 16.

[15] George Bent to Hyde, January 27, 1914, Coe Collection.

Bent says the Cheyennes did not make lodges until after they crossed the Missouri into the lands where buffalo and elk were plentiful. Elk skins were also used for lodge covers then, and lodge poles were obtained near the Black Hills. It was when the Cheyennes reached the Black Hills that they began to have fine, large tipis and to prosper.

[16] George Bent to Hyde, February 19, 1914, Coe Collection.

Standing Rock, near present-day Fort Yates, North Dakota. Here, again, they planted corn, beans, and squash.[17]

Archaeological evidence, plus Sioux and Cheyenne tradition, indicates that the Cheyennes occupied sites on the Missouri between 1750 and 1780. Elk River, the venerable Northern horse catcher, stated that the people built two such villages. The first was "above the Standing Rock." From this area some of the Cheyennes moved toward the Black Hills, following the buffalo herds and seeking other game. The remainder of the tribe moved south and built a village near the mouth of Cheyenne River. Elk River's mother, who was born about 1786, pointed out this village in 1877. The old woman stated that the people still lived and planted gardens there when she was a girl.[18]

Trade was carried on, the Cheyennes taking horses, meat and robes to the Mandans, Hidatsas, and Arikaras. They exchanged these goods for corn, dried pumpkin, tobacco, guns, and European goods. The Cheyennes then carried these wares out to the Black Hills or, later, down to the Platte just above its forks. There the Kiowas and Comanches would meet the people for a trading fair. The southern tribes brought horses and some Spanish goods—especially the gaudy striped blankets the northern tribes prized so greatly.[19]

These were times of insecurity, also. In the old earth-lodge villages, holes were dug, some of them three or four feet deep. Around the holes, poles were placed, bent over at the top, and covered with tall grass and dirt. These were their breastworks. Throughout the night, all the Cheyennes stayed within these walls in case of an attack. When evening arrived, the old men would cry out to warn the warriors to prepare for enemies. Women and children were instructed to put on their moccasins, in case they had to flee. The women carried awls and skins, so that if they were forced to run, raw material for new moccasins would be with them.

17 Will and Hyde, *op.cit.*, 44 f.
18 *Ibid.*, 44n.
19 *Ibid.*, 184 f.

They had been attacked by the Assiniboines so often and driven
from their homes [that]everyone had their things all ready at the
head of their beds.

Men and women sat up all night watching their children . . . .
In the daytime the old people slept. The old timers said they had
hard times in olden times.[20]

It was "near the pipestone quarries in a land of lakes" that the
Cheyennes and Suhtaio traditionally first met.[21] The language of
the Suhtaio or Buffalo People was a dialect recognizable to the
Tsistsistas, but rougher, harsher, and more gutteral.[22] Fire Wolf,
who at his death in 1966 was the oldest of the Northern Suhtai
Buffalo and Sun Dance priests, recalled the tradition concerning that meeting:

The Tsistsistas used to head north in the season when the birds
shed their feathers. During one of these trips, Tsistsistas and
Suhtaio met and fought.

In the midst of the battle, a Tsistsistas warrior named Wise
Buffalo recognized the Suhtai language was almost the same as his
own. After talking together, crying out from a distance, four of the
Desert People and four of the Suhtaio came out. They motioned
to each other to come on, and to meet in the middle.

The Tsistsistas said, "We are Desert People." The Suhtaio said,
"We are Suhtaio."

After that—nobody remembers how—they came together. A

[20] George Bent to Hyde, May 22, 1914, Coe Collection.

[21] Fire Wolf to the author, 1959. For further Cheyenne statements see Appendix VII.

Cf. Berthrong, op. cit., 10. Berthrong states that the Suhtaio joined the Cheyennes while the Cheyennes were living on the Missouri. Cf. also, John R. Swanton,
The Indian Tribes of North America, B.A.E. Bulletin 145, s.v. "Suhtaio," 258.

[22] Tsis tsis' tas (Zezestas: Petter) is the name of the Cheyenne proper.
Anciently, they called themselves Desert or Sand Hill People. This name is still
used to designate them in the sacred ceremonies.

Cf. Petter, Dictionary, s.v. "Cheyenne," 228, and "Indian," 582.

Also, George Bird Grinnell, "Some Early Cheyenne Tales," J.A.F.L., Vol. XX,
No. 78 (July–September, 1907), 169; and ibid., Vol. XXI, No. 82 (October–December, 1908), 303.

The Cheyennes call the Suhtaio (singular, Suhtai) (Sota; Sotaeo: Petter) the
Buffalo People, because the Suhtai ceremonies traditionally derive from the Buffalo themselves, and are related to the calling and renewing of these animals.

long time after, they roamed together, south and west. They crossed the Missouri long before the white man came west.[23]

As late as 1830 or 1831, the Suhtaio continued to camp by themselves.[24] They still regarded their Cheyenne allies as a different tribe, and continued to speak their old language. Intermarriage was practiced among the Suhtaio; not, however, with the other Cheyenne bands.[25] Suhtai women wore skin dresses, with suspender-like straps over the shoulders. One tradition says that the Suhtaio brought the painted tipis with them. Like the Cheyennes, they camped in a circle, their lodges opening toward the sunrise. "More constant; less flexible," the Suhtaio described themselves, contrasting their conservatism with the fluidity that was characteristic of the Cheyenne sacred ways and tribal customs. Many years later, Wolf Chief stated that by 1833, the Year the Stars Fell, the two tribes were united.[26]

The Suhtaio's greatest gift to the Tsistsistas was Is'siwun, the Sacred Buffalo Hat. With the Hat came her related ceremonies, the Sun Dance, Sweat Lodge, and Buffalo ceremonies. The Tsistsistas and Suhtaio were now one Cheyenne tribe. Thenceforth, with the Sacred Arrow and Sacred Hat ceremonies growing in power, the importance of the older agricultural ceremonies diminished under the ascendancy of the hunting and world-renewal rites.

Cheyenne oral traditions mirror this transition from farming to hunting. There is, for instance, the account of the two young men who visited the old woman in the spring:

When we first got corn, two young men dressed alike heard a

23 Fire Wolf, 1959.
24 George Bird Grinnell, "Social Organization of the Cheyennes," International Congress of Americanists Proceedings, Vol. XIII, 135; Grinnell, Cheyenne Indians, I, 87.
25 Grinnell, Cheyenne Indians, I, 86ff.
26 Truman Michelson Notes, Smithsonian Institution, National Anthropological Archives, August 11, 1913, and August 13, 1913. Interviews with Wolf Chief and Wrapped Hair.
George Bent stated that in 1865 there were about seventy-five lodges of Suhtaio. By 1914, only about twenty Suhtaio lodges remained in Oklahoma. George Bent to Hyde, November 7, 1914, Coe Collection.

noise in the mountains. They went there. One said, "Why did you follow me to this big spring?" The other said, "Because I am going too!"

They went down into the spring. There was an old woman, pounding corn, making hominy.

The Cheyennes were starving. The old woman said, "I am Grandmother Earth."

She gave them bags and said, "When you get back, call the people. Let the orphans eat first; then the rest. For four days, let the buffalo come to the camp. Do not kill them until the fourth day!"

That is why the Cheyennes call her the Earth Mother: because she gave the Cheyennes everything—corn, buffalo.[27]

The names of these young men are those of the Suhtai and Cheyenne culture heroes, Erect Horns and Sweet Medicine. However, in this account they also possess second names: Red Tassel or Standing on the Ground (as corn does), and Rustling Corn Leaf or Sweet Root Standing.[28] The fact that they possess both names indicates the reidentification of the older agricultural traditions with the later bearers of the Arrows and Hat, sacred objects related to the hunt. This account links the old cornfields along the Missouri to the buffalo and the high plains.

The Cheyennes, then, adapted their earlier ceremonies to the new life west of the Sacred Mountain, out in the clear, dry air of the prairies. The People did what others have done before them; they carried their holy places with them.

For example, at least one Cheyenne tradition speaks of a sacred mountain and a large spring far to the east. This is the site described in the account of the two young men who visited Grandmother Earth in the spring of water.

[27] Mary Inkanish to the author. Cf. parallel accounts in Grinnell's "Some Early Cheyennes Tales" loc. cit., Vol. XX, No. 78, By Cheyenne Campfires, and Cheyenne Indians. Also, George Dorsey, The Cheyenne: Ceremonial Organization, Field Museum Publication 99, Anthropological Series, Vol. IX, No. 1, (March, 1905), 39f. (Hereafter referred to as The Cheyenne, I).

[28] "The name Red Tassel refers to a stalk of maize in bloom. Rustling Corn Leaf refers to the sound made by the corn leaves as they rub against each other in the wind." Rufus Wallowing to the author, 1957.

Fire Wolf recalled other sacred sites:

> The Suhtaio came from the north across the Missouri river. There were several medicine mounds where the Indians fasted. However, there was one principal mound: Nowah'wus, the Sacred Mountain.[29]

Since there are glimpses of holy mounds or mountains in the traditions from the days before the Sacred Mountain was known to Cheyenne eyes, it must have been from one of these earlier high places, later identified with Nowah'wus, that the Prophet brought the Sacred Arrows. Their acquisition, as we have said, preceded the union of the Tsistsistas and Suhtaio into one Cheyenne tribe.

There are earlier traditions relating to the Arrows, also. One states that their shafts first were made from trees growing in the East.[30] Mahuts's points are of stone rather than of the later metal brought by the white traders. The Cheyennes believe that stone possesses some of the attributes of eternity. At the Sacred Mountain, itself formed from stone, Maheo and the Powers had told Sweet Medicine to choose one of four Persons present to be himself: that is, he should choose the Person he would most like to resemble. The culture hero made the wrong choice. When he did so, Maheo and the Sacred Persons groaned, saying that Sweet Medicine would have lived forever had he chosen the Person who really was stone.[31]

The Kit Foxes are traditionally the oldest of the Cheyenne warrior societies. Their origins are said to extend back beyond the Missouri crossing. One of the Kit Fox songs often was sung by warriors facing certain death in battle. The words stress the theme of the eternity of stone, for they say,

> *Nothing lives long—*
> *Except the rocks.*[32]

[29] Fire Wolf.
[30] Grinnell states that the shafts are of currant bush. "The Great Mysteries . . .," *loc. cit.*, 558.
[31] Grinnell, *Cheyenne Campfires*, 274f.
[32] John Stands in Timber, a member of the Kit Fox Society, to the author, 1956.

Originally, nothing coming into the presence of the Arrows, Buffalo Hat, or sacred warbonnets should have been touched by white man's metal. Nothing eaten in the sacred feasts should have been killed by iron or gunpowder.[33]

On the plains, only fragments of these agricultural and woodland traditions remained with the Cheyennes. However, the eagle catchers still carried corn balls into the pits with them when they waited in hiding to capture the great birds. Eagle catching was sacred work, because the breath feathers represented the Sacred Powers themselves. Eagle tail plumes fluttered from the warbonnets, the plumes possessing the same holy symbolism as the breath feathers. Eating corn balls in the pit was part of the sacred ritual which brought the catcher both a blessing and success.[34]

Finally, even after the Cheyennes reached the prairie, their calendar designated May and the beginning of June as Enanoeshe, "the Planting Moon."[35]

The corn dances continued, even though they were overshadowed by the ceremonies related to Mahuts and Is'siwun. The dancers were young girls and women. Men singers accompanied their dancing, keeping time with gourd rattles representing the squash. One woman led the dancers. It was she who bore the ear of sacred corn, carrying it by means of a stick fitted into the butt of the ear. In later years, the corn dance was largely social, or it was held as a sign of rejoicing when a war party continued.[36]

There are also accounts of the Cheyennes farming on the Grand River and the Little Missouri, North Platte, and Laramie rivers. George Bird Grinnell wrote that Cheyenne testimony affirming that they farmed up to the year 1865 is too general to be ignored.[37]

[33] Grinnell notes that until recent times there were older Cheyennes who would not eat or drink from the metal dishes made by whites. *Cheyenne Indians*, I, 171.

[34] Will and Hyde, *op. cit.*, 161.

[35] Petter, *Dictionary*, s.v. "Moon," 718.
W. P. Clark, *Indian Sign Language*, 261.

[36] Grinnell, *Cheyenne Indians*, I, 251 ff.

Cf. Robert Anderson, "Notes on Northern Cheyenne Corn Ceremonialism," *The Masterkey*, XXXII, No. 2 (March–April, 1958), 58ff.

Bridge, Sleepy Jack Rabbit, and a few other medicine doctors used Ree and Mandan gourds and medicine for healing. An ear of Ree or Mandan corn was also used in the same ceremonies:

One woman or more danced. They had in each hand [a] prairie dog skin that contained some medicine. Every little while, the women would lay down on the ground, would raise the skins, and point them at whoever they were doctoring. They supposed the medicine would enter into the sick person's body and cure him.

Cheyenne medicine [men] used rattles filled with coarse gravel. Rees and Mandans filled their rattles with different kinds [of] sand.[38]

Recollections of a corn dance held at Fort Keogh, Montana, in 1890 still remain. The ceremony was given when Little Chief's band arrived there after years of detention at Pine Ridge Agency. Little Creek and Strong Left Hand gave the dance.[39] John Stands in Timber recalled these details:

When the Cheyennes were through, they passed out corn in a wooden dish. Everyone present, small and big, took two or three kernels of corn, and ate them. When they finished, they claimed the corn never disappeared from the dish. It stayed the same.

The corn ceremony was used at planting time, when the people planted along the Cheyenne river. Some Cheyennes say they used elk horns. They cut them off at the prongs, except the last prong by the root of the horn. Then they held the horn upside down, and used it as a hoe.

Those things were used to plant corn in a sacred way; but it's not like the corn we see now.[40]

[37] Grinnell, *Cheyenne Indians*, I, 253.
Cf. *Ibid.*, 30, 251, 253f.; George Bent to Hyde, February 10, 1915, February 18, 1915, and October 26, 1916, Coe Collection.
[38] George Bent to Hyde, November 9, 1916, Coe Collection.
[39] John Stands in Timber to the author, 1959. Strong Left Hand was said to possess such power that he could kill animals simply by throwing bones or stones at them.
[40] John Stands in Timber to the author, 1960.
Dan Old Bull, who was eight years old at the time, stated that the Cheyennes had a corn dance the summer after their surrender at Fort Keogh in 1877. Bridge, the last survivor of the Ree Society, led it. Robert Anderson, "Notes on . . . Corn Ceremonialism," *loc. cit.*, 60.
John Stands in Timber also stated that the Cheyennes claim they were the first

The last ears of sacred corn disappeared among the flames of Morning Star's camp. Raised from the original seed carried from Grandmother Earth's lodge below the spring, this corn had been watched over by Bridge himself.

Thus it was on the prairies that the Sacred Arrows, with their power over men and over animals, rose to full ascendency. Now hunting and dominance over the enemy were more important than agriculture. Tradition linked the Arrows to a holy mountain, and so Nowah'wus became the focal point of the Cheyenne sacred ceremonies and tribal life.

Veneration for the corn lingered on into the twentieth century, nevertheless. A 1913 letter from George Bent to George Hyde gives us a glimpse of this observance. Bent writes:

> ... My son is going to plant that corn and other seed you send me. I told old Cheyennes that was the corn that Cheyennes planted on Missouri river way back. They took one grain of this corn in their hands, rub themselves with it all over their bodies. Then hung their heads down and prayed . . . .[41]

Even the Arrows, the Sacred Mountain, and the Buffalo Hat could not completely erase the memories of those days "before we came to the buffalo."

---

to plant corn, then the other tribes took it from them. The Rees were the first to obtain corn from the Cheyennes.

[41] George Bent to Hyde, May 23, 1919, Coe Collection.

A sacred object often is rubbed over the body in order to cover one's entire being with the blessing of the holy thing. The grain of corn was rubbed over their bodies because of its sacred connotation. Cf. the rubbing of Sweet Medicine's hair over the bodies of the worshippers during the Arrow ceremonies in 1960.

3. The Whole Camp Was Crying

The Pawnees long had been the bravest enemies of the People. The two tribes had been fighting ever since the first Cheyenne bands moved into the country of the Yellowstone and the Platte. Old people said they were like two buffalo bulls battling in spring, their robes caked with dried mud. First one animal gained the advantage over his adversary, pushing him back until the very weight of the enemy slowed down his offensive. Then, with a sudden burst of strength, the second bull rallied. His hind legs churned the damp prairie soil as he threw back his opponent. The advantage shifted back and forth until exhaustion left the bulls with heaving sides, foam-flecked mouths, and no further strength for fighting—at least for the moment.

It was the same way in the wars with the Wolf People, as the Cheyennes named the Pawnees. First one tribe pushed back the warriors of the other. Then the second tribe retaliated with fresh raids against the villages of the enemy.

It was the summer of 1830, the season when the wild cherry bushes bent under the weight of ripening fruit, and this year's raiding would be no ordinary matter.[1] This time the Sacred Arrows were leading the Cheyennes against the Pawnees, only the third such move of Mahuts in tribal history. The entire tribe was following, for no one remained behind when the Sacred Arrows were carried against an enemy. Some of the Sioux had smoked the war pipe also, thus signifying their willingness to join this attack on a mutual foe.[2]

At the head of the Cheyenne tribe rode White Thunder, the Keeper of Mahuts.[3] Watchful riders from the military societies were guarding him, because his was the most sacred position among the People. The Cheyennes were a tribe spiritually nourished by sacrifice, consequently their spiritual leader bore scars on his arms, shoulders, legs, chest, and back.[4] A flint knife had been used for this cutting, this offering of the Arrow Keeper's own flesh to Maheo and the four Sacred Persons.[5] The symbols of the Sun and Moon were carved on White Thunder's chest; for when a Cheyenne sacrificed his body, he usually stood with his eyes turned toward the Sun. He was "standing against the

[1] Grinnell, "Great Mysteries . . . ," loc. cit., 556; George E. Hyde, The Pawnee Indians, 126f.

Bent, however, places the event in 1833. Cf. George Bent to Hyde, February 6, 1905, Coe Collection; George Bent, "The Battle of the Medicine Arrows," The Frontier, Vol. IV, No. 5 (November, 1905), 3; George E. Hyde, Life of George Bent, 49ff.

[2] Six such moves behind the Sacred Arrows were made in Cheyenne history. Cf. Appendix III.

[3] Also called Gray Thunder or Painted Thunder. He was the father-in-law of William Bent, founder of Bent's Fort.

[4] Cf. drawing in Grinnell, "Great Mysteries . . . ," loc. cit., 545.

[5] Ibid., 544ff.

Sun," as a warrior stood against the enemy; and he continued to do so until the Moon, the "Sun of the Night," appeared. Such a sacrifice won the pity of Maheo, the Sacred Persons, and the Maiyun. It also won the man a share in the Sun's own life-giving and life-renewing power.

White Thunder's wife rode beside him. In ordinary times, it was she who kept the sacred tipi neat and spotless. Now she was bearing the Sacred Arrow bundle on her back, just as Sweet Medicine's woman first bore Mahuts from the Sacred Mountain. The faces and hands of White Thunder and his wife were covered with red paint, because red is the life color. Again, this was in obedience to the instructions Maheo and the Sacred Powers gave the first Arrow Keeper and his woman inside the Holy Mountain.[6]

The Cheyennes moved on across the prairies, with the Sacred Arrows leading them. Families walked carelessly, traveling in small groups. Off to one side, the Sacred Hat Woman carried Is'siwun on her back. She moved slowly, out of respect for the Buffalo Hat that Erect Horns first wore as he led the herds to the starving Suhtai camp. The Cheyennes traveled in this fashion until they reached a spot where the South Platte flows into the North Platte, at the mouth of Kingfisher water.[7] Somewhere ahead of them, the Skidi Pawnees had assembled to sacrifice a captive maiden to the Morning Star.[8]

Scouting parties had been dispatched to locate the enemy, but they reported no sign of the Pawnees. Then a larger war party was sent ahead of the main camp. This party scouted for several days, but it, too, was unsuccessful. Four of the scouts were ordered back to the main Cheyenne village. They bore word

[6] George Bent to Hyde, July 6, 1914, Coe Collection.

[7] George Bent to Hyde, February 6, 1905, Coe Collection.
Cf. George Bent, "The Battle of the Medicine Arrows," loc. cit., 3; also, Grinnell, "Great Mysteries . . . ," loc. cit., 556.
Grinnell, using a Pawnee source, gives the site as near the South Loup. Luther North states that White Eagle, a Skidi born c. 1820, gave the site as the mouth of the Birdwood, twenty miles above North Platte City. Cf. "Life and Experiences of Captain Luther H. North of the Pawnee Battalion," Correspondence with George E. Hyde, 1928–34, Yale University Library, 31.

[8] Grinnell, "Great Mysteries . . . ," loc. cit., 551.

that the main body should cut across country to a designated spot rather than follow the war party. Meanwhile, the other scouts continued their search for enemy signs.[9]

Suddenly sounds of excitement broke out at the head of the main column. Wailing rose above the noise of other voices. The four scouts had been located. They were dead, and their rotting bodies showed signs of having been dragged about. The Pawnees obviously were near, and the presence of the Cheyennes had been detected.

Now the Cheyennes were impatient for revenge and they pushed forward throughout the entire day and night. Finally, late at night, they reached the Skidi village. They drew up in a line near it, but remained out of sight. Early next morning, scouts discovered a number of Pawnees making preparations for a buffalo chase. The Cheyennes waited, hoping that these men would leave the village. However, when some of the enemy rode near them, warrior patience cracked, and the Cheyennes charged.[10] Men hastily uncovered their shields, offering them to Maheo and to the Sacred Persons before slipping them on their left arms. War bonnets were removed from their painted parfleches. They were shaken out, offered to the Sacred Persons, and hurriedly laced beneath warrior chins. Some of the fighting men spat sacred sweet root upon the hoofs of their war ponies, thereby blessing the animals and making them swift and sure-footed for the fighting ahead.

The charge occurred so swiftly that White Thunder had no opportunity to hold the blinding ceremonies.[11] There was no time for him to place a bit of sweet root in his mouth, to chew it fine, and then to blow the root toward the four directions, the homes of the Sacred Persons. Next, he should have blown sweet root towards the Pawnees themselves. Then they would have been blinded by the power of the root into which Sweet Medicine had transformed himself.

[9] *Ibid.*, 556.
[10] *Ibid.*
[11] George Bent, "The Battle of the Medicine Arrows," *loc. cit.*, 3.

34

White Thunder should have exposed Mahuts upon a bed of sacred white "man" sage. Beginning at the height of the enemies' feet, the Keeper should have elevated the Arrows slowly until the stone points were aimed at the hearts and finally at the heads of the Pawnees. He should have sung,

There you lie helpless,
Easily to be wiped out!

as he performed this ceremony.

The Keeper should have been dancing as he chanted this song, his left foot extended and keeping time to the music. He should have made short thrusting motions with the Arrows, aiming them at the foe as he danced. The Cheyenne warriors should have formed a line behind him. Each man should have danced as the Keeper danced, his left foot forward, thrusting at the enemy with his weapon, just as the Keeper did with Mahuts. The warriors should have shouted at each thrust with the Arrows, just as they shouted in charging the enemy. Finally, after White Thunder had pointed Mahuts toward the Skidi four times, he should have thrust the Arrows toward the earth. Then he would have been ready to fasten Mahuts to the lance of the man who would bear the Arrows into battle.

Throughout this ceremony, the Cheyenne women and girls should have taken seats behind the men. Their heads would have been covered and their faces averted, since no woman is allowed to gaze upon Mahuts.

Elsewhere, the Keeper of the Sacred Hat should have placed Is'siwun upon the head of another brave warrior, tying the chin string to hold the Hat in place. Then the bearers of the two Great Mysteries of the Cheyennes should have charged ahead, in advance of the line of warriors.[12]

Normally, the bearer of Mahuts galloped toward the right side of the enemy line, because the Arrow lodge always stood on the inner south side, the right side, of the Cheyenne camp circle. The Sacred Hat wearer charged toward the left of the

[12] Grinnell, "Great Mysteries . . . ," *loc. cit.,* 571–72.

35

enemy line, because Is'siwun's lodge was located to the left of the Arrow tipi within the camp circle.[13] Then, as they neared the Pawnees, the bearers of the Great Mysteries should have passed each other, changing positions as they continued around the rear of the Skidi line. The Pawnees would have been confused and blinded by the power of the Arrows and the Hat, and the bearers would gallop triumphantly back to the advancing Cheyennes.[14]

However, on this occasion there was only time for White Thunder to lash Mahuts to the lance of Bull, a priest-warrior. The Keeper fastened the Arrow bundle just below the spear point, rather than tying the Man Arrows and Buffalo Arrows to the lance in separate pairs. Moreover, instead of confidently leading the Cheyenne charge, Bull found that he had been left behind in the confusion.

The Skidi warriors were drawn up in a line facing the Cheyennes across a wide flat. They appeared far from blinded or terror-stricken. The Skidi village was in plain view of the Cheyenne women and children, who were waiting in a circle behind the men, much as they did when the Cheyennes were about to pitch camp. The Skidi women and children looked on from the roofs of their earth lodges. Some Pawnee women were making the trill, encouraging their warriors onward.

Now, among the Skidi, there was a sick man who believed that this was a good day to die. His friends had borne him in a robe to a position in advance of the Pawnee line. The sick man sat there, singing his death song, his bow and arrows before him as he waited to sell his life dearly.[15] The sick Pawnee was still chanting his death song when Bull finally pulled away from the

---

[13] The sacred tipis were pitched on the south side of the Cheyenne camp circle, forty or fifty yards beyond the innermost circle of lodges. The Arrow tipi was easternmost, with the Hat tipi to the west of it. No other lodges were allowed within the inner circle unless a major dance, council, or great feast was in session. In such cases, a large double lodge would be erected in the center.

[14] Grinnell, "Great Mysteries . . . ," *loc. cit.*, 573.

[15] George A. Dorsey, "How the Pawnee Captured the Cheyenne Medicine Arrows," A.A., N.S., Vol. V, No. 4, 645.
Cf. Grinnell, "Great Mysteries . . . ," *loc. cit.*, 551 f.

Cheyenne line. Some Cheyenne warriors already had struck the Skidi with their lances and coup sticks as they rode by. They shouted to Bull, "Do not go near him. He has already been killed!" meaning that coups already had been counted upon him.

Bull ignored the shouts. He attempted to ride over the Pawnee and to touch him with his lance. Unfortunately, Bull's horse shied. When the Cheyenne attempted to strike the sick enemy, the Pawnee quickly moved the trunk of his body, avoiding the thrust. Then the Skidi grabbed the extended lance and wrenched it from Bull's hands. The Cheyenne was nearly unhorsed by the power of that pull. He released the lance rather than face death in hand-to-hand fighting on the ground.[16] The sick man, looking at his prize, spied the Arrow bundle. "Come here quickly and take this! Here is something wonderful!" he cried.[17]

Bull's wailing was drowned in the triumphant shouts of the Skidi who raced to surround the seated victor. The Cheyennes charged too, but the Pawnees were faster. The Cheyennes did succeed in killing the brave invalid.[18] By that time some of the Pawnees had galloped back to Big Eagle, a noted Skidi chief, and handed him the sacred trophy. Then Big Eagle charged, brandishing the lance with its Arrow bundle. The despirited Cheyennes melted before his onslaught like snow melting before the Chinooks in the north country.

Elk River, the venerable Northern Cheyenne horse catcher, later recalled the sorrow of the journey home:

A young man of the Cheyenne went back to their camp where the old men, the women, and the children were, and told them that the medicine arrows had been captured. The men, women, and children all cried. Soon after this the fight stopped, and the Cheyenne moved back away from the Pawnee camp. How many were killed on either side was not known. The whole camp was crying all the time as it moved along, mourning over the loss of

[16] Grinnell, "Great Mysteries . . . ," *loc. cit.*, 551 f.
[17] *Ibid.*
[18] Details differ. One Pawnee account states that he was killed two years later, during a Cheyenne attack on the Pawnees.
Cf. Dorsey, "How the Pawnee Captured the . . . Arrows," *loc. cit.*, 651.

the medicine arrows more than over the loss of the people who had been killed.

The Cheyenne kept traveling until they returned to the place from which they had started—their own country. When they made camp, a lodge for the medicine arrows was pitched in the usual place, but it was empty: the arrows were gone.[19]

We have noted that the Suhtaio refer to the Tsistsistas, the Cheyenne proper, as being more fluid and less constant than themselves. In the face of this crisis the Tsistsistas displayed the profound spirituality coupled with down-to-earth practicality that is typical of the old Cheyenne attitude toward life. About four years later, the Chiefs, the Sacred Arrow Keeper, and the Keeper's four assistant priests all gathered. The leaders of the military societies sat nearby, listening. All of them knew that the People could not exist without the supremely holy objects whose power bound the Cheyennes to the Creator Himself. Therefore, they decided to consecrate four new Arrows. Box Elder and Crazy Mule, both famous holy men, were honored by being chosen to prepare the shafts of the new Mahuts. The ceremonies were marked by the same devotion manifested by the Cheyennes during the renewing of the original Arrows.[20]

Then, about 1835, White Thunder and his wife, Old Bark, his woman, and Doll Man, crossed the enemy-infested prairies to the Skidi village on the Republican River.[21] Here they were given sanctuary in Big Eagle's own lodge, where they begged the chief to return Mahuts to the Cheyennes. However, the Pawnee chief would give them only one Buffalo Arrow.[22] Big Eagle and

[19] Grinnell, "Great Mysteries . . . ," loc. cit., 558.

[20] John Stands in Timber stated to the author in 1966 that Box Elder and Crazy Mule held a Spirit Lodge ceremony. There, a Maiyun told them to keep the two original Mahuts and to make the two substitutes. This, of course, contradicts the sequence of events given by Grinnell.

Cf. Grinnell, "Great Mysteries . . . ," loc. cit., 559; George Bent to Hyde, February 6, 1905, Coe Collection; Bent, "The Battle of the Medicine Arrows," loc. cit., 4; Hyde, George Bent, 51.

[21] Hyde, Pawnee Indians, 139f. Bent gives the date as 1835, two years after their capture in 1833. George Bent to Hyde, February 6, 1905, Coe Collection. Grinnell, Cheyenne Indians, I, 48f., also gives 1835 as the year for White Thunder's visit to the Pawnees.

the other Skidi returned with White Thunder's party to the Cheyenne camp pitched near Bent's Fort on the Arkansas. The People showered over a hundred horses and many other gifts on the Pawnees, but the Skidi returned no more Arrows.[23]

In 1837, the Brulé Sioux attacked a Pawnee village. During the fighting, the Sioux recovered one of the Man Arrows for their Cheyenne allies.[24]

After the recovery of the two original Mahuts, two of the new Arrows were prepared as sacrifices to Maheo. They were wrapped in a bundle of gifts, and the Keeper and priests bore them to the Sacred Mountain and placed them in a crevice in the rock. Several years later, they had disappeared. Today, Cheyenne Arrow Lodge priests state that two spare shafts preserved in the Sacred Arrow bundle are the substitutes.[25] In any case, two of the new Arrows fashioned by Box Elder and Crazy Mule still rest beside the original Mahuts. Conservative Cheyennes believe that the fullness of Maheo's power continues to reside in all four Arrows.

In spite of the fact that Mahuts's spiritual power had been restored, there still remained the matter of the stain upon Cheyenne national pride. Two of Sweet Medicine's Arrows still lay in the hands of the bitterest enemies of the People. Repeated attempts were made to regain them. In 1866, Black Kettle and Big Head, through the agency of Edward W. Wynkoop, promised to make peace with the Pawnees and to give them a hundred fine horses

[22] Grinnell, "Great Mysteries . . . ," *loc. cit.*, 561. Cf. George Bent to Hyde, February 6, 1905, Coe Collection.

Details differ concerning the return of the Arrows. Cf. Dorsey, "How the Pawnee Captured the . . . Arrows," *loc. cit.*, 646–51.

[23] George Bent to Hyde, February 6, 1905; December 5, 1913, and December 18, 1913, Coe Collection.

Cf. Hyde, *Pawnee Indians*, 139.

[24] This may be the fight described as a Cheyenne attack in Dorsey, "How the Pawnee Captured the . . . Arrows," *loc. cit.*, 651. Cf. Grinnell, "Great Mysteries . . ," 550.

He Dog, the Oglala chief, told Hugh Scott that the Brulé recovered the Arrow. Hugh Scott papers, National Anthropological Archives, Smithsonian Institution. Cf. George Bent to Hyde, February 6, 1905, and February 20, 1905, Coe Collection.

[25] Jay Black Kettle and Ralph White Tail to the author, 1960.

plus other gifts if the Skidi would release the captured Arrows. The offer failed.[26]

Fire Wolf recalled a Spirit Lodge ceremony in which the question of regaining the Arrows was put to the Maiyun:

> When the Arrows were renewed in 1877, about the time the Northern Cheyennes were taken to Oklahoma, there was a medicine man named Old Crow.[27] He put on a Spirit Lodge. In it, he claimed he was told by the Maiyun: "You have already got two substitute Arrows. That makes four. Now it is a complete bundle. You cannot get the two original Arrows from the Pawnees. If you do, you will have too many. It is best to allow the Pawnees to keep two."[28]

During the 1890's, about three hundred Cheyennes visited the Pawnees with the avowed purpose of recovering the missing Arrows. Most of them were Dog Soldiers, led by Flying Hawk. The Pawnees entertained the Cheyennes at a dance and gave them many presents—horses, blankets, calico, and food. However, the Skidi would not relinquish the Arrows. They went so far as to state that if the Dog Soldiers proved to be worthy friends after a proposed visit of the Pawnees to the Cheyennes the next summer, then they might listen to a proposal from the Cheyennes. But nothing came of this, either.[29]

Jay Black Kettle, the Keeper of Mahuts from 1957 to 1962, recalled a Pawnee offer to release the Arrows about 1930. However, when the matter was discussed in the Sacred Arrow lodge, Hollering Eagle, a Spirit Lodge priest, objected. "No one dared to insist on it because Hollering Eagle was also an Arrow priest. No one can argue in the Sacred Arrow lodge. So Hollering Eagle had his way," Jay Black Kettle recounted.[30]

[26] Berthrong, op. cit., 58f.

[27] This is evidently the Suhtai Old Crow who, about 1914, was Little Man's choice to succeed him as Keeper of Mahuts. However, the Cheyennes said Old Crow was ineligible because he was Suhtai. Bent to Hyde, June 26, 1914, Coe Collection.

[28] To the author, 1959.

[29] "Sacred Arrows—Pawnees Captured Them and the Cheyennes Want Them," a clipping from the Kansas City Times, in the "Cheyenne Indians" files of the archives of the Museum of the American Indian.

In May, 1931, General Hugh Scott stated that the Arrows were still in Pawnee hands; also, that the Skidi had refused a Cheyenne offer of a hundred dollars and a horse to buy them back.[31]

Even today, some of the Cheyennes still hope for the return of the original Arrows. However, the Pawnee attitude seems to remain that of the old Skidi who said of them in 1960, "Those are Pawnee arrows now!"[32]

Two grooved and featherless shafts, their heads missing, still hang suspended beneath the Skidi Morning Star bundle in Oklahoma. They continue to be venerated as the Arrows captured that summer of 1830, when the Cheyennes wept as they rode away from Kingfisher stream.

[30] To the author, 1960.

[31] From a letter dated May 3, 1931, and written at the Pawnee agency, Oklahoma. Hugh Scott papers, National Anthropological Archives, Smithsonian Institution.

[32] In 1960 and 1962 the author visited the Pawnees and was shown the Morning Star bundle with the two shafts. These were identified by the bundle keeper as the arrows captured from the Cheyennes. Cf. George Dorsey, *Traditions of the Skidi Pawnee*, 52ff., 338n.

4. Two Arrow Keepers Are Dead

Outwardly, all seemed peaceful again within the Sacred Arrow tipi. The two ancient Mahuts and the newly consecrated Arrows, wrapped in their kit-fox quiver, hung suspended from the pole erected near the place of honor. The Cheyennes bore offerings of beautifully tanned and painted robes into the sacred lodge; and gifts of tawny panther skins, fine horses, and black-and-white eagle feathers were given to White Thunder. Even so, the memory of the Skidi capture of Mahuts weighed heavily upon the Keeper's mind.

Ever since Sweet Medicine's passing, the Keepers of Mahuts had been venerated as men who shared the holiness of the Prophet himself. Prior to his departure from earth, the culture hero described the qualifications his successors should possess. Sweet Medicine pointed to a pipe that rested upon the earth as he spoke of these things to the Cheyennes:

> Now you must select a good man; one who is good-natured and of good character in every way. He will be the man to take charge of the Arrows. He will be the man to take the pipe in his hands.
>
> This you must remember: in his daily prayers, beginning at daylight, he will smoke four times. In his prayers he must not forget to pray for the people, for their food, and for all the game, that the animals may be plentiful. All the animals living in the water must also be remembered in his prayers these four times.
>
> No one will be in the tipi when he prays in the morning. That is strictly forbidden. And the Maiyun will be with him during the time he is alone.[1]

The Cheyennes obeyed Sweet Medicine's admonition by respecting the person and the position of the guardian of Mahuts. "'He keeps us. He owns us.' That is the way we describe the Keeper. Through the Sacred Arrow tipi, the Keeper holds the Cheyennes together, just as if he was holding them in his hand." This statement by a contemporary Cheyenne reflects the honor long accorded the successors of Sweet Medicine.[2]

However, not even the holiness of the Keeper's office saved White Thunder from the anger of the Bow String society.

The trouble began about 1836 when a Cheyenne killed a fellow tribesman, thus bringing blood upon the Arrows. The unity between Maheo, Mahuts, and the Cheyennes was so perfect that, traditionally, flecks of blood appeared upon the Arrows when blood was spilled within the tribe. Sweet Medicine had admonished the Cheyennes to keep Mahuts fresh and clean, always. Therefore, after such a murder one of the Chiefs pledged the renewing ceremonies, since the Chiefs bore the responsibility for maintaining the unity of the People.[3] The murderer was not

---

[1] Baldwin Twins, Keeper of Mahuts, 1936–56, to the author, 1960.

[2] Sam Buffalo to the author, 1965.

[3] Baldwin Twins, Little Face, and John Stands in Timber all stated that orig-

put to death, because an execution within the tribe would only further stain Mahuts and further disrupt the unity of the People. Before Mahuts were renewed, the Chiefs would order the murderer into exile. This banishment generally lasted from two to ten years.[4]

After the 1836 killing, the Chiefs pledged the renewing ceremonies. Then all war expeditions ceased, since no war party had any chance of success without the blessing of the Arrows. White Thunder was awaiting a propitious time and place for the renewing rites when the Bow Strings came to him. They were anxious to move against the enemy and they demanded that the Arrow ceremonies be held at once. White Thunder counseled patience until the ceremonies could be offered properly, at the right time and place. "Do not raid the enemy until the renewing is over," was the Keeper's advice.

The Bow Strings refused to listen. Insolently, they ordered White Thunder and his four assistants to renew Mahuts at once. The Keeper refused; whereupon the Bow Strings beat him with their quirts and quirt-handles, whipping Sweet Medicine's successor just as they would lash some ordinary miscreant who had violated the tribal hunting rules. White Thunder was well over seventy years old, and he finally bowed to their wishes. The renewing rites were held, but before the ceremonies began, White Thunder warned the Bow Strings that misfortune would strike them the first time they went to war. "Wherever you go,

---

inally only the Chiefs pledged the renewing of the Arrows. Not until the reservation era was an ordinary warrior permitted to do so.

Karl N. Llewellyn and E. Adamson Hoebel, *The Cheyenne Way*, 132, state that there are sixteen recorded killings within the tribe during the two generations 1835–79.

Cf. George Bent to Hyde, February 17, 1912, and February 10, 1914, Coe Collection.

[4] The length of such an exile is disputed. Fire Wolf stated that it was four years, Little Face said from two to four years, John Stands in Timber said four years.

Cf. Llewellyn and Hoebel, *op. cit.*, Ch. VI, "Homicide and the Supernatural"; also, *ibid.*, 137, states that the ban was in the nature of an indefinite sentence with commutation possible on several grounds.

you will be powerless!" he said. Issuing from the Arrow Keeper's lips, the warning was also a curse.[5]

Shortly thereafter, in 1837, some forty-two Bow Strings rode against the Kiowas and Comanches. The Cheyennes were wiped out. Not one warrior escaped to bear home news of the disaster. Later, some Arapahoes and a Sioux were visiting in the Kiowa, Comanche, and Apache camps. There the Arapahoes recognized the scalps of certain of the Bow String warriors, and they carried news of the tragedy to the Cheyennes.[6]

The dead Bow Strings had to be avenged, so early that winter of 1837 Porcupine Bear, chief of the Dog Soldiers, carried the pipe to the scattered Cheyenne camps. At each camp he extended the stem in supplication to the Chiefs and principal men, begging them to smoke. Each man smoked, thus signifying his willingness to join the Dog Soldiers in punishing the Kiowas.

Porcupine Bear also carried whisky with him—a gift for the same Chiefs. But when he reached the large Northern Cheyenne camp on the South Platte, American Fur Company traders had arrived there before him. The village already was on a great drinking spree. Following his arrival, Porcupine Bear visited in the tipi of some of his relatives. Inside, everyone was drunk, and soon a fight arose between Little Creek and Around, two of Porcupine Bear's cousins. Around was getting the worst of the battle, and he called upon Porcupine Bear to jump on Little Creek. For a while, Porcupine Bear watched in a drunken stupor, singing Dog Soldier songs. Suddenly he moved into action. Pulling his long butcher knife from its scabbard, he stabbed Little Creek two or three times. Then he forced Around to finish off Little Creek.[7]

The Chiefs immediately deposed Porcupine Bear, outlawing his relatives with him for their share in the killing. The Dog

[5] Ralph White Tail and John Stands in Timber to the author, 1960. Similar accounts are recorded in Hyde, *Life of George Bent,* 72; Grinnell, *The Fighting Cheyennes,* 45; Llewellyn and Hoebel, *op. cit.,* 146; and Berthrong, *op. cit.,* 81.

[6] Hyde, *George Bent,* 74; Grinnell, *Fighting Cheyennes,* 48.

[7] George Bent to Hyde, June 2, 1914, Coe Collection. Cf. accounts in the sources listed above.

Soldiers shared their leader's disgrace. They had been honored by having been chosen to bear the Arrows against the Kiowas and Comanches, with the entire tribe following. Now they watched their head chief deposed as a murderer. Porcupine Bear bore the stench of Little Creek's death upon his own person; for a Cheyenne begins to decay within himself when he kills one of his own people. The other Cheyennes could detect the smell of putrified flesh. So could the animals, for the Cheyennes say game disappeared after an intra-tribal killing. Then the people faced starvation, and no war party could succeed until the Arrows were renewed. In order to remove the stigma, the Chiefs exiled Porcupine Bear's outlaw band from the presence of the tribe and from the immediate presence of Mahuts. The exiles moved away to a spot a mile or two from the main village.

For the second time in two years, flecks of blood covered the Sacred Arrows. Once more, Mahuts had to be renewed.

Old Little Wolf, chief of the Bow Strings, now bore the war pipe to the scattered soldier bands.[8] By spring of 1838 the re-organized Bow String Society was entrusted with the task of moving Mahuts against the Kiowas, the fourth such recorded move of the Arrows against the foe and the first move since their capture by the Skidi.

The Cheyenne village moved south, down the Arkansas River, far below Bent's Fort.[9] The Chiefs sent scouts ahead, men who were fast runners. At the head of Wolf Creek, Pushing Ahead, Howling Wolf, and two other scouts spotted a Kiowa war party coming down Wolf Creek on horseback. The four Cheyenne scouts watched the enemy from a hill, noting the direction the Kiowas were traveling. Then they returned to the Cheyenne village, now pitched on Crooked Creek. When they reached the

[8] This is the Southern Cheyenne who died c. 1886, age 92. Cf. Grinnell, *Fighting Cheyennes*, 42; Hyde, *George Bent*, 75.

[9] This account is drawn principally from George Bent to Hyde, Coe Collection, letters for the following dates: June 23, 1905; June 2, 1914; June —, 1914; July 29, 1914; August 7, 1914.
Cf. accounts in Hyde, Grinnell, and Berthrong. Also, James Mooney, *A Calendar History of the Kiowa Indians*, B. A. E. *Seventeenth Annual Report*, 271–73.

camp, they were summoned to the center of the village, where the Chiefs had assembled to hear their report. Afterward, criers carried the news throughout the large camp.

The night, Gentle Horse and two other scouts were dispatched south to Wolf Creek with instructions to find the trail of the Kiowa war party and follow to where Pushing Ahead and his party had seen the enemy. The main Cheyenne village continued its move south. The scouts had been told where the daily camps would be made.

One day, while Gentle Horse and the others were lying on a hill between Beaver and Wolf creeks, they spotted a large party of Kiowas riding up a nearby slope. There was a herd of buffalo between the Cheyenne scouts and the Kiowas, so the Cheyennes knew that their enemies were after buffalo. Gentle Horse and the others crawled to a small creek, where they lay hidden in the water that flowed through the rushes. A Kiowa mounted on a fine mule chased a buffalo close by them. However, the hunter was watching his game and did not see the Cheyennes. After the Kiowas had packed the buffalo meat on their horses and headed for camp, the Cheyennes followed their trail. Presently they came in sight of a stretch of timber near Wolf Creek. Gentle Horse's party could see horses grazing on the prairie all around. However, the Cheyennes could not locate the Kiowa lodges, which were hidden by the timber.

Gentle Horse and his companions ran all night until they reached the Cheyenne village, now pitched beside the Cimarron. After the scouts reported to the Chiefs, criers again circled the village, telling what the scouts had seen. At this point, the Cheyennes and Arapahoes were camped together in one great circle, the Arapaho lodges located at the northeast end.

Next day the Cheyennes moved to Beaver Creek, at the forks of Wolf Creek. There the warriors readied themselves for battle, the men singing their war songs and preparing themselves and their horses for the fighting ahead. The entire village made ready to move, because the Sacred Arrows were being carried before the Cheyennes. No one was to remain behind, and the move was to be made in darkness, in order to catch the enemy by surprise. Now the Cheyenne women erected scaffolds within their tipis, placing their belongings upon the scaffolds in order to protect them from the wolves. The lodge skins were rolled up all around so the wolves and coyotes could not chew the bottoms of the tipi covers while the people were absent. Meat was prepared for the meals ahead; and buffalo tripe containers were filled with the water that would be drunk at sundown.

The Chiefs led the march, with a screen of scouts far in advance of them. The women, children, older men, and horses all traveled in a body. Children too young to ride horseback were tied to the travois baskets, so they would not fall out while they were sleeping. The soldier societies, marching in their regular organized bands, rode along each side of the column and covered the rear. The military societies were ready to quirt anyone who dropped from the column. As they rode through the darkness, the military men were singing their war songs. Thus the movement south continued, with the Cheyennes and their Arapaho allies marching together. However, as the darkness wore on and the traveling became more difficult, they divided into at least two main parties, marching independently. When dawn came, the Cheyennes were still on the high prairie and not yet within sight of the stream along which the enemy was camped. They were still too far east, and downstream from the Kiowa village.

Porcupine Bear and his outlaws had been camped about two miles above the main village, and were aware of all that was happening. There were seven warriors among the outlaws; and they had moved forward alongside the main body of Cheyennes. While the larger village traveled southeastward, the outlaws headed straight south. They marched by themselves, off to one side of the main column. Moving in from a westward position, Porcupine Bear's men approached Wolf Creek directly opposite the Kiowa camp. Just after the dusk of morning lifted, Porcupine Bear spotted buffalo hunters, both men and women, riding over a hill in front of him. He called to his men to keep out of sight. Then he began to ride backward and forward in front of the Kiowas, making the sign that buffalo had been seen. The Kiowas took him for one of their own and followed him into the ravine where his warriors were hidden. Then the Cheyenne outlaws charged, lancing or shooting down every one of the thirty Kiowa men and women. Porcupine Bear killed twelve himself, Crooked Neck killed eight.[10] Porcupine Bear's men were the first to strike the enemy, but the Cheyennes did not recognize these coups. Porcupine Bear was an outlaw. He had brought blood upon the Sacred Arrows. Therefore, the honor of the first coup was awarded to Walking Coyote, who counted first coup in the general battle an hour or two after Porcupine Bear's men struck the Kiowas.

The main body of Cheyennes did not make their charge upon the enemy village until between ten and eleven A.M. By that time, the Cheyennes were divided into several parties. Some of them crossed Wolf Creek at the south, and others charged into the village. The warriors who crossed the creek charged into the timber. There they discovered some enemy women gathering sap from the trees. They also found some Kiowa men courting their sweethearts among the trees. The Cheyennes killed many enemies at this place. Then they charged on toward the village.

The Kiowa camp was pitched along the north bank of the stream, and many Kiowa, Comanche, and Apache warriors crossed Wolf Creek to intercept the Cheyennes on the other side. They drove the Cheyennes back on the south side of Wolf Creek, killing five Cheyennes and one Arapaho. Six Cheyennes fell in the fighting on the north bank.

Again Porcupine Bear's lawlessness brought sorrow to the Cheyennes. He and his outlaws had attacked before the blinding ceremonies could be performed against the enemy with the Arrows and Hat. Lacking the protection afforded by the ceremonies, the Cheyennes lost many brave men in the fight. The most noted of these was White Thunder himself. He had con-

[10] Grinnell, *Fighting Cheyennes,* 56f.

tinued to taste the bitterness of the Pawnee capture of Mahuts. "I will give the people a chance to get a smarter man to guide them. They have been calling me a fool," he had remarked. During the fighting, a large party of Kiowas and Comanches had rushed the Arrow Keeper and his companions, riding over them and killing White Thunder and Big Breast as they did so. White Thunder was the first of the Chiefs to be killed. Grey Hair was next, then Deaf Man, an older man who was one of the Servants of the Red Shield Society. Altogether, eleven Cheyennes and one Arapaho died. Among the slain was Porcupine Bear's own son, Porcupine, who was cut down after he himself had slain several Kiowas.[11]

The enemy losses were heavy, between fifty and sixty dead, with the Kiowas suffering the greatest number of men and women killed. The fighting around the village continued until the sun was low in the west. Then the older people began to call out that the Cheyenne warriors should cease fighting.

While the Arapahoes and Cheyennes were pulling back, a small party of Kiowas and Apaches met some Arapahoes near the edge of the Kiowa village. The Kiowas begged for peace, but the Arapahoes said they could make no peace as long as their Cheyenne allies refused to make peace.[12]

Peace was concluded in the summer of 1840. From that time on, war ceased between the Kiowas, Comanches, and Apaches on one side, and the Cheyennes and Arapahoes on the other. The treaty site was the wide bottom that stretched along both sides of the Arkansas River about three miles below Bent's Fort. The Cheyennes named the spot "Giving Presents to One Another Across the River" in honor of the occasion.

Shortly thereafter, a group of Kiowa warriors held a great war dance in the Cheyenne village on the north side of the Arkansas. The Kiowas recounted their killing of the forty-two Bow Strings. A few days later, the Bow Strings returned the compliment by riding over to the Kiowa camp, where they held a dance of their

[11] *Ibid.*, 59.
[12] *Ibid.*, 61; Hyde, *George Bent*, 82.

own. In the midst of the celebrating, Porcupine Bear, mounted upon a fine horse, rode boldly into the midst of the dancers. There, unrepentant to the last, he proceeded to count some twenty coups that he had won during the battle at Wolf Creek.[13]

Fortunately, prior to the fight with the Kiowas, White Thunder had placed the Arrows in the hands of a medicine man, who bore them into battle.[14] When the fighting ended, Tail Woman, White Thunder's wife, assumed temporary custody of the Arrows. She bore them back to the Arkansas, where the Cheyennes camped near the fort of William Bent, White Thunder's son-in-law. There, Mahuts were placed in the hands of a new Keeper.[15]

There is a conflict as to whether White Thunder's successor was Elk River or Lame Medicine Man.[16] Concerning Elk River, little is known except that he possessed power in the Spirit Lodge ceremonies. During the winter of 1838, he demonstrated that power in the presence of the Chiefs.

Earlier that winter, Chief Medicine Snake and four other warriors had headed toward the Solomon River. Their plan was to capture horses from the Pawnees. However, as the days passed nothing was heard from them and no one knew what had happened to them.

[13] George Bent to Hyde, June 2, 1914, Coe Collection.

[14] Hyde, *George Bent*, 80.

[15] George Bent to Hyde, June —, 1914, and June 26, 1914, Coe Collection; Grinnell, *Fighting Cheyennes*, 62.

[16] Grinnell appears to contradict himself concerning the succession of Arrow Keepers. In *Fighting Cheyennes*, 62, he states that White Thunder's widow bore Mahuts to the Arkansas, where Lame Medicine Man was given temporary charge of the Arrows. In *Cheyenne Campfires*, 15, he states that Lame Medicine was Keeper in 1838.

However, in "Great Mysteries . . . ," *loc. cit.*, 544, he lists Elk River as White Thunder's successor, with Lame Medicine succeeding Elk River. In *Cheyenne Campfires*, 32, he links Elk River, who he says was Keeper, to the Spirit Lodge ceremony performed during the winter of 1838.

Adding to the confusion, Grinnell states in "Great Mysteries . . . ," *loc. cit.*, 544, that Elk River died in 1838, from the effects of swallowing the root sacred to Mahuts. George Bent, writing to George Hyde, November 9, 1916, and May 11, 1917, Coe Collection, states that it was Lame Medicine Man who died from swallowing the medicine root.

The author's informants failed to throw any definite new light upon this problem.

51

Now, among the Cheyennes, the priests of the Spirit Lodge possessed power to summon the Maiyun, the Sacred Powers. At night, a small lodge was erected within a larger tipi. The Spirit Lodge priest entered the small lodge. His fingers, toes, hands, feet, and throat were encircled with a long rawhide rope. Outside the Spirit Lodge, eight men were seated: four on each side of a trail of white sage leading to the lodge. Each group took one end of the rawhide rope, which extended from beneath the lodge cover. The fire was extinguished. Four sacred songs were sung in the darkness. Then, as the fourth song began, the eight men pulled upon the rope with all their might. Sometimes they pulled so hard that the priest was lifted from the floor of the Spirit Lodge. Suddenly the men dropped the ends of the rope, and the priest lay there as if dead. Then voices were heard from within the Spirit Lodge. These were the voices of the Maiyun, who gave the priest information concerning events of which nothing had been known.[17]

Elk River was noted for his power in the Spirit Lodge. Finally the Chiefs decided to ask the Arrow Keeper to summon the Maiyun, and to ask the Powers what had happened to Medicine Snake and his men. The Chiefs wept in supplication as they walked in a line toward the Sacred Arrow lodge. At the center of the line, one Chief held an extended pipe. When the Chiefs entered the lodge, Elk River smoked the pipe, thereby expressing his willingness to carry out their petition. Mahuts were hanging inside the tipi, hearing all that was said. Elk River now was bound to use his supernatural power to the utmost in summoning the Maiyun.

The Keeper entered the Spirit Lodge and sat there bound hand and foot. In the darkness, Sun Flower, one of the Maiyun, was heard speaking. First his voice sounded from up where the Spirit Lodge poles were joined, saying that he was coming down to learn what Elk River and the Chiefs wished to know.

---

[17] This is an abbreviated version of the ceremony as described to the author by Ralph White Tail, Jay Black, James Medicine Elk, and John Stands in Timber in 1960. Cf. the detailed version in the Sacred Arrow section of this book.

The earth shook as the Maiyun touched it. The Chief who bore the pipe to Elk River was standing outside the lodge. He begged Sun Flower to take pity on the Chiefs, for one of their number was missing. He said that Medicine Snake and his men had been missing all winter, and their relatives were anxious about them.

The Maiyun's voice replied that the missing men were long dead. They had been killed by the Pawnees, and their bodies were lying beside one of the streams that flowed into the Solomon. When the Chiefs heard these words, they began weeping —mourning for Medicine Snake and his companions.

Later, a war party of Sioux told the Cheyennes that they had come upon an old Pawnee camp on the Solomon. There, on a big white log, they had discovered a charcoal drawing that depicted the killing of five persons by the Pawnees. When he heard this report, Standing on the Hill assembled a war party to investigate the drawing and its message. The Cheyennes located the log. Nearby, Standing on the Hill also found a few scattered bones, all that remained of Medicine Snake and his men.[18]

Elk River's Spirit Lodge power had been shown again.

It has been mentioned that the Arrow Keepers sit in the place of Sweet Medicine, who also bears the names of Sweet Root or Sweet Root Standing. Tradition says that when the culture hero left the People he transformed himself into the sacred plant whose name he bears.[19] Thus, a piece of sweet root rests within the Sacred Arrow, the Sacred Hat, and the Sun Dance bundles. Sweet root is the principal holy object within the Chiefs' bundle, the bundle that Sweet Medicine gave the Cheyennes at the beginning when he first blessed them with the Sacred Arrows. "Do not forget me. This is my body I am giving you. Always think of me," he had said to them.[20]

Throughout the Cheyenne sacred ceremonies, the priest-instructor often bites a tiny fragment from a piece of sweet root.

[18] Grinnell, *Cheyenne Campfires*, 31 ff.
[19] The plant is Actaea argutta. Cf. Grinnell, *Cheyenne Indians*, II, 174; Petter, *Dictionary*, s.v. "Arrow," 59.
[20] Little Wolf's killing of Starving Elk during the winter of 1879–80 brought the smell of death to the Chiefs' bundle.

53

Then he reverently spits this root upon the hands and bodies of the priests assisting in the rites. They avert their faces as he does so, because the sacred sweet root would blind them if it touched their eyes. To swallow the root would bring sure death. Sweet Medicine also gave the Cheyennes this ceremony. They call it, "throwing it at him" because, through the holy root, Sweet Medicine's blessing and power is thrown at the priests and participants in the sacred ceremonies.

On one occasion, Elk River was preparing to administer the "throwing it at him" ceremony. However, instead of spitting out the fragment of sweet root, the Arrow Keeper chewed it and swallowed the juice. Soon he was dead.[21]

Thus, within the year 1838, the tragedy of Mahuts's capture had touched even Sweet Medicine's successors, men who, like the culture hero, normally lived to peaceful old ages.

Lame Medicine Man, leader of the Issio me'taniu or Hill band, succeeded Elk River as Keeper later in 1838. He had been the keeper of one of the Ox'zem, or sacred wheel lances. Prior to 1833, he had been involved in a display of the concealing power of that sacred object.[22]

Lame Medicine Man had dreamed that he bore his Ox'zem on a war expedition against the Crows on the Big Horn River. His dream also showed that he and his companions took many horses there. A man was bound to follow such a sacred portent. Therefore, Lame Medicine called High Wolf to his tipi and recounted his dream. High Wolf listened, and then he thanked Lame Medicine; for the Cheyennes believed that such a dream would come true. As soon as the women could make enough moccasins, the

[21] Grinnell, "Great Mysteries . . . ,"*loc. cit.*, 544.

[22] Grinnell indicates the existence of a plural number of Ox'zem (Hohk'tsim) bundles. Cf. *Cheyenne Campfires*, 6ff., 15ff., 27ff.; and *Cheyenne Indians*, I, 186f.

It is probable that originally there were four such Ox'zem bundles. Fire Wolf and John Stands in Timber could recall two that had been handed down into recent times. One had been kept by the father of Limpy. Fire Wolf stated that at Limpy's death the Ox'zem either was buried with Limpy or left in the hills. The only sacred wheel lance known to survive is the one cared for by Box Elder, the Northern Suhtai holy man.

war party was on its way. High Wolf and Lame Medicine carried the pipes, because they were the leaders. There were nine warriors in all.

One day, two scouts already had been sent ahead and the other seven men were following. High Wolf and Lame Medicine walked in advance of the rest, as was proper for the leaders of the party. Suddenly one of the men in the rear called out for them to drop to the ground. A horseman was on the hill, he said. The Cheyennes fell to the earth. When they looked up, they could see a warrior on horseback. They crept to a nearby hollow. When High Wolf lifted his head again, he could see that the hill was covered with Crows. Soon the enemy was moving toward the hollow where the Cheyennes were lying. However, the Crows had not yet spotted them.

High Wolf instructed his men to keep close to the earth. Then he spoke to Lame Medicine, telling him that he always had believed him to be a strong medicine man. "Take pity on our men now and help us, so that the Crows will not find us," he begged. "As for me, when I get back to the village, I will wrap a fine blanket about the Medicine Arrows," he continued. Then High Wolf prayed to Mahuts: "Although you are a long way from us, we always believe, O Arrows, that you listen when anyone speaks to you. I ask you to make these Crows blind, so that they may not see us."

The Crows were continuing their advance as Lame Medicine crept to a position ahead of where his companions lay. There, he thrust the point of the Ox'zem into the earth, leaving the sacred wheel lance in full view of the enemy. He was singing a holy song as he did so, one that had power to cover the Crows' eyes and turn them from the Cheyennes. Lame Medicine continued singing as the enemy rode so near that the Cheyennes could hear them singing and talking. But not once did the Crows look toward the place where Lame Medicine and his companions lay. The Ox'zem had thrown its protective power over the Cheyennes.

Toward evening, the two scouts dispatched earlier returned.

They had found a great Crow village on the Big Horn, with many horses grazing on both sides of the river. They also had seen the hunters that had passed by their comrades. Now the Cheyennes vowed the sacrifices they would offer if they were allowed to return home successful. Some pledged the renewal of the Arrows; others promised they would wrap Is'siwun with fine blankets. Others vowed to paint white blankets with the sacred paint that came from the home of the Arrows.

All agreed that they would return to the place where Lame Medicine left the Ox'zem thrust into the ground. They left their guns behind; taking with them only their lariats, bows and arrows, and small twisted hair ropes for bridles. Later, all returned, leading or driving fine horses. Crooked Neck captured the largest and finest herd of ponies. He did not wait for the others; but headed back to the Cheyenne village. He did this so that his big herd would not slow up the movements of his companions. The other Cheyennes reached home a day after Crooked Neck's arrival. The Crows had chased them, but failed to overtake them.

After the Cheyennes had rested, they prepared the sacrifices they had pledged. High Wolf carried a fine blanket to the Arrow lodge, where Mahuts hung suspended above the doorway. High Wolf wept as he stood before the Arrows. Then he walked four paces, and proceeded to wrap the blanket around Mahuts. High Wolf entered the sacred tipi, where he smoked with the Arrow Keeper. He thanked Mahuts for blessing him. Then he invited the Keeper to his own tipi. There High Wolf fed him and presented him with one of the Crow horses he had captured.

Nearby, at Is'siwun's lodge, Crooked Neck wrapped a fine blanket about the Sacred Buffalo Hat. Thus he thanked Is'siwun for the blessing and protection she had given him during the expedition on which Lame Medicine carried Ox'zem against the Crows.[23]

Lame Medicine guarded Mahuts until 1849. That was the year

23 Grinnell, *Cheyenne Campfires*, 15ff.

in which the creaking white wagon trains bore the swift-killing cholera to the Plains tribes. When the disease hit, most of the Northern Cheyennes were living on the Platte River. Comparatively few of them died. Many of the Southern Cheyennes were camped south of the Arkansas. They were attending the Kiowa Sun Dance on the Cimarron, and the great village was filled with Cheyennes, Arapahoes, Kiowas, Comanches, Apaches and Osages. Cholera broke out in the midst of the Sun Dance ceremonies. The Indians fled in every direction, with most of the Southern Cheyennes and Arapahoes stampeding towards the Arkansas.[24] The Indians possessed little or no immunity to the dreaded disease. Nearly two thousand Cheyennes—almost two-thirds of the tribe—died within the year. Several bands were nearly exterminated.[25]

Lame Medicine died in 1849, but after the cholera epidemic.[26] His successor was Stone Forehead. The whites would call the new Keeper Medicine Arrows, naming him for the sacred objects he protected.[27]

Stone Forehead, like White Thunder, was an Ivistsinih'pah or Aorta man. As Elk River had before him, the new Keeper also possessed Spirit Lodge power to an unusual degree. Sometimes while Stone Forehead was talking with the Maiyun, the spirit would call out, "Make a light!" Then, when the fire in the lodge had blazed up, the other Cheyennes would find that Stone Forehead had disappeared. Sometimes, however, his rattle would be seen moving through the air, sounding as if it were being shaken by a person.

Stone Forehead could exert his power in other ways. On occasion he would dance through the camp carrying a pole in one

[24] George Bent to Hyde, February 2, 1915 and October 26, 1916, Coe Collection.

[25] Grinnell, *Cheyenne Indians,* I, 101; Mooney, *Cheyenne Indians,* 378. Cf. Hyde, *George Bent,* 96f.

[26] Grinnell, "Great Mysteries . . . ," *loc. cit.,* 544.

[27] He was also known as O Wine Site, from the manner in which he walked with his toes outward. Cf. "Legends of the Cheyenne and Arapahoe Indians," a manuscript written by Ben Clark in 1889. Now in the Fred Barde collection, Oklahoma State Historical Society.

hand, a drum in the other. He would toss the drum in the air. It would fly for a great distance, then suddenly return, come to the end of the pole, and slide down the pole to Stone Forehead's hand. He also possessed a ball which he could make fly about in a similar fashion.[28]

Along with his Spirit Lodge power, Stone Forehead was noted for his success as a leader of war parties. About 1826, he and White Antelope carried the pipes at the head of a twenty-man expedition bent on stealing horses from the Comanches and Kiowas. They returned with the largest herd ever captured by a Cheyenne war party.[29]

In 1837, the year before the great fight at Wolf Creek, the Cheyennes were camped on South Platte River. Stone Forehead and Pushing Ahead led fourteen men south to capture horses from the Kiowas and Comanches. They located the enemy village at the head of Big Sand Creek, which flows into the Red River of Texas. The Cheyennes waited until night, then they entered the village in pairs. Stone Forehead and Angry moved through the darkness together. They passed one tipi behind which a shield hung suspended from a pole. Angry unfastened the shield, and slung it on his own back. Then he and Stone Forehead continued their search for horses. Finally they located a bunch of fifty or sixty head, which they drove off.

When Stone Forehead and Angry reached the spot where the Cheyennes had agreed to meet, six warriors had not yet arrived. Little Wolf, Mouse's Road, and Walking Coyote were among the missing. Stone Forehead said they could wait no longer, they must start home. The Cheyennes moved out, with Stone Forehead and Rushing Ahead covering the rear, for they were the leaders. The country was so rough that the Cheyennes could drive the captured horses only at a slow pace.

About the middle of the day, the Cheyennes spotted a party of some thirty Kiowas pursuing them. The Cheyennes caught

[28] Grinnell, *Cheyenne Indians*, II, 114.
Cf., Grinnell, *Cheyenne Campfires*, 6, where Old Lodge makes a stolen Ox'zem bundle return in this fashion.
[29] George Bent to Hyde, October 22, 1908, Coe Collection.

58

Little Wolf, the Sweet Medicine Chief, ca. spring 1868. This is one of the two earliest-known portraits of Little Wolf, and it was taken at the time of the Fort Laramie Treaty of 1868.

The photographer was Alexander Gardner, whose pictures form the most complete pictorial record of the Fort Laramie Treaty councils extant. Gardner also witnessed the signatures of the Chiefs and head-men of the Northern Cheyennes, Northern Arapahoes, and Crows, and also the government officials who signed the treaty. Identification of the place and date of this Little Wolf portrait was first made by Doctor Raymond J. De Mallie, Associate Professor of Anthropology, Indiana University, Bloomington.

Photograph courtesy of the Edward E. Ayer Collection, The Newberry Library, Chicago.

Cheyenne Survivors of the Custer Fight, 1926. John and Josephine Stands in Timber gave the author the following identifications in August, 1964. *Standing, left to right:* Medicine Bear (?), Kills Night, Walks Last, Hollow Wood, Black Stone, Stump Horn, Sun Bear, Braided Locks. *Seated, left to right:* Little Sun; Little Wolf II; Porcupine; Bob Tail Horse; Pine; Thomas Flying; Squint Eyes.

This photograph, copyrighted by Elsa Spear Byron, of Sheridan, Wyoming, is printed here with Mrs. Byron's permission. This copy made from a print in the possession of John Stands in Timber.

Little Man. He was the son of Stone Forehead's sister, and thus the cousin of Black Hairy Dog. At the latter's death, ca. 1883, Little Man succeeded him as Keeper. His last years were filled with sorrow at the death of his wife and most of his children. About 1914, he attempted to turn the Keeper's responsibility over to Old Crow, a Suhtai priest. This transfer was refused by the Chiefs, the Arrow priests and the leaders of the military societies. They held fast to Sweet Medicine's rule that the Arrow Keeper must be Tsistsistas. Jay Black Kettle stated that Little Man permitted peyote to be placed in the Sacred Arrow bundle. He died ca. 1917.

Mower or Cut Grass. He succeeded as Keeper of Mahuts ca. 1920. Hugh Scott stated that Mower was elected by the soldier societies because Little Man had no sons. Fire Wolf added that neither Little Man nor Mower were Sacred Arrow priests, even though they guarded Mahuts. In such cases, a qualified Arrow priest was delegated to carry out the renewal ceremonies.

Photograph courtesy of the Smithsonian Institution, National Anthropological Archives, Bureau of American Ethnology Collection.

Baldwin Twins or Scabby, as a young man in 1908. Twins was chosen
Arrow Keeper in 1936. He carried Mahuts back to the Sacred Mountain
in 1945, and he watched over the Arrow lodge until 1956.

*Photograph courtesy of the Smithsonian Institution, National Anthropological
Archives, Bureau of American Ethnology Collection.*

White Frog or Fringe. A respected Northern Suhtai Massaum and Sun Dance priest, he was the father of Henry Little Coyote, Keeper of Is'siwun.

Photograph courtesy of the Smithsonian Institution, National Anthropological Archives, Bureau of American Ethnology Collection.

64

Porcupine. The priest and doctor who carried the Ghost Dance to the
Northern Cheyennes.

*Photograph courtesy of the Smithsonian Institution, National Anthropological
Archives, Bureau of American Ethnology Collection.*

The Northern Cheyenne Delegation to Washington in 1914. *Left to right, standing*: Willis T. Rowland, Lone Elk, Samuel Little Sun. *Seated*: Jacob Tall Bull, Thaddeus Red Water, and Big Head Man. When they asked Washington for permission to hold the Sun Dance, they were told that the Northern Cheyennes must give up both the Medicine Lodge and Massaum ceremonies.

Photograph courtesy of the Smithsonian Institution, National Anthropological Archives, Bureau of American Ethnology Collection.

the fastest horses and proceeded to bunch up the captured herd. Two young men were sent ahead on horseback, one on each side, to hold the herd together. Then the other Cheyennes stopped to face the enemy. One warrior dismounted and fired at a Comanche, hitting the enemy's horse. The Comanche escaped by jumping up behind one of his comrades. Then the Cheyennes charged, and the Kiowas and Comanches wheeled and rode away. After that, there was no further trouble. Stone Forehead and Pushing Ahead got both men and horses safely back to the Cheyenne village.

However, the six missing men did not fare as well. Little Wolf and Walking Coyote had taken only a few horses when they saw a large party of enemies riding in two bands. The Cheyennes dismounted and hid in a ravine. The Kiowas could have found them had they looked carefully, but just then they spotted Mouse's Road and his three companions and charged them. Little Wolf and Walking Coyote remained hidden in the ravine until nightfall. Then they started home on foot.

Mouse's Road and his companions dismounted and bravely faced the enemy on foot. It did not take the Kiowas and Comanches long to wipe out all but Mouse's Road. The enemy numbered almost a hundred warriors, but Mouse's Road faced them like an angry bear. First he killed a Comanche chief with the enemy's own lance. Then Lone Wolf, a noted Kiowa chief, charged. A Mexican captive was riding close beside him. Mouse's Road ran to the Mexican, dragged him from his horse, and knifed him to death. Next he turned to Lone Wolf, who ran toward him with his lance held high above his head to that he could strike a blow of great power. Mouse's Road ducked under the lance, caught the Kiowa by his left shoulder, and stabbed him in the hip. Lone Wolf turned to run, but Mouse's Road caught him by his silver hair ornament. The Cheyenne plunged his knife into the Kiowa again, but the blade snapped as it hit one of the metal hair plates. Mouse's Road continued to stab Lone Wolf with the stump of the knife until the Kiowa leader fell, pretending to be killed. After that, another Comanche chief charged and

67

Mouse's Road proceeded to finish him off with Lone Wolf's own lance.

The Kiowas and Comanches never had seen such bravery, and they offered to spare the life of Mouse's Road. He signed back to them that his brothers had been killed, and if he were to go home he would be mourning these men constantly. "You must kill me," he signed. Then he charged.

The Kiowas and Comanches began to run. However, two Kiowas with guns had ridden up behind the main body. They dismounted, sat down, and waited until Mouse's Road was close to them. Then they fired. The Cheyenne fell from his horse, his thigh broken by one of the rifle balls. He sat there upon the earth, defending himself with his lance, and defying the enemy to take him. Finally an enemy sneaked behind Mouse's Road and shot him in the back. The Kiowas and Comanches rushed in upon the fallen enemy and cut off his head. When they did that, Mouse's Road raised himself and sat upright.

The enemy fled back to their village in terror. There they told the people that they had killed a medicine man who had come back to life and who was coming to attack them. The women packed in panic, and the camp moved away, leaving many lodges still standing.

Thus death overtook four of Stone Forehead's men. But the Kiowas and Comanches long remembered Mouse's Road as the bravest warrior they ever faced or ever knew of.[30]

Stone Forehead would fight the Kiowas and Comanches one last time at Wolf Creek.[31] Then, when the Sacred Arrows were placed in his care, he abandoned the warpath for the Keeper's life of peace. Nevertheless, in doing so Stone Forehead entered into the very years in which there would be no peace for the People. The first emigrant trains had moved up the Platte River in 1841, opening up the Oregon Trail. By 1846 the flood of white settlers to Washington and Oregon was flowing in earnest. The

[30] Grinnell, *Fighting Cheyennes*, 13ff.
[31] George Bent to Hyde, September 5, 1914, Coe Collection.

68

year of Lame Medicine's death, 1849, also saw the discovery of gold in California.

Stone Forehead would live to see that first trickle of whites transformed into a river of soldiers and settlers, a river that would engulf the Cheyennes, their lands, and the way of life their Sacred Arrows blessed.

5. Is'siwun Is Mutilated

Before his departure, Erect Horns
prophesied sorrow ahead. He admonished the Suhtaio never to
quarrel with one another, never to harm each other. Many men
would care for the Buffalo Hat, he said. Those Keepers would
die, but Is'siwun never would wear out. Then Erect Horns
warned the Suhtaio:

You must tell whoever you pass it [the Buffalo Hat] over to,
that he must take good care of it, and never injure it in any way.
*If, in any manner, the Hat is abused or hurt, the buffalo will dis-
appear, because Is'siwun is the head chief of the buffalo.*

The Suhtai culture hero told the people that in the future

70

Sweet Root would bring them another medicine. He concluded:

> When you have driven the buffalo away, you will live on spotted animals [cattle]. You will not be healthy as you are now, but disease will come often. All the medicine power of this Cap will be lost. You will marry early, and people will have their hair turn gray when young. Sweet Root will tell you a great deal more than I do. Always tell the others. Do not forget what I tell you. Do not forget what you have been told. I have spoken.[1]

Then Erect Horns disappeared.

Throughout all the troubles flowing from the loss of the Arrows, the tipi of the Sacred Hat remained a place of peace. No blood stained Is'siwun, and her Keeper, Erect Horns's successor, was careful to see that this state of affairs continued. There were some near escapes, though.

About 1820, the Crows killed Red Robe's two sons. When he heard the news, the grief-stricken father gave away his entire herd of horses. He left himself destitute. When the camp moved, he was the last person to follow. He had nothing with which to make camp, and he remained out in the open, mourning the death of his boys. This continued for three or four months. Finally, the Elks, Kit Foxes, Bow Strings, and Dogs gathered. They all approached Red Robe, and one or two men spoke to him, begging him to come in among the people again. Red Robe remained unmoved. Finally, Two Twists, one of the Bow String chiefs, promised war against the Crows if Red Robe would return. "I accept," the old man responded at last.

Two Twists carried the pipe to all the warrior societies, and everyone smoked. So great was the response that the entire tribe moved against the Crows. The Sacred Hat and the Sacred Arrows were leading the way.[2]

---

[1] Grinnell, "Some Early Cheyenne Tales," *loc. cit.*, Vol. XX, No. 78, 193f. This account contains numerous details concerning Is'siwun's care, including the ceremonies of exposing the Hat. It also describes the origin of Nimhoyoh, the Turner, and the decoration of the Sacred Hat tipi.

Cf. Grinnell, *Cheyenne Campfires*, 262f.

[2] This is the 1820 movement of the Arrows against the Crows in retaliation

When the Cheyennes neared the enemy village, Two Twists rode through the camp with a crier following him and calling for everyone to listen. Two Twists announced that he was about to follow Red Robe's sons. He would never return from this raid, he vowed.

Meanwhile, the Crows had spotted the Cheyennes and had warned their camp. The enemy quickly erected a breastwork of all their tipis, arranging them in a semicircle.

Next morning, Two Twists rode through the Cheyenne village again. "People behold me! This is my last time to walk on earth," he announced. Then he rode to the Sacred Hat lodge, where he begged the Keeper for permission to wear Is'siwun into battle. The Keeper remained silent. Finally his wife voiced disapproval:

> You are going to war never to return. I do not think it right to give you the Hat. You will get it bloody. You will bring us great trouble. Blood on the Hat would mean blood for all the tribe.

Even without Is'siwun, Two Twists led the charge against the Crows. Armed only with a saber, he rode alone into the breastwork, slashing off a Crow head as he burst through. The Cheyennes saw him disappear among the enemy as he fought the Crows hand to hand. Then the other Cheyennes charged, and a great battle ensued, but Two Twists was not killed. He fought so bravely that the people said he had done his work; he did not have to fulfill his promise to die. Red Robe adopted him in the place of his dead sons. Sometime later, Two Twists was made one of the Council of the Forty-four.[3]

The Cheyennes won a great victory against the Crows that day, with the power of the Arrows and the Buffalo Hat blessing them. Almost the entire Crow camp was captured, and many

---

for the Crow annihilation of some thirty-two men, most of them Crooked Lances, the year before.

[3] Llewellyn and Hoebel, op. cit., 3ff.

Here is another indication of woman's importance in relationship to Is'siwun. The Sacred Hat woman is allowed to voice final disapproval, and to say that the spilling of blood on Is'siwun will bring blood upon the entire tribe. No woman, not even the Arrow Keeper's wife, would be allowed to make such a decision regarding Mahuts.

prisoners were taken. Among them was the son of the Crow head chief. The son eventually married a Cheyenne girl, and he refused his father's subsequent attempts to induce him to leave his wife's people.[4] After this 1820 victory, so many captive women were married by Cheyenne warriors that many of the Cheyennes have possessed Crow blood ever since.[5]

Several years later, the Cheyennes were camped on Horse Creek, on the south side of the North Platte River. One day a young Crow warrior emerged from the hills and rode alone right to the edge of the Cheyenne village. He had lost many relatives in the 1820 fight, and was ready to throw his life away. Some of the older Cheyennes suspected an ambush and called out that everyone should wait until all the warriors were mounted and ready to ride. Nevertheless, twelve young men, all relatives of the Sacred Arrow Keeper, charged after the Crow. The Crow decoyed them back into the hills where his companions were hidden. Suddenly the enemies charged out. The Cheyennes wheeled and galloped back toward the village, but the pursuing Crows struck down eight of them. A countercharge by the main body of Cheyennes drove the Crows back into the hills, and several of them were killed.

After the battle, the women brought the dead bodies of the young Cheyennes into camp. Eight beds were erected in the lodge of the Arrow Keeper, and the bodies of the dead men were placed upon them. The Crows had mutilated the Cheyennes, but the women reassembled the remains as best they could.

Cheyenne fury was aroused. After the great fight in 1820, the families of these dead men had adopted several Crow prisoners. The old rule was that once a prisoner had eaten with his captor in the captor's camp, the prisoner could not be killed. The tipis of the Sacred Arrows and Buffalo Hat were both places of sanctuary. An enemy was as safe within them as he was in his own

---

[4] George Bent to Hyde, February 10, 1914, Coe Collection.

[5] John Stands in Timber, Frank Waters, James Medicine Bird, and others gave the author many examples of Cheyennes descended from captives taken that day. John Stands in Timber's own maternal great-grandmother, Pretty Lance or Blackbird Woman, had been a captive taken in that fight.

tipi. Above all else, no blood was to be spilled in or near those sacred lodges.

But now the families of the dead Cheyennes turned upon the Crow captives they had adopted as relatives. They killed eight of the Crows, an act which, under the old rule, amounted to killing their own natural relatives. The Crow corpses were piled around the edge of the Sacred Arrow lodge like logs were laid along the border of a tipi cover to keep out the wind.

Not only had the blood of kinsmen been shed, but it was shed upon the very cover of the Sacred Arrow tipi. Older Cheyennes said that this was the greatest crime ever committed against Mahuts. When the Arrows next were renewed, they were found to be stained with the blood of those eight Crow prisoners.[6]

However, no blood was spilled upon Is'siwun or upon the Sacred Hat lodge.

Then, in 1852, Alights on the Cloud, a much-respected warrior who owned a famous suit of chain mail, was killed by the Pawnees. An enemy arrow caught him in the right eye—the one vital area that the armor did not cover. Many other Cheyennes were killed that day. The next year, in retaliation for these deaths the Sacred Arrows and Buffalo Hat were moved against the Kitkahahki Pawnees. Arapaho, Kiowa, Brulé Sioux, and Apache warriors rode with the Cheyennes on this expedition.[7]

Stone Forehead held the blinding ceremonies four or five miles from the Pawnee village. Is'siwun was placed upon a bed of sacred white "man" sage, so that she faced the earth lodges of the enemy. Then Stone Forehead handed one of the Sacred Arrows to Wooden Leg. Wooden Leg moved out in front of the line of men. There, with the Arrow pointed toward the enemy, he sang the first of the sacred blinding songs. He danced as he

---

[6] George Bent to Hyde, February 17, 1912, Coe Collection; Grinnell, *Fighting Cheyennes*, 31. Cf. Hyde, *George Bent*, 26ff.

Details differ in these accounts. Grinnell gives the above description of the disposition of the bodies. Bent states that the Cheyennes were laid upon scaffolds erected within funeral tipis. Then the Crows were killed and their bodies laid outside the lodges in which the dead Cheyennes lay.

[7] The following is from Grinnell, *Fighting Cheyennes*, 84–94.

74

did so, thrusting the stone point toward the enemy. Behind him, the other men stamped their feet in time to the song. At the same time, they were thrusting their weapons and shields toward the Pawnees in unison with Wooden Leg's thrusting of the Arrow. As Wooden Leg completed the fourth song, all the men whooped. Then Wooden Leg reverently handed the Arrow to Stone Forehead, the feathers toward the Keeper, for death awaits anyone who stands before the exposed points of Mahuts.

When the preliminary blinding ceremonies had ended, Long Chin rode to the Sacred Hat Keeper, requesting permission to wear Is'siwun during the charge of the Great Mysteries against the enemy. The Keeper lifted the Buffalo Hat from the bed of sage, offering her to the warrior. Just as Long Chin was tying the leather chin string, the string snapped. Here was trouble! Immediately, Long Chin pledged a woman to be passed "on the prairie."[8] He re-tied the string. Then he rode off to join Black Kettle, who bore the Arrows tied to his lance. Together they

[8] The custom of putting a woman "on the prairie" is the great exception to the prevailing respect the Cheyennes had for womanhood, chastity, and marriage. It was a husband's right to make a "free woman" of an adulterous wife, providing the woman had been unfaithful more than once. The phrase "on the prairie" refers to the fact that the aggrieved spouse might invite his military society or his cousins to gather at a spot on the prairie for a feast. The feast was the unfaithful wife, who was raped by all present.

The procedure of putting a woman on the prairie sometimes was applied to a captive woman by an entire war party. Captive women, being foreigners, were not entitled to the same respect as the women of the People.

On this 1853 occasion, however, Long Chin's vow to Is'siwun implies an older sacred significance to this act. The Buffalo Hat is the sacred living symbol of female renewing power. The name Is'siwun means a herd of buffalo. The great holiness of the Hat derives from her power to renew the herds.

As we shall see in the following chapters, a woman—the Sacred Woman—offers the sacrifice of her body in the Sun Dance and Buffalo ceremonies. Both of these ceremonies are of Suhtai origin, and both are derived from the Sacred Hat. It is probable that Long Chin vowed a woman to be offered in this context. Erect Horns had warned the Suhtaio that the Hat must never be abused or hurt. If this happened, the buffalo would disappear. Long Chin could well have pledged this woman in reparation to the Hat, offering the woman "on the prairie" because it is on the prairie that the buffalo live. The sacrifice of a woman in this context becomes a sacrifice for the renewing of both the herds and the prairie upon which the herds subsist. It could also be a sacrifice for the renewing of the Sacred Hat herself.

Cf. Llewellyn and Hoebel, *op. cit.*, 169–211, "Marriage and Sex."

charged the Pawnees, completing the ceremonies that should have rendered the enemy blind and helpless.

However, while these ceremonies were still under way, Big Head and seven others had slipped off to strike the Kitkahahkis first. Once again, the impatience of impetuous warriors destroyed the blinding power of the Great Mysteries. The Pawnees were far from demoralized, and their Potawatomi allies came to their assistance in the fighting. At least seventeen Cheyennes and four Arapahoes were killed. Both the Arrows and the Buffalo Hat escaped harm.

The year 1853 saw further misfortune for the Cheyennes. Now that peace existed with the Kiowas and Comanches, the Cheyennes could raid much farther south. A large Cheyenne war party raided down into Mexico, where they tangled with Mexican lancers. All but three of the Cheyennes were killed.[9]

Yet, with the exception of the broken chin string, no disaster had befallen the Buffalo Hat. Life in the Hat tipi continued to be peaceful until about 1869. Then, in the country near the Little Big Horn, Half Bear, Keeper of Is'siwun, lay dying.[10]

When either the Arrow Keeper or Hat Keeper died, his next male relative traditionally succeeded to the position of Keeper. The relative might be a son or a younger brother of the deceased Keeper, or, again, a nephew. Prior to his death, the Keeper himself might designate a successor, and his choice would be respected. The Keepers of the Arrows must be Tsistsistas; those of the Buffalo Hat, Suhtaio. If there was no male next of kin, the Chiefs and the soldier societies chose the new guardian of Mahuts or Is'siwun.[11]

---

[9] Mooney, *Cheyenne Indians*, 379.

[10] The dates of these incidents are disputed. Grinnell, "Great Mysteries of the Cheyenne," says that Half Bear died about 1869. Llewellyn and Hoebel, *op. cit.*, 154, gives the date as c. 1865.

Coal Bear also is known as Charcoal Bear or, occasionally, Black Bear.

[11] For example, Stone Forehead's son, Black Hairy Dog, succeeded him as Keeper of Mahuts. Black Hairy Dog was succeeded by his cousin, Little Man.

The Cheyenne kinship system makes the Anglo Saxon uncle-nephew relationship into a father-son relationship. Male cousins are considered to be a man's

At Half Bear's death, the care of the Buffalo Hat should have passed on to Coal Bear, his son. Coal Bear, who was an extremely young man to hold so sacred an office, happened to be absent at the time. However, Broken Dish or Crow White, a friend of the dying Keeper, was present. He had been instructed in some of the mysteries of the Buffalo Hat. Therefore, Half Bear placed Is'siwun in Broken Dish's temporary care, with the understanding that the Hat would be given to Coal Bear upon his return.

After the old Keeper's death, camp was moved to the Little Big Horn. There, some four years later, Coal Bear returned.[12] He bore gifts to Broken Dish, and he reminded the older man that his appointment was temporary. The military societies joined in offering horses and other suitable presents. In this way they tried to make the exchange a peaceful one—one in which Broken Dish would not lose face. However, Broken Dish remained seated by Is'siwun, who hung suspended from her tripod at the head of his bed.

The military societies gathered again. Their decision was to march to Broken Dish's tipi, to take Is'siwun from him, and to restore the Hat to Coal Bear, the rightful Keeper.[13]

Charles Sitting Man, who was born in 1866, recalled these details of the affair:

When they came to Broken Dish, they told him: "We have come

brothers among the Cheyennes. Thus, in the choice of Keepers, there was some latitude within the framework of these fixed rules.
Cf. Fred Eggan, "The Cheyenne and Arapaho Kinship System," *Social Anthropology of North American Tribes*, (ed. by Fred Eggan), 41–75.

[12] Mooney, *Cheyenne Indians*, 369f., places the dispute over Is'siwun at the beginning of the outbreak of 1874. Grinnell, "Great Mysteries . . . ," *loc. cit.*, 566, states that the Hat came to Coal Bear c. 1873.

[13] The author's informants did not identify the military bands involved in the move. Grinnell, "Great Mysteries . . . ," *loc. cit.*, 566 states that the Foxes marched with the Chiefs to Broken Dish's lodge. Elsewhere, in "When Broken Dish Lost the Hat," Southwest Museum MS No. 70, Grinnell identifies the Foxes and Crazy Dogs with the return of Is'siwun to Coal Bear.
George Bent to Hyde, October 30, 1913, Coe Collection, identifies the Foolish Dogs as those who offered horses and other gifts to buy back the Hat. Llewellyn and Hoebel, *op. cit.*, 154, identifies the marchers as Shield Soldiers.
It is interesting that the Elks, the traditional protectors of the Sacred Hat, are not mentioned in this connection.

here to take back the Sacred Hat because you did not care for it in a perfect way. We will choose another qualified man."

Broken Dish said, "It's all right. Come back tomorrow." So the military believed him, that he would let the tipi go. However, that same night Broken Dish and Ho'ko, his wife, took off one of the horns.

Next morning the military got together and marched to Broken Dish's tipi. Broken Dish and his wife were willing to return the bundle to them. In the meantime, the horn was already cut off. Broken Dish's wife kept the horn, wrapped up under her dress.

When the military got the bundle, they marched back to the village and took it to the tipi of Coal Bear. He was the only one appointed at a very young age to become Keeper of the sacred tipi. The military men put the bundle outside the tipi, above the door, on the breast of the tipi. . . .

Broken Dish, Ho'ko, and their family slipped from the camp in disgrace, spending many of their later years in exile among the Sioux.[14] However, that was not the end of the affair. Sitting Man continued:

> Even when Is'siwun was given to a new man, the people realized that all things seemed to turn out wrong. Sickness, blindness, headaches: such things were beginning to come to every person. And game became scarce. . . .[15]

Is'siwun had not been opened at the time of the transfer, so the cause of these troubles remained unknown for a long time.

[14] George Bent to Hyde, October 30, 1913, Coe Collection. Bent states that "Broken Dish himself was willing to give the cap up, but his wife would not part with it, as by custom *she was owner of it* . . . ." (italics mine).

Grinnell, in "When Broken Dish Lost the Hat," *loc. cit.*, adds details concerning the Cheyenne attitude toward Broken Dish afterwards: "The hat was taken on the Little Big Horn River. Some time afterward the Cheyenne village was camped near Fort Laramie and Broken Dish's outfit was camped across the Laramie from them and there was a little fight between the two camps. Some shots were fired. White Hawk tells this . . . ."

Grinnell, "Social Organization of the Cheyennes," *loc. cit.*, 145, states that Broken Dish's little band was named Anskowi'di—"narrow across the bridge of the nose" or "eyes close together." Beaver Heart, a member of this band, was present in 1876 when William F. Cody killed the Cheyenne leader Yellow Hand. Don Russell, *The Lives and Legends of Buffalo Bill*, 234f.

[15] Charles Sitting Man, Sr., to the author, 1959–60.

Finally Coal Bear summoned the Chiefs, the Buffalo priests, and the leaders of the military societies. Criers carried news of the anticipated opening of Is'siwun to the people. One Horn was chosen to perform the rites. First he prayed to Maheo and to the Sacred Powers, vowing that he would soon offer the formal veneration ceremonies to the Hat. Then, after making the four motions, One Horn untied the strings of the buffalo-hide pouch. Is'siwun was inside—but one of her horns was missing. The piece of sacred sweet root also had disappeared.[16]

Erect Horns had warned the Suhtaio that they must never injure the Sacred Hat in any way. "If the Hat is abused, the buffalo will disappear," he had told them. Such a sacrilege could only bring misfortune. The Buffalo priests predicted ill luck ahead for all the Cheyennes, but especially for Ho'ko's own family. The prediction came true. In the years following, all the children of Broken Dish and Ho'ko died except one son who repudiated his parents' deed. Broken Dish finally came south with Little Wolf and Dull Knife in 1877. However, the effects of his crime followed him even then.[17] Fire Wolf described Ho'ko's fate:

[In Indian Territory] the Southern Cheyennes used to get their rations. They called out the family's name, let the beef run out of the corral, and then they killed it.

When they did this, there was one of those black and yellow steers. The steer came out and started to run out to the tipis nearby. It started towards Broken Dish's wife. She started to run toward the tipi. The steer caught her, hooked her, and threw her into the air. Then the steer got away in the brush.

When the Northern Cheyennes camped at Hammer mountain, one of the priests put on the Spirit Lodge. The Maiyun spoke. He said, "Your Image [Is'siwun] has only one horn. But your Image

---

[16] Josie Head Swift Limpy, Temporary Keeper of Is'siwun, 1952–58, to the author, 1957.

[17] Grinnell, *Cheyenne Indians*, I, 97, states that Broken Dish (White Crow) lived in the north and later came south with Dull Knife. George Bent to Hyde, October 16, 1906, Coe Collection, lists Broken Dish among the Northern Cheyenne chiefs coming to Darlington Agency, I.T., in 1877.

shall have both horns again. The one who took the horn from the Hat has been killed by a steer."[18]

Ho'ko died about 1906. By that time, Wounded Eye was guarding the Sacred Hat in Montana. In present-day Oklahoma, the women preparing Ho'ko's body for burial discovered the missing horn—worn like a pendant around the dead woman's neck. Her sister, who was the wife of the Suhtai priest Dragging Otter, took possession of the sacred object. Later, at his wife's death, Dragging Otter himself assumed custody of it. The horn hung in his lodge, stored in a buffalo hide bundle and covered with offering cloths. Occasionally, the sacred object was exposed for veneration. Dragging Otter's troubles soon began. His favorite daughter, Minia or Shell Woman, (the name designates an extremely pretty woman) died. Her death was followed by the deaths of most of Dragging Otter's family. Only a son, Three Fingers, survived. When Dragging Otter died, Three Fingers, who was then titular chief of the Southern Cheyennes, received the horn.[19]

Is'siwun's horn was carried home some thirty-four years after Ho'ko's sacrilege. In 1908, Wounded Eye, Coal Bear's successor as Keeper, made the long journey to Oklahoma.[20] There, Three Fingers placed the shaved horn, its surface covered with red paint and carved with the sacred "man power" design, into the Hat Keeper's hands.[21]

When Wounded Eye arrived back in the Tongue River country, Charles Sitting Man was among those who watched the

[18] Fire Wolf, to the author, 1962. Verified by John Stands in Timber and Wesley Whiteman.
[19] Grinnell, "When Broken Dish Lost the Hat," loc. cit.; also, "Great Mysteries . . . ," loc. cit., 568ff.
[20] Fire Wolf and Sitting Man, to the author.
However, Grinnell, "Great Mysteries . . . ," loc. cit., 567, states that Three Fingers carried the horn north in 1908. Cf. George Bent to Hyde, October 30, 1913, Coe Collection.
[21] Cf., Father Peter Powell, "Issiwun, Sacred Buffalo Hat of the Northern Cheyenne," Montana (Winter 1960). Also, Grinnell, "Great Mysteries . . . ," loc. cit., 569.

ceremonies of restoring the horn. Years later, he recalled of that occasion:

The village was here at Lame Deer agency when he [Wounded Eye] arrived, bringing back the horn belonging to Is'siwun. There were many tipis here. I remember they were calling in the old men, the priests from the various ceremonies. After all these men filled the tipi, they did not have any trouble, because they were all old people who understood these sacred things.

The priests of the Buffalo ceremony restored the horn.[22] The old men who were watching, told the man opening the Hat to watch Is'siwun closely; to tie the other one on in the same way. That was a very serious thing: the watching, and the way they opened the Hat bundle.

The man who tied the horn back on, tied it the same way [as the other horn]. The holes were there also—where the horn was originally tied. Then they carefully put the Hat back in the same position [in the buffalo hide pouch], hanging it where it belonged, on a tripod at the rear of the Keeper's bed.

Then all the men marched to their homes.

However, Is'siwun did not rest easy. Sitting Man concluded:

Even though the horn was tied on just like before, ill health continued to come to the people in many ways. They did not find life the way it was before the horn was taken off . . . .[23]

Ho'ko's sacrilege long had disturbed the peace of the Cheyennes. The Buffalo priests' predictions of misfortune came true in a multitude of ways. The final wars with the whites followed hard upon the theft of the horn. Coal Bear's assumption of the

[22] John Stands in Timber stated to the author that Hershey Wolf Chief and two other "qualified men" (i.e., Buffalo priests) restored the horn to Is'siwun. This is the same Wolf Chief who later opened Is'siwun for General Hugh Scott.

[23] Sitting Man explicitly stated that the Sacred Hat was preserved with one horn missing until Wounded Eye went to Oklahoma to retrieve the horn. John Stands in Timber and Fire Wolf verified this.

Cf. Llewellyn and Hoebel, op. cit., 156, states that a substitute horn was added earlier than 1908. According to Hoebel's informants, the original horn was enfolded in the bundle with the Hat. Then, during a Spirit Lodge ceremony, the Maiyun told the Cheyennes that Ho'ko's horn was a lifeless husk. The horn was finally buried in the hills.

81

Keeper's duties marked the beginning of the final years of Cheyenne freedom. There were the sorrows of the Northern Cheyenne exile to Indian Territory, where so many of the people quickly died. Then Little Wolf and Morning Star led the flight home. During that terrible trek, the Cheyennes suffered warfare, sickness, and death. There was the outbreak and the killing of Morning Star's people as they fled the barracks at Fort Robinson, where they had been imprisoned in the bitter cold, with all food and water taken from them.

Even Is'siwun's Keeper did not escape the consequence of the sacrilege. Prior to Ho'ko's deed, the Sacred Hat guardians lived lives of nearly a century. But Coal Bear, the youngest of Erect Horns's successors, died at the forks of the Lame Deer in 1896. He died before even seventy winters had passed for him.[24]

[24] Sitting Man, Fire Wolf, and John Stands in Timber all stated that Coal Bear was the youngest of the Sacred Hat Keepers.

The Tongue River census records give varying ages for Coal Bear. The 1886 census lists his age as fifty, making his birthdate 1836. However, the 1891 census lists his age as sixty-four, making his year of birth 1827. The Lame Deer Probate Records, copied by Mari Sandoz in 1949, lists Coal Bear as having been born in 1828.

6. The End of Southern Cheyenne Freedom

Is'siwun's mutilation marked the beginning of the last years of Cheyenne freedom.[1] Ever since the arrival of the horse among the Plains Indians, it had been possible for the entire tribe to assemble at Sun Dance time or when the Sacred Arrows were renewed. However, by the 1870's, the white settlements and forts formed a barrier that made the offering of one united Sun Dance impossible. No longer could the people gather in one huge half-moon camp circle in order to worship Mahuts.

Shortly after Ho'ko's deed, the Southern Cheyennes revolted.

[1] Mooney, *Cheyenne Indians*, 369–70, places the desecration of the Buffalo Hat at the beginning of the outbreak of 1874.

They had many grievances in addition to the steady loss of their lands. White hide hunters already had decimated the buffalo herds north of the Arkansas River. By 1872, the whites were penetrating the range west of the Cheyenne and Arapaho reservation. At least 7,500,000 buffalo were shot between 1872 and 1874.[2] The Cheyennes demanded that this indiscriminate slaughter stop; but the killing went right on.

Unlicensed traders were moving through the Cheyenne camps, and the whisky trade was especially active. Some of the warriors were trading robes for liquor rather than for food, trade goods, guns, and ammunition. These men, numbed by alcohol, did little hunting, therefore their families starved. By 1874, band after band had moved in close to the Cheyenne and Arapaho Agency, where rations ran short as the result of this sudden influx of hungry families.

The Kiowas were ready for fighting. White horse thieves plundered the Indian herds, some of them stealing horses within sight of the agency. The Cheyenne chiefs warned John D. Miles, their agent, that they would not be able to restrain their young men unless this horse stealing ceased.[3] Early in 1874, some young warriors did raid into Kansas in retaliation, capturing horses and mules from the settlers there. In mid-May, a party of white surveyors fired on a band of friendly Cheyennes, wounding one warrior. The Cheyennes threatened retaliation.

The Kiowas had been offering war pipes to the Cheyennes, but the chiefs of the Council of the Forty-four held out for peace. Nevertheless, after the Southern Sun Dance of 1874, the influence of the Council chiefs no longer prevailed. Now the power of the military societies grew stronger.

By June of 1874 fighting was being waged in earnest, with the Comanches, Kiowas, and some of the Cheyennes attacking the buffalo hunters and the trading settlement at Adobe Walls. Soon Suhtai Chief Gray Beard and Medicine Water, a noted fighter,

[2] Berthrong, *op. cit.*, 382.
[3] See Upper Arkansas Agency records, National Archives, Letters Received, 1871–74, Microcopy 234, Rolls 881 and 882; also, Cheyenne and Arapaho Agency records, 1875, National Archives, Microcopy 234, Roll 119.

accepted the Kiowa and Comanche war pipes. Most of the young Cheyenne warriors followed them.

John D. Miles, the agent for the Southern Cheyennes and Arapahoes, summed up the situation in a letter to the Commissioner of Indian Affairs. The letter was dated September 30, 1874.

... The lack of power to administer the law; to remove improper characters from the reservation; to break up the various bands of dissolute white men horse and cattle thieves—known to be operating in the vacinity—is the prime cause that may be assigned for the serious outbreak among the Cheyennes on their reservation ...

The Cheyennes and Arapahoes were assured by the President on their recent visit to Washington that improper white men and Buffalo Hunters should be kept from their country at all hazards, and they very naturally expected that some effort would be made to keep that promise, but they looked in vain—and the Cheyennes being the most restless of the two tribes grew tired and endeavored to avenge their own wrongs . . . .[4]

General Philip H. Sheridan dispatched five columns of troops against the warring bands. For the next ten months, fighting continued throughout the southern plains.

Medicine Water and his band were the most active of the fighting faction. In August, he and his warriors killed a surveying party near Fort Dodge. Then, in September, 1874, Medicine Water led the warriors who killed John German, his wife, and his oldest daughter. The four younger daughters were captured. Two were subsequently released by the Cheyennes, but Catherine and Sophia, the older girls, remained captives. Chief Stone Calf continually sought their freedom, but not until March 1, 1875, were they released.[5]

[4] Agent Miles to Edward Smith, Commissioner of Indian Affairs, September 30, 1874, Upper Arkansas Agency records, Microcopy 234, Roll 882, M 1209.

[5] Upper Arkansas Agency records, Letters Received, 1874, Microcopy 234, Roll 882; also, Cheyenne and Arapaho Agency records, Letters Received, Microcopy 234, Rolls 119 and 120, especially correspondence of January 3, 1875, January 20, 1875, February 24, 1875, March 2, 1875, March 18, 1875, March 19, 1875, April 3, 1875, May 28, 1875, and October 6, 1875.

85

On March 9 of the same year, most of the Southern Cheyenne bands came in. Stone Calf led them in surrendering. Many of the other chiefs were with him: Gray Beard, Heap O'Birds, Lean Bear, High Back Wolf, Red Moon, Bull Bear, Eagle Head and Bear Shield. Medicine Water surrendered too, and he was immediately placed in chains.[6]

Thirty-two men were identified as leaders in the outbreak and the fighting that followed. So was Mochi, a woman, who was pointed out as the one who had struck down Mrs. German.[7] Chiefs Gray Beard, Heap O'Birds, Bear Shield and Minimic were among them. Medicine Water, Long Back, Big Moccasin and other leaders of the warrior societies also were included. Lean Bear and Howling Wolf were listed too, even though the agent stated that they "were said to have been in favor of peace." Ten other warriors were noted as having "no special charge against them." However, all were selected for imprisonment at Fort Marion, Florida.[8]

Even after the surrender, there was another flare-up. On April 6, 1875, Black Horse, a warrior whom the whites considered dangerous, was being shackled in leg irons. Goaded by the taunts of the women, he attempted to break loose. The soldiers opened fire, some of the bullets flying into the camp of the surrendered Cheyennes nearby. These Cheyennes fled across the North Canadian River to the sandhills there. In the fighting that followed, nine men and two women were killed by the soldiers. A number of Cheyennes were wounded, and some of them died.[9]

Under cover of darkness, about 252 men, women, and chil-

---

[6] Cheyenne and Arapaho Agency records, Letters Received, 1875, March 9, 1875.

[7] Mari Sandoz, *Cheyenne Autumn*, 85–86, says that Mochi had become a warrior woman after all her men had been wiped out at Sand Creek. Later her new husband and her cousins also were killed. She is said to have carried her grandfather's gun, a present from two gold miners whom he had saved from starvation on the Smoky Hill trail.

[8] Cheyenne and Arapaho Agency records, Letters Received, 1875, Agent Miles to Commissioner Smith, April 29, 1875.

Ibid., Covington to Enoch Hoag, September 20, 1875, adds: ". . . That a number of innocent parties were selected there can be no doubt."

[9] *Ibid.*, Covington to Smith, April 10, 1875.

dren slipped from the camp. Eighty-four of these fled to the Antelope Hills, while the rest camped about ninety miles north-west of the agency. Three companies of the Sixth Cavalry were dispatched up the Cimarron River, headed for this larger camp. When the soldiers approached, some of the younger men and women hurried to join the Cheyennes camped near the Antelope Hills, most of whom were warriors who never had surrendered at Darlington Agency.[10]

This group headed toward the Northern Cheyennes. Major H. A. Hambright, Nineteenth Infantry, the commandant at Fort Wallace, Kansas, was ordered to intercept and return them.

Lieutenant Austin Henely was then dispatched from Fort Wallace with forty men of the Sixth Cavalry. They were joined along the way by some buffalo hunters who were interested in plunder. The hunters led the soldiers to a secluded spot on Sappa Creek, in northwest Kansas. One of the fleeing Cheyenne bands was camped here. They were Little Bull's people, part of Gray Beard's Suhtai band. The soldiers surprised the Cheyennes at daybreak on April 23, 1875.

The people were camped on a low projection of land at the bend of the Sappa. A sharp bluff rose behind them, with the plains and pony herds beyond. When the firing began, some of the Cheyennes fled across the bluffs to the horse herd. The soldiers rushed across the creek, arranging themselves so that they could pour cross fire into the camp. The buffalo hunters were firing their heavy, long-range guns, and these cut down many of the people. So many women and children were killed that Little Bull and Dirty Water went out to parley with the soldiers. A sergeant came out to meet them. White Bear, Black Hairy Dog's stepson, was hidden near the creek bed. As the sergeant moved out, White Bear shot him down. Then the soldiers opened fire on Little Bull and Dirty Water, killing both of them.

Henely's men continued to pour their fire on the Cheyennes. Then, after a time, the soldiers rode off in the direction taken by

[10] *Ibid.*, April 16, 1875.

the Cheyennes who had fled. As the troopers moved off, White Bear stood up and fired at them. They turned and shot him down.

Seven men and twenty women and children were killed at the Sappa that day. Black Hairy Dog, Stone Forehead's son, was among those who escaped. His wife fled with him.[11] They joined one of the small bands of Southern Cheyennes that found their way to the vicinity of Red Cloud Agency, the agency for the Northern Cheyennes and Oglalas. Some of the Southern escapees eventually returned to Indian Territory. Others remained with their Northern relatives for a longer time. Black Hairy Dog, Lame White Man, and their bands were among those who stayed in the Powder River country.

For the Southern Cheyennes, the old days of freedom were over.

[11] Hyde, *George Bent,* 368–69. Cf. Berthrong, *op. cit.,* 404; Sandoz, *Cheyenne Autumn,* 90–95.

George Bent to Hyde, February 5, 1914, Coe Collection, states that there were twelve lodges in this camp. Cf., Cheyenne and Arapaho Agency Records, Letters Received, April 28, 1875. This verifies Bent's statement concerning the twelve lodges. However, the letter notes that, ". . . Nineteen warriors, including two chiefs and one medicine man, were found among the dead, the balance, eight in number, being Indians not engaged in the fight . . . . The remainder escaped with a small portion of their stock . . . ."

Lieutenant Henely reported that nineteen men, eight women and children were killed. Berthrong, *op. cit.,* 404.

7. Is'siwun Is Renewed

Stone Forehead's band of thirty-three men was among those who fled northward. When they had reached the middle of Kansas, the Cheyennes spotted a cloud of dust behind them, the sign of soldiers approaching. The Cheyennes scattered out, in order to leave no trail. A few miles farther on, they came together again. They could see the troops still following. Stone Forehead told the people to dismount and to hold the horses by their ropes. He told them to turn their robes so that the hair side was out, as a buffalo wears his robe. The Cheyenne horses were of many colors, white, black, and spotted. These ponies were in poor condition, and the Cheyennes had no hope of escaping by outrunning the soldiers.

When the people were seated according to his instructions, Stone Forehead took the Sacred Arrow bundle in his arms. He was wearing his robe with the hair side out. Then the Keeper walked the sacred four times around the people and their horses. As he did so, he was singing:

> *My weapon I use.*
> *Skin of rattle snake,*
> *Skin of bull snake;*
> *I use water snake.*

The soldiers continued their advance, passing within half a mile or so of the Cheyennes. They were so near that it should have been easy for them to see the many-colored Indian ponies. The plain was perfectly level, with no trees and no buffalo in sight. Nevertheless, after looking around for a time, the soldiers rode on. When the Cheyennes heard the sound of the troops passing, they looked up, watching the soldiers until they disappeared. Then they mounted and continued their journey north. It is still believed that while the soldiers were passing the Sacred Arrow Keeper transformed the Cheyennes into buffalo.[1]

Stone Forehead's band finally reached the villages near Camp Robinson, close to the agency for the Northern Cheyennes and Oglalas. The Keeper bore Mahuts to the camps on Powder River. There he died in 1876.[2]

Black Hairy Dog, Stone Forehead's son, was far to the south at the time of the Keeper's passing, therefore the father was unable to offer his son's flesh in the old sacred fashion, using a flint

---

[1] Grinnell records this event in "Cheyenne Miscellany," MS No. 20, Southwest Museum archives. He states that Stacey Riggs was his informant. Elsewhere, in "Great Mysteries . . . ," *loc. cit.*, 574, Grinnell describes the event. He identifies his informant—presumably Riggs—as one of the Cheyennes involved in the event. In "Cheyenne Miscellany," Grinnell dates the event 1875 and identifies the Keeper as Black Hairy Dog. However, elsewhere he states that Black Hairy Dog did not succeed Stone Forehead as Keeper until 1876.

In 1960, Baldwin Twins recounted the same episode to the author, giving the words of the Arrow Keeper's song as recorded here. Twins identified the Keeper on this occasion as being the father of Black Hairy Dog, i.e., Stone Forehead.

[2] Cf. Appendix regarding the death of Stone Forehead.

knife to carve the Sun and Moon symbols on Black Hairy Dog's chest. From that time on, this sacrifice of the Arrow Keeper's own flesh to Maheo and to the Sacred Powers was discontinued.[3]

The days of Northern Cheyenne freedom were limited now. The Laramie Treaty of 1868 had established the Great Sioux Reservation, upon which the Lakotas and their Northern Cheyenne allies were to remain. These lands stretched from the Missouri River west to the Big Horn Mountains and south to the North Platte River. After the Laramie Treaty, many of the Sioux gave up fighting, choosing instead to draw their rations at the agencies along the Missouri River. However, most of the Northern Cheyennes continued to draw their rations with the Oglalas, at Red Cloud Agency in northwestern Nebraska.

Sitting Bull and his Hunkpapas had chosen freedom in the unceded lands of the Powder River country. There was much movement of Sioux and Cheyenne bands between the agencies and these still-rich hunting grounds to the west. Some fighting continued. The Chiefs of the Council of the Forty-four generally spoke for peace. They were the older men. The members of the warrior societies, most of whom were younger men, remained eager for coups and for glory. Some of them joined the Sioux in raiding along the Platte and the Yellowstone. Thus they brought on charges by the whites that the Indians were violating the promise to keep the peace that they had made at Laramie.

In 1874, Colonel (Brevet General) George A. Custer led an expedition into the Black Hills, part of the Great Sioux Reservation. Gold was discovered, and the government attempted to purchase the lands. The Indians refused to sell. Meanwhile, miners invaded the area, arousing public sentiment in favor of taking the hills away from the Indians. Now the Sioux and Northern Cheyennes accused the whites of bad faith and of violating the Laramie Treaty.

Grievances continued to mount. Finally, in a move to stop the warrior raids and, incidentally, to pressure the Sioux and Chey-

[3] Grinnell, "Great Mysteries . . . ," *loc. cit.*, 545.

ennes into selling the Black Hills, General P. H. Sheridan ordered all Indians living in the unceded area to be at their agencies by December 31, 1876. They were to come in or be treated as hostiles. In the dead of that winter, many of the Northern Cheyennes never heard the edict until the deadline was past, but it was doubtful if they would have surrendered anyway. They were upon lands they believed to be their own.

Thus began the Sioux War of 1876. General Crook was to initiate a three-pronged movement of troops against the Indians. Crook's campaign moved from the south, and it began in the dead of winter. Among his officers was Colonel Joseph Reynolds. In the spring, Colonel John Gibbon was to lead a column moving in from the west. At the same time, General Alfred Terry's column was to move from the east, with George Armstrong Custer's Seventh Cavalry among them. The army's task was to round up or destroy the roving bands of Sioux and Cheyennes. These were the bands among which Coal Bear still traveled, his wife bearing the Sacred Buffalo Hat upon her back.

It was in February of 1876 that Last Bull, chief of the Kit Foxes, first shouted the warning of soldiers coming to the Cheyennes in Old Bear's village on Powder River.[4] Old Bear was one of the four Old Man Chiefs, the priestly chiefs who were the head Tribal Chiefs of the people. Mystically, they represented the Maheyuno, the four Sacred Persons who dwell at the cardinal points of the universe. Maheo had created the Maheyuno to be the special guardians of his creation. The four Old Man Chiefs, the earthly representatives of the Sacred Persons, were the special guardians of the Cheyennes. Thus, the Old Man Chiefs served the people in both a political and a religious capacity.

Forty other chiefs served under the Old Man Chiefs. Two were designated Doorkeepers or Servants. The other thirty-eight were undifferentiated among themselves. Together, they formed

4 Thomas B. Marquis, *A Warrior Who Fought Custer*, 160.
Identification of this village is from W. P. Clark, "Report of W. P. Clark on the Sioux War," Department of the Platte, Letters Received, 1877, Doc. No. 4601, DP 77.

the Council of the Forty-four. Every ten years, membership in the Council was renewed. The Old Man Chiefs chose their successors from among the retiring forty. The other chiefs chose successors from outside the Council.

Among the chiefs, it was the Sweet Medicine Chief whose position was the most sacred.[5] He sat in the place of honor, and presided over the meetings of the Council of the Forty-four. His seat represented the heart of the world, the home of Maheo himself. Some Cheyennes considered his office to be the holiest in the tribe, for he bore, under his left arm, the parfleche cylinder containing the sweet root that mystically represents Sweet Medicine himself. Prayers were offered before the Chiefs' bundle, for Sweet Root Standing was present there. "Sweet Medicine does not answer your prayers in words; but he hears everything you say," Frank Waters, a later Keeper of the Chiefs' bundle, stated.

Little Wolf was the Sweet Medicine Chief at this time, and his tipi stood among the other lodges in the camp. Chiefs of the military societies rarely retained their former office when they were advanced to the Council of the Forty-four. Little Wolf was the exception, for he remained an Elk Society leader even after he was named Sweet Medicine Chief. He had been a brave and tough leader in his earlier days, one who was noted for his sternness in disciplining his own men, and respected as a leader and

[5] Traditionally the Sweet Medicine Chief was the forty-fifth Chief. However, by the 1876 period, Wooden Leg mentions Little Wolf's name among the four Old Man Chiefs: Morning Star, Little Wolf, Black Moccasin (Dirty Moccasin), and Old Bear. Thus, he makes the Sweet Medicine Chief one of the lesser Old Man Chiefs. It is possible that one of the Old Man Chiefs had died at about this point. In the midst of the wars, there would have been no time in which to gather the entire tribe for the formal reorganization ceremonies for the Council of the Forty-four.

John Stands in Timber wrote the author in February, 1967:

"In Little Wolf's time there were 44 chiefs but only 4 principal chiefs. These chiefs were organized and acted as a unit, not separately. One of the four chiefs held the medicine bundle. It was not given to a fifth man. Little Wolf was one of the keepers of this medicine a little before 1884. Little Wolf violated the law that says, 'Thou shalt not kill.' He killed a man named Starving Elk and Little Wolf was cast out and became an outlaw . . . ."

Cf. Llewellyn and Hoebel, *Cheyenne Way*, 67–98; John Stands in Timber and Margot Liberty, with Robert M. Utley, *Cheyenne Memories*, 42–57; Dorsey, *The Cheyenne*, I, 1–15.

an organizer. He always led the Elks into battle; he always counted the first coup. Now, during the sessions of the Chiefs, Little Wolf represented Sweet Medicine himself, and the Prophet's presence in the Chiefs' bundle continually guided the deliberations of the forty-four men who governed the Cheyennes.

There were other prominent men in Old Bear's village. Box Elder, the Suhtai holy man, was there. It was he who made the shafts of the new Arrows after Mahuts's capture by the Pawnees. Above the doorway of Box Elder's lodge hung the Ox'zem, the sacred wheel lance made by his father, Horn or Blind Bull. Box Elder also possessed one of the four straight pipes, the holiest of Cheyenne pipes.[6]

Box Elder possessed the power of prophesy to a remarkable degree. This knowledge came to him through the wolves, the messengers of the Maiyun. The wolves told Box Elder that he would never be killed in battle. He would die of old age, they said. Box Elder also possessed bullet-proof power, and he was famed for his ability to summon the Maiyun in the Spirit Lodge.[7] At this time, he was a blind old man, well over seventy-five years of age. The Cheyennes say that his blindness only helped to deepen Box Elder's contacts with the spirit world.

White Bull was present, too. The Cheyennes also called him Ice, from his power to eject ice from his mouth during the sacred ceremonies. Years before, in 1857, he and Dark had used their bullet-proofing power against Colonel Sumner's cavalry, who were pursuing the Cheyennes in Kansas. The soldiers tricked

[6] Box Elder is also named Maple, Maple Tree, Dog on the Range, Dog on the Ridge, Dog Standing, and, in his last days, Old Brave Wolf. He was born c. 1795 and died c. 1892, near present Birney, Montana. No old-time holy man was more venerated by the author's informants.
Cf. Grinnell, Cheyenne Indians, II, 112f., 223, 272, 292, 315.
Some indication of Box Elder's importance is indicated by the fact that Bent identifies this village as consisting of eighty lodges "under Maple Tree (Box Elder)." Bent to Hyde, March 13, 1914, Coe Collection.
Cf. Father Peter Powell, "Ox'zem: Box Elder's Sacred Wheel Lance," in press.
[7] George Bent calls Box Elder a ventriloquist, an apparent reference to his power in summoning the Maiyun who spoke from the Spirit Lodge. Bent to Hyde, March 13, 1914, and September 5, 1914, Coe Collection. Also, Bent to Hyde, April 2, 1914, George Bent Letters, Western History Dept., Denver Public Library.

White Bull that day, for they charged with drawn sabers, rendering Ice's medicine powerless.[8] White Bull also made the horned warbonnet that protected Roman Nose from enemy bullets. That protective power was broken, too, when a spoon made from the white man's metal touched the food Roman Nose was eating. Shortly thereafter, the Elk Society leader was shot down by Major George A. Forsyth's men at Beecher's Island.

White Bull had joined the Crazy Dogs in his youth, but in 1858 he had been expelled from that society under unusual circumstances. His uncle shot at a man who had shot at his dog. The uncle did not even wound the man. Nevertheless, the Crazy Dogs proceeded to expel White Bull for his relative's action. That same day the Elks invited Ice to join their society. He did, and remained an Elk for the rest of his warrior days.[9]

Two Moon was present, also. At this time he was one of the lesser chiefs of the Kit Foxes. Some Oglala and Minniconjou Sioux were camped with the Cheyennes. They numbered at least fourteen lodges, under the leadership of He Dog, the Oglala scalp shirt wearer. The Cheyenne tipis numbered at least forty, and they were scattered along the west side of Powder River, not far above the mouth of the Little Powder.[10]

Last Bull had ridden into this village shouting, "Soldiers are coming to fight you!" He went on to say that the whites would fight all the Cheyennes and Sioux who were off the reservation. He did not know from what forts the soldiers would come, nor who their leaders would be. After he delivered this news, Last Bull and his family joined Old Bear's camp. Soon other Cheyennes followed.[11]

For several reasons, Last Bull's warning went unheeded. The leaders of this village were Elks, and Last Bull was chief of the

[8] Hyde, *George Bent,* 102ff.

[9] Edward S. Curtis, *The North American Indian,* VI, 105.
Cf. George Bent to Hyde, January 19, 1905, July 12, 1912, and January 24, 1906, Coe Collection.

[10] The size of the camp is variously estimated at from 40 to 105 tipis.

[11] Marquis, *Warrior Who Fought Custer,* 159.
Cf. J. W. Vaughn, *The Reynolds Campaign on Powder River,* 123ff.; Grinnell, *Fighting Cheyennes,* 347n.

Kit Foxes. Last Bull was also a woman stealer, a notorious tough who made little attempt at concealing his pleasure as he quirted his own men or struck some hapless lawbreaker.[12]

For years the Kit Foxes and the Elk Scrapers had been rivals. Both societies traced their origins to Sweet Medicine himself, but among the Northern Cheyennes at least, the Foxes claimed superiority over the other military societies. When a list of the warrior bands was announced, the name of the Kit Fox Society usually was mentioned first. The Foxes had been powerful when the Arrows and Hat first were borne across the Missouri. Older Cheyennes spoke of them as the "Preparing the Place Ones," the men who moved ahead to locate and make ready the spot where the sacred ceremonies were held after that first Missouri crossing. When Sweet Medicine received Mahuts, the Arrows were wrapped in a kit fox skin quiver. Thus, the Foxes long had considered themselves the special protectors of the Arrow tipi, its Keeper, and its sacred contents.[13]

On the other hand, by 1876 Last Bull's men had become arrogant and overbearing in the eyes of the other societies. Many Cheyennes called them, "Woman Stealers, Wife Stealers, Beating-up Soldiers," because the Kit Foxes were all too eager to strike down any offender with their bows or quirts.[14]

Angry and contemptuous of the Foxes, the Northern Elk Society men had increased both in power and in respect among the people. Elk Scraper Society membership was largely Suhtai, and they regarded themselves as the special protectors of the Sacred Buffalo Hat. Three of the four Northern Old Man Chiefs

12 For some additional insights into Last Bull's character cf. Llewellyn and Hoebel, *op. cit.*, 117f., 119ff., 204f., 220 ff., 266. Wooden Leg adds a kindly note in Marquis, *Warrior Who Fought Custer*, 166, 300. Last Bull's character was well recalled by the author's informants. Later he was deposed as Chief of the Kit Foxes and went into exile among the Crows.

13 Details are from John Stands in Timber, Henry Little Coyote, and James Medicine Elk. Both Little Coyote and John Stands in Timber were Kit Fox Society members. Cf. Dorsey, *The Cheyenne*, I, 20.

14 For example, c. 1854, White Horse, Chief of the Kit Foxes, stole Walking Coyote's wife. Llewellyn and Hoebel, *op. cit.* 140 ff. About 1866, Last Bull was accused of stealing the wife of American Horse, adding strength to the nickname "Wife Stealers." Mari Sandoz to the author, April 16, 1962.

had been Elks: Little Wolf, Black Moccasins (Dirty Moccasins), and Old Bear. Elks were leaders in the Fetterman fight, where they had received the nickname of "Blue Soldiers" from their victory over the blue-clad cavalrymen.[15] Elks headed the charge against the Platte River bridge in 1865. Their membership cut across tribal lines, for it included Young Man Afraid of His Horses, one of the four scalp shirt wearers of the Oglalas. White Bull, White Shield, Left Hand Shooter, Bob Tail Horse, Lame White Man, the Southern Cheyenne leader—all were Elk Scraper Society members. White Antelope and Roman Nose (Bat) had been Elks prior to their deaths.[16]

Thus Wooden Leg, himself an Elk Society man, expressed the prevalent sentiment when he said, "We did not believe Last Bull's report. The treaty allowed us to hunt here as we wished, so long as we did not make war upon the whites."[17] Last Bull, Chief of the Kit Foxes, smoldered under the humiliation of being ignored by his society's arch rivals.

Soon the Cheyennes heard the warning again. This time the word came from Spotted Wolf, Twins, and Medicine Wolf, as they and their families joined Old Bear's camp. "Soldiers will come to fight you!" they said. Now the Elks were willing to listen. Every hunting party watched for soldiers. The women and old people were ready to flee. Wooden Leg and Yellow Hair,

[15] Grinnell, *Cheyenne Indians*, II, 48.

[16] For Roman Nose's membership in the Elks, cf. Bent to Hyde, June 10, 1904, June 20, 1904, and August 9, 1904, Denver Public Library. Accounts of the death of Roman Nose are to be found in Grinnell's *Fighting Cheyennes*, Hyde's *Life of George Bent*, Stands in Timber's *Cheyenne Memories*, Grinnell's *Cheyenne Indians*, Berthrong, *The Southern Cheyennes*, Brady, *Indian Fights and Fighters*, and others.

Clark, *Indian Sign Language*, 355, states that Roman Nose led the Medicine Lance band (Elks), but after his death in 1868 "this band lost its prestige and wasted away in numbers." Clark, however, indicates that his informants are Southern Cheyennes, not Northerners. A study of the military society membership of Northern Cheyenne leaders during the final wars certainly indicates that the prestige of the Northern Elk Society remained high, even though the membership was diminished by the battles with the soldiers.

The Elks, with their Suhtai affiliation, were not prone to talk about themselves to whites. The Kit Foxes were just the opposite. After the rise of Two Moon, the Foxes regained much of their prominence in the north.

[17] Marquis, *Warrior Who Fought Custer*, 160.

his brother, located a soldier camp. They hurried back with the news. Then criers moved through the Cheyenne-Sioux village, summoning the leaders to council. The Chiefs' decision was to keep moving, to keep away from the soldiers.[18]

Daybreak usually found the older Cheyennes awake for prayers. Often a priest would move through the camp crying, "Don't let the Sun find you in bed!" Thus, it was an old man's cry that first shattered the cold daybreak of March 17, 1876. "The soldiers are right here! The soldiers are right here!" he cried, as Colonel Joseph Reynolds's troopers attacked.

Cavalrymen on white horses charged in first, sweeping between the tipis and the horse herds. The soldiers had eluded ten Cheyenne scouts who had been appointed to find them just the evening before. Now the screams of women and children carried far in the cold, dry air, the sound rising above the duller reports of the rifles. Some Cheyennes slashed the sides of their lodges in their rush to escape. Older people hobbled along, fleeing the bullets that scorched the lodge skins in their flight.

Then soldiers riding bay horses charged the village from another direction. Warriors grabbed whatever weapons they could find. Women were struggling with packs of their most treasured possessions. Mothers hurried to the adjacent ravines and rocky bluffs, dragging or carrying their children, while the men covered their retreat. From their hiding places, the Cheyennes watched yellow flames streak the dark colors of the winter dawn. Flares marked the explosion of the gunpowder stored in some of the tipis, and the crack of exploding cartridges cut through the other sounds of destruction.

Reynolds's cavalry were soon gone, driving almost a thousand horses before them. Behind they left the stench of burned buffalo skin lodges, beadwork, robes, dried meat, and furs. All were

---

[18] Details of the Reynolds fight are from Clark, "Report on the Sioux War" *loc. cit.;* Marquis, *Warrior Who Fought Custer,* and Thomas B. Marquis, *She Watched Custer's Last Battle.* Additional details are from the author's Northern Cheyenne informants listed earlier. Cf. Harry F. Anderson, "Cheyennes at the Little Big Horn—A Study of Statistics," *North Dakota History,* Vol. 27, No. 2 (Spring, 1960), 83–85.

reduced to black piles, smoldering against the melting snow. One tipi remained standing. An old woman was huddled within it, unharmed by the troops.

That night, the power of Box Elder's sacred wheel lance was proved to be strong. After Reynolds's attack, the blind priest invoked Ox'zem's concealing protection to cover the movements of the Cheyennes as they attempted to recapture their horses. The warriors were successful in recovering most of the herd. This Cheyenne victory resulted in General Crook's later claim that the Reynolds campaign was a failure because of the loss of the pony herd, a charge leveled against Colonel Reynolds during his subsequent court-martial.

After the battle, the Cheyennes moved northeast. At night, there was the cold and the wailing of children muffled in robes for the fleeing. By day, mud and the water of melting snow made the march miserable. Early the fourth day, the Cheyennes reached Crazy Horse's Oglala camp, far up a creek east of Powder River. The Cheyennes were cared for there. Then the Cheyenne and Oglala leaders gathered in council. Their decision was to move on to the Hunkpapa camp to the northeast. When they reached it, they were generously received by Sitting Bull.

After the battle on Powder River, there were Suhtaio who believed that Is'siwun should be renewed. Sacrifices were needed to atone for the dissension between the Elks and the Kit Foxes. Both Sweet Medicine and Erect Horns had warned against such dissension. The Elks and the Kit Foxes were the special guardians of the Arrows and the Hat. By their bitter rivalry with each other, the two societies had weakened the strength of the people who were blessed by Mahuts and Is'siwun.

Like the Arrows, the living symbols of male power, the Buffalo Hat could be renewed. The renewing ceremonies for Is'siwun, the symbol of buffalo herds and of female power, were simpler than those of the Arrows. Sacrifices of a Cheyenne's own flesh, of an enemy scalp, or of a fine robe or blanket were offered to Is'siwun, and a new tipi was erected above the sacred bundle.

However, before this was done some people believed that a great victory was needed, also, one that would demonstrate the tribal unity made possible through the power of the Hat. After such a display of Cheyenne unity, the formal renewing ceremonies could be held. Sacrifices would be offered to Is'siwun, and all would be well again.

After the Cheyennes and Oglalas joined Sitting Bull, the villages continued to grow. The Minniconjous, under Chief Lame Deer, were the next to arrive. Later, the Sans Arcs, the Arrows All Gone People, came. At Powder River, the Blackfoot Sioux, the Sihasapa, joined the others. Soon they were followed by some of Inkpaduta's Santees, the Waist and Skirt People. Lame White Man, one of the Southern Chiefs, arrived at Powder River.[19] He and his band had traveled there from Red Cloud Agency. A few days later, on Tongue River, another band of Northern Cheyennes arrived. Dirty Moccasins, one of the Old Man Chiefs, was leading this group. His arrival appears to have been early in May.[20]

The six great camp circles lay in close proximity to each other. The younger warriors, many of whom were untried men eager for war honors, were anxious to be fighting the soldiers. The Council Chiefs and the older men urged them to hunt instead. However, the tension remained.

By the middle of May, the circles of lodges were pitched along Rosebud River, six or eight miles up from the Yellowstone. The villages were Cheyenne, Hunkpapa, Oglala, Minniconjou, Sans Arc, and Blackfoot Sioux. The Santees camped with the Oglalas. Some Brulés pitched their tipis with the Blackfeet and Oglalas;

[19] Wooden Leg describes Lame White Man as being one of the Old Man Chiefs of the Southern Cheyennes, but says that he was not a chief among the Northerners. "He was a wise and good man. For this reason he had much influence among us, even as an advisor to our Chiefs." Marquis, *Warrior Who Fought Custer*, 183. Later, on page 211, Wooden Leg describes him as "the most capable warrior chief among us" at the Little Big Horn, and lists him as the chief of the Elk Society men there.

John Stands in Timber described Lame White Man as being one of the Council Chiefs.

[20] Marquis, *Warrior Who Fought Custer*, 177ff.; H. H. Anderson, "Cheyennes at the Little Big Horn," *loc. cit.*, 85.

while a few Assiniboins, those long-time enemies of both the Cheyenne and Sioux, were camped with the Hunkpapas and Blackfeet. A handful of Arapahoes were also present.

About May 19th, Coal Bear's wife bore Is'siwun into the Cheyenne village. The Sacred Hat tipi was pitched at the usual place, on the south side of the inner camp circle, well in front of the other lodges. The sight of Is'siwun's tipi put good thoughts and good feelings into the hearts of the people, Wooden Leg later recalled.[21]

By June there were two villages of Cheyennes near the Rosebud.[22] The larger village was on Reno Creek, but Magpie Eagle's village of fifteen to twenty lodges was at the head of Trail Creek. American Horse, the Cheyenne chief, was there, and so were Crazy Horse and Jack Red Cloud, son of the Oglala Bad Face leader. Scouts were sent south from this village, and they traveled as far as Powder River. These "wolves" watched Crook's men moving down Coal Creek, following it to the divide between that creek and the head of the Rosebud. Then the scouts returned to Magpie Eagle, saying that they expected the soldiers to continue their movement down the Rosebud.

The larger Cheyenne camp on Reno Creek also had been warned. The Chiefs had chosen the Elks to furnish scouts for this village. Little Hawk was one of the Elk chiefs, and he called the society together. He said he would take charge. The Elks appointed three men to go with him: Yellow Eagle, Big Wolf, and White Bird. They rode toward the Rosebud, following it up to the rough country at the head of the creek. Then they followed the Tongue River side toward the north, heading back toward the Rosebud again. At this point they met Crooked Nose and an Arapaho named Little Shield. These men were from Magpie Eagle's village on Trail Creek.

At the Big Bend of the Rosebud, these men found a herd of

21 Marquis, *Warrior Who Fought Custer,* 187; H. H. Anderson, "Cheyennes at the Little Big Horn," *loc. cit.,* 86.

22 John Stands in Timber, to the author, 1957–66.

Cf. Stands in Timber, Liberty, and Utley, *op. cit.,* 181–90; Grinnell, *The Fighting Cheyennes,* 328–44; Marquis, *Warrior Who Fought Custer,* 199.

buffalo. They killed one, and were preparing to roast the meat when they noticed other buffalo stampeding north from the Rosebud. The scouts climbed the hill. There they saw Crook's forces moving down toward the bend of the river. The Cheyennes watched the soldiers until they made camp late that afternoon. Next day the scouts headed back to the camp on Reno Creek, arriving there by evening. The scouts howled like wolves four times. Then they rode into the village, where they reported the soldiers on the Rosebud. Meanwhile, the scouts from Magpie Eagle's village already had reported.

Little Hawk, an Elk Society man, was first to sight the soldiers. In recognition of this honor, he later was chosen to scout out the center pole for the Sun Dance lodge.

When the wolf howls of the returning scouts were heard, the combined Sioux and Cheyenne Chiefs gathered in council. Criers called the Chiefs' words throughout the camps: "Young men, leave the soldiers alone unless they attack us."

But again warriors slipped away in the darkness. Most of them were younger men, but there were older warriors present, also. Little Hawk led a party which cut across the Wolf Mountains. Young Two Moon led almost two hundred men, both Cheyenne and Sioux. One woman rode with them. She was Buffalo Calf Road Woman, the sister of a Southern chief, Comes in Sight. They traveled throughout the night, and toward morning warriors from both the Reno Creek and Trail Creek camps came together. They waited until daybreak, then they sent out scouts once more. These men were Young Two Moon, White Bird, and four others. As the scouts moved ahead, the men behind them prepared their shields, warbonnets, and the sacred ornaments they wore into battle.

By the time Young Two Moon and his companions approached the enemy, their comrades were ready for battle. There is a high hill where Corral Creek comes into the Rosebud. The Cheyenne scouts were halfway up it when they met some of the Crow scouts coming over the other side. Shots were exchanged, and one Sioux horse was wounded. The scouts hurried back to their respective forces. Not far from the Big Bend of the Rosebud, the Cheyennes and Sioux charged the soldiers.

The fighting moved back and forth all day. At the mouth of present Corral Creek, called Bear Creek by the Cheyennes, the Shoshones and soldiers attacked one party of Cheyennes, driving them back to Ash Creek, near the present OD ranch. Just then a large force of Sioux and Cheyennes arrived from the Reno Creek camp, and they pushed the soldiers and Shoshones back in a running fight.

There was a large, flat divide at one point where the fighting was heavy. Some of the Sioux and Cheyennes used huge flat rocks to build breastworks there. Then they fired out at the enemy from behind these breastworks. Crook's men, however, drove them from these fortifications, pushing them across the divide. Finally the Cheyennes and Sioux made a stand behind the north side of the ridge, less than half a mile across the divide. The soldiers attacked from the south side, and the fighting became hand to hand. One soldier was killed at the site the Cheyennes call Coney Hill. Then the soldiers retreated south, taking a stand behind the ridge there.

More fighting was in progress down nearer the river. Some of the soldiers dismounted there and scattered in three directions. Young Two Moon, White Bird, Young Black Bird, Chief Comes in Sight, Louis Dog, and Limpy all had taken a stand behind some sandrocks. They were unaware that the soldiers were coming up from the pocket where they had left their horses. The troopers had almost surrounded these Cheyennes when a Sioux shouted, "Soldiers are coming behind you!" Then the troopers opened fire.

The Cheyennes decided to make a run for a hill about two hundred yards away. One at a time, they raced their ponies to this hill that rose to the northwest. One started out, and when he was halfway across, the next man started. Limpy was the youngest, and he was last. Just as he was ready to start, his horse was shot. Limpy was a cripple, with one leg shorter than the other, and now he was afoot.

The soldier scouts saw him all alone down there, and some of them started down to count coup on him. Young Two Moon saw what had happened, and he started back to help Limpy. He rode toward Limpy shouting, "Get ready! When you run, make a curve toward the north. Then stop quickly!" He rode over close to Limpy. However, the bullets were so thick that Two Moon's horse shied and Limpy was unable to jump up behind his friend. Two Moon rode out for another turn. Again he shouted, "Get ready!" There were large sandrocks twenty-five or thirty yards away. Limpy hobbled toward them and managed to climb up on one. When Two Moon charged toward him this time, Limpy was able to jump down behind him, and both men rode away to safety.

At that point, a party of Sioux warriors arrived. They drove the soldiers back down to the pocket, where their horses had been left waiting. The troopers mounted and retreated to a nearby ravine. Here they again opened fire on the Sioux and Cheyennes.

Chief Comes in Sight was one of many who fought bravely that day. He, Young Black Bird, White Bird, Low Dog, and Jack Red Cloud had been riding back and forth, allowing the soldiers to shoot at them. Suddenly Comes in Sight's horse somersaulted, struck by a bullet. Comes in Sight landed on his feet, and he immediately began to zigzag as he ran toward his friends. The soldier scouts charged at him. All at once a figure on horseback appeared, moving out from the trees and rocks on the north side of the battlefield. The horse and rider passed Comes in Sight, wheeled, and pulled up by the Chief's side. He quickly jumped up behind the brave rider, who was Buffalo Calf Road Woman, his sister. They galloped away from almost certain death.

Black Moon was killed that day. He had been wounded already at Beecher Island and again at Summit Springs. Before the Rosebud fight, he had tied to his scalp lock a sacred lizard, one that darted quickly across the rocks. Then he painted his entire body yellow, the color of the Sun himself. During the fight, a bullet struck Black Moon from behind, tearing a wound through his left side. Nevertheless, he managed to stay on his horse while Wooden Leg led him from the battlefield. Black Moon died that night, the only Cheyenne fatality in the Rosebud fight.[23] Limpy was wounded, but he recovered in time to ride against Custer's men. White Wolf's thigh was broken by an accidental discharge from his own repeating rifle. He, too, recovered. Several other Cheyennes were wounded. Finally the Cheyennes and Sioux had enough. They were tired and hungry, and they withdrew after about six hours of fighting. General Crook pulled back his forces to Goose Creek, near present Sheridan, Wyoming. Now his planned juncture with Custer and Terry was an impossibility.

The Cheyennes, however, knew nothing of General Crook's campaign plans. When they reached their camp at Reno Creek, the women prepared skins for the new covering of Is'siwun's tipi. Tanned buffalo hides were spread out upon the earth, fitted, but not sewn together. Then the bravest warriors were invited to gather around the spot where the skins lay.

Young Black Bird, an Elk soldier, was chosen to count coup over the new cover, for he had been the bravest in the Rosebud fighting.[24] Spotted Wolf, his father, had prepared him for the battle. The older man had been taught by the Maiyun who appeared as a kingfisher. Therefore, before they left camp, Spotted Wolf painted the figure of a kingfisher upon the shoulders and

---

[23] John Stands in Timber stated to the author that Scabby was the only Cheyenne killed. However, Grinnell, *The Fighting Cheyennes*, 365, states that Scabby was wounded during the attack on Dull Knife's camp in November, 1876, and died two days later.

Kate Big Head, Marquis, *She Watched Custer's Last Battle*, 6, describes Scabby as being alive during the Custer fight, and showing off his spirit power there.

Cf. Stands in Timber, Liberty and Utley, *op. cit.*, 187.

In 1930, Wooden Leg drew a picture of himself leading the wounded Black Moon from the battle field. The original is in the Custer Battlefield Museum, Catalogue No. 1951, Accession No. 12. A photograph of this picture appears on page 202 of Marquis, *Warrior Who Fought Custer*.

The same event is shown in a ledger book of paintings from Little Wolf's band, now in the author's possession. Here it is Calling Elk (Whistling Elk?) who is depicted as being the warrior who led the wounded Black Moon from the Rosebud battlefield.

[24] John Stands in Timber to the author.

flanks of his son's horse. As a result, the horse would not lose his wind; he would charge as quickly as the kingfisher does in diving toward the water.[25]

Then, just before the attack on Crook, Spotted Wolf painted Young Black Bird's body yellow. He faced his son's horse toward the south. Then he tied a scalp to its lower jaw. He placed his own war shirt upon his son. Then he took the stuffed skin of a kingfisher, the symbol of the Maiyun. Holding it up to the Sun, he sang a sacred song. Then Spotted Wolf said:

> My son, this is the song sung to me when the Maiyun took pity on me. If the kingfisher dives into the water for a fish, he never misses his prey. Today I wish you to do the same thing. You shall count the first coup in this fight.

After that, he tied the kingfisher to Young Black Bird's scalp lock, and he hung an eagle-wing bone whistle around his neck. He blew medicine and earth upon the horse's feet, and rubbed horse medicine over his son's quirt. Finally, Spotted Wolf said:

> If you see anyone ahead of you and whirl your quirt above your head, the man's horse may fall. When you charge, try to keep on the right-hand side of everyone. Take pity on everyone. If you see some man in a bad place, from which he cannot escape, help him if you can. If you yourself get in a bad place, do not get excited, but try to shoot and defend yourself. That is the way to become great. If you should be killed, the enemy, when they go back, will say that they fought a man who was very brave; that they had a hard time to kill him.

Young Black Bird followed his father's advice, and he saved the life of Young Two Moon during the battle. He also rode back and forth, drawing the soldier bullets to himself and away from his comrades. He killed three of Crook's men, and shot down one of the Shoshone scouts. He also captured a revolver.

Now Young Black Bird charged the whitened buffalo hides. He counted coup over them, recounting the victories he had

---

[25] Grinnell, *Fighting Cheyennes,* 337–39; Stands in Timber, Liberty, and Utley, *op. cit.,* 184f.

won at the Rosebud. When he finished, the best tipi makers among the women could safely walk upon the hides. When the stitching, the painting, and the decorating of the lodge cover was completed, the women spread it out to dry beneath the life-giving rays of the Sun.

Then Coal Bear blessed a crier who rode through the village, calling out that all who wished to receive a blessing now could walk across the new cover of Is'siwun's lodge. This walking not only blessed the people, it also drove sickness away. After the Cheyennes had walked across the cover, it was stretched in place over a framework of newly-peeled tipi poles. Now the cover of the Sacred Hat tipi had been renewed.[26]

For four nights the victory dances continued in the camp on Reno Creek. The faces of the Cheyennes were painted black, the color of victory, of enemy fires extinguished and enemy lives snuffed out. The victory songs rose with intensity, the trilling of the women echoing above the deeper voices of the men.

In the midst of this celebration a crier rode through the Cheyenne village, calling out a message from the parents of Young Black Bird: "The name of Young Black Bird is thrown upon the ground. Hereafter, he shall be called White Shield!"[27]

Coal Bear carried the Sacred Hat bundle from the new lodge, and he tied Is'siwun above the doorway. Then the scalp of one of Crook's Shoshone scouts was offered to the Buffalo Hat.[28] Now

[26] This ceremony continued down into the 1970's. However, in more recent days, it is the old lodge cover that is spread upon the earth. The people who desire a blessing stand at the edge of the cover, their faces turned toward the Sacred Mountain to the east. The Hat Keeper prays. Then he offers the pipe to Maheo, to the Earth, and to the Persons at the four directions. Then, in single file, the Cheyennes walk across the old lodge cover, heading toward the east as they do so. Little children are led by the hand. The author observed this ceremony during the years when Josephine Head Swift Limpy and Henry Little Coyote cared for the Sacred Hat, and again in August, 1970.

[27] John Stands in Timber to the author.

[28] The author's older Cheyenne informants stressed that a white man's scalp was never offered to the Sacred Hat or to the Arrows. John Stands in Timber stated that the Shoshone scalp preserved in the Sacred Hat bundle is the scalp offered to the Hat on this occasion.

Phillip Wells, the mixed-blood interpreter for the Indian scouts at Wounded Knee, made the same point to Judge Ricker. He stated that, among the Sioux,

both Is'siwun and her lodge were renewed. With this renewing, there was hope that the Cheyennes would be strong and united once more.

"whites are never spoken of as enemies and therefore were not scalped as a rule, for it is not honor to scalp any but an enemy. [A] white man's scalp was never exhibited at an event such as a council." Phillip Wells Interview; Judge Ricker papers, Nebraska State Historical Archives, Lincoln.

8. The Fight with Long Hair

The Cheyennes and Sioux knew that more soldiers were on the way. In fact, after the Rosebud fight, some of them expected an attack the next day. After the battle with Crook, Magpie Eagle's camp of Cheyennes, Sioux, and a few Arapahoes left the head of Trail Creek. They moved on toward the Little Big Horn, camping one or two nights at the forks of Reno Creek. It was near this campsite that Crazy Horse later climbed a low butte and carved upon its surface the figure of the horse that was his namesake. Above the horse he carved a snake with lightning marks.

Soldiers were reported near, so Magpie Eagle moved on to the large village on the Big Horn. Crazy Horse and Jack Red Cloud were with him.[1]

As usual, the Cheyenne camp circle was pitched in the form of a crescent moon, opening toward the east. Is'siwun's new tipi stood on the south side of the open space at the center of the camp. The Sacred Arrow lodge should have been pitched to the east of the Hat tipi. However, that spot was empty.[2]

Only a few of the Northern Cheyenne Council Chiefs were absent. Two of the four Old Man Chiefs sat smoking their long-stemmed pipes during the councils. Old Bear had fought his way out of the Powder River village during the Reynolds attack in March. Dirty Moccasins had joined the other Northerners at the Rosebud River. Only Morning Star and Little Wolf were absent. Most of the thirty chiefs of the Kit Foxes, Elks, and Crazy Dogs were present.[3]

White Bull was in camp. Several days before, he had been present at the Hunkpapa Sun Dance on the bank of the Rosebud, not far from the carved deer rocks. Sitting Bull had pledged that Sun Dance, vowing a hundred pieces of flesh to Wakan Tanka, the Great Mysterious. Jumping Bull, his adopted brother, had cut fifty pieces of skin from each of the Chief's arms. Then Sitting Bull had taken his place in the Sun Dance lodge, his eyes staring up at the Sun. Blood ran down his arms and shoulders as he endured throughout the night and day. About noon the following day, the crowd saw that he was weakening.

Black Moon, a Sioux priest, aided by some others, laid Sitting Bull upon the ground. The Chief was nearly unconscious, so they threw water upon him to revive him. Soon Sitting Bull's eyes cleared. He had seen a vision. Then Black Moon moved

---

[1] Unless otherwise noted, the details of this battle are from John Stands in Timber, to the author, 1957–66.

Cf. Stands in Timber, Liberty, and Utley, *op. cit.*, 191–211.

[2] Stands in Timber stated that there were about fifty lodges in the Cheyenne camp. Harry Anderson, "Cheyennes at the Little Big Horn—A Study of Statistics," *North Dakota History*, Vol. XXVII, No. 2 (Spring, 1960), gives the figure as about seventy. Wooden Leg states that there were about three hundred. Marquis, *op. cit.*, 210.

[3] Marquis, *Warrior Who Fought Custer*, 205f.

before the center pole of the Sun Dance lodge. There he called
out in a loud voice:

> Sitting Bull wishes to announce that he just heard a voice from
> above saying, "I give you these because they have no ears."
> He looked up and saw soldiers and some Indians on horseback
> coming down like grasshoppers, with their heads down and their
> hats falling off. They were falling right into the camp.

After that vision, the Sun Dance came swiftly to an end, and
the Hunkpapas moved on toward the Little Big Horn.[4]

Box Elder had seen a vision, too. Afterward, he dispatched
a crier to ride through the Cheyenne camp warning the people
to tie their horses close to their tipis. "In my dream I saw soldiers coming!" the blind holy man warned them.[5]

Magpie Eagle's followers arrived in the main village on June
24. That evening, the Sioux Chiefs invited the Cheyenne Chiefs
to a council. There they decided to send out the military societies
to patrol the camp, and to keep the young men in. They also
decided what to do if the soldiers came. "If the soldiers want
peace, we will talk to them. If not, we will fill them up with
fighting," was the decision.[6] Then the Chiefs appointed the Sioux
and Cheyenne military societies who would guard the camp.
Each society called in its members, and they rode out on duty
about sunset, patrolling both sides of the Little Big Horn.[7]

That evening, the Cheyenne women and girls prepared the
ground for a social dance. Some of the young men carried a
long, slender pole into the center of the dance area. Then Coal
Bear bore Nimhoyoh, the Turner, from the Sacred Hat tipi. The
Keeper lashed Nimhoyoh to the end of the long pole and ordered

[4] Stanley Vestal, *Sitting Bull*, 148ff.
[5] *Ibid.*, 155.
[6] John Stands in Timber, to the author.
[7] Cf. Marquis, *Warrior Who Fought Custer*, 212, where Wooden Leg states
that the Kit Foxes were on duty as camp police. Grinnell, *Fighting Cheyennes*,
347f., states that Last Bull, chief of the Kit Foxes who were then on camp duty,
saved the lives of seven Arapahoes who were suspected of being spies for the
soldiers.

the pole raised above the crowd. The Turner swung in the breeze, blessing the dancers and turning away sickness and death from those who were celebrating in the light of the bonfire below.[8]

A crowd was gathering in one of the Sioux camp circles. Spotted Elk and Crooked Nose, who were boys then, decided to see what was taking place. When they arrived, they heard that a group of young Sioux and Cheyennes had vowed the Suicide Warriors Dance, also called the Old Man's Charm or the Dying Dance.[9] Some of the boys had lost relatives at the Rosebud. Now they were pledging to throw away their lives—to never return from the next battle.

Five Cheyennes were among them, all young men, most of them less than twenty years old. Noisy Walking, White Bull's son, was about fifteen. Cut Belly, son of Roman Nose, was less than twenty. The other three boys were Closed Hand or Fist, Long Roach's boy; Roman Nose, the son of Red Robe; and Limber Hand or Limber Bones, whose father was Horse Roads or Chicken Hawk.

As Spotted Elk and Crooked Nose watched, the young men began to move into the dance circle. The first suicide fighter took his place there and began to dance. Men were singing strong-heart songs, and women making the trill. An old man was encouraging the boys. He said that their names soon would be forgotten if they died natural deaths, but if they died in battle, their names would be long remembered. The noise was so great that Spotted Elk and Crooked Nose could not hear themselves talk. Then a second boy joined the first, both of them dancing within the circle formed by the densely packed crowd around them. One by one, the other suicide warriors joined in the dancing. Relatives called out that they were giving away presents in honor of these brave boys: war clothing, robes, horses, moccasins, clothing for everyday wear.

Whenever the suicide boys danced, it was customary to an-

---

[8] Marquis, *Warrior Who Fought Custer*, 215.

[9] Details on the suicide fighters are from John Stands in Timber to the author, 1959. Cf. Stands in Timber, Liberty, and Utley, *op. cit.*, 194–204, where he lists only four: Little Whirlwind, Cut Belly, Closed Hand, and Noisy Walking.

nounce a parade for the following morning. Thus, it was still dark the morning of June 25 when the criers rode through the camps waking the people, telling them to watch the young men who had pledged to throw away their lives.

The parade began to form above the Sioux camps. The men arrived on horses that had been staked out the night before because the people knew that soldiers were in the vicinity. The line of warriors began moving down into the main camp. Two old men rode on either side of the line of suicide fighters. They were calling out the names of the men who had vowed their own deaths, announcing to the people whose sons these brave boys were. "Look at these boys! The next battle they will not come back. They will never be seen again!" the criers shouted.

Lame White Man, the Southern chief, was in the village. He had been one of the bravest fighting men at the Rosebud. There he had ridden back and forth in the open, drawing the soldier fire to himself as he rallied the younger warriors. Now, when he saw the preparations on the hill, he got his horse ready. Then he told his wife Twin Woman, "I must go up there and come down in the parade with my boys. I must follow my boys."

Other chiefs climbed the hill and joined the parade led by the suicide fighters. Lame White Man was singing a chief's song as he followed the young men. Other chiefs were singing with him. Magpie Eagle, American Horse, and Bobtail Horse, were among them, and so was Two Moon. They followed the suicide fighters down to the lower end of the Cheyenne village, where they marched before the tipis, swung around behind the lodges, and rode back to where the parade had begun. Then the warriors scattered to their respective lodges.

When Lame White Man reached his own tipi, he saw that Tall Sioux was erecting a sweat lodge down near the river. The chief tied his horse and walked down, joining the other men who entered the lodge. While they were there, sounds of excitement burst from the valley above the village, where Reno had begun attacking the Hunkpapas. The men crawled from the sweat lodge and ran to the aid of their families.

When he reached his tipi, Lame White Man found his horse waiting. Twin Woman caught a horse for herself, the chief hurriedly threw Red Hood, their small son, up behind his mother, and Crane Woman, their daughter, rode along on another horse.[10]

Lame White Man, still stripped for the sweat bath, did not have time to dress in his war clothing. He tied a blanket about his waist, grabbed a belt, a gun, and moccasins, and jumped on his pony, riding him bareback. Together the family rode off toward the western hills, the direction in which many other Cheyennes were running. About halfway there, Lame White Man called to his wife, "I must go across. I must follow my boys!" He left his family, and Twin Woman and the children rode on to a hill from which other women were watching the battle. Many were singing strong-heart songs as they followed the course of the battle across the river. Then someone was shouting, "There are more soldiers coming from the opposite side!"

In spite of their fear of the patrolling warrior societies, there were still young men eager to gain the first war honors for themselves. Wolf Tooth and Big Foot, two cousins, were among those who wanted to strike the enemy first.[11] They planned to slip through the line of soldier society guards, cross the river, and be in position to meet the soldiers first. The evening of June 24 they hobbled their horses out beyond the camp, on the west side of the Little Big Horn. There the ponies would be handy for later use by the young men.

After midnight, Wolf Tooth and Big Foot slipped out to their horses. They rode west from the village, heading in the direction of present Crow Agency. When they reached the river they had difficulty in crossing because the horses made so much noise in the water. However, they reached the other side safely. There they hid in the brush all night. As daylight approached they

10 Crane Woman became John Stands in Timber's mother. Her brother Red Hood is also known as Red Hat.

11 Wolf Tooth was the step-grandfather of John Stands in Timber.

could see the scouts all along the hill, guarding the west side of the river. They knew that if the patrols caught them they would be punished. They might be whipped with quirts, or their horses and property might be destroyed.

Wolf Tooth and Big Foot waited until the scouts moved out of sight. Then they rode on, keeping under cover. As they rode, they saw other riders slipping out of the brush—first a few, then more and more, until there were nearly fifty men. These warriors all followed the dry creek north of present highway 212. After they had ridden some distance, they heard a shout. Looking back, they saw a rider on top of a ridge that ran along the south side of the dry creek. He was signaling them back, and they rode to him as quickly as their horses would gallop. When they reached the rider, the Cheyennes saw that he was a Sioux boy. Big Foot spoke some Sioux, and he caught the boy's words: "The soldiers are already at the village!"

The Cheyennes then raced back up the creek until they could follow the divide. As they rode along the divide they saw the last of Custer's troopers preparing to ride into camp. The soldiers were just going down toward the river, and they were almost out of sight. Reno's men had already attacked the Hunkpapa end of the villages, but these warriors did not know that.

The Cheyenne fighting men split into two groups. One rode down the south side of the divide, and the other down the north, until they nearly reached the bottom. Some of the warriors chased the soldiers, while the others circled around to cut them off. The soldiers opened fire, and the Indians moved back behind the troops, allowing them to move on down toward the river. They followed the troopers into the dry gulch above the head of Medicine Tail Creek, close to the present battle monument. The Cheyennes and Sioux were thus behind the cavalry, cutting them off in case they attempted to retreat to the north.

Custer and his men followed the ridge down to a level place, near the present cemetery site. Two warriors, Yellow Nose and Low Dog, were the first to cross the Big Horn River.[12] Now they

12 Yellow Nose was a captive Ute who was raised as a Cheyenne. Low Dog was half Cheyenne, half Sioux.

rode back and forth in front of the soldiers, firing at them. This slowed down Custer's advance. More warriors joined Yellow Nose and Low Dog, and the soldiers began pulling back, moving on down toward the river, across from the Cheyenne camp. Other Cheyenne fighters had moved out from their village, concealing themselves in the brush along the river bottom, and they fired out at the cavalrymen. The soldiers then turned north, riding back in the direction from which they had first come until they reached the place where the cemetery is located today. Here they made a long pause.

Wolf Tooth, Big Foot, and the other warriors had moved in behind the ridge above the soldiers and were firing down at Custer's men. Then Custer retreated, riding toward a dry gulch and following it up to the center of the basin, below where the monument now stands. This gave the Indians time to cover the ridge, so that the soldiers could not retreat in that direction. Custer moved toward the lower bank of the basin, then his men dismounted. The soldiers of the Gray Horse Company got off their mounts and began to move up on foot. Some soldiers lay down on the ground, firing from that position. Others advanced for a distance, running, covered by the rifles of the men already hugging the earth. Some of the troopers fired from behind their dead horses. By this time, the Indian fire was heavy from both sides.

Twice, Sioux criers came along behind the warrior lines, shouting to them:

Watch those suicide boys! When they attack the soldiers, the soldiers will turn and fight the boys. When the soldiers turn, all you warriors jump over the hill. Shoot at the soldiers. Don't give them a chance to reload. Then we will fight them hand to hand, before they have a chance to reload!

The suicide warriors were the last ones to enter the battle. The Cheyennes had been watching for them, and at last they rode out into view. The soldiers were grouped near the monument site, with a number of them in the ravine. The suicide boys galloped up the level area where the National Cemetery now stands. Some of them turned and stampeded the horses of the soldiers. Their comrades charged right into the midst of the troopers, with the others following as soon as the horses were stampeded. Some of the soldiers jumped on their horses and attempted to ride farther up, toward the site of the monument. However, the suicide boys cut them off, turning them back toward the north about a quarter of a mile from where the soldiers remaining near the monument site were finally killed. Then the suicide boys moved in for hand to hand fighting. When that happened, Wolf Tooth, Big Foot, and the Indians on the ridge swarmed in from the other side. The Sioux and the Cheyennes were in among the soldiers so quickly that they had no time to reload or even to aim.

Yellow Nose fought well that day. He had been captured from the Utes as a child. However, he grew up "all Cheyenne." As he charged in, the dust suddenly cleared. He saw a guidon rising above the sagebrush in front of him. He grabbed it. Then he rode on into the thick of the fighting, using the guidon to count coup on a soldier. Black Bodied Man (Black George) captured a saber. Hand to hand fighting was going on everywhere—all along the ridge, down toward the river—filling the basin with struggling men.

Iron Shirt spotted a trooper wearing a buckskin jacket. The soldier had fallen to his hands and knees and was crawling along the prairie. Iron Shirt wanted that jacket. He threw the soldier over on his back, attempting to unbutton the shirt, but blood was clotted below the trooper's neck, staining the front of the coat, so Iron Shirt left him and moved on into the thick of the fighting.

After the suicide warriors charged in, the battle did not last long—not even half an hour.

White Necklace, Wolf Chief's wife, later recalled:

> I had a small hatchet under my belt. I saw a soldier lying there, stripped. I jumped off my horse. This was the same type of white man who cut off my niece's head at Sand Creek. When they (the Cheyennes) found her there, her head was cut off. I jumped off my horse and did the same to him. I cut off his head!

Other women hacked the bodies of the dead troopers because they, also, remembered how Colonel Chivington's men had mutilated the bodies of their relatives during the Sand Creek massacre. Later, White Necklace and Yellow Hair Woman saw other women dancing nearby, singing victory songs. They walked up to a place where several dead soldiers were lying. Then they saw a pole pushed into the earth. An enemy head was stuck on top of the pole, a head with long hair that fell the length of a man's neck.

There were no victory dances in the camp along the Little Big Horn that evening. Even with the soldiers wiped out, there were still dead Cheyennes to be mourned.

After the fighting, Tall Bull, Lame White Man's brother-in-law, rode to the hill where Twin Woman and her children were waiting. "My brother-in-law is one of those killed. Prepare a travois for him," he said quietly. They made ready a travois, stripping it to the bare skeleton of poles, making a flat surface upon which the body could be tied. When they reached Lame White Man's corpse, his body was covered with dust. A small part of his scalp was missing, because some of the Sioux had killed him, mistaking him for one of Custer's Indian scouts.[13]

[13] John Stands in Timber, to the author, 1959. Cf. Marquis, *Warrior Who Fought Custer*, 261 f.; also, Marquis, *She Watched Custer's Last Battle*, 4 ff.

We have noted that Wooden Leg is not clear concerning whether Lame White Man was a Council Chief or an Elk Society chief. Wooden Leg calls him "the most capable warrior chief among us," Marquis, *Warrior Who Fought Custer*, 211, 245. Kate Big Head, White Bull's sister, calls Lame White Man, "the bravest Cheyenne warrior chief" and "the most important war leader among the Cheyennes" in the Custer fight. Marquis, *She Watched Custer's Last Battle*, 4, 6.

Wooden Leg explains Lame White Man's presence in the battle by stating that any older man who had a warrior son was expected to stay out of battles, thereby giving his son a chance to gain honors. "Lame White Man . . . went into the fight because of his having no son . . . . I do not know of any tribal chiefs or old men having mixed into the battle. My father stayed in the camps, but his staying there was not on account of personal fear." *Ibid.*, 383.

This statement underlines a fact that many persons do not realize: namely, that most Chiefs of the Council of the Forty-four, as well as Chiefs of Sitting Bull's stature, retired from the active warpath when they became Council Chiefs. They already had proved their bravery. Now, in the councils, they could demonstrate their wisdom. Chiefs and warriors of Lame White Man's age were not considered cowards for sending young men fifteen to thirty years old into battle. "Old men for council; young men for war," was a Plains Indian maxim.

Lame White Man's last words to his wife had been, "I must follow my boys into battle." So he had ridden after the suicide fighters. Now his mourning family carried his body back to the Cheyenne camp. There they dressed him in a fringed buckskin shirt and leggings, and then they bore his body to the sand rock across the river, on the north side.

White Bull also found sorrow in that day. Noisy Walking, one of the suicide boys, was his only son. The boy had been badly wounded, hit by three bullets and stabbed in the side as well. He had been carried to a bed of buffalo robes, with a willow dome shelter to protect him from the heat of the sun's rays. He lay there, pleading for water. "No! Water will kill you!" White Bull's voice broke as he forbade his son this kindness. His power, that was so strong in helping others, was not sufficient to save his own son's life.[14]

All the suicide fighters died, either during the battle or afterwards from wounds received in the fighting. The Cheyennes knew that they could kill more soldiers in hand to hand fighting than they could shoot down from a distance. In the fight with Reno, the Indians stayed back, firing at the troopers. However, in the battle with Custer the suicide boys charged in, drawing the soldier fire to themselves and beginning the hand to hand fighting that finally finished Custer's men.[15]

The Northern Cheyennes had no idea whose soldiers they were fighting. However, as the women moved back and forth among the dead troopers, two Southern Cheyenne women recognized Custer's body. They also recalled his visit to Stone Forehead's village on the Sweetwater.

Kate Big Head gave Lame White Man's age as thirty-seven. Wooden Leg says he was about thirty-eight. In describing Lame White Man's role in the Rosebud fight, Wooden Leg refers to him as, "Chief Lame White Man, the old [sic] Southern Cheyenne." Marquis, *Warrior Who Fought Custer*, 201. For a Cheyenne fighting man, thirty-eight years often was old!

[14] Marquis, *Warrior Who Fought Custer*, 256. The Cheyennes placed marker stones on the site of Noisy Walking's mortal wounding. According to John Stands in Timber, the spot is about 150 feet south of where Lame White Man's marker is today.

[15] For comparative statistics and names of the Cheyennes killed at the Little Big Horn, see Appendix VI.

That was in March, 1869, after Custer's attack on Black Kettle's camp on the Washita. After that battle, the captured women and children had been taken to Fort Hays. One of the women, an elderly person named Red Hair, had been taken on to Fort Sill. Later she had been sent back to the Cheyenne camps in order to encourage the people to move to Fort Sill and to make peace once more.

However, after Red Hair's departure, Custer himself learned the location of the Cheyennes. He also learned that they had two captive women in their camps. Instead of waiting for the Cheyennes to come in, Custer rode to Stone Forehead's camp himself. As he was approaching the camp, he met a hunter named Sand Hill. It was Sand Hill who took Custer to the Sacred Arrow lodge. The Chiefs had gathered there, and they made room for Long Hair, placing him directly beneath the Sacred Arrow bundle. Stone Forehead offered the pipe to the sacred Persons, to Maheo, and finally to the Arrows themselves. Then he handed the pipe to Custer. The two leaders smoked there, under the Sacred Arrows.

Custer asked the meaning of the ceremony. One of the Cheyennes replied that when a man smoked before the Arrows, he was swearing to tell the truth; he was swearing to keep his promise. Custer replied, "I will never harm the Cheyennes again. I will never point my gun at a Cheyenne again."

When the pipe had burned out, Stone Forehead took his wooden pipe tamper and deliberately scraped the ashes from the pipe bowl, causing them to fall directly on Custer's boots. Again, the officer asked the meaning of this procedure. "If you break your promise, you and your soldiers will go to dust like this," was the Arrow Keeper's reply. Custer repeated, "I will never kill another Cheyenne."[16]

[16] The account of Custer smoking under the Arrows was repeated to the author by Little Face, Charley Hawk or Buffalo Hair Ornament, Mary Little Bear Inkanish, and John Stands in Timber. It also appears in the Sand Crane MS, Mari Sandoz papers. Cf. George Bent to Hyde, September —, 1905, Colorado State Historical Society archives.

Custer's own account appears in his *Wild Life on the Plains and Horrors of*

Then Custer rejoined his command, which was camped near the Cheyenne village. He told the Cheyennes that he wanted their chiefs to come to the soldier camp to discuss the return of the captive white women. However, Custer's real plan was to capture as many Cheyenne men as possible, thus forcing the surrender of the entire village. Only three Cheyennes were taken by this trick, two older men and a middle-aged warrior.

When Custer got back to Camp Supply, the three captives were sent to Fort Hays. The women and children taken at the Washita were still held captive there. At Fort Hays, the commanding officer, who was acting without an interpreter, decided to transfer the men from the prison stockade to a guardhouse, as a security measure. When the Cheyennes saw guards with fixed bayonets entering the stockade, they thought they were about to be executed. The three Cheyenne men drew their knives and rushed the guards. Big Head was shot down, and Slim Face received a mortal wound from a bayonet. Little Bear was stunned when a guard struck him with a rifle butt.[17]

Later that spring, the Southern Cheyennes and their Arapaho allies moved on to Fort Supply. There they made a peace that lasted until the outbreak of 1874. There, also, Custer's Cheyenne captives from the Washita were finally returned to their relatives.

Now, at the Little Big Horn, it was seven years after Custer had ridden into Stone Forehead's camp. Even so, the two Southern Cheyenne women, both of whom had known him in the south, recognized his body lying there on the battlefield. When they saw Custer, they pushed a sewing awl into each of his ears and on into his head. Now his hearing would be improved, the

Indian Warfare, St. Louis, 1891, 306ff. Custer stated that he was deprived of the services of Romeo, his interpreter, during the meeting with the Arrow Keeper and the Chiefs.

Cf. Charles J. Brill, *Conquest of the Southern Plains*, 219ff.; Berthrong, *op. cit.*, 337f.; Grinnell, *Fighting Cheyennes*, 307; Hyde, *George Bent*, 324–26; Marquis, *Warrior Who Fought Custer*, 322ff.

[17] The names of the three captives vary. Slim Face is also called Lean Face or Dull Knife. Curly Hair is also known as Big Head. Cf. George Bent to Hyde, December 11, 1912, Coe Collection; Berthrong, *op. cit.*, 308; Custer, *Wild Life on the Plains*, 306ff.

women said—since it seemed that he had not heard the Chiefs' words when they smoked together under the Arrows. Long Hair had not heeded the warning that if he broke his promise, if he fought the Cheyennes again, Maheo would cause him to be killed.[18]

[18] Little Face, Mary Little Bear Inkanish, and John Stands in Timber to the author. John Stands in Timber said that he heard the account from Magpie, one of the Southern Cheyennes who fought at the little Big Horn. Magpie was near the Arrow Lodge while Custer was within.

Cf. Marquis, *She Watched Custer's Last Battle*, 8. Here Kate Big Head adds the note that some Sioux men were about to dismember Custer's body. The Cheyenne women who were nearby remembered Me-o-tzi (Monasetah), the Cheyenne girl who is said, by some informants, to have borne Custer a child. The Southern Cheyenne women made signs to the Sioux, saying, "He is a relative of ours." The Sioux men cut off one joint of Custer's finger. Then the Cheyenne women pushed the awl into his ears.

9. Blood on Is'siwun's Lodge

In the excitement following victory, few of the Cheyennes noticed further confusion in the Sans Arc camp. There the Sioux were crowding around a group of newly arrived Indians. Some of the Sans Arcs were shouting, "Kill them!" Others were calling, "Wait! See if they are really enemies." Rising above the Sioux outcry, some of the Cheyennes recognized a familiar voice protesting that he was "all Cheyenne." Little Wolf, the Sweet Medicine Chief, had arrived. Seven lodges of people were with him

But even some Cheyenne voices were raised in accusation. White Bull, shaken by the strain of Noisy Walking's fatal ordeal, shouted out that Little Wolf should have joined the people long before this. Little Wolf should have been there for the fighting, instead of remaining on the reservation so long, Ice exclaimed angrily. Wooden Leg, one of Little Wolf's Elks, spoke a little of the Sioux language. Now he interpreted for the Chief, in order that the Sans Arcs could understand what was being said.

The afternoon before, Little Wolf's band had seen the soldiers camped on the upper Rosebud. The Cheyennes hid in the hills and watched the whites as they moved toward the divide leading to the Little Big Horn. Then Little Wolf's band pushed on, alternately traveling and resting throughout the night. Scouts were sent ahead to watch for the soldiers. Early next morning, some of these scouts discovered a box discarded by the troopers. While the Cheyennes were examining it, the soldiers appeared and opened fire upon them, but the scouts were able to make their escape.[1]

Little Wolf's band continued to follow the troops, keeping themselves concealed as they moved along. Finally the Cheyennes heard the sound of guns echoing from the hills above the Little Big Horn. From a distance, they also could see the general movements of the fighting. At first it appeared to them that the Indians were fleeing. When the shooting died down, Little Wolf's band looked over the hilltops again. This time they saw that the tipis were still standing, and that the Indians were still in possession of the valley. Thereafter the Cheyennes had advanced cautiously until they reached the Sans Arc camp.

The grumbling continued even after the onlookers heard Little Wolf's account. There were still mutterings that he should have been with them long before this. However, the crowd finally scattered, and Little Wolf carried the Chiefs's bundle into the Cheyenne camp. Now Morning Star was the only Old Man Chief who was absent.[2]

Custer's men had been completely wiped out by this time. The village was alive with activity. Burial parties were leaving, and

---

[1] John Stands in Timber identifies Red Cherries and Medicine Bull as being with this party. Cf., Marquis, *Warrior Who Fought Custer*, 250.

[2] Marquis, *Warrior Who Fought Custer*, 251.

warriors were still riding out to keep an eye on Reno's men, who were pinned down across the Big Horn River. The Cheyenne tipis were pulled down, since it was customary to move camp after a death. There had been many deaths that day, with Lame White Man and the suicide boys all killed in battle. Now the Cheyennes chose a new campsite about a mile to the northwest.

On the afternoon of June 26, wolves reported more soldiers moving up the valley of the Little Big Horn. These men were the forces of Terry and Gibbon. The Sioux and Cheyenne Council Chiefs gathered. Their decision was to move toward the south-west. Two or three Cheyenne bands left the great village at this time, but most of them continued to travel with the Sioux. By late afternoon, the tribes were in motion again. The Cheyennes led the column, with the Hunkpapas guarding the rear. Scouts watched the new band of soldiers approach the river where the fly-blown bodies of Custer's men still lay sprawled on the hillside above its banks. Next day the tribes arrived at a campsite near present Lodge Grass. All six camps were pitched in the same arrangement as before. Here they finally paused to celebrate.[3]

Some of the Sioux paraded the morning after their arrival. Warriors had ridden through the villages collecting the gray horses captured from the soldiers. Now the Sioux marched proudly, mounted on the captured horses. Many of the warriors wore soldier uniforms and hats. Some were blowing captured bugles, and guidons waved above the heads of others. When the fighting had begun, Without Weapon had loaned White Elk a horse to ride into battle. When White Elk returned, he was leading two gray horses. He gave one of these soldier ponies to Without Weapon. Now she proudly watched a Sioux warrior parade by on her gift horse. Afterwards, the warrior led the gray horse back to her.[4]

That evening the Cheyennes held their own celebration. It was a small affair. No women danced; too many had sore legs from the gashes that had been made in mourning. Coal Bear carried

3 *Ibid.*, 274.
4 John Stands in Timber.

Nimhoyoh from the Sacred Hat tipi again. He lashed the Turner to a long pole which was erected in the center of the Cheyenne camp. The Cheyenne warriors danced around Nimhoyoh, counting the coups they had won against the soldiers.[5] However, this was a short celebration, because so many of the people were still in mourning. Some of Sitting Bull's Hunkpapas silently watched from the edges of the dance circle, but it would be another two days before the Hunkpapas celebrated.[6]

Next day, the tribes continued moving up the valley of the Little Big Horn. Here trouble struck again. This time Coffee was killed by his own rifle as he dismounted from his horse near the sacred tipi. Although he was a Southern Cheyenne, for many years he had lived in the north, assisting Coal Bear in the care of Is'siwun's lodge. Coffee never had married, because he believed that such holy work required the power that came with chastity. However, Coal Bear himself was married, as the Hat Keeper before him had been.[7]

The combined Sioux and Cheyenne villages remained together about sixteen days, until they reached Powder River. At Powder River they camped four or five days, the Cheyennes gathering daily. The danger from soldiers seemed to be gone, and game was growing scarce in the wake of so many people. The ponies were getting thinner, and the soldier horses were wearing out faster than the Cheyenne ponies. Indian herds could live on grass alone, but the army horses needed oats and corn. At Powder River, the Chiefs decided it was time to separate.[8]

The Cheyennes had begun to scatter even before the move to the Lodge Grass. One band had headed east, toward the Black Hills. Magpie Eagle led this group, and White Elk was with them.[9] A second band, White Bull and White Wolf (Wounded

[5] Marquis, *Warrior Who Fought Custer*, 274.
[6] Vestal, *Sitting Bull*, 183.
[7] Marquis, *Warrior Who Fought Custer*, 276. Wooden Leg states that Coal Bear had a wife and two children at this time. In later chapters he has two wives.
[8] *Ibid.*, 280. Wooden Leg and Kate Big Head both state that sixteen sleeps passed before the division of the tribes.
[9] The entire account of the killing of the Sheep Eater is from John Stands in Timber to the author.

in the Head) among them, moved down Tongue River.[10] Then they swung north, toward the Black Hills. As they traveled, they met other small Cheyenne bands scattered all the way to Belle Fourche Creek. At the Belle Fourche, White Bull's band paused to camp for a time. Some of the Sioux were traveling with each of these Cheyenne bands.

Two Moon, the Kit Fox little chief, moved his band down Tongue River and then back to the Powder. About twenty-five miles from present Broadus, Montana, is a small range of mountains the Cheyennes named the Pemmican Mountains. Many years before, the Cheyennes had captured a Crow village there. At Pemmican Mountains, Two Moon's followers found good hunting, with buffalo and other game plentiful. Chokecherries for making pemmican were abundant, also. Two Moon's band decided to camp nearby for a while. It was now early July.

In the meantime, the largest band of Cheyennes followed a wide trail running along the top of a divide in the Big Horn Mountains. Many of the Chiefs rode with this group. The Cheyennes soon found themselves in the country of the Sheep Eaters.[11] The Cheyennes considered the members of this small tribe to be dirty and wild. They often lived in caves in the mountains, eating wild sheep and goats. They also were a constant bother to the other tribes who camped in the Big Horns.

At one of these mountain camps, a Cheyenne warrior left the village to look for elk. While he was hunting, he saw two strangers who were peering down into the village. He carried this news to the camp, and the Cheyennes began to keep close watch on their horses again.

That evening, a small group of warriors scouted along the edge

[10] John Stands in Timber to the author.
Cf. Grinnell, *Fighting Cheyennes*, 383. Here Grinnell states that Black Moccasin was White Bull's father, thereby disagreeing with the author's informants, who, with the exception of Rufus Wallowing, stated that North Left Hand was the father of White Bull or Ice.
[11] The Sheep Eaters are the Tukuarika (Tukuaduka), a mostly non-equestrian branch of the Shoshones. They ranged from the area of Yellowstone Park to the middle course of the Salmon river in Idaho, and spent much of their time in the Big Horns.

of the nearby timber. Wolf Tooth and Big Foot always traveled together, and they were members of this party. Above the camp there was a meadow surrounded by timber. The Cheyennes scattered all along the edge of the timber to keep watch. Wolf Tooth and Big Foot were looking out from the brush when they saw a man moving along the creek that flowed near the village. Wolf Tooth moved closer in order to see if the man was a Cheyenne or an enemy. As he drew near, Wolf Tooth could see that the stranger was peering down into the camp. He went to Wrapped Hair, one of the Kit Fox little chiefs, and reported that someone was coming down close to the camp circle. Then he returned to do some more scouting.

Chief Plum Man also had seen the stranger skulking nearby. He walked up close to him and called out: "Who are you? Tell me, or I am going to shoot you!" But the Sheep Eater fired first, and his shot killed the chief. The Sheep Eater moved into the Cheyenne camp circle and shot another warrior. Then he slipped behind the Sacred Hat tipi, where he met Young Box Elder. They fired simultaneously, and Young Box Elder fell. However, his bullet hit the Sheep Eater, who fell against Is'siwun's tipi. Later, his blood was found splashed on the lodge cover itself. The Hat tipi was pitched near the stream, so the wounded Sheep Eater crawled into the brush growing near the water.

The Cheyennes surrounded the area, and waited for a long time. Finally, Wolf Chief and Medicine Bird began to crawl along on their hands and knees. They moved up the creek, pausing to listen every few minutes. Suddenly they saw a pair of feet protruding from the bushes. The enemy had died and was lying hidden there. Medicine Bird shouted, "Hi yi! I count the first coup!" Wolf Chief counted the second coup. Then they dragged the body from the brush.

Chief Bobtailed Horse recently had vowed the renewing of the Sacred Arrows, so the other warriors called him over to where the dead Sheep Eater lay. Bobtailed Horse scalped him and carried the scalp over to Is'siwun's tipi, where he tied the offering to one of the wooden lacing pins above the doorway.[12] Medicine Bird was honored for his counting of the first coup. Now he was given the name White Moon.

When daylight came, many of the Cheyennes came to view the gift Bobtailed Horse had offered the Buffalo Hat. The front of the sacred tipi was covered with lice "as thick as an anthill." The Cheyennes burned the Sheep Eater's scalp in disgust.

The three dead Cheyennes were buried in the rimrock near the camp. In anger and grief, their friends threw the Sheep Eater's body into the fire. Then the Cheyennes moved camp.

Morning Star reached the village in the Big Horns after a difficult trip from Red Cloud Agency. Throughout the spring and summer months of 1876, the government had been pressuring the Northern agency Cheyennes to join the Southern bands in Indian Territory. The Northern agency bands were filled with growing uneasiness at the military campaigns against their relatives. The influence of the army officers was growing at Red Cloud Agency as well as at the other Sioux agencies. Therefore, early in July the Cheyenne bands at Red Cloud Agency began to move north, seeking the camps of their free relatives in the Yellowstone country.

Colonel Wesley Merritt's Fifth Cavalry learned of these preparations. The Cheyennes already had dispatched about forty-five warriors as wolves. These scouts were riding in advance of the main band on the trail from Red Cloud Agency to the Powder River country. On July 17, 1876, at Warbonnet Creek, an advance force from Merritt's cavalry intercepted the Cheyenne scouts. Yellow Hand was killed, presumably by Buffalo Bill Cody.[13] The other Cheyenne scouts dashed back to the main body, which turned back toward Red Cloud Agency. They soon left that trail and headed for Spotted Tail Agency, a short ride to the southeast. However, before reaching Spotted Tail, the Cheyennes separated again.

Morning Star and his band continued in the direction of the Big Horns. Finally, late in July, they located the village there.

12 In the absence of the Arrows, the scalp was offered to Is'siwun.
13 Russell, *op. cit.*, 214 ff.

Now, all four of the Old Man Chiefs were present. The Sacred Hat tipi stood in the Big Horn camp, and Coal Bear had erected the lodge at each camping spot along the way. The sight of the tipi, with the buffalo head painted on its side, was a constant reminder of Is'siwun's presence among the Northern Cheyennes.[14]

After their separation from Morning Star's band, the other agency Cheyennes had returned to Red Cloud. Chiefs Living Bear, Standing Elk, Black Bear, Turkey Legs, and Calfskin Shirt were the leaders. These bands still were camped near Red Cloud Agency when the Black Hills Commission visited there. These Cheyennes joined the Sioux agency chiefs in "touching the pen." Thus they signed away the Black Hills. However, late in October, the bands of Standing Elk, Black Bear, and Turkey Legs slipped away from Red Cloud. They arrived in Morning Star's camp in the Big Horns shortly before the end of November.[15]

Other bands had been moving in also. Black Hairy Dog, Stone Forehead's son, rode ahead of one group. His wife was riding beside him, the Sacred Arrows bundle on her back. During their journey from the south they had been chased by soldiers. The Keeper and his wife had separated, with each of them taking two Arrows. A few days later, their band was reunited on upper Powder River.

Once again the tipis of the Sacred Arrows and the Buffalo Hat were side by side in the center of Morning Star's village. Their doorways still faced east, the direction of Nowah'wus, the Sacred Mountain. Nevertheless, in spite of the victory at the Little Big Horn, these were the last weeks in which Mạhuts and Is'siwun would bless the Cheyennes as a free people.

[14] Marquis, *Warrior Who Fought Custer*, 282.
However, Cf. Grinnell, *Fighting Cheyennes*, 383, which states that Black Moccasin was absent; that he and his band remained with the Sioux after the separation of the tribes.
[15] H. H. Anderson, "Cheyennes at the Little Big Horn," *loc. cit.*, 90 f. Anderson states that a crisis at Red Cloud Agency caused these heretofore peaceful bands to leave. The question of removal to the south may have arisen again. More likely they fled after hearing news of the disarming of Red Cloud's Sioux in October.

Cheyenne War Scenes

Drawings from Spotted Wolf's ledger book of battle scenes, 1889. The originals are in the National Anthropological Archives, Smithsonian Institution, catalog number 166,032.

Spotted Wolf's notations state that some of these drawings depict the war honors of Yellow Nose, the warrior who captured the soldier guidon at the Little Big Horn. Identifications of the paintings shown here are by the author.

Buffalo Calf Road rescues her brother during the Rosebud fight. Soldier bullets fly before them as they charge away from the troops. This event caused the Cheyennes to name this battle "Where the Girl Saved Her Brother."

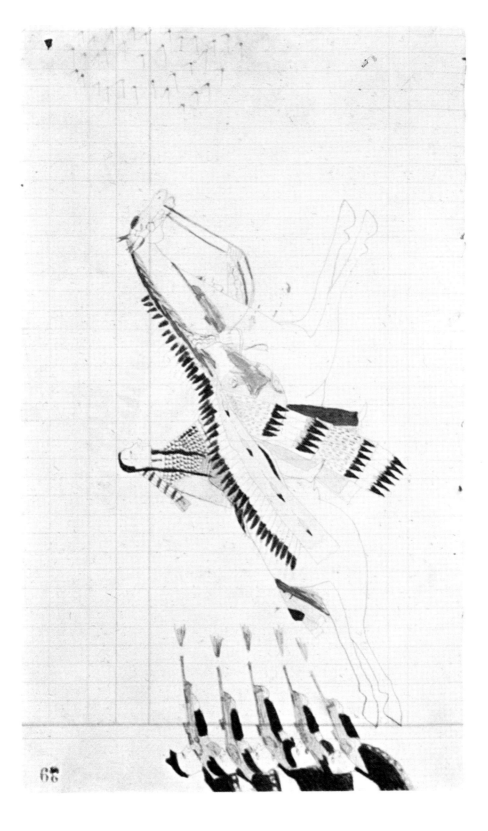

Yellow Nose counts coup with his captured guidon during the fight with Long Hair's men.

63

A Cheyenne warrior throws an army scout (buckskin outfit) from his horse.

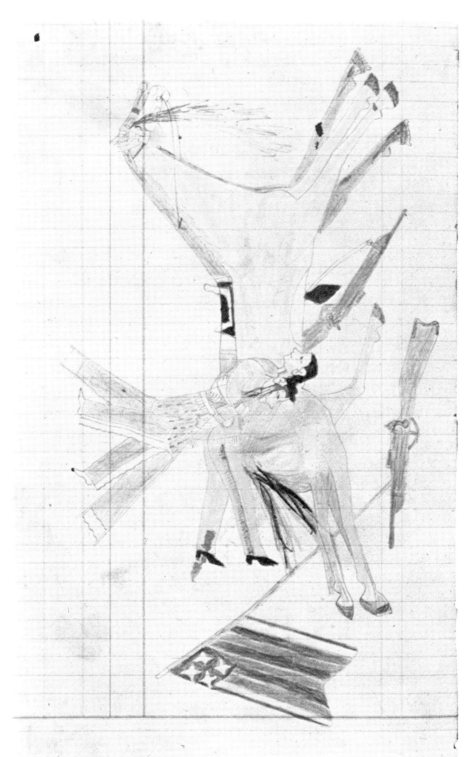

Hand to hand fighting with the soldiers, as a Cheyenne warrior wrestles a trooper to the ground.

99

Soldier scouts shoot a Cheyenne warrior from his horse. His companion, who carries what appears to be a Contrary lance, charges off amidst a rain of soldier bullets.

10. Three Fingers' Campaign[1]

"Three Stars" Crook had rallied
from the fight at the Rosebud. By early winter he was moving

[1] Fire Wolf, John Stands in Timber, and Henry Little Coyote are the major
Cheyenne informants for this and the following chapters.

The major written sources are the Billy Garnett Interviews, Books I and II,
dated January 10 and January 15, 1907, Judge Ricker Papers, Archives of the
Nebraska Historical Society. Billy Garnett was born in 1855, the son of General
William Garnett, former commanding officer at Fort Laramie, and a Sioux girl.
General Garnett fought in the Confederate army and was killed at Gettysburg.
Billy Garnett was active, both as scout and as interpreter, during the 1876–77
campaign. He spent his later years at Pine Ridge.

In addition, the author has drawn upon the account of Jerry Roach, the New
York Herald correspondent who accompanied Mackenzie; and also, the correspondence from Major General Henry Ware Lawton to R. G. Carter, U.S.A.,
dated November 29, 1876, Ayer Collection, Newberry Library.

troops from Camp Robinson to Fort Laramie, and then on to Fort
Fetterman. Crook chose "Three Fingers," General Ranald Mackenzie, to lead the eleven companies of cavalry that left Fort
Fetterman on November 14, 1876.[2] Some four hundred Indian
scouts rode along: Pawnees, Arapahoes, Sioux, Shoshones, and
Bannocks. William Rowland, who had married a Southern Cheyenne girl about 1850, was interpreter for the Cheyennes in the
group.[3] They were Hard Robe, Little Fish, Crow (Old Crow),
Cut Nose, Thunder Cloud, Bird, Blown Away, Wolf Satchel,
and Black Bear. Black Bear had married a Sioux girl, and he
was sergeant of scouts.[4]

The scouts from Morning Star's village were aware of the

[2] Crook had a hard summer following the Rosebud fight. Both he and Terry
received reinforcements and spent the summer months looking for hostiles.
Crook's troops made their "starvation march," fought American Horse's Sioux at
Slim Buttes, and ended the starvation march in the Black Hills in September.
Then Crook organized the winter campaign, of which the major action was
Mackenzie's attack on Dull Knife's camp.
"Three Fingers" was so-named because he had lost some of the fingers on his
right hand during the Civil War. The Cheyennes also called him "Bad Hand."
The expedition against the Cheyennes was composed of eleven companies of
cavalry from the Second, Third, Fourth, and Fifth Regiments, under Mackenzie.
There were four companies of the Fourth Artillery, dismounted, under Colonel
Richard I. Dodge. The campaign was under the personal orders and supervision
of Major General George Crook. John G. Bourke, *Mackenzie's Last Fight With
the Cheyennes*, 3.
[3] William Rowland originally had settled in Southern Cheyenne country not
far from Denver. Among his wife's brothers were Hard Robe, Roan Bear, and
Little Fish—all of whom rode with him against Morning Star's village.
During his Colorado days, Rowland had shot one of his brothers-in-law during
an argument. Another brother-in-law retaliated by hitting him on the head with
a tomahawk. Then the Cheyennes burned Rowland's ranch, leaving him for dead.
However, he revived and got to a doctor, who patched his head with a silver
plate. Eventually he located his wife in one of the Cheyenne camps on the North
Platte above Fort Laramie. About 1878, Rowland settled on Muddy Creek, on
the present reservation. John Stands in Timber to the author, 1961.
William Rowland interpreted for Grinnell. His son Willis, High Forehead,
interpreted for Grinnell and for Hoebel, *q.v.*
Cf. Mark H. Brown and W. R. Felton, *Frontier Years*, 105f.; Maurice Frink
and Casey Barthelmess, *Photographer on an Army Mule*, 91, 94, 108, 112.
[4] This is a composite list from John Stands in Timber to the author, 1961. John
G. Bourke, *On the Border with Crook*, 391; Garnett Interviews, II; Grinnell,
Fighting Cheyennes, 372.
Bourke, *Mackenzie's Last Fight*, 13, notes that Sitting Bear, another Cheyenne,
had been sent from Red Cloud Agency in advance of the expedition. He bore an
ultimatum to the alleged hostiles, asking them to surrender without bloodshed.

soldier activities. They knew that Crook was enlisting scouts from the tribes and that Black Bear, a Cheyenne, was one of them. The Cheyenne wolves knew that Crook was preparing for war. They carried news that the soldiers were leaving Fort Laramie, and that their route would be by way of Fort Fetterman. As Crook's column moved out from Fetterman, the Cheyenne scouts were watching.[5]

Almost a hundred Shoshone scouts had joined the soldiers at old Fort Reno, on Powder River. Chief Washakie's two sons and a nephew were among them.[6] At Fort Reno Crook had left the Powder, swinging in the direction of Crazy Horse's camp. When the Cheyenne wolves reported this, the people said among themselves that Three Stars did not know where to find them. Crook's course from Fort Reno indicated that he was planning to strike the Oglala camp under Crazy Horse. The Cheyennes were temporarily lulled into a false sense of security.

Meanwhile, fourteen of Crook's Sioux and Arapaho scouts had captured Many Beaver Dams, a Cheyenne.[7] From him they learned the present location of Morning Star's village. They also learned the whereabouts of the villages of Crazy Horse and Sitting Bull.[8] Many Beaver Dams was captured about forty miles northeast of Reno. The army scouts were then heading in the supposed direction of the hostile camps.

Crook also had his spies, and there were Cheyennes among them. General Mackenzie had dispatched them before the Powder River expedition had even begun.[9] Sitting Bear was one of

[5] Garnett Interviews, I and II. Cf. Grinnell, *Fighting Cheyennes*, 369ff.

[6] Bourke, *On the Border With Crook*, 390.

[7] Garnett Interviews, I. Cf. Grinnell, *Fighting Cheyennes*, 362; Bourke, *Mackenzie's Last Fight*, 11.

[8] Garnett Interviews, II. Cf. Grinnell, *Fighting Cheyennes*, 362, 377. Grinnell states that he was one of a small party camped on upper Powder River. Many Beaver Dams escaped and was in Morning Star's village by the time the soldiers attacked. However, he was nearly killed by the Cheyennes, some of whom suspected that he was among those who led the soldiers to the village.

[9] Garnett Interviews, I. Garnett stated that Crook had Indian spies among the Northern holdouts, one of them in Crazy Horse's camp. This man remained with the Crazy Horse people until after their surrender. "It is not known that they rendered any particular service, for the occasion of such service never came, as

these spies, a Cheyenne with a Sioux wife at Red Cloud Agency. However, the few Cheyennes remaining with Crazy Horse's Oglalas had spotted him for what he was. They denounced Sitting Bear as a traitor and warned him to leave the camp or be killed. Sitting Bear reasoned that if a fragment of his people could detect him, he would be in worse danger if he attempted to infiltrate the main Cheyenne camp. He headed back toward the whites.[10]

Sitting Bear carried news of the location of Morning Star's camp, now in a spot different from that described by Many Beaver Dams.[11] The spy also bore word that Crazy Horse and the Cheyennes were split into two camps, almost a hundred miles apart at that point. Sitting Bear added that Crazy Horse knew every movement of the army—everything that was being done by the soldiers.

When they heard this report, Crook's Sioux scouts formed their own plan of action. Their advice was that Crook should move against the Cheyennes while they were distant from the Oglalas. The troops should "use them up, and then turn on the Sioux and finish them, thus destroying the hostiles in detail."[12]

The Sioux army scouts then advised Crook to move the soldiers camped on the Crazy Woman fork of Powder River.[13] These

they had been commissioned to slip away from the Indians when Crook should approach and press them, and give him advice as to the direction in which they were contemplating escaping."

The two spies were Lone Bear and Iron Bear. Both had been dispatched before the Mackenzie expedition began. Lone Bear returned ahead of Iron Bear, coming with some Northern holdouts riding in advance of Crazy Horse.

[10] On November 23, he arrived back at Crook's camp.

Cf. Bourke, *Mackenzie's Last Fight*, 13.

[11] *Ibid.* Sitting Bear reported that "the capture of the young Cheyenne warrior (Many Beaver Dams) had alarmed his village, which had started over the hills to join Crazy Horse . . . ."

Cf. Grinnell, *Fighting Cheyennes*, 362.

[12] Garnett Interviews, I.

[13] Crook moved here on November 22.

Cf. Grinnell, *Fighting Cheyennes*, 362.

Crazy Woman Creek derived its name from an incident that occurred when a large party of Northern Cheyenne and Sioux warriors bore many Crow scalps to a Cheyenne village camped there. The young women in camp were so excited that a number of them ran off with the young men while the scalp dance was in

troops should be dispatched in two or three directions, the Sioux said, because the hostiles were watching their movements. Then the main body of troops and Indian scouts should be moved back so far that the hostiles could not see their movements. The hostiles thus would be unable to spot Mackenzie's column moving out from the camp, the Sioux scouts concluded.

Three Stars followed their advice. On November 23, before noon, the main body of Indian scouts marched out, Mackenzie's cavalry following them.[14] That evening, when camp was made, four Sioux and four Arapahoes were dispatched to locate the Cheyenne village. The larger force of Pawnees and Shoshones followed behind them.

Next morning, the twenty-fourth, the command was again in motion. Leading the column was Sharp Nose, the Arapaho chief who also headed the scouts from that tribe.[15] At noon, dinner was eaten in the cold; fires would have revealed their position. Mackenzie dispatched pickets to the hills, men who would scout while the others ate.

Suddenly, "Boots and Saddles" rang through the air. The soldiers raced for their horses. A trooper was running down the hill, reporting that Indians were approaching. The Indian scouts charged ahead, only to discover that these were two of their own men. As they moved out in a body, the scouts began singing war songs. A stick was forced into the frozen ground and a blanket draped over it. Charging in, the two advance scouts knocked over the blanket, thus signaling that they would truthfully report what they had seen.

They had discovered seven lodges camped in a valley, they recounted. Many horses were there—so many that more tipis must be nearby. Four scouts, two Sioux and two Arapaho, had

progress. Hence they acted like "crazy women." George Bent to Hyde, October 2, 1905, Western Collection, Denver Public Library.

[14] Mackenzie had all but one troop of cavalry. There were eleven hundred officers and men, with a third that many Indian scouts. Cf. Bourke, *Mackenzie's Last Fight*, 13.

[15] Garnett Interviews, I, states: "Sharp Nose led Mackenzie all through the night march before they fell on the Cheyennes. Garnett says Sharp Nose was the best scout he ever knew. Gruard is not to be compared on a night march."

147

remained behind, and they were moving in to investigate further. These advance men would later meet the main force at a pre-arranged location.

At this news, Mackenzie's command had moved out. The advance scouts were located that night, and they reported that it was indeed the main Cheyenne village. There were two hundred or more lodges and thousands of ponies.[16]

The Indian scouts turned their horses loose before stripping themselves for the battle ahead. Then they mounted war horses. Sharp Nose was again leading as they marched on. At his heels rode Lieutenant W. P. Clark, "White Hat" to the Cheyennes. Throughout the night hours, riders continued to pass back and forth between the advance scouts and Mackenzie's main force.

The scouts had left their horses on a flowing stream, one of the main branches of Powder River. For a while, the column followed this stream. Then the men crossed over to the south side, retracing part of their course. Turning almost directly south, they moved along a high ridge for a distance of almost two miles. Eventually, scouts and soldiers descended into a dry valley. Here sharp ears first detected the faint rhythm of drums in the village ahead, the sound echoing through the dry night air of the mountains. Riding back and forth with the new information, the scouts reported scenes of revelry in the Cheyenne camp.[17]

The column proceeded slowly, picking its way along, the men sometimes moving single file through the narrow valley. When the soldiers emerged from this valley, they discovered at its head a pass between two mountains. From this point they could look down into another valley below, one heavily timbered with cottonwoods, box elders, willows, and other softwoods. Moving down the gentle descent, the soldiers and scouts reached the creek upon which the village was located, a bit farther up. Now they could see the great horse herds. This sight warmed the hearts of the Indian scouts, because they had been promised

[16] Bourke, *With Crook*, 392, says 205 lodges. W. P. Clark, "Report on the Sioux War," *loc. cit.*, says 180 lodges. H. H. Anderson, "Cheyennes at the Little Big Horn," *loc. cit.*, 91, says the camp numbered 175 lodges.
[17] Garnett Interviews, I.

horses as rewards for victory. The column was now advancing from the northeast, moving down an incline toward the southwest, in a widening gap.

As soon as Mackenzie reached the center of this pass, he halted the column, and issued his orders to the scouts. He told them he wanted them to take the horses belonging to the village; but not to shoot unless the Cheyennes shot first. "If they do not shoot, we will capture them without shooting."[18]

Light was breaking. Songs and laughter were echoing from the village, still unconscious of the presence of enemies.

Scraper, the only member of old Conquering Bear's Oglalas among the scouts, was determined to count the first coup. He had not been made a noncommissioned officer, since he was the only member of his band with Crook's forces. This slight had rankled, because he was a brave man. Now he intended to show his courage in the thick of the fighting.[19]

Another Sioux, Sergeant Three Bears, was attempting to hold back the other Indian scouts. While the sergeant was thus occupied, Scraper rode down toward the village. Billy Garnett and Big Bat Pourier, regular army scouts, were also serving as interpreters for the soldiers.[20] These two, accompanied by Sergeant Fast Thunder, were now dispatched to catch the lone warrior. Scraper refused to fall back, so all four men advanced together, guided by the sound of the music. The others were following them.

Finally, this advance group struck the trail to the camp. From then on, they rode among the Cheyenne horse herds. They could see that they were in a park in the mountains, an ideal camping and grazing place for Morning Star's people and their ponies. Many of the horses around them wore boots of buffalo rawhide to protect their feet from the stones which covered this mountain country.

Garnett, Big Bat, Scraper, and Fast Thunder were now four

18 *Ibid.*
19 *Ibid*, I and II.
20 Baptiste Pourriere (also spelled Pourier).

or five hundred yards in advance of the others. The Sioux scouts were wearing their warbonnets, while Garnett and Pourier were in civilian clothing. Suddenly they spotted the first Cheyenne, a warrior out looking for his horses. The Cheyenne gazed at them for a few moments, then suddenly realized they were enemies. He fired at them, then turned and raced for the village.

Billy Garnett shouted: "He fired first. Now fire!"[21]

The battle was on.

[21] Garnett Interviews, II.

11. Box Elder's Warning

                             Morning Star's camp was a natural fortress, almost completely surrounded by rock. The tipis were pitched along the Red fork of the Powder, a swiftly flowing stream that wound west to east through groves of willows, cottonwoods, and box elders. There were three possible entry points into the valley. On the southeast side, a trail entered through a sheer wall of grooved, red, naked rock. At the northeast corner, a dry run cut through an almost perpendicular height of sheer stone dotted with scrub pine. Finally, the north end of the valley was pierced by a narrow trail flanked on both sides by steep, rolling hills. Mackenzie's men would enter here, passing through a grove of cottonwoods just before they came into full view of the main village. Tall red buttes towered on the west, sprinkled with sage and scrub pines. At the northwest, these buttes disappeared and rimrock formed the face of high, rolling, pine hills, gashed by ravines of red soil.

Had they suspected immediate danger, the Cheyennes could easily have defended the valley. However, after watching Crook's troops leave old Fort Reno apparently headed toward Crazy Horse's village, the wolves had carried back word that the danger had passed, at least for a time.[1]

Later a Cheyenne hunting party discovered the tracks of many horses traveling down the Powder on the divide south of the river. The Chiefs appointed Hail, Crow Necklace, Young Two Moon, and High Wolf to discover what the tracks meant. These scouts located the soldier camp on Powder River. Then they infiltrated the enemy lines, capturing three horses from the Arapahoes. They also recognized two Cheyennes, Crow and Wolf Satchel, among the soldier scouts. When they returned, the wolves rode to the center of the village. There they reported to the Chiefs the presence of many soldiers and Indian scouts. Young Two Moon added, "If they reach this camp, I think there will be a big fight."

When the Chiefs heard this news, Black Hairy Dog, the Sacred Arrow Keeper, wanted to move the village along the foot of the mountains to the location of the large Sioux village,—no great distance away. However, Last Bull, the Kit Fox chief, spoke out against it. "No. We will stay here and fight," he declared.

Meanwhile, the Cheyenne scouts had maintained a watch on the soldiers. Four nights after the report of Young Two Moon and his companions, word came that the soldiers were near. That evening the Chiefs themselves decided that the people should move up on the mountainside. Breastworks could be built there for the protection of the women and children. Last Bull disagreed again. His Kit Foxes recently had returned from a war expedition. They had fallen upon a Shoshone hunting party and had

---

[1] The description of the valley was made during a visit to the battlefield in August, 1968. Cf. Garnett Interviews, II.

taken thirty scalps. Now Last Bull was determined to celebrate. "No. We will stay here. We will dance all night," he arrogantly told the Chiefs.[2]

Dry wood was hauled from the trees growing along the river. The Elks and Crazy Dogs piled the lumber in the form of a tipi-shaped fire, a "skunk." Kindling was packed inside. Then, when darkness came, the wood was set afire. The Kit Foxes forced many families to go to the celebration, and a crowd soon gathered. When the dancing started, some of the mothers fastened strings to their daughters' belts, lacing the girls together. This was to keep the men from grabbing a girl and running off with her during the celebration.[3]

There were signs of danger, nevertheless. During the evening Sits in the Night reported that he had seen someone stealing his horses. "I think soldiers are there, for farther down the stream I heard a rumbling noise," he told the people. A crier announced this news through the camp, and he warned the Cheyennes to build breastworks.

Crow Split Nose, chief of the Elks, sent a crier to tell the women and children to tear down the lodges and move to a near-by cutbank where they could build breastworks. In a short time, many people were packed and ready to move. However, Last Bull had his own crier summon the Kit Foxes. When his men had gathered, the chief ordered them to stop anyone attempting to leave the village. Then the Foxes rode out to stop those who had followed Crow Split Nose's advice. They told the people to turn back and to unpack. Last Bull again commanded, "We will stay up all night and dance!"

A short while later, Crow Split Nose and Last Bull met face to

[2] Garnett Interviews, II; Grinnell, *Fighting Cheyennes*, 373.

[3] Fire Wolf, John Stands in Timber, and Henry Little Coyote to the author, 1961.

Garnett Interviews, II, says that this tying was "partly for sport and partly to keep the dancers there and from going off to their lodges."

The Cheyenne informants listed above added that this tying was also to protect the young girls who might be carried away by the enthusiasm of the victory dance like the girls who gave Crazy Woman Creek its name.

Cf. Grinnell, "Cheyenne Stream Names," *loc. cit.*, 16f.

face. The Kit Fox chief had not forgotten the Elk rejection of his warning before the Reynolds attack at Powder River. Now he taunted the Elk chief, saying, "You will not be the only man killed if we are attacked by the white soldiers. What are you afraid of?"

Crow Split Nose answered that he did not care about himself; that he was thinking about the women and children. "I want to get them up there where they will be safe, so that only we men will be left in camp to fight," he added. Last Bull snapped, "You will know in the morning what is to happen. Wait 'till morning."[4]

Thus, the Kit Fox chief arrogantly disregarded the authority of the Elk leader whose society was in charge of the safety of the village at this time. Again, the old Kit Fox–Elk society rivalry would bring trouble to the Northern Cheyennes.

There had been yet another warning of danger. That morning, Box Elder had been gazing toward the sunrise when he saw a vision. He saw soldiers and enemy scouts moving from the direction of the sunrise. They were attacking the village and killing the people. Box Elder called his son, Medicine Top:

> Go out and tell the Crier to warn the families that this camp will be attacked early in the morning. Now the women should go toward the high cliffs and build breastworks. They should stay there. Then they will be saved![5]

When the Cheyennes heard Box Elder's warning, they began to saddle up their horses. They got their buffalo robes and other belongings ready to camp out in the rimrocks to the north side

---

[4] There is an apparent conflict in sequence between the account given to the author by Fire Wolf, John Stands in Timber, and Little Coyote and the one given in Grinnell, *Fighting Cheyennes*, 373–75.

Fire Wolf et al. has the Kit Fox intervention taking place as the people begin moving after Box Elder's warning. Grinnell's account places the Kit Fox intervention after Crow Split Nose's warning.

The explanation seems to be that there were at least two such attempts to leave camp, with Last Bull's men breaking up both of them. The Foxes were keeping an eye on the entire camp and were prepared to stop any movement away from the village.

Cf., Llewellyn and Hoebel, *op. cit.*, 120 ff.

[5] Fire Wolf, 1961. Verified by John Stands in Timber and Henry Little Coyote.

of the village. However, at about that point the Kit Fox crier
came along shouting that the Foxes were in charge of the camp.
No one was to leave. Then Last Bull and Wrapped Hair rode
up with some of their men. The Kit Foxes began to cut the saddle
cinches of those who were ready to move from camp. They threw
the saddles on the ground. Then Last Bull shouted, "No one will
go away! The people will dance the victory dance all night!"[6]

Throughout the night, the scalp dancing continued. The
sounds of singing carried far on the cold, clear night air. In the
darkness beyond Morning Star's village, Three Bears, chief sergeant of Mackenzie's Sioux scouts, was preparing for action. He
rode up and down before his men, holding them back, as their
bodies strained against his own body in their eagerness to count
the first coup on the Cheyennes below.

Daylight was just beginning to show when the soldier attack
came. Black Hairy Dog, the Arrow Keeper, had untied his horses
and was leading them up on the hill. Suddenly he was heard
shouting: "Get your guns. The camp is charged. They are coming!" There was the flash of shooting and the sound of rifles
firing down the valley.[7]

The dancing was ending when those first shots were heard.
Looking up, the dancers could see horsemen on the ridge above
the camp. These were the Shoshone scouts. Then, as the dancers
looked down the valley, they could see the Cheyenne horse
herders running back toward the main camp. Women were
screaming as they broke to run. Some girls were still tied together
for the dancing. Now they were thrown down, tumbling each
other in piles in their hurry to escape. Finally someone cut the
girls apart, and they fled out into the cold beyond the fire. Then
the Cheyennes saw the army scouts charging up the creek bed.
Some were wearing war clothes; others were dressed in soldier
uniforms. The Cheyennes scattered. Some headed for their tipis;
others ran toward the hills beyond the village.[8]

[6] *Ibid.*
[7] Grinnell, *Fighting Cheyennes*, 375.
[8] Fire Wolf et al.; Garnett Interviews, II.

When the noise of fighting began, Box Elder asked for his sacred wheel lance.[9] He was joined by Medicine Bear, Curly, and a handful of warriors who kept him in their midst as they hurried toward the Sacred Hat lodge. When they reached it, Coal Bear already had placed the Sacred Hat bundle on his wife's back. Both were calm, but they were ready to leave by the time Medicine Bear and the others arrived. One of the warriors said, "Let the woman walk ahead; and let Coal Bear walk not too close to her, a little to the right."

Then Medicine Bear lifted Nimhoyoh, the Turner, from the tripod at the head of the Keeper's bed. He jumped on a horse, carrying the Turner on his arm, much as he had carried his shield in other battles. The other warriors scattered to either side of Coal Bear and his wife, forming a protective guard. The Sacred Hat Woman was walking naturally, just as she walked while she carried the bundle in the camp movings. Box Elder had to be led as he followed her and the Hat Keeper. The blind priest was carrying the sacred wheel lance in his arms. Ox'zem's power protected them as bullets poured in from the north and south.

Medicine Bear rode back and forth, waving the Turner from side to side, covering the rear of the procession. Nimhoyoh's power was turning away the soldier bullets as the Cheyennes continued their flight. Finally a low, dry creek bed came into sight. They followed it until they came upon some other Cheyennes, huddled together in the cold.

Box Elder turned to Medicine Top, his son. The blind priest asked if there was a knoll nearby. He instructed Medicine Top and Spotted Blackbird to lead him to the top of the knoll. The three started out, with Box Elder carrying his pipe and his tobacco pouch. When they neared the top of the knoll, the priest ordered the two men to release his arms. "You stay behind," he said. Then he finished the climb alone. At the crest, Box Elder sat down. Then he calmly filled his pipe from his tobacco pouch.

[9] Fire Wolf, John Stands in Timber, Henry Little Coyote, and Wesley White Man provided corroborating details of the actions involving Box Elder, Long Jaw, and Medicine Bear.

From below, the Cheyennes could hear Box Elder singing, his voice rising above the noise of the fighting. Then the holy man got down on his knees. He offered the pipe to the Persons at the four directions and to Maheo. Suddenly the pipe began to burn. "No one knew how he lighted the pipe. It looked like he did it from the sun," John Stands in Timber stated.

Soldiers were on a high knoll about a hundred and fifty yards away. Their bullets were flying around Box Elder. Suddenly a warrior moved out along a ridge to the northwest, a red cloth whipping up and down upon his shoulders as he ran. This was Long Jaw. A dog was running beside him as he jumped back and forth, drawing the bullets to himself. Long Jaw ran for about a hundred yards; then he dropped out of sight. In a few minutes he reappeared, moving on toward the knoll where Box Elder was sitting. Long Jaw paused there, facing the northwest for a minute or so. The women were singing strong-heart songs from their shelter behind the rocks. Then Long Jaw went on, the dog with him. When the fighting was over, the people saw that the scarlet cloth was riddled with bullet holes.

Years later, Long Jaw's son asked his father what kind of power he had used that day. Long Jaw answered:

> I didn't have any power. All I know is that I thought about the Creator as I did this. Every jump I made, I asked to be saved. Many bullets hit the dust in front of me and between the dog and me. That dog must have some power too, or he would have been hit. Many soldiers were shooting.[10]

As Coal Bear, his wife, and the other women and children continued, they came to a small ridge leading to another small creek. Making their way along this ridge, they were exposed to enemy bullets. Once more, Medicine Bear rode to their assistance. Again, he waved the Turner back and forth over their heads, protecting them as they escaped. Thus, Box Elder, Long Jaw, and Medicine Bear drew the enemy bullets to themselves as the Sacred Hat and her Keeper moved on to safety.

[10] John Stands in Timber to the author, 1961.

John Stands in Timber later commented:

Box Elder, Long Jaw, Medicine Bear: the soldiers were shooting at them, rather than at the women and children, as the women moved across the flat to safety behind the rimrock. The Cheyennes say that was the most wonderful thing Box Elder ever did. He saved the women and children during that fight.[11]

The Sacred Arrow Keeper escaped also. After he had raised the first alarm, Black Hairy Dog had hurried back to the Arrow tipi. There he lifted the sacred bundle from its pole and headed toward a vantage point above the village. Other men joined him along the way.

When they reached the vantage spot, Black Hairy Dog opened the Arrow bundle. He spread white sage upon the earth. Then he slid Mahuts from their kit fox skin wrapping and laid them in a row upon the sacred sage. The Keeper and the men faced toward the soldiers and enemy scouts in the village below. Black Hairy Dog stamped the ground four times, grunting like a buffalo bull as he did so. The other men were twanging their bow strings and shouting defiance in unison with the buffalo sounds the Keeper was making. A few men had guns, and they pointed them at the soldiers and the enemy scouts. Black Hairy Dog and the men cried out, pawing the earth with their moccasins like an angry buffalo does before he charges. When the Cheyennes below them heard these sounds, their courage returned. Now the power of the Sacred Arrow was turned against the enemy.[12]

Black Hairy Dog returned Mahuts to their bundle. Then he and his wife joined a band of eighteen families who fled the burning camp.[13] Most of these people were relatives of the Arrow

[11] *Ibid.*

[12] John Stands in Timber, Henry Little Coyote, and Wesley White Man to the author, 1961.

John Stands in Timber and James Medicine Bird stated to the author that all Mackenzie's Cheyenne scouts were dead by 1885 because the Arrows were turned against them on this occasion.

[13] This list of names from Little Coyote, Stands in Timber, and White Man. John Stands in Timber stated to the author that Black Hairy Dog and these eighteen families left for the south immediately after the burning of Dull Knife's camp. However, cf. Stands in Timber, Liberty, and Utley, *op. cit.*, 223.

Keeper. Brave Wolf, Big Horse, White Buffalo, Turkey Legs, Yellow Calfskin Shirt, Star, Magpie, Leaving Bear, Stands on the Cloud, Little Spring, and Porcupine Bear were among them. They headed south, traveling along the east side of the Big Horns until they reached the country near Hammer Mountain (Pike's Peak) in Colorado. From there, they moved on to the Southern Cheyenne villages in Indian Territory. Then the Sacred Arrows were safe.

12. Attacking Morning Star's Camp

Billy Garnett, Big Bat Pourier,
Scraper, and Sergeant Fast Thunder had continued their march
toward Morning Star's village. General Mackenzie had issued
orders to seize the horse herd, so the four pressed on up the
valley, attempting to move between the ponies and the camp.
At the same time, the four men were trying to hold and to drive
back the Cheyenne warriors, thereby giving the main body of
soldier scouts further opportunity to run off the horses.

Garnett and his companions kept moving in a westerly direction, forcing back the Cheyenne horse herders until the scouts
reached a rocky ridge.[1] Scraper and Fast Thunder now separated

[1] This ridge is east of, and parallel to, the dry run where Lieutenant McKinney
afterward was killed. Garnett Interviews, II, 6.

from Garnett and Big Bat, who were joined by Jim Twist, a half-blood scout, and a second man known to Pourier. The Cheyennes were facing them in increasing numbers now, for the Indian army scouts had attacked the village near its southeast corner. The Cheyennes were being driven up the valley. Meanwhile, the cavalry continued to advance up the same valley which the troops had entered from the north.

Garnett and his companions dismounted before they reached the top of the ridge, tying their horses out of range of the Cheyenne bullets.[2] However, at the same time, a number of Cheyennes were firing at the cavalry from a higher ridge, opposite and some distance on the other side of the valley. Their bullets were passing over the heads of the four army scouts. Then the cavalry mistook Garnett and his companions for Cheyennes and opened fire on them. The four quickly scattered in order to avoid being hit.

However, just before they separated, a lone Cheyenne warrior appeared. He cantered up to within a few feet of them before he discovered that they were not Cheyennes. As he halted, the four army scouts fired. The warrior wheeled his horse and galloped toward the main dry run forming the center of the valley. Garnett aimed at the Cheyenne's pony, and the bullet brought down the horse. The Cheyenne raised himself up from the ground, and Garnett fired again, felling the warrior, whom the scout now believed to be dead. Later he discovered that this was Little Wolf himself. The Sweet Medicine Chief would receive at least six wounds during the fighting that day.[3]

When the four scouts scattered, Garnett dashed in the direction of the village. On the way he met Three Bears, the chief sergeant of the Sioux. Three Bears' horse had been shot from under him, and he was riding a big horse loaned to him by Lieu-

---

[2] *Ibid.*

[3] *Ibid,* II, 8. After the Cheyenne surrender at Red Cloud Agency, Garnett gave a feast for the chiefs. This warrior, whom he supposed to be dead, was present. It was then that Garnett discovered Little Wolf's identity.

Mari Sandoz, *Cheyenne Autumn,* xiii, states that Little Wolf received seven wounds that day.

tenant W. P. Clark. Three Bears asked Garnett to ride with him to General Mackenzie, who was busily writing orders. The Sioux sergeant said to the commanding officer:

> Stop your paper fighting and let the soldiers fight as Indians do. If you don't, we are all going to leave you; and if we do, you will all be killed as Long Hair was.[4]

Three lieutenants were rushing toward Mackenzie as Three Bears said this. The General immediately changed his tactics, issuing orders that the men were to fight as they saw fit.

Garnett later stated:

> From the moment that Mackenzie's order to the soldiers to fight at will took effect, different results followed. The men protected themselves from the shots of the Indians; better success attended their exertions; and few casualties occurred afterwards. The Cheyennes scattered southwestward and northwestward, promiscuously westward. The greater number were killed along the main dry run; their dead were widely spread around. Some of the tribe had started, in the beginning, down the stream from the village, when the scouts were coming up at the outset. Some of their dead, lying below the village, was evidence of the encounter of the two sides early in the morning.[5]

It was during the interval in which Garnett left the ridge and reached Mackenzie that Lieutenant John A. McKinney, Fourth Cavalry, was killed. General Mackenzie's intention had been to send some of his cavalry on a charge through the village. These cavalrymen were to take possession of the upper end of the valley. Meanwhile, other soldiers were to hold the end through which Mackenzie's men entered. In this way the Cheyennes would have been boxed in and forced to surrender. However, the camp had been alarmed before the cavalry could move up in force. Many of the Cheyenne fighting men had scattered into the ravines.

Nevertheless, Lieutenant McKinney led Company M, Fourth

[4] Garnett Interviews, II. 9.
[5] *Ibid*, II, 11–12. Punctuation is mine.

Cavalry, in an attempt to seal off the lower end of the valley.[6] They charged over the ridge and down to the dry run. Some of the Cheyenne warriors had moved up to the rim of the ravine opposite the ridge, and here McKinney ran directly into them. His sword was in his hand when their bullets cut him down. All the way from Fort Fetterman, McKinney had been boasting that he would kill any Indian who came within reach of that sword. He had begun to fulfill that pledge by assaulting the Cheyennes on the ridge of the dry run. However, he was unaware of the nearby ravine, and unaware that the Indians were moving up through it from the village. The Cheyennes were the same warriors Garnett and his party had been standing off until fire from their own soldiers forced them to scatter. Now the Cheyennes were sheltered by a bank. Their bullets cut down McKinney as he rushed down toward them in plain sight, after the unexpected dry run had stopped his advance.

The lieutenant received a number of wounds, four of which were mortal. His troops dismounted and charged the ravine, killing all the Cheyennes who remained there. White Shield, Yellow Eagle, and Bull Hump had been among these warriors. Fortunately, however, the three had left before the soldiers charged.[7]

McKinney's bugler (or orderly) had his horse shot at the same time and place. Later, when the soldiers were gathering up their dead, the seemingly lifeless orderly suddenly asked if the Indians were gone. When he heard that they were, he immediately arose from the ground, announcing that he was unhurt.[8]

At least forty Cheyennes died in the fighting that day. Crow Split Nose, chief of the Elk Society, was among them. So were

[6] Henry Ware Lawton's letter to R. G. Carter, November 29, 1876. Lawton blamed the failure to seal off the valley on "the impetuosity of our Indians. The alarm was given before the cavalry had come up the path [it] being such that they had to come in single file and the Indians had time to get into the ravines . . . ." It was Lieutenant Lawton who carried Mackenzie's order to McKinney.

[7] Details of McKinney's death are from Garnett Interviews II, 11; Grinnell, *Fighting Cheyennes*, 365. Cf., Bourke, *Mackenzie's Last Fight*, 23, and Lawton's letter to R. G. Carter, November 29, 1876.

[8] Garnett Interviews, II, 11.

two of Morning Star's sons. One had been shot down by Captain Luther North at the beginning of the fighting. The Pawnee scouts counted coup on his body as they charged toward the village.[9]

The body of another son was found fallen across a stream flowing southwest of his father's camp. The dead warrior was a handsome man, with unusually long hair, tinged with golden hues. A fine red and blue blanket was doubled and suspended from his waist. A belt was around his body, holding his army rifle in place. He appeared to be peacefully sleeping when Garnett and Louis Shangrau, another mixed-blood scout, came upon him. They dismounted, striking the warrior with their quirts, counting coup on Morning Star's boy. The Shangrau took his gun and stripped off his beautifully beaded moccasins.[10]

During a lull in the fighting, Bill Rowland, with a small party of Cheyenne soldier scouts and mixed-bloods, crawled up close to the Cheyenne position. Morning Star and two companions approached near enough that they could talk. The Old Man Chief told Rowland that he had two sons killed in the fighting, and that he was personally willing to surrender now. However, Little Wolf, Old Bear, Roman Nose, and Gray Head would not hear of it, he said. Then Morning Star and his companions called out to the Indian army scouts: "Go home, you have no business here. We can whip the white soldiers alone, but can't fight you too."[11]

The destruction of the village continued throughout the after-

[9] Grinnell, *Fighting Cheyennes*, 364, 366.
Lawton wrote that Mackenzie "would report only 25 Indians killed, although I am positive there were more than twice that number." The army dead were Lieutenant McKinney and six enlisted men.
Bourke, *Mackenzie's Last Fight*, 27f., says that thirty Cheyenne dead fell into army hands. Later, at Red Cloud, the Cheyennes submitted a list of forty killed.
[10] Garnett Interviews, II, 21.
[11] Bourke, *Mackenzie's Last Fight*, 27. Cf. Bourke, *With Crook*, 393.
Garnett states that two of Dull Knife's sons died in the fighting; also, that Dull Knife had three sons and three daughters by his two wives. All were noted for their handsomeness. One of these "sons" was probably a nephew.
Sandoz, *Cheyenne Autumn*, xiv, states that Dull Knife lost a son and son-in-law in this battle. Bourke, *With Crook*, 402, notes the son-in-law's death.

noon and into the darkness. The army scouts were allowed to take whatever they wanted. One trophy was High Wolf's famous necklace of enemy fingers. This was found by Big Bat Pourier, who presented it to Captain John G. Bourke, of Crook's staff.[12] There were also reminders of the Rosebud and Big Horn: cavalry horses branded U.S. and 7C; a pillowcase made from a Seventh Cavalry guidon; an officer's Macintosh cape; and a buckskin jacket lined with taffeta, supposed to have been that belonging to Captain Tom Custer. The hat of Sergeant William Allen, Company I, Third Cavalry, killed with Crook's forces on the Rosebud, was there; as was a Guard Roster of Company G, Seventh Cavalry. There was also a letter to a young lady in the East, already stamped and ready for mailing.[13]

Plates, chinaware cups and saucers, spoons, knives, forks, scissors, pillows, even mattresses—all were destroyed by the soldiers and army scouts. Axes, spades, picks, shovels, hammers, and knives were burned. Holes were smashed in the bottoms and sides of kettles, pans, and canteens before they were thrown into the fires. Cheyenne saddles were smashed, bridle reins cut, and bits broken before their final destruction in the flames.

At least a thousand buffalo robes were taken from the village. Tons of buffalo meat were destroyed, thrown into the fires alongside blazing saddles and steaming fat, adding their crackling sounds to the noises of exploding captured ammunition. Skins of many kinds were found in abundance, as well as beaver traps and dozens of bottles of arsenic with which to poison wolves. Many weapons of excellent make were seized. These and the buffalo robes were spared from the fires. "Lodge poles, not more than half burned, were broken into smaller fragments, and thrown upon what it is no rhetorical flourish to call the funeral pyres of Cheyenne glory."[14]

[12] A photograph of the necklace appears in John G. Bourke, "The Medicine Man of the Apaches," B.A.E., *Ninth Annual Report*, 408. Cf. Bourke, *Mackenzie's Last Fight*, 31 and Bourke, *With Crook*, 402. Another necklace of fingers was buried on the battlefield.

[13] Bourke, *Mackenzie's Last Fight*, 30–32 gives a full inventory.

[14] Bourke, *Mackenzie's Last Fight*, 29.

The sounds of Shoshone grief were mingled with the other noises of destruction. The Snake scouts recognized the scalp of one of their own men, killed at the Rosebud. Shoshone saddles were mute evidence of the earlier Cheyenne victory. There were also many reminders of Last Bull's destruction of the Snake hunting party, including a buckskin bag containing the right hands of twelve Shoshone babies and the severed hand and arm of a woman of their tribe. Half wild with grief, their hair worn loose in mourning, the Snake scouts were weeping and singing as they moved about, destroying the village of the very Cheyennes who had destroyed their relatives. The Shoshones even refused to assume the new names most Plains warriors received after such a great victory as this.[15]

When the destruction was finished, Mackenzie's column was ordered to saddle up and ride back to rejoin the infantry, still moving toward the village. Captain Bourke wrote:

> As the March was taken up it began to snow heavily. Two or three Cheyennes entered their ruined village almost the moment our men had withdrawn and sat down and bewailed the spectacle of their desolated home. They were not molested. They were, of course, not a bit more affected than the others of their tribe, but possibly represented them all.[16]

Most of the old Northern Cheyenne material beauty died in the flames of Morning Star's camp. Two hundred tipis, nearly all of canvas, but some of buffalo hide, were destroyed. Among them were the elaborately decorated lodges of the military societies, their linings covered with vividly colored paintings of men and horses moving in battle. Exquisitely quilled and beaded clothing, the sacred shields, scalp shirts and war bonnets—all were carried off or burned. Mackenzie's men threw the last two ears of sacred corn into the flames. This was the same corn which, by tradition, Grandmother Earth first gave Erect Horns and Sweet Medicine. Brave Wolf's Contrary lance was destroyed, as

---

[15] *Ibid.*, 32; and Garnett Interviews, II, 26.
[16] Bourke, *Mackenzie's Last Fight*, 29.

were many of the sacred bundles owned by individuals. Never again would Northern Cheyenne material culture reach the heights of richness and splendor that the people knew before that bitter day in the Big Horns.

Fortunately, the Sacred Arrows and the Buffalo Hat were saved. Their supernatural power and the spiritual richness of their ceremonies remained to give Cheyenne life both beauty and meaning in the hard, new days ahead.

The Cheyennes were unaware of all this as they struggled to survive in the cold. Soldier thermometers fell to nearly thirty degrees below zero that night.[17] Soon after dark, snow began falling. The storm continued for almost two days, leaving snow over a foot deep. At least 750 Cheyenne horses were captured by Mackenzie's men.[18] As many more ponies were killed, wounded, or slaughtered by the Cheyennes during the night following the battle. Some of them were eaten by the hungry fugitives. Others were killed so that the half-naked older men and women could place their hands and feet in the steaming entrails, thus finding the only warmth they would know that night.[19] Eleven babies froze to death in their mothers' arms during the first night in the mountains. Three others perished the next evening.[20]

The night before, the sounds of the Kit Fox victory dances had filled Cheyenne ears. Now, as they moved deeper into the mountains, the people heard other noises. There was the dull beat echoing from a sacred drum, now in Shoshone hands. The clear, cold air carried the music of the Cheyenne sacred flutes. The sound of holy songs played upon these flutes carried a blessing to the person who heard them. But now the flutes were being played by Pawnee medicine men riding at the head of the Paw-

[17] *Ibid.*, 27f.

[18] Garnett Interviews, II, 29. The horses were divided among Mackenzie's Indian scouts. Billy Garnett was allowed to take two horses captured in the Custer fight.

[19] Bourke, *With Crook*, 392.

[20] *Ibid.*, 393.

nee soldier scouts as they rounded up the horses of their Cheyenne enemies.[21]

So the fugitives straggled on through the bitter cold. The few warriors who had robes gave them to the women and children. Only a few of the Cheyennes had escaped with moccasins. Most of them had to wrap their feet in loose pieces of cloth, skin, or strips of green horse or buffalo hide. Fourteen persons were badly frozen during that flight.[22]

White Frog and his wife, Comes Together, were among Morning Star's fleeing people. White Frog's body ached from three bullet wounds. Comes Together already had suffered at the hands of the Pawnee scouts who were burning the village.

In August, 1867, she had been with Spotted Wolf's party when they derailed the Union Pacific train. In the midst of the celebration afterward, the Pawnee scouts surprised the Cheyennes, capturing Comes Together, a boy, and two other women. Because Comes Together was a woman, the Pawnees handed her over to a young boy who was with them. She could see that the boy was afraid, so she suddenly bolted. The Pawnees charged her, trying to count coup on her before they recaptured her. One rode at Comes Together waving a hatchet. She wrenched it from his hand, knocking him off his horse. Another Pawnee fired at Comes Together, but the bullet glanced off the rear of her high-pommeled saddle, lodging in the broad, heavy leather belt she was wearing. A third Pawnee cut her across the face with his quirt, scarring her for life. Nevertheless she still made her escape.

Now Comes Together was hugging her baby to her, giving him the heat that remained in her body. She did not know then that he would someday be Keeper of the Sacred Buffalo Hat.[23]

[21] Ibid., 392f.

Cf., Hyde, Pawnee Indians, 264 ff.; George B. Grinnell, Two Great Scouts and Their Pawnee Battalion, 253ff.

[22] W. P. Clark, "Report on the Sioux War" loc. cit., Sand Crane MS; Henry Little Coyote and John Stands in Timber to the author.

[23] Henry Little Coyote, son of Comes Together and White Frog (Fringe) to the author, 1959.

Cf. Grinnell, Fighting Cheyennes, 265–68; Grinnell, Cheyenne Indians, II, 44; Stands in Timber, Liberty, and Utley, op. cit., 175f.; Henry M. Stanley, My

Finally, below the mouth of Hanging Woman Creek, a party of their own tribesmen spotted the fugitives. Wooden Leg, Yellow Weasel, Black Hawk, and seven other warriors had been searching for Crows when they discovered Morning Star's people.[24] Near Beaver Creek, Crazy Horse's village finally came in sight. The Cheyennes were hospitably received. They were fed well, even though the Oglalas were by no means rich. The Sioux also gave them gifts of robes, blankets, tobacco, and horses. Every married woman received enough buffalo hides for a family lodge. For the first time in eleven days, no Cheyenne went to bed cold or hungry that night.[25]

Early Travel and Adventures in America and Asia, I, 154–56; Donald F. Danker (ed.), *Man of the Plains: Recollections of Luther North, 1856–1882*, 58–60, 73f.

[24] Marquis, *Warrior Who Fought Custer*, 287f.
Cf. Stands in Timber, Liberty, and Utley, *op. cit.*, 217–19.
[25] Marquis, *Warrior Who Fought Custer*, Sand Crane MS.
Garnett Interviews, II, 65, adds, "The Cheyennes were helped at Crazy Horse's camp; but there were too many of them. And there was not much in the camp and the Sioux could not help them much. So they started to the agency . . . ."

13. The Fight at Belly Butte

The Cheyennes rested for a few days in Crazy Horse's village, then both tribes traveled slowly up Tongue River. The deep snows and sub-zero weather continued. Morning Star's people were gathering meat and hides for new lodges as they moved along. However, buffalo were becoming scarce, and it was increasingly difficult to feed such a large village.[1]

Meanwhile, the army had been attempting to negotiate with the free bands who refused to come into the agencies. Early in December, 1876, two Minniconjou subchiefs, Important Man and Foolish Bear, left Cheyenne River Agency for Crazy Horse's

[1] Marquis, *Warrior Who Fought Custer*, 288f.

village. They carried the army's terms for surrender: the Cheyennes and Sioux were to give up their horses and firearms in return for promises that they would not be punished for wiping out Custer's men. Foolish Bear and Important Man rode into Crazy Horse's village about December 22. At that time, the combined Sioux-Cheyenne camp was pitched on the upper reaches of Tongue River.

There were already some Sioux in the village who favored discussing surrender with the whites. The leader of this peace faction was Sitting Bull, the Oglala leader from Red Cloud Agency. He long had been a peacemaker. In 1875, President Grant had presented him with an engraved repeating rifle in recognition of his friendly attitude. The whites nicknamed him Sitting Bull the Good, contrasting him with the Hunkpapa chief who led the great camp on the Little Big Horn.

In spite of his friendliness toward the whites, Sitting Bull had opposed the sale of the Black Hills. During the signing of the treaty he had become disgusted with the pressure tactics of the government commission and had left Red Cloud Agency for Crazy Horse's village. By December, Sitting Bull had become the leader of the peace faction there. The arrival of Morning Star's starving people seems to have strengthened the arguments of this faction. Now they could point out that the Cheyenne defeat was the kind of fate that faced anyone who continued to hold out against the soldiers.[2]

Consequently, on December 16, 1876, a peace delegation from Crazy Horse's village rode into the vicinity of Colonel Nelson A. Miles's Tongue River Cantonment. Their trip had been a quiet one. Along the way, they had met groups of white cattle herders and some wood-chopping parties from the soldier fort. The

[2] Harry H. Anderson, "Indian Peace Talkers and the Conclusion of the Sioux War of 1876," *Nebraska History*, Vol. 44, No. 4, 234–37.

Cf. Harry H. Anderson, "Nelson A. Miles and the Sioux War of 1876–77," *The Westerners Brand Book, Chicago*, Vol. XVI, No. 4 (June, 1959), 26; Harry H. Anderson, "The War Club of Sitting Bull the Oglala," *Nebraska History*, Vol. 42, No. 1 (March, 1961), 55f.; Mari Sandoz, *Hostiles and Friendlies*, "The Lost Sitting Bull," 87ff.

whites had been friendly, so the Sioux peace delegation had moved on. Sitting Bull was chosen to lead a small party who rode in advance of the others, bearing a flag of truce, in order to arrange for a council with Miles. Bull Eagle and three other chiefs rode with him. As the peace seekers approached the cantonment, they could see the log huts of the soldiers on their left. On the right, a number of Crow tipis had been pitched beside the frozen river. The Crow army scouts rode out from these lodges, making signs of friendship. Suddenly the Crows turned on the advancing Sioux. They pulled Sitting Bull, Bull Eagle, and the three other chiefs from their horses and shot them or stabbed them to death. The rear guard of the peace delegation wheeled their horses and rode away at a gallop. The Crows fled to the hills in the opposite direction. They attempted to hide the Sioux truce flag, but the peaceful nature of Sitting Bull's visit soon was discovered.

Miles was furious. He dismissed the Crow scouts on the spot and seized their horses and other personal property. These were sent with an explanation in an attempt to reopen negotiations with the Sioux. However, nothing came of these overtures.[3]

Meanwhile, back at Crazy Horse's village, the difficulty of finding sufficient food continued. Finally, at the mouth of Hanging Woman Creek, the Cheyennes and Sioux decided to separate. White Bull, Two Moon, and most of the Cheyennes moved on up Tongue River. The main body of Sioux, with a few Cheyennes, rode up Hanging Woman Creek.[4]

[3] H. H. Anderson, "Nelson A. Miles and the Sioux War of 1876–77," loc. cit., 26; Virginia Johnson, The Unregimented General, 136.
Cf. Don Rickey, "The Battle of Wolf Mountain," Montana, Vol. XIII, No. 2, 46; Sandoz, Cheyenne Autumn, 106f.
For the Crow version of the killing of the peace delegation see Thomas B. Marquis, Memoirs of a White Crow Indian, 269–71.

[4] Wooden Leg says that it was decided that the Oglalas would go eastward up Hanging Woman Creek. The Cheyennes planned to continue up Tongue River valley. A few Cheyennes joined the Sioux. Among them was Crooked Nose, Wooden Leg's sister, who was later with the women captured by Miles's Crow scouts. These started out.
However, Crazy Horse, Water All Gone, and a few other Oglalas came with the Cheyennes. Just as the tribes were about to separate, scouts brought word

When news of Sitting Bull's death reached the Sioux village, plans were made for war. A plan was made to send fifty Cheyennes and Oglalas down to Miles's cantonment to draw out the soldiers. These warriors were instructed to keep firing on the soldiers; and to draw them on toward the main village, where the main body of warriors would be waiting. This plan was kept a secret, and it was not known to the women and children.[5] After the decoy party had ridden towards Miles's cantonment, the Sioux village moved up Tongue River to the mouth of Prairie Dog Creek. This spot offered a good defensive position at which to encounter the soldiers.

Now the attacks on Miles's cantonment increased. The Cheyenne-Oglala decoy party captured both horses and mules from the soldiers. Then they drove off about 150 head of cattle from the beef contractor's herd.[6] These attacks had the desired effect. On December 27, the first of Miles's infantry units started up Tongue River. The main force followed two days later. There were five companies of the Fifth Infantry and two of the Twenty-

of soldiers coming. The two bands began to come together again, and the warriors fought as one tribe. The women, children, and older people moved on up the Tongue. The warriors covered their retreat. Then someone brought Wooden Leg word that the soldiers had captured a band of women, his sister among them.

Evidently, Wooden Leg has combined the movements of several days in this single brief account.

Cf. Marquis, *Warrior Who Fought Custer*, 289f.

[5] Details of the decoy are from Red Horse, a Sioux who participated in the councils in the Sioux camp. The decoy failed because of the subsequent capture of Sweet Taste Woman and the others. As soon as word of their capture was received in the camp, a war party formed. This party attacked Miles's troops, stopping them at Hanging Woman (Suicide) Creek rather than drawing them into range of the main body of warriors.

It is not clear whether or not this decoy is the same one described by John Stands in Timber later on in this narrative. The Sioux plan was a variation of the decoy party maneuver, one of the few bits of military strategy used by the Plains tribes. The annihilation of Fetterman's men is the best example of its successful use by the Cheyennes and Sioux.

These details are from Red Horse's statement after his surrender. The interviews are in the Report of Colonel William H. Wood, Post Commander at Cheyenne River Agency, to the Assistant Adjutant General, Department of Dakota, February 27, 1877. National Archives.

[6] H. H. Anderson, "Nelson A. Miles and the Sioux War," *loc. cit.*, 26 and Johnson, *op. cit.*, 250, state that 250 cattle were captured.

Second, with Miles personally in command. A few white scouts rode along, Liver Eating Johnson, Yellowstone Kelly, and Thomas Leforge among them. There were two Crow scouts and a Bannock named Buffalo Horn. Miles's command totaled 436 officers and men. There were also two field guns hidden beneath the canvas-covered bows of a wagon moving at the end of the train as if it carried ordinary supplies.[7]

The Cheyenne-Oglala decoy party continued to move back in the direction of the main village. These warriors skirmished with the soldiers on January 1 and 3, 1877. One soldier was killed on January 3. His grave was dug in the trail, and the wagons rolled across it, obliterating any signs of a burial. Early on the morning of January 6, a blinding snowstorm struck the soldiers. Ahead of them, the Sioux and Cheyenne decoys continued their withdrawal up the valley of the Tongue.

During the afternoon of January 7, the Crow scouts captured a small party of Cheyenne women and children. Sweet Taste Woman, White Bull's sister-in-law, was the oldest among them. Two of her daughters, Crooked Nose Woman and Fingers Woman, were with her. So were Twin Woman, Crane Woman (Buffalo Cow) and Red Head (Red Hood)—Lame White Man's widow and children. Black Horse, a young boy, also was taken.[8]

John Stands in Timber recalled the details of this capture as told to him by his mother and grandmother. He also recalled warrior accounts of the Battle of Belly (Battle) Butte that followed.[9] The following paragraphs contain his account.

[7] Nelson A. Miles, *Personal Recollections and Observations*, 236.

[8] John Stands in Timber and his mother-in-law, Mrs. Ethel Bear Chum Ridgewalker, to the author, 1966. Sweet Taste Woman's husband had been a Negro captive, named Black Man by the Cheyennes. He had been dead for many years at this time.

Cf. Marquis, *Warrior Who Fought Custer*, 295f.; Grinnell, *Fighting Cheyennes*, 384.

[9] To the author, 1958, 1966. John Stands in Timber stated that he had heard these details from Chief Medicine Bear, Chief White Elk, Wooden Leg, Medicine Top, Hershey Wolf Chief, Big Head (Sweet Taste Man), Young Bird, and Headswift. All were in the battle.

The number of persons in the party is variously given. Miles, *op. cit.*, states that there was one young warrior, four women, and three children.

Cf. Marquis, *Warrior Who Fought Custer*, 293; Grinnell, *Fighting Cheyennes*,

These women and children had been camping with one of the Sioux bands that were living near the Belle Fourche River. Twin Woman and her children had been staying with Tangle Hair, the head man of Lame White Man's family.

At that time, Two Moon's large Cheyenne camp was on Tongue River. Big Horse, a scout from the village, had traveled as far as this Sioux camp, which was pitched near the Sacred Mountain. While he was in camp, Sweet Taste Woman and the others heard that he planned to return to the camp on the Tongue. The Cheyenne women were lonesome for their relatives, so they asked Big Horse if they could go with him.

This band traveled across country until they came near the Tongue River. Their last camp was on the east fork of Hanging Woman Creek, about nine miles from the main Cheyenne village. Bob Cat Creek flowed nearby, and they followed it up to the top of the divide. Now they were near the head of Wall Creek, which empties into the Tongue. From the top of this divide they could look down over the west side of Tongue River. They could see where the village had been located, but the tipis were no longer there. Then they saw smoke rising below the camping spot. Big Horse told the women, "I do not believe they moved camp such a short distance. This could be soldiers, I'll look closely." Then he told the others to move on down Wall Creek; but to do it slowly, so he could catch up with them.

Big Horse left the women traveling north along the divide. He moved in the direction of the smoke, but went too far. Then he returned to the divide and started out again. It was then that he spotted a camp filled with soldiers. The camp was near the foot of Belly Butte. He ran back to the divide, attempting to

384; Marquis, *She Watched Custer's Last Battle*, 8; W. P. Clark, "Report on the Sioux War," *loc. cit.*; Rickey, "Battle of Wolf Mountain," *loc. cit.*, 48; H. H. Anderson, "Nelson A. Miles and the Sioux War," *loc. cit.*, 27; G. W. Baird, "General Miles' Indian Campaigns," *The Century Magazine*, Vol. XLII (1891), 356; Sand Crane MS; Charles B. Erlanson, *Battle of the Butte*, 12; Johnson, *op. cit.*, 145f.; Stands in Timber, Liberty, and Utley, *op. cit.*, 219-21.

Thomas Leforge claimed to have captured Sweet Taste Woman and the others. He stated that there were four women, two girls, and a boy in the party. For his version of this and of the fight at Belly Butte, cf. Marquis, *Memoirs*, 271-75.

find the women. Then he hurried back to the middle of Wall Creek. He saw the women's tracks there, so he moved on. Then, from a distance, he saw the women and children surrounded by Indian scouts. They had seen the women coming and had hidden, taking the women by surprise.[10]

Big Horse saw that he could do nothing, so he traveled back to the divide. He followed it toward the southwest. Finally he located the main Cheyenne village at the mouth of Deer Creek, a spot now covered by Tongue River Dam. It was sundown, and he howled like a wolf as he approached. When the Cheyennes heard that sound, they came from their lodges. Big Horse pulled his horse sideways, facing one of the four directions. Then he howled like a wolf again. Moving on farther, he pulled up his horse. He faced another direction. Again he howled. He did this four times, facing each of the directions where the Sacred Persons live. Then Big Horse rode on down into the village.

When Big Horse reached the camp circle, the Cheyenne Chiefs had gathered. They were singing the song used to greet a returning wolf. Some Sioux chiefs also came to listen. A pipe was filled; and it was handed to Big Horse to smoke. "Tell the truth. Tell nothing but the truth!" one of the Chiefs said. Then Big Horse reported how he had left the Sioux village near the Sacred Mountain, and how Sweet Taste Woman and the others had come with him. He also told the Chiefs what had happened; how the soldier scouts had captured the women.

When the Chiefs heard this, they decided to turn the matter over to the leaders of the military societies. The military societies elected to send a war party to rescue the women and children. It was arranged that they would attack the soldiers early in the morning. The Cheyennes and Sioux started out after midnight.

---

[10] Kate Bighead recalled that that night some of the Cheyenne wolves moved in close to the soldier camp. There they heard an old woman singing. "That sounds like a Cheyenne song," the scouts said among themselves. They listened carefully and heard, "Get ready to go with the soldiers. There are too many of them for you to fight. They are feeding us and treating us well." But the Cheyennes did not surrender to the soldiers. Marquis, *She Watched Custer's Last Battle,* 8.

They rode to the Tongue. Then they followed the river, which was covered with ice. When they reached the soldier camp, it was nearly daybreak.

Now the Cheyennes planned to trap the soldiers. The Sioux joined in most of this planning, and took charge of this attack. The plan was for the main body of warriors to go to the mouth of Wall Creek. Then decoys were to be sent to draw the soldiers into the trap. There is a bench-like formation that rises between Wall Creek and Belly (Battle) Butte. The plan was to bring the soldiers out from their camp, lure them over the ridge, and bring them down on the other side of the ridge into the basin below. Then the Cheyennes and Sioux would cut them off from both directions.

A group of young men moved up the east side of this ridge, coming down near the soldier camp. They moved down the creek bed near where Big Crow was later killed. However, these young men showed themselves too quickly. They let the soldiers see that this was a trap. Then the big band of warriors that was holding back, waiting for the ambush, moved up to attack. (This happened before Big Crow was killed.) This group of warriors was on the west side. They moved down to where the soldiers were making breastworks.

At this point, the soldiers were on the west side of the river, about a hundred yards from the soldier camp. The camp was across the river, on the east side. The Cheyennes opened fire on the tents below. However, no one came running out. Then they saw the soldiers were up near Belly (Battle) Butte. The women prisoners were with them. They were trying to call out that the soldiers were gathering; and that they were ready to move. The women were so close to the Cheyennes that they could hear their words. Then the soldiers began to fire back at the Cheyennes from that location.

Sweet Taste Woman and Twin Woman saw all this. Later, they told how the soldiers prepared (for attack) the day before. They saw a team of mules pulling the big gun to the top of Belly Butte. Soldiers helped to push the big gun up on top. While the

177

fighting was going on, the women were brought up on top, and they crouched behind the cannon. Later, they told how the arrows reached up to them, and how the arrows flew over the top of the cannon.

On the west side of the river, some of the soldiers had made breastworks in the red shale. They made a depression there, where they placed the second big gun. The Sioux came on from both sides. They pushed the soldiers out of the breastworks on the west side of the river, where the gun was located. Then they forced the soldiers up near Belly Butte.

It was at this point that Chief Medicine Bear attacked. When the fighting began, he had hurried to the Sacred Hat tipi. There, Coal Bear gave him Nimhoyoh, the Turner.[11] Medicine Bear had charged in from the north, galloping along the west side of Tongue River. The soldiers were about a quarter of a mile away, firing at him from across the frozen river. Medicine Bear rode across on the ice. Then he charged along a ridge, swinging the Turner back and forth above his head. He was drawing the soldier fire to himself, just as he had done in Morning Star's village. The power of Nimhoyoh turned away the bullets.

Suddenly an artillery shell hit the flank of his bay horse, throwing the pony on his haunches. The shell did not explode, and the horse got to his feet again. Medicine Bear was not touched. The horse's wound was about the size of a shell. The hair peeled off; then it grew back in. Later, when the wound was healed, white hair grew in over the spot the shell had burned. Medicine Bear rode back to the sacred tipi, still swinging the Turner back and forth as he galloped along.

The Sioux and Cheyennes were fighting up and down both sides of the river. Some warriors moved down on the east side of Dry Creek. There is a high, sloping hill there, one that is flat on top. Here, Big Crow came out within sight of the soldiers. He was wearing a long-tailed warbonnet, and he was waving a

[11] Rufus Wallowing, John Stands in Timber, and Charles Sitting Man gave the author similar accounts of this incident. Details from all three informants are included here. The incident also is noted in the Sand Crane MS. However, Sand Crane says the horse was yellow.

Springfield rifle captured from one of Custer's men. Big Crow jumped up and down as he moved along the ridge, daring the soldiers to hit him. Then he ducked back to where some of the warriors lay under cover of the rocks. He had used up his bullets firing at the soldiers. He asked his friends for more. Then, with his cartridge belt filled again, Big Crow moved out in sight of the soldiers once more. Again, he jumped up and down as he moved across the exposed ridge. Again, he was untouched. A third time he appeared before the soldiers. This time he was almost halfway across the flat when the soldier fire hit him, throwing him to the ground. Wooden Leg and two Sioux warriors crawled to his rescue. They dragged the mortally wounded Big Crow across the snow to the cover of the rocks.[12]

Almost immediately after this, the Cheyennes saw the soldiers and army scouts moving up from the bottom in a line. They were firing at the Cheyennes and Sioux, heading toward them as the Indians fired back from the rocky area above.

The warriors in this area withdrew, carrying Big Crow on a blanket. They moved about half a mile along Dry Creek, to a place where there were large sandrocks on the north side. Big Crow begged the warriors to put him up against the rocks. He said, "I am going to die anyhow. Leave me here. Wrap me in a buffalo robe. Go back to the rest of the warriors. Tell my people I have done my share to rescue the prisoners taken by the soldiers."[13]

The warriors left Big Crow wrapped in a buffalo robe there in the sandrock, close to Dry Creek. There is a high pocket there, and they placed him in it. Later that spring, Wooden Leg and some other Cheyennes returned. They found Big Crow's body there, still wrapped in a buffalo robe.[14]

[12] Details from John Stands in Timber to the author; Marquis, A Warrior, 290f. Cf. Sand Crane MS; Miles, op. cit., 238; George Bent to Hyde, April 9, 1913, Denver.
Wooden Leg stated that Big Crow was the only Cheyenne casualty, but that two Sioux were killed. W. P. Clark, "Report on the Sioux War," loc. cit., agrees. However, H. H. Anderson, "Nelson A. Miles and the Sioux War," loc. cit., 27, mentions the death of Long Hair, another Cheyenne.
[13] John Stands in Timber to the author, 1966.
[14] Ibid.

After Big Crow's death, the fighting continued throughout the day. After dark the fighting stopped. Most of the warriors left during the night. Some of the Oglalas already had gone up Hanging Woman Creek. Crazy Horse and Water All Gone, with many of their people, again joined the Cheyennes. The Cheyennes then continued to travel up Tongue River.[15]

A council was held at the mouth of Wall Creek. Crazy Horse told the Cheyennes to go back, because their horses were not in good shape. The Sioux said that they would follow the soldiers; they would try to recapture the women. Ten Sioux warriors with good fat horses were chosen for this scouting. The others moved back to Deer Creek, where the large Cheyenne and Sioux village was located. The ten Sioux warriors watched Miles's men all the way down to the mouth of Tongue River, where the soldier fort was located. Several days later they rode back into the village. There they reported that they could not get near the captured women.[16]

[15] Marquis, *Warrior Who Fought Custer*, 292.

The Sand Crane MS adds: ". . . As they [the Cheyennes] were fighting [they] heard Sweet Woman was calling that these soldiers is not doing anything to us . . . They heard her singing a song, and she said to let them go [the soldiers]. They [the Cheyennes] obeyed her. They quit right there."

Cf. Miles, *op. cit.*, 238; H. H. Anderson, "Nelson A. Miles and the Sioux War," *loc. cit.*, 27; Rickey, "The Battle of Wolf Mountain," *loc. cit.*, 49ff.; Johnson, *op. cit.*, 149.

[16] John Stands in Timber to the author, 1958, 1966.

14. Before Surrender

After the fight with Miles, the
Cheyennes and a few Oglalas traveled far up Tongue River.
There were plenty of buffalo, so the hunting was good. Then the
Cheyennes cut west to the upper Little Big Horn. They camped
and hunted there for a while. Then they traveled farther west
to the mouth of Rotten Grass Creek, where they remained
briefly. Finally they returned to the Little Big Horn. The hunting was good, and no soldiers bothered them.

Most of the Northern Cheyennes were encamped there on
the Little Big Horn. The four Old Man Chiefs were present; so
was the Sacred Hat. Coal Bear had guarded Is'siwun throughout
all the weeks of fighting and wandering. The Sacred Hat lodge

again had been renewed. With the buffalo plentiful, the Cheyennes had been able to renew most of their tipis as well. Now the village displayed some of the old beauty that the people had known before the burning of Morning Star's village.[1]

Just before the grass of early spring came up, two riders suddenly appeared at the edge of the village. They galloped into the camp circle, heading their horses for the Sacred Hat tipi. The Cheyennes came running from their lodges as the horsemen pulled up before Is'siwun's tipi. One rider was a white man, the other a Cheyenne woman. Sweet Taste Woman had returned. She had brought with her Big Leggins, John Bruguier.[2]

Bear Coat Miles had treated his captives well during their stay at the Tongue River fort. He had given them a tent, warm clothing, and plenty to eat. When spring was near, Miles called Sweet Taste Woman to him. He asked her how he might contact the Cheyennes without anyone else being killed—without any more trouble.

Sweet Taste Woman answered that one plan would be successful. She told Miles about the Sacred Hat tipi; of how it stood in a special position in front of the other lodges in the camp circle. She explained how, if there was fighting inside the village, an enemy could duck into Is'siwun's home. If he did so, the fighting would stop. "If this can be done, I believe that all will turn out well," she said.

Then Miles ordered a troop of soldiers with pack mules to ride with Sweet Taste Woman. The mules were loaded with sugar, flour, bacon, hardtack, and tobacco. Big Leggins rode along also. Miles sent them up Tongue River.[3]

John Stands in Timber described the events that followed.[4]

[1] Marquis, *Warrior Who Fought Custer*, 293f.

[2] These details are from Rufus Wallowing and John Stands in Timber to the author, 1959.

Bruguier was also called White by the Cheyennes. He and Sweet Taste Woman had left Miles's Yellowstone cantonment on February 1, 1877.

[3] Miles, in *Personal Recollections* . . . , states that he sent two captives with Bruguier. However, Wallowing, Stands in Timber, Wooden Leg, and Grinnell mention only Sweet Taste Woman.

Sweet Taste Woman and the others rode up the river to Belly Butte, where they crossed the divide. They rode on as far as the old soldier camp, the place where the women had been captured. Near Wall Creek the soldiers scattered to look for the Cheyennes. They found the village just above the mouth of Lodge Grass Creek.

Next day, they moved across country to the opposite side of Lodge Grass Creek. One group of soldiers stayed back and watched the village through field glasses. Sweet Taste Woman, Big Leggins, and the other soldiers moved down to the Little Big Horn. The troopers, leading pack mules, stayed behind. Then Big Leggins and Sweet Taste Woman crossed the river. On the other side, they waited for daylight. Sweet Taste Woman told Big Leggins, "Ride fast to the Sacred Hat tipi. Get off right away. The Keeper of the Hat may come out. If he doesn't, go right in."

There were about a hundred tipis in the camp. Sweet Taste Woman and Big Leggins climbed the river bank and rode fast to the Sacred Hat tipi. When they reached the front of the tipi, Big Leggins jumped off his horse. Coal Bear came out. Since the Keeper was standing near the doorway, Big Leggins tried to shake hands with him, but Coal Bear would not shake hands. Then Sweet Taste Woman made a motion toward the door with her head. Big Leggins jumped behind the priest and jumped into the tipi. The warriors arrived then, but he was already inside.

The white soldiers had stayed back to see what would happen. When nothing did, they turned back toward Miles's fort, as had been planned.

Then Sweet Taste Woman told the Cheyennes, "We left pack mules over there by the river. Go bring them up." Several men went out, and they led the mules to the Hat tipi, where they unloaded them. There was a big pile of gifts, sent by Miles.

The Cheyennes called the army generals "Big Chief." Now Sweet Taste Woman told Coal Bear, "All that you see here is sent to you and the Chiefs, your military men, and the women

4 Rufus Wallowing also gave the author his own account of these events. It agreed with that of Stands in Timber in all the major details.

183

and children as well, by Big Chief Bear Coat." Then Coal Bear told the military societies to take charge of the gifts; to divide them up so that all the families got a share. Whatever was left was to be used for a meal for the Council. The tobacco was to be set aside for the use of the Chiefs.

The Chiefs then gathered in the Sacred Hat tipi. Sweet Taste Woman told them that their friend Bear Coat wanted them and their people to surrender. All would be well if the Cheyennes would do this. No one would be harmed, and the women prisoners would be returned. Then the Chiefs called the military societies to come to the sacred tipi. There the Chiefs turned the whole matter over to the military. When they heard that decision, the chiefs of the military societies agreed to meet later.[5]

Sweet Taste Woman and Big Leggins explained why they had come. First of all, they reported that the captives were well treated. Sweet Taste Woman said, "They fed us well. We had a good place to live in. The guards watched us. Nobody bothered us. Bear Coat told me, because I was the oldest: 'I don't want to fight the Cheyennes. I don't want any harm to come to

[5] This is characteristic Cheyenne legal procedure. The relationship between the Council of the Forty-four and the military society chiefs was one of mutual deference and careful politics. The Council Chiefs had the supernatural sanction and power deriving from Sweet Medicine's own presence in their sacred bundle. They also possessed seniority and social position. However, the military society chiefs were the men of direct action. Their co-operation was necessary in order to carry out the directions of the Council of the Forty-four, a fact that was recognized and respected by the Council Chiefs.

Ultimate legislative power rested in the hands of the Forty-four. The power might be delegated, as in this instance, but it was the right of the Council Chiefs alone to initiate such delegation. Under any circumstances, a unanimous consensus would be sought before a decision was announced to the people.

During the latter wars with the whites, this legislative power began to shift back and forth between the Council and the military societies. During the Southern Cheyenne outbreak of 1874–75, the influence of the military societies finally outweighed that of the Southern Council Chiefs, so the Southern Cheyennes went to war. In the north, Last Bull and his Kit Foxes defied the Council Chiefs in Morning Star's camp. Rather than spill Cheyenne blood, the Chiefs and the leaders of the Elks gave in to Last Bull. The result was the surprise and destruction of the village.

This fluctuation of authority and power between the Council of the Forty-four and the military societies, plus the rivalry between the Northern Elks and Foxes in particular, consistently prevented a united Cheyenne "front" in their dealings with the whites.

them. I want to make peace terms with them. I want the Cheyennes to come in, and I will meet with them peacefully. I want to make friends with them; to "recognize" [make a treaty with] them. There will be no more harm done to them.' "

Sweet Taste Woman said her answer to Bear Coat was: "There is a tipi that sits in front of the line of tipis. This is the medicine tipi—the Buffalo Hat tipi. Any enemy who steps inside that tipi cannot be touched. There may be a fight in the village. If any enemy runs into that tipi, the whole fight stops. That is the reason he sent Big Leggins and me. Now the Chiefs must decide whether the people will move into the fort. Everything will be prepared there."

Sweet Taste Woman and Big Leggins had met with the Chiefs first. After the Chiefs turned the matter over to the military, a double tipi was put up. That afternoon there was a big gathering in it. The tipi was filled with men. Many people stood outside, listening. Then the discussion began. Last Bull, Wrapped Hair, Two Moon, Little Old Man, and others spoke for the Kit Foxes. Crawling, Roan Bear, Long Roach, Magpie, Tall Sioux, and others represented the Elks. Strong Left Hand, White Bird, She Bear, Brady, and others represented the Crazy Dogs. There were twelve men representing each military band.

Right from the start, they [the Elks and the Kit Foxes] were divided because the army had destroyed their village at the mouth of Powder River. They argued almost all night. Next morning, they gathered again. They argued again. The night of the second day, they decided to turn the decision back to the Chiefs. Whatever the Chiefs decided, the military said they would support.

Again the Council gathered. All the military were there to listen to the Chiefs. Standing Elk's talk was remembered by the old people:

> Listen to me my friends. Ever since our Chiefs made a treaty with the white men, what did they do? They started shooting at us the day after we made a treaty with them. [This is the 1851 treaty at Horse Creek.] Then, the next time, Little Wolf and the

185

other Chiefs made another treaty of friendship. The white men did the same thing again. They destroyed our village and killed many Chiefs and military men. They also shot and killed women and children [Sand Creek]. Only nine years ago, we made an agreement with the white men. After that, what did Three Fingers do to us? He captured our tipis and horses, and he also killed our women and children.

If we go into this fort and sign another treaty, they will maybe kill us all. These are all the Cheyennes left. The white man way of making friendship is no good. The Indian way is best. We have never broken our friendship. The white man did. We had to protect ourselves, or they would have killed us all. I will never go to the fort!

The Chiefs did not decide anything that afternoon. The next session began with divided opinions. Right from the beginning, Two Moon was doing much talking. He told of a council he had been to at Red Cloud Agency: "Many of the Indians who came had seen white people coming towards the west. They said, 'It is like ants covering the whole country.' I have been told by Long Knife [William Rowland] that too many people are coming. Too many whites are coming. It is better to be friends with them; to make a treaty with them. I am going in as Bear Coat asked. Right now I ask for volunteers who will follow me there. Those who don't want to come, can choose wherever they want to go."

Crazy Head said there were too many white men to fight now. The Cheyennes could not kill them all. He would follow Two Moon. White Wolf (Shot in the Head), Medicine Bear, White Elk, White Hawk, Howling Wolf, and Old Wolf (Cut Foot) said the same.

Standing Elk stood up again: "Very well. Two Moon has made his decision to join with the army, to make another treaty. I have already refused, and I still say I will not go. Instead of going to the fort at the mouth of Tongue River, I want volunteers to follow me to Red Cloud Agency to join the Sioux. Red Cloud and Crazy Horse both have Cheyenne wives. Once our Chiefs agreed to live together like relations with the Sioux Chiefs, and they claim the land which we are on as their own. I refuse Bear Coat's offer!"

Within two days, a Cheyenne council party was heading for Miles's fort. Old Wolf and Crazy Head were the leaders, because they represented the Council of the Forty-four. Two Moon and Little Creek rode with them. They were little chiefs of the Kit Fox and Crazy Dog societies. White Bull rode along too, and so did Sleeping Rabbit, Iron Shirt, White Wolf, Little Chief, Black Bear, Crazy Mule, White Thunder, Roan Bear, and others. Hump led the Sioux who had remained with the Cheyennes. A few women were with them.

White Bull was an Elk Society member. However, the Elks sent no chief to represent them. As a whole, the Elk Scrapers were opposed to surrendering to Miles.[6]

Here John Stands in Timber resumes the narrative.

Sweet Taste Woman and Big Leggins rode with this delegation. At Tongue River, Big Leggins left the others and rode in a day ahead in order to report to Miles that they were coming. When he came back, he told the Cheyennes that Bear Coat was happy to hear that they were coming. He wanted them to dress in their war clothes, but he did not want them to bring guns.[7]

Big Leggins said, "I am an Indian myself. I don't want to see my Indians killed. If Miles rides a roan horse, he is on his war

[6] This is a composite list from Wallowing, Stands in Timber, and Wooden Leg. Cf. Grinnell, *Fighting Cheyennes*, 384 ff.; Marquis, *Warrior Who Fought Custer*, 297.

Miles, *op. cit.*, 240, says there were nineteen Indians in all. They reached the fort on February 19. However, Johnson, *op. cit.*, 158, differs in details. Here, in a letter dated February 19, 1877, Miles says that Bruguier returned with twenty-nine Indians. He speaks of seven prominent Indians in the same delegation. Wallowing and Stands in Timber said there were more than twenty-nine in this party. However, their figure also included the woman and scouts who had stayed back in hiding in case Miles attacked.

[7] Wallowing and Stands in Timber agree that Miles said no guns, but Grinnell, *Fighting Cheyennes*, 385f., seems to imply that they kept their arms.

horse. If he is on a roan horse, you can shoot at him as he comes close. But if he rides a white horse, he comes in peace."

Then the Cheyennes hid out in the hills and along the river bank. They were preparing an ambush if Miles rode out on a roan horse. If he did, all the scattered groups would move in on him. However, when they saw he was riding a white horse, they knew he was peaceful.[8]

There was a big flat on Tongue River three or four miles from the soldier fort. Big Leggins told the Cheyennes that Bear Coat wanted them to line up on one side of the flat, with the principal chiefs in front. Then Bear Coat would line up with his troops. He and his officers would be in front. Then both sides would ride out to the middle, and they would shake hands.

Miles rode out with his soldiers. He stopped at a distance. The soldiers were lined up with the officers in front. Miles gave a signal. Big Leggins waved to the Cheyennes to come on. Then they rode out to the middle.

Crazy Head, Two Moon, Brave Wolf, and White Wolf rode out ahead of the other Cheyennes. Miles rode up to them. He grabbed each of the chiefs by the wrist, raised his arm up, and let it drop. The chiefs were surprised. Later they understood that Miles meant this as a signal that they were prisoners of war.

Then Miles told the chiefs to follow his army. He took off his hat and waved it. The troops turned and marched toward the fort, with the Cheyennes following them. When they got to the fort, Big Leggins told them that Miles wanted them to dismount, and that the soldiers would feed their horses.

The Cheyennes were fed. Then they walked over to a building nearby. There they had a council. Miles said he was happy that they had surrendered. "There will be no more fighting between the army and the Cheyennes. You will be well protected," he said to the chiefs.

Miles asked Two Moon to let him have all his warriors. "We know the Cheyennes are good fighters. Give me all your warriors as scouts," he said. Two Moon said, "I will have to talk to my

[8] Grinnell, *ibid.*, says the horse was gray.

warriors. Let the warriors decide for themselves. I cannot just give them to you."[9] Then Two Moon talked to the others in Cheyenne. Two or three of the military society men were willing to surrender and join the army as scouts.

Big Leggins translated this answer. Miles jumped up and said: "You are my good friends now!" He shook hands with Two Moon then, but this time he shook hands with all the men "in a good way." He did this to show they were friends now. They were no longer prisoners of war. "The Cheyennes are in the army now. No more fighting between soldiers and Cheyennes," he said.

Miles then told the Cheyennes: "There are a few hostile tribes still left. You and I will go together against any other tribes on the warpath. You will get horses and guns. You will be given all you need. If you help win this war, I will see that you will be allowed to choose your own place for a reservation—anywhere from Yellowstone River south."[10]

Then Miles said, "Now we will have a feast." Dinner was all

[9] John Stands in Timber and Wallowing said that Miles addressed this question to Two Moon. The reader will also note the prominence that Two Moon is given in this account.

However, in his letters to his wife, Miles constantly mentions White Bull and Little Chief as the outstanding leaders of the Cheyennes coming to the cantonment. Indeed, Miles makes no mention of Two Moon at this time. Cf. Johnson, *op. cit.*, 158, 162, 165ff.

Two Moon's ascendency begins at this time. Prior to this he was merely one of the Kit Fox little chiefs. His later association with Miles and the whites gave him a prestige that most of his own contemporaries did not accord him. A number of Cheyennes, both then and now, consider Two Moon a prize story-teller—especially concerning his role in the Custer fight. (For one example, see Wooden Leg's statement in Marquis, *Warrior Who Fought Custer*, 360.)

Conservative Cheyennes, especially the Elk Society members (who were strongly Suhtai), held that Two Moon sold out to the whites. To this day, the sharp difference of opinion concerning Two Moon's character continues.

Rufus Wallowing was a nephew of Two Moon. John Stands in Timber was a Kit Fox Society leader. Thus theirs was a natural affinity for the importance of Two Moon and his role in later Cheyenne history.

[10] Miles's promise is still vividly recalled and frequently quoted by the Northern Cheyennes. Two Moon is frequently given credit for bringing about this promise from Bear Coat—a promise which many Northern Cheyennes believe made it possible for them to own Tongue River Reservation.

There are references to such a promise being made to the Northern Cheyennes in the *Annual Report of the Commissioner of Indian Affairs* for the years 1879 (p. xviii) and 1880 (p. 68). However, the source of the promise is not given.

ready. But, before this, a soldier brought in a jug of liquor. "Before we eat, we'll drink, feel good," Miles said. Two Moon said, "Take that jug away!" Then a soldier came and took the jug into another room. Right after the feast, Miles said, "Now you are free to visit the prisoners." So the Cheyennes went and visited the women. All took turns in doing this.

In the meantime, the soldiers were busy putting up tents and shelters down along Tongue River, near the present Range Rider Museum. The Cheyennes went there.

Miles said, "After you and your horses have rested, go back to the main village. Bring your families here, so they will be protected. I want two warriors to stay here with us while you go back for your families." The Cheyennes had a hard time getting volunteers. At last White Bull said he would stay. Then the soldiers took White Bull back to the fort. The next morning they brought him back to camp. He had on an army uniform, with a rifle on his back. The soldiers did this to show that the Cheyennes would be safe.

The Cheyennes slept well that night. The next morning, the chiefs started back towards the main village. That same day, Crooked Nose, one of the captive women, shot herself because her husband had not come to see her when these others had been visiting.[11]

While Old Wolf, Crazy Head, Two Moon, Little Creek, and the others had been riding toward the Tongue River fort, the main body of Cheyennes continued moving eastward. At Powder River the Oglalas separated from the Cheyennes. A few of the Sioux continued down the Powder. However, most of them went on to Red Cloud Agency, where they surrendered. The Cheyennes pitched camp on the west side of Powder River, near

[11] Marquis, *Warrior Who Fought Custer*, 298, quotes Wooden Leg as saying she did it from grief that she never again would see her people. However, Miles, *op. cit.*, 240, states she did it because of sorrow that her beloved had not thought enough of her to come with the others in the peace mission. John Stands in Timber and Mrs. Ethel Bear Chum Ridgewalker, his mother-in-law (b. 1876), corroborated Miles's statement.

the spot where Reynolds's soldiers had burned their camp the previous March.

Here the four Chiefs found them. They told the people that Bear Coat had received them kindly. Some of the Cheyennes were not happy at the news of White Bull's enlistment. Wooden Leg later remarked that it was one thing to surrender to the soldiers, if that seemed wise. However, Ice's offer to assist the troops in killing friends showed that he had a bad heart.[12]

Seven Cheyennes from Red Cloud Agency also had reached the village. They urged the people to surrender at the White River Agency, as the Cheyennes called Red Cloud. The visitors said that the Indians there were well fed and well treated. Also, that no one was being punished for attacking the soldiers.

The Chiefs gathered again. Their decision was that each person was free to decide for himself where he would surrender. The Cheyennes discussed the matter for two or three days. Then the division of the tribe began.[13]

Old Wolf (Cut Foot), Crazy Head, Little Creek, Two Moon, American Horse, Little Chief, and their followers rode off toward the Tongue River fort. Sweet Taste Woman was with them, and so were White Bull's relatives. White Wolf, Medicine Bear, Howling Wolf, and White Elk also were in this party. So was Black Bear, who, the year before, had joined Spotted Elk and the Sioux agency chiefs in signing away the Black Hills and the Sacred Mountain. Hump led the Sioux who decided to surrender to Miles.[14]

Smaller bands also left the Powder River camp. White Hawk, one of the Elk Society little chiefs, led a group who planned to join Lame Deer's Minniconjou Sioux. At that time, the Sioux were camped near present Lame Deer Creek.

Last Bull, the Kit Fox head chief, struck off on his own for a

[12] Marquis, *Warrior Who Fought Custer*, 297.
[13] *Ibid.*, 298.
[14] A composite list from Cheyenne informants; Johnson, *op. cit.*, 161, indicates that this band reached the Yellowstone cantonment about March 17, 1877. Black Bear appears in the 1885 Tongue River census as a member of Two Moon's band. Cf. H. H. Anderson, "Cheyennes at the Little Big Horn," *loc. cit.*, 91.

time. There were thirty-four people in his band. The men represented all three of the Northern Cheyenne warrior societies. Among them were Black Coyote and his wife Buffalo Calf Road Woman, the brave girl who saved her brother's life at the Rosebud and then went on to charge Custer's men at the Little Big Horn.[15]

One small band decided to join the Northern Arapahoes and the Shoshones under Scar Face, Chief Washakie. Some of these men were Cheyennes who had married Arapaho girls. Little Shield, All Around Chief, Runs Behind, and Sage were among them. By Cheyenne custom, a man lives with his wife's people. Therefore, these Cheyennes now joined the Arapaho warriors in this band: Charcoal (Black Coal), Shakes the Spear, Yellow Calf, and others. Little Raven (Little Crow) and Black Horse also rode along.[16]

The four Old Man Chiefs—Little Wolf, Morning Star, Dirty Moccasins, and Old Bear—all chose to give themselves up at Red Cloud Agency. Coal Bear said that Is'siwun and her sacred tipi would follow them. Their choice influenced the majority of the Cheyennes.[17] Standing Elk, Black Wolf, and Spotted Elk were among the Chiefs who followed. Box Elder and most of the northern Suhtaio came also.[18]

[15] Marquis, *Warrior Who Fought Custer*, 299f.; also, Marquis, *She Watched Custer's Last Battle*, 7.

[16] John Stands in Timber to the author, 1957. The Northern Arapahoes were given formal government permission to join the Shoshones on Wind River Reservation at about the same time that Little Wolf's people were taken to Indian Territory.
Cf. *Annual Report of the Commissioner on Indian Affairs*, 1877, 19–20.

[17] Marquis, *Warrior Who Fought Custer*, 299.

[18] Stands in Timber, Liberty, and Utley, *op. cit.*, 223, notes the departure of Black Hairy Dog and a band of Southern Cheyennes at this division of the tribe. However, there is a conflict in Stands in Timber's own information on this subject. In 1957 he told the author that Black Hairy Dog and these families left directly after the destruction of Morning Star's village. Cf. the chapter, "Box Elder's Warning."
Probably Stands in Timber was correct in saying that the Arrow Keeper left then. Wooden Leg makes no mention of Black Hairy Dog's presence among the Northern Cheyennes during the weeks after the Mackenzie fight. He does refer

With Is'siwun leading them, the Old Man Chiefs rode in to surrender at Red Cloud Agency.

---

to the Keeper coming north (on page 322 of Marquis, *Warrior Who Fought Custer*). However, he does not specify when Black Hairy Dog returned south.

Wooden Leg is meticulous in noting Is'siwun's movements, and it is not likely that he would fail to mention Black Hairy Dog's presence if the Keeper was in the Northern Cheyenne camp after the Mackenzie fight.

15. To the South, Then Home Again

The Old Man Chiefs reached Red Cloud Agency on April 21, 1877. There were 524 of the people who surrendered altogether. Other smaller bands continued to straggle in until, by May 15, Lieutenant W. P. "White Hat" Clark listed 869 Northern Cheyennes at the agency.[1]

The Cheyennes were detained at nearby Camp Robinson. They were well treated, and life seemed peaceful for a time. Soon however, both the agent and the army officers were urging them to move on to Indian Territory. At that time, both the gov-

[1] W. P. Clark, Census of Cheyennes surrendered at Red Cloud, dated May 24, 1877, National Archives. The first band, that of Big Foot and his family, had come in as early as February 24. Small bands continued to straggle in until May 15, when Medicine Wolf and his party, 57 persons in all, surrendered.

ernment and public sentiment favored the removal of as many tribes as possible to the south. The Northern Cheyennes already had relatives in Indian Territory, and the whites used this as an added argument for their removal. During previous years, the Northern bands often had visited the Arkansas River country and the land south of it. However, they loved the high, dry lands of the Yellowstone, Tongue and Platte. Here in the north the Sacred Mountain was nearby, its very presence a constant source of power and blessing for the people.

Crook and Mackenzie continually were meeting with the Chiefs, discussing with them what was to be done with the people. Crook offered the Cheyennes three solutions to choose from: move south to Indian Territory, move to the Shoshone and Arapaho Agency at Fort Washakie, or remain at Camp Robinson for a year. Then, at the end of a year, the authorities would decide what was to be done with the people. The vast majority of the Cheyennes wished to remain at Camp Robinson.[2]

Standing Elk was a fine speaker, and the Chiefs chose him to speak for all of them during these sessions. They instructed him to say that the people would not consider going south. Therefore, during the meetings with Crook and Mackenzie, Standing Elk was often on his feet. At one of these councils, he suddenly announced that the people were willing to move south. The other Chiefs were so astonished and confused that no one spoke out against him. Finally, the dazed Chiefs agreed to accept what Standing Elk had said, and to move to the south.[3]

[2] Grinnell, *Fighting Cheyennes*, 400; Marquis, *Warrior Who Fought Custer*, 308.

[3] Standing Elk was a favorite of the officers and there are many indications that he curried the favor of the whites at Fort Robinson. Later he led the so-called progressive faction at Pine Ridge. The Cheyennes were not particularly enchanted by Standing Elk, especially after this betrayal. Cf. Marquis, *Warrior Who Fought Custer*, 308f.

John Stands in Timber stated that the soldiers offered him many gifts, including a fine saddle horse, to influence the Cheyennes to moving south. Whatever the case, Standing Elk's history—from his signing away of the Black Hills until his death—was one of constant capitulation to the whites.

Cf. Martin F. Schmitt, *General George Crook, His Autobiography*, 217; Grinnell, *Fighting Cheyennes*, 400 ff.; Bourke, *With Crook*, 402; H. H. Anderson, "Cheyennes at the Little Big Horn," *loc. cit.*, 91–92; Verne Dusenberry, *The*

The army wasted no time after that. On May 28, 1877, 937 Northern Cheyennes rode out of Red Cloud Agency escorted by Lieutenant Henry W. Lawton, Fourth Cavalry.[4] Seventy days later they reached Darlington Agency, headquarters for the Southern Cheyennes and Arapahoes. For several days there was a period of feasting and rejoicing. Soon, however, troubles began.

After over forty years of separation, the Northern and Southern Cheyennes again were united. Throughout those two generations, the Cheyennes had maintained their spiritual identity as the People. They had come together for the renewing of the Sacred Arrows and for the offering of the Sun Dance. However, political differences had developed. The Southerners had been at peace since March, 1875. The people of Little Wolf and Morning Star were still mourning for relatives killed in the constant fighting of the past year and a half. Now the Northern Cheyennes had been betrayed into moving south. They were in no mood to trust the whites, neither in Indian Territory nor anywhere else.

Many Northern Cheyennes camped at a distance from their Southern relatives, refusing to affiliate with them. The Northern bands held that the more passive Southern Cheyennes were receiving preferential treatment in the form of better rations. The people of Little Wolf and Morning Star were poor. Their wealth had disappeared in the flames of soldier fires. The Southern Cheyennes still were a rich people, and some took to lording it over their poorer relatives. The people of Little Wolf and Morning Star were still warriors, and they refused to consider the farming projects being pushed by Agent Jonathan Miles.

Deadliest of all, there was the terrible heat of Indian Territory, with its dampness and malarial diseases—the "coughing sickness" so dreaded by the Northern bands. Nearly two-thirds of the people were sick within two months after their arrival. Over forty persons were dressed for burial during the first winter in

Northern Cheyenne, 6; *Annual Report of the Commissioner of Indian Affairs,* 1877, 19f.

[4] The exact figure is variously given. This is from the *Annual Report of the Commissioner of Indian Affairs,* 1877.

the south. That was more than had been killed since Reynolds attacked Old Bear's camp on Powder River. There was a doctor for the Cheyennes, but he had almost no medicine. Rations soon were cut, and the Northerners argued that what food they did get was not fit to eat.

Agent Miles wrote:

> In council and elsewhere [they] profess an intense desire to be sent north, where they say they will settle down, as the others have done.[5]

An old Northern woman, dying of malaria, voiced this longing for the pine hills rising along the valleys of the Rosebud and the Tongue. In the midst of her fever she murmured, "Up north, the pines make a rustling sound in the wind, and the trees smell good." Then she fell back and died.[6]

By September, 1878, the misery and homesickness could be endured no longer.[7] Again, it was Little Wolf and Morning Star who went before the people, carrying their long-stemmed pipes as the Chiefs should. Old Bear rode with them also. Of the Old Man Chiefs, only Dirty Moccasins was absent. There were 284 of the people in all. Eighty-seven could be considered fighting men; although there were very young and very old men among them. Wild Hog, one of the Chiefs, was among the principal leaders; so was Tangle Hair, Chief of the Dog Soldiers. Bridge, the old Ree doctor who had kept the last ear of sacred corn, followed, as did Black Coyote and his wife Buffalo Calf Road Woman. So did Old Crow, a former scout for Mackenzie. Almost two hundred of the people were women and children.

Little Wolf was bearing the Chiefs' bundle under his arm, so Sweet Medicine's presence was with them. However, neither

[5] *Annual Report of the Commissioner of Indian Affairs*, 1878, 56f.

[6] John Stands in Timber to the author.

[7] Major written sources for the following section are Grinnell, *The Fighting Cheyennes*, Sandoz, *Cheyenne Autumn*, and Edgar Lee Bronson, *Reminiscences of a Ranchman*.

The Cheyenne informants who furnished details were John Stands in Timber, Henry Little Coyote, Weasel Woman, Charles Whistling Elk, and Henry Tall Bull.

the Sacred Arrows nor the Sacred Buffalo Hat were along to bless them. Nimhoyoh, the Turner, was not there to turn aside the soldier bullets, because both Coal Bear and Black Hairy Dog remained behind, believing that too much blood had been shed near the sacred bundles already. Box Elder stayed in the south, also. Now the fleeing people would not have the concealing power of the Ox'zem bundle—power that could have hidden them from the whites, who covered the country on all sides of them. Many of Little Wolf's people feared that something bad surely would happen now.

They fled the Cheyenne and Arapaho Agency on September 9, 1878. They followed the Cimarron north until they reached Two Medicine Lodge River some two days later.[8] Here, in the late afternoon, they were caught by troops of the Fourth Cavalry under Captain Rendlebrock. Little Wolf warned his young men not to shoot until the soldiers had fired first. He said that he would meet the troops and try to talk to them. "If they kill any of us, I will be the first man killed. Then you can fight," he told the others.[9]

The soldiers pulled up in sight of the Cheyenne camp. Then Ghost Man, an Arapaho scout, rode out, shouting the names of Little Wolf, Morning Star, Wild Hog, and Tangle Hair. When the Cheyenne leaders came within hearing, the Arapaho told Little Wolf that the soldier chiefs wanted him to turn back. The Cheyennes would be fed and treated well if they would give up and return, he said.

Little Wolf answered that the people did not wish to fight, but they would not go back. "We are going to our old home and stay there," he said. Ghost Man repeated the offer. Little Wolf again replied, "No. We are going back to the country where we were born and brought up."

The Arapaho wheeled his horse. Again Little Wolf rode toward the soldiers. However, before he reached them, they began to

---

[8] Grinnell, *Fighting Cheyennes*, 405, gives this location. Sandoz, *Cheyenne Autumn*, 276, dates the fight September 13–14 at Turkey Springs.

[9] Grinnell, *Fighting Cheyennes*, 404f.

advance and they fired on the Chief. Now the Cheyennes charged out. The fighting began about four in the afternoon, and continued until dark. The people watched the soldiers all night, keeping them shut in a ravine, their horses and wounded with them. A few shots were exchanged in the darkness.

Early in the morning, the fighting broke out again. Firing back and forth continued all day, with the Cheyennes holding the strongest position. Finally, toward evening, the soldiers remounted, heading their horses back down the river toward Fort Supply.

After that, Little Wolf and the warriors moved down to the place where the troops had made their stand. They found the bodies of two soldiers, one of them a sergeant. The Arapaho messenger lay there dead, also.[10] The Cheyennes lost no men, but five of the people were wounded. One was a little girl, an orphan of about six. She had been hit in the foot, and thereafter the people called her Lame Girl.

The women skinned the dead soldier horses. Everyone rested in camp that night. Next morning the Chiefs led them north again. That day, on the north side of the Cimarron about forty miles northeast of Camp Supply, they came across a cow camp. It is not clear who fired the first shot. However, fighting broke out, and two white men were killed. The Cheyennes took their horses and butchered several cows. Then they moved on again.[11]

It was impossible for such a large band to move across country without being detected. Shortly after the fight at the cow camp, the Chiefs divided the people into smaller parties. They were to travel as rapidly as possible by night, and keep out of

[10] George Bent to Hyde, October 16, 1906, says the messenger was wounded. Stands in Timber, Liberty, and Utley, op. cit., 233, gives a slightly different version of the meeting between the Indian scouts and Cheyennes.

[11] George Bent to Hyde, October 22, 1906, Coe Collection. Red Berry, who was with Little Wolf's band, was Bent's informant.

This appears to be the fight described by Sandoz, Cheyenne Autumn, 49–50, which says that Little Finger Nail and some other men in search of horses had ridden into a white camp to buy horses. The whites opened fire on them, killing Black Beaver. Now the first Cheyenne had been killed by settlers, rather than by soldiers. Some of the Cheyennes wanted revenge on the settlers. Little Wolf talked against this.

sight during the day. Even so, there was danger of running into settlers, for the country was filling up with whites as the Cheyennes moved north.

Suddenly, two or three days after the fight with Rendlebrock, soldiers on gray horses appeared. The Cheyennes were moving across the flat Kansas prairie when the troopers charged in from the north. There were not as many as before, and again the people drove them back, this time in the direction of Dodge City. One soldier was killed. The shooting did not last long, and the Cheyennes paused to camp nearby.

About noontime the next day, the soldiers suddenly were at them again. The troops rode in from the direction of the Arkansas, the direction of Fort Dodge and Dodge City. This time there were cowboys with them. The Cheyennes bunched up and waited, since there was no place to hide on the prairie. Again the soldiers fired first. The fighting continued only a short time before a bugle sounded, and the soldiers and cowboys pulled back. It was as if they had no heart for fighting.

Several soldiers were wounded and one died in this battle. Old Sitting Man was wounded too, the bullet passing through his thigh, breaking the bone. Bridge doctored the leg, using the old Ree healing ceremonies. He stroked the wound with sacred white "man" sage, sprinkled it with puffball dust, and bound it. Then he set the leg by covering it with the green hide of a dead horse.

Up to this time, Little Wolf had been able to keep the young men under control. He insisted that the people were to fight only when attacked, and that they were to let the soldiers shoot first. He told the warriors that they were not to kill settlers; they were to leave them alone. They should kill all the soldiers they could, for the soldiers were trying to kill the people. But they were not to trouble the settlers, Little Wolf insisted.[12] The Cheyennes already had killed cattle and captured horses along the way; but this was necessary if the people were to survive.

The younger men were always difficult to handle, for many

[12] Grinnell, *Fighting Cheyennes*, 413.

were more eager for plunder and for coups than they were thoughtful for the good of the people. After this fight, it was clear that the cowboys and settlers, as well as the soldiers, were ready to kill the people. Now not even Little Wolf could hold back the wildest of these young men.

The next day, Cheyenne scouts found that two warriors left behind to watch the retreating soldiers had been killed close to where the cowboys had been shooting. Here was another excuse for striking back at the whites. The young men slipped out in small parties. One party discovered a cow camp on Crooked Creek, some forty-five miles southwest of Fort Dodge, Kansas. Here they killed four white men and captured both horses and mules.[13]

More whites were killed as the young men scattered to capture more horses, guns, and cattle. They also took bedspreads, blankets, and dresses for the women, as well as some pretty pictures for the smaller children. Little Wolf was angered by the killings and looting, but he could do nothing.

As the Cheyennes approached Dodge City, the town was in an uproar. The young warriors continued their raiding along the Dodge trail. There were several skirmishes with settlers and cowboys, and more whites were killed. Food was captured from a store. Several houses were burned within three miles of Dodge City. Sheep herds were scattered. Cattle were captured and driven into camp, where they were quickly butchered to feed the hungry people.[14]

After the last fight with the soldiers, the main band of Cheyennes had come together. Then they moved northward again.

[13] George Bent to Hyde, October 22, 1906, Coe Collection.
This may be the fight described in Sandoz, *Cheyenne Autumn*, 54. Mari Sandoz says that two of the horses had been stolen from the Cheyennes the year before. One had belonged to Black Coyote. The Cheyennes killed one rider and let the other man go. They returned to camp with six horses—two of their own and four others.

[14] Bronson, *Reminiscences of a Ranchman*, 146.
For a biased white account that nevertheless gives details concerning settlers that were killed, cf. Dennis Collins, *The Indians' Last Fight on the Dull Knife Raid*, 245–53, 255–58.

Suddenly the soldiers and the cowboys were back, in greater numbers than before. Raiders out for guns and horses were signaled in. Evening was near, and the soldiers, again under Rendlebrock, circled their wagons on a section of Sand Creek. The cowboys camped with them. There was no real fighting that night, although some of the cowboys skirmished with the Cheyenne scouts guarding the shallow canyon where the women and children were resting. At sunset, both soldiers and Cheyennes went into camp. Little Wolf and Morning Star sent scouts ahead to the Arkansas to locate a safe crossing for those who wanted to escape this fighting. Then the Cheyennes slipped some three miles west, to another sandy creek. There the people slept that night.

Early the next morning, Cheyenne wolves climbed a high hill to watch the troops. They could see the soldiers breaking camp and moving up toward them. The troopers were both infantry and cavalry, and they had between thirty and forty wagons along. The cowboys were riding with them.

The warriors mounted, but they did not charge. They were able to hold back the infantry for a time. The cowboys were charging in and out, making more noise than they caused damage. However, the people were in an exposed place, and finally the Chiefs instructed them to pull back into the broken hills nearby, where there was better protection.

The soldiers moved in below them. The wagons were drawn up side by side in a long line, their tail gates facing the people. The Cheyennes hastily dug rifle pits. The soldiers were close enough for the people to see their actions clearly. The cavalrymen dismounted close to the wagons. Then the infantry began moving in a skirmish line beside the dismounted cavalry. The soldiers moved forward, running, dropping to fire, then rising again to move up nearer the people. As the steady firing continued, the Cheyenne women were becoming frightened. The warriors were excited, too. Nevertheless, Little Wolf remained calm as the troopers continued their advance. "Let no man fire a shot; and do not get excited. They have plenty of ammunition.

We have very little. Lie hidden and wait," he quietly told the warriors.[15]

When the soldiers were within easy rifle range, Little Wolf ordered his men to fire. A soldier was shot down. As he fell, the others dropped to the ground, firing up at the people along the slope above them. The Cheyennes returned their fire with only an occasional shot. Then they saw twenty of the soldiers rise and walk back toward the line of wagons, where they jumped on their horses and headed them around behind the hill, attempting to encircle the people. Little Wolf, with some of his Elks and some Dog Soldiers, charged these soldiers. They shot down one trooper as they drove the others back toward the wagons.

Then Morning Star ordered a charge down the slope of the hill. The soldiers and cowboys scattered, heading back to the safety of the wagons. They quickly mounted and retreated, the mules loping as they pulled the bouncing wagons away.

Some of the young men tried to overtake the soldiers, but Little Wolf called them back, shouting, "Stop! Stop! The grass is not very high and our horses are not strong enough to stand a long run." Then the warriors quickly moved down to look for rifles and ammunition. They found a wooden box of cartridges near where the wagons had waited, and half a box more where the soldiers had been lying.

That evening the Chiefs and head men gathered for their usual smoke, the passing of the pipe that carried the petitions of the people to Maheo even during such hard times. "My friends, there are too many troops here for us to fight," Little Wolf said. "We must run away. We must move out this night and try to get away from here."

Soon after dark, the people started north again.

Next evening, when they were near the Arkansas River, they surprised a group of buffalo hide hunters. The Cheyennes had every cause to hate such men. They had slaughtered the buffalo herds, and some of them had joined the soldiers in shooting

[15] Grinnell, *Fighting Cheyennes*, 407. All of the Little Wolf and Tangle Hair quotations are from this account.

down Little Bull's people at the Sappa three and a half years before. However, Little Wolf again told his men not to kill the whites if they would give up their guns. The hunters surrendered. The Cheyennes carried off their powder, lead, and bullet molds —all of which could be used in making bullets or reloading cartridges. They also carried off the eighteen buffalo cows the hide hunters had killed.

The Cheyennes paused long enough to cook some of this buffalo meat in a big draw some distance back from the Arkansas. After the people had eaten and rested a bit, the scouts sent out earlier led them toward the river. They crossed the Arkansas the night of September 23, at a spot near the Cimarron crossing west of Fort Dodge. They hurried on to a little creek beyond the river, where they kindled fires, roasted some meat, and rested for the night.

Buffalo were near, and some of the men rode out to hunt them the next day. Some of the women moved out along Punished Woman Creek. Here they dug breastworks, overlooking the canyon of Punished Woman, a short distance above Fort Dodge. The people lingered here in the creek bottoms, preparing meat for the journey ahead.

The second night after the crossing, soldiers were reported a few miles behind them. These were the troops under Lieutenant Colonel W. H. Lewis. Lewis was commanding the nineteenth Infantry out of Fort Dodge, with cavalry and Indian scouts as well. They were followed by wagons.

The morning of September 27, the soldiers came nearer. The Cheyennes crossed Punished Woman Creek, camping where the women already had dug breastworks with their knives. The Cheyenne wolves told the camp all that was happening, and the people formed a line along the ridge where the breastworks had been dug. The Cheyenne horse herders drove in the ponies—the captured horses running with the Indian ponies. A few wild, unbroken horses kicked and squealed among them. The women, children, and old people hurried into a rocky draw, the bottom of which was filled with grass and running water.

Little Wolf had his fighting men in place by the time the soldiers came in sight. Lewis, the soldier chief, was riding at the head of the column. The wagons rolled slowly behind the soldiers. When the troopers were near, the Cheyennes opened fire. Three soldiers fell. Then the warriors quickly pulled back to their breastworks. The troops hurried across the ridge that the Cheyennes held. At the next creek, they corraled their wagons. The soldiers spread out from the wagons, the cavalrymen leaving their horses in order to move up on foot.

A company of infantry was ordered out around the Cheyennes and across the dry creek. They were to move in on the bluffs along the other side of the people. Here the women, children, and horses had remained hidden. A soldier scout located the horses, and some of the troopers fired down on them. Some of the ponies stampeded, the Cheyenne pack horses among them.

As the afternoon wore on, the soldiers closed in, moving up on foot from both sides until they had the Cheyennes nearly encircled. Still Little Wolf would not allow his men to fire. Colonel Lewis was on horseback, swinging his saber as he urged his men on. The soldier bullets were flying so close that they kicked up the dirt around the waiting Cheyennes, covering them with dust. Still Little Wolf sat there calmly, smoking his long-stemmed pipe, the Chiefs' bundle resting beneath his arm. "Do not get excited," he called out to his men. "Keep cool and listen to what I say to you." Tangle Hair, the Dog Soldier leader, sat next to him. "Little Wolf did not seem like a human being. He seemed like an animal—like a bear. He seemed without fear," Tangle Hair later recalled.

Then, as some of the soldiers were climbing the hill where the warriors waited, Little Wolf told his men to get ready. "Let every shot you fire count for a man," he said. The warriors opened fire. Some of the soldiers fell wounded. The others retreated, some of them running hard. One of the Cheyenne bullets caught Colonel Lewis in the leg, piercing his femoral artery. The soldier chief bled to death in the ambulance that hurried up to carry him back to the fort. By the time night had fallen, most of the soldiers had returned to the wagons.

That night Little Wolf again spoke to the people. "My friends, we must try to get through here without so much fighting, or we may all be killed. We must go faster!" he urged.

So the Cheyennes crawled up the draw in which many had been hiding. Two warriors had been killed, and many others wounded. The soldiers also had captured many horses. A few more Cheyennes were lost in the darkness as the others hastily moved on.

By the next morning, they were far away. Later they stopped long enough to butcher some captured cattle. Some of the wolves found the main band that day, and they reported that the soldiers had shot the pack horses they captured from the people. They also had burned the bundles of Cheyenne belongings that the horses were carrying.

Now the people were traveling harder than ever, moving two or three days without stopping. Some became so exhausted that they fell asleep on horseback. When they came to water, they fell from their horses, and the fall did not even awaken some of the most exhausted ones. Instead of lighting fires, the people often lit bunch grass. They wrapped a piece of meat around the blazing grass, doing this until the meat was cooked. They were moving fast, and this was the quickest way to prepare food.[16]

Now they were near the Sappa and Cheyenne Hole, the place where Lieutenant Henely and the buffalo hide hunters had shot down Little Bull and his people. The Cheyennes had not forgotten that twenty-seven of the people, many of them women and children, had been cut down there. Now the younger warriors, such as Little Finger Nail and Roman Nose, struck back at the settlers along the Beaver, the Frenchman, and the Sappa, avenging the people who had died while they, too, were fleeing north in 1875. For two days the young men raided. On September 30, they killed nineteen whites—the same number as the Cheyenne men the whites had reported dead at the Sappa. The Cheyennes also captured over two hundred horses.[17]

[16] Medicine Woman and Brady to their grandson, Henry Tall Bull. Tall Bull to author, 1959. Both came north with Little Wolf.

206

As the main band neared the Cheyenne Hole country, a herd of captured horses was driven in. Soon scouts signaled soldiers coming, and the old men, women, and children hurried to load the ponies. As Short One, Morning Star's favorite wife, was preparing to mount one of the captured horses, the animal began to buck. Short One was thrown under the horse's hoofs, and she died on a travois while the people fled. She was hastily buried, and then Morning Star and his sorrowing family rode on with the others.

So the Cheyennes pushed on. Sometimes they traveled both night and day. Sometimes they moved north in the darkness, pausing to rest when daylight came. Many were on foot, carrying what remained of their belongings on their backs. Limpy's parents, Buffalo Chips and his wife, were among those traveling on foot. A scout reported a loose horse roaming nearby, and the three turned off from the main band to catch the pony. Some cowboys surprised them, cutting them off as they tried to rejoin the others. Limpy's mother and the scout managed to escape. However, the cowboys shot down Buffalo Chips. When Limpy heard this, he rode out to avenge the killing. Limpy himself returned safely and lived to be an old man in the north.

Gradually the raiding parties that had struck along the Sappa came in. They brought back more horses, food, blankets, and clothing for the women. At night, the Cheyenne head men led the women and children across the Sappa divide. They moved down into the long, deep draw that opened into the valley of the Beaver. Here they hid and rested for a while.

Late that afternoon, Captain Mauck and his soldiers found them. The people were in a strong position, and Mauck soon pulled out. The Cheyennes got away quickly, leaving one man

---

[17] Bronson, *Reminiscences of a Ranchman,* 149, states that two separate engagements were fought on October 2. In one, along the Sappa, eighteen ranchmen were killed and five wounded. In the other, Lieutenant Brodenck, Twenty-third Infantry, was wounded. Corporal Steward, Company I, and five other soldiers were killed.

Cf. Sandoz, *Cheyenne Autumn,* 194f. Also *ibid.,* 90–95, for a description of the death of Stone Forehead and the Sappa fight.

out and a boy whose leg had been hit by soldier fire. Searchers looked for them later, but could not find them in this country that was filled with white men now.

Again the people moved on, the soldiers in steady pursuit. By the time the Cheyennes reached the breaks of the Republican valley, most of the younger men had abandoned their raiding. The people crossed the Republican and camped for the night. Next morning, Little Wolf hurried them on again. They crossed Frenchman's fork of the Republican, in southern Nebraska, and kept on northward. About October 2, just north of Frenchman's fork, the soldiers charged them again. Suddenly the troopers stopped. There were some shots exchanged, but no real fighting. Again the Cheyennes fled northward. The soldiers soon followed, firing at the people until darkness forced them to make camp. When the exhausted Cheyennes finally stopped, they found that more of their band had been lost.

There was not a soldier in sight when the Cheyennes reached the South Platte two days later. They crossed the river at noontime October 4, about four miles west of Ogallala, Nebraska. Then they hurried on across the Union Pacific tracks. The news that they had crossed the tracks was wired to Major Thornburg at Sidney Barracks. By four in the afternoon the soldiers reached Ogallala, and they immediately struck out on the trail of the people. Captain Mauck's cavalry followed shortly after. Mauck had been chasing the people ever since their bullets had struck down Colonel Lewis in Punished Woman Canyon.

On the same day, General Crook ordered Major Carlton to leave Camp Robinson with five troops of the Third Cavalry. They were to scout the sand hills, and they were to attempt to hold the Cheyennes until Thornburg's column could strike the people from the rear. Then Crook dispatched his orders to the Seventh Cavalry, in cantonment near the Sacred Mountain itself. They were to form a barrier some two hundred miles north of Camp Robinson. This was the fourth military barrier thrown up against the Cheyennes since they had left Indian Territory.[18]

Of all this the people knew nothing. After crossing the Union Pacific tracks, they hurried on to the North Platte, where they forded the river near the mouth of White Clay Creek. Then they paused to rest. Now they were home.

Even here the scouts soon reported soldiers within sight of the camp. But again, the soldiers did not attack.

Now the Cheyennes were not far from old Red Cloud Agency, the place they had left to begin their exile almost a year and a half before. It was October, and the winter would be upon them soon. Morning Star, who was always more like a Sioux, wanted them to continue on to Red Cloud Agency. He believed that nothing bad would happen now, for they were back in their own country. Little Wolf was a Suhtai. His ancestors had led the first Suhtai people into the Yellowstone country. He wanted to continue north until they reached the Yellowstone and Powder River country again. "I think it will be better for us if the people are not divided," he said.[19]

In the party was a medicine woman who had discovered her power during the flight north. One evening the Cheyennes had been ready to stop for their meal. The woman had gone apart from the others when she heard a voice. She stopped to listen. The voice said, "Don't stop to eat. Keep on going. There are soldiers behind you." The woman hurried back to camp to tell this strange happening. When Little Wolf heard her story, he told the people to keep moving on.

After that, when the others were preparing to camp for the night, the woman moved apart from them to listen. If she did not hear the voice, the people would stop. Many of them had come to depend upon this woman, because she was guided by the Above Powers.

When this break between Little Wolf and Morning Star was threatening, Little Wolf said, "Let us ask this woman for a sign or guidance. We will go by her decision." Morning Star an-

[18] Bronson, *Reminiscences of a Ranchman*, 150.
[19] The account of the medicine woman is from John Turkey Legs, who was with Little Wolf's band, to Rose Little Bear, his daughter. She repeated it to her son-in-law, Henry Tall Bull. Tall Bull to author, 1959.

swered: "We cannot listen to this woman. We are men—leaders. My mind is made up. Whoever wants to follow me can do so." Then he rode off to one side. Wild Hog and Tangle Hair joined him. So did some of the others.

When Little Wolf and his followers arose the next morning, Morning Star and his people had slipped away. They had gone sorrowfully, for on the earth they had left gifts—a buffalo robe, some powder, and a little heap of ammunition.

Little Wolf led his people down the Running Water to the Sand Hills country of Nebraska. Most of the Elk Society men followed him. So did Starving Elk, Black Coyote, Buffalo Calf Road Woman, and Black Crane. There were 126 persons altogether, 40 men, 47 women, and 39 children. They wintered in a protected valley near the forks of the Niobrara. The hunting was good, and although soldiers came near, the people never were discovered.

In March they started toward the Yellowstone. No soldiers chased them, and there was little raiding by the young men. However, trouble still followed. They were camped near the Little Missouri when Black Coyote rode in with some army stock, branded with the U.S. government brand. The Chiefs wanted no further trouble with the soldiers, and this stealing endangered them all. The few remaining members of the Council gathered, and Black Crane was chosen to tell Black Coyote that he must return the horses. Black Coyote was known for his quick anger, and when Black Crane told him their decision, he refused to obey the Chiefs. So Black Crane quirted him for disobeying the Council. Black Coyote's anger flared, and he shot Black Crane down. Sweet Medicine's law said that a murderer must leave the people, so Black Coyote was driven from the camp. Seven others rode into exile with him: Buffalo Calf Road, his wife; Whetstone, his brother-in-law; and five others. Now the number of Little Wolf's people was even smaller.[20]

[20] Sandoz, *Cheyenne Autumn*, 260; Bismarck *Tribune*, April 19, 1879.

Cf. Marquis, *Warrior Who Fought Custer*, 328f., and Stands in Timber, Liberty, and Utley, *op. cit.*, 45–47.

On April 5, warriors from this exiled band attacked a party of the Second

Meanwhile, Lieutenant W. P. Clark—White Hat—had been dispatched from Fort Keogh to intercept Little Wolf. Clark and the Chief had known each other at Red Cloud Agency, and Little Wolf trusted this officer who sign-talked so well. White Hat had a hundred men with him, as well as Indian scouts. Two Moon, Brave Wolf, and others from Miles's Cheyenne scouts rode among them.

South of Charcoal Butte, some fifty miles north of Belle Fourche, three of Clark's scouts were captured by Little Wolf's people. The soldier scouts were Billy Jackson and George Farley (or Fleury), both mix bloods, and Red War Bonnet, a Sioux. They pretended to be friendly, and they told the Cheyennes that they were from Sitting Bull's camp in Canada. However, Little Wolf was not fooled.

The next morning while camp was being moved, Red War Bonnet said that he was riding out to hunt antelope. As soon as he was out of rifle range, he galloped off to locate Lieutenant Clark. Little Wolf said to Farley, "I know you, and everybody knows me. Go tell the soldiers that I am here." So Farley rode off. Red War Bonnet reached the soldier camp first, and Farley arrived late that night. Billy Jackson did not catch up until the next day.[21]

Cavalry on Mizpah Creek. They killed a private, wounded a sergeant, and captured their horses. These Cheyennes were captured on April 10 by soldiers, men of the Second Cavalry and three Indian scouts from Keogh.

Black Coyote, Whetstone, and three others were locked up in chains. During the weeks of her husband's imprisonment, Buffalo Calf Road Woman died of diphtheria. When he heard of her death, Black Coyote went wild with grief. He had to be beaten and tied when they took him out to hang him. Marquis, *Warrior Who Fought Custer*, 329–30.

The Bismarck *Tribune*, July, 1879, reports that the last of the five captives committed suicide by hanging himself. The *Tribune* reported that three others had hanged themselves, the third one just seven hours before he was scheduled to die.

William Jackson, the scout, described the suicide of the three men in *Forest and Stream*, Vol. 49 (August 7, 1897), 102–103.

[21] There are conflicting details between the account given by Grinnell in *Fighting Cheyennes*, 410–11, and the account given by Jackson himself. Jackson claimed that Red War Bonnet and Farley escaped by slashing their tipi cover the night they were captured. They got to the horse herds and rode off. Jackson also claimed to have been kept in Little Wolf's own lodge. The next morning

Little Wolf moved camp to a spot north of Charcoal Butte, on the west side of the Little Missouri.

Clark did not want to fight Little Wolf. He already had discussed the matter with his Cheyenne scouts, telling them that he would not ask them to fight their own people. However, he added that if they did not wish to do so, he wanted to know it now. Brave Wolf answered that Little Wolf was his own brother-in-law, and that he liked his own people. Nevertheless, he had been at the soldier fort for two years, and he found that the whites had kept their word. He would go against Little Wolf with the soldier chief, and if Little Wolf did not surrender, he would fight him as hard as the white soldiers did.[22]

Clark decided to send Young Spotted Wolf, White Horse, Little Horse, Hump, and Wolf Voice ahead with a message. They left that night, with orders to send back a man when they found Little Wolf and his people.

Little Wolf's camp was near Box Elder Creek. It was so well concealed in the bushes that Wolf Voice was practically in the midst of it before he knew where he was. He quickly called out, "I am Cheyenne!" When the people heard that, they scattered to catch their horses. Then Wolf Voice was taken to Little Wolf, and he told the Chief that he was with the soldiers, but he did not say how close Clark's men were.

The next morning they started off, with Little Wolf riding ahead of the people, as the Chief should. His people had moved to a high bluff nearby. It was a natural fortress, with a flat top and lowlands surrounding the base. Soon Little Wolf saw two

---

he went hunting with the Cheyennes and escaped by pretending to be chasing an antelope. The Cheyennes fired at him, but he had a good horse and got away. The next morning he reached Clark's column. Farley was already there.

The author has used the Grinnell account here, as being the Cheyenne version. Jackson's account appears in *Forest and Stream*, Vol. 49, August 7, 1897, 102–103.

Farley's name was actually George Fleury, also spelled Florey. He had accompanied General D. S. Stanley's Yellowstone expeditions of 1872 and 1873. He was hired as a scout at Keogh in October, 1877.

[22] Bismarck *Tribune*, April 19, 1879.

Grinnell, *Fighting Cheyennes*, 411, says "Brave Wolf was eager to fight . . . ."

men coming. One called out, "I am White Hat!" Then Little Wolf could see two troops of cavalry drawn up in a line behind the soldier chief. Clark was seated on his horse, with Seminole, his interpreter, on a horse beside him.

White Hat spoke first. "I have prayed to God that I might find my friend Little Wolf; and now I have done so," he said. The two men shook hands. Then they rode into Clark's camp to discuss the surrender of the people. White Hat said that he had come as a friend. He asked Little Wolf and his people to turn over their arms, and to ride to the Tongue River fort with him.

Brave Wolf also spoke to his brother-in-law. He said that there was no use fighting the soldiers. The rivers could not be crossed, and the country was full of troopers. Little Wolf was quiet after he heard that. Finally he went back to talk over things with his people, while Clark moved his column up close to Little Wolf's camp on the high bluff.

After a time the Chief sent for White Hat. Before Clark left his camp, he is said to have told his officers: "You needn't go with me unless you want to. If you do, you must go unarmed. As for me, I am going; and I will show them by my acts that I mean good faith. If it is treachery, I can't help it."[23]

So Clark and Brave Wolf rode into Little Wolf's village unarmed. They met with the Chief and his warriors, and they talked over the terms of surrender. That night the Cheyennes were well fed. The next day, Little Wolf's people moved down from the high bluff and headed for the soldier camp. Of the people who started north, only 114 were left: 33 men, 43 women, and 38 children. They had about 250 horses. White Hat, with his usual thoughtfulness, waited for three days before he asked the people to give up their arms.[24]

Little Wolf's people surrendered on March 25, 1879. About three days later, they pulled up their tired horses along the gray bluffs of the Yellowstone. They sat there quietly, looking down

[23] Bismarck *Tribune*, April 19, 1879.
[24] Bismarck *Tribune*, April 19, 1879; Grinnell, *Fighting Cheyennes*, 412.

upon the tree-lined valley through which Elk River flowed. Suddenly the high, clear trilling of a woman filled the air. It was the old cry of victory and joy that had not been heard for a very long time. The horses moved forward, and Little Wolf, the Sweet Medicine Chief, led his people home at last.

16. Morning Star's Surrender

A blinding snowstorm swept the country as Morning Star's band reached the lands lying between White River and a small branch of the Running Water. On October 23 they were crossing a ridge, headed for a camping spot by a stream. Suddenly they glimpsed soldiers moving in the same direction. Some of the Cheyenne warriors quickly put on their war bonnets. Brandishing their rifles and arms, they prepared to meet the soldiers.[1]

[1] The principal source for this and the following chapter is the "Proceedings of a Board of Officers, convened by virtue of the following special order: Headquarters Department of the Platte, Fort Omaha, Nebraska, January 21, 1879,

The cavalrymen were Companies B and D of the Third Cavalry, patrolling the Niobrara country out of Camp Robinson. Captain J. B. Johnson was their commanding officer. When they discovered the Cheyennes, the soldiers prepared to attack. However, the Cheyennes waved their hands and hats; signaling that they wanted to talk. Then Lone Bear and Two Lance, both Sioux army scouts, rode out. They reported back to Johnson that the Cheyennes did not wish to fight, that they had asked to council with the soldiers instead.

Earlier, after crossing the Platte, Morning Star had moved through the camp warning his men that there was to be no more fighting with the whites. Now he, Wild Hog, and Old Crow rode out.[2] When they met the soldiers, the Cheyennes shook hands with them. Morning Star repeated that the people did not wish to fight. They wanted to move on to Spotted Tail Agency, he said. "We have come back home to our old agency. You can return at once (to the soldier camp). We shall go to the agency as soon as we can get there," he told Johnson.[3] The Cheyennes did not know that the Sioux agencies had been removed from Camps Robinson and Sheridan.

The captain's reply was that the Cheyennes would have to come with him to the soldier camp. If they refused, they would have to fight him, he added. Then he gave Morning Star, Hog, and Old Crow time to discuss his position with the people. Soon they were back. They would go with the soldiers, they said.

The army camp was pitched on Chadron Creek, near the road

Special Orders, No. 8." *Records of the U. S. Army Commands, Record Group 98,* National Archives.

Cf. Stands in Timber, Liberty and Utley, *op. cit.,* 231–37.

[2] This is the same Old Crow who had scouted against his own people at the time of the Mackenzie fight. He had continued to fight for the soldiers afterward. He, too, had become tired of the sickness and death of Indian Territory, and he started north with Morning Star.

[3] Grinnell, *The Fighting Cheyennes,* 414.

Mari Sandoz writes of messengers from Dull Knife's band who slipped through to Red Cloud, asking the Oglala chiefs' aid and protection. Red Cloud was powerless to help, so the Cheyennes decided to head for Spotted Tail agency. Sandoz, *Cheyenne Autumn,* 133–36.

running from Camp Robinson to Camp Sheridan, the post near old Spotted Tail Agency. Morning Star's people reached there after dark, with the storm still raging around them. Major Caleb Carlton, the commanding officer, was absent. He had ridden to Camp Sheridan to discuss scouting the country with the commander at Spotted Tail. Captain Johnson assumed temporary command in Carlton's absence.

That night, the Cheyennes camped in a thicket about three hundred yards from the soldiers. A fire was lighted for them, and they were fed hard bread, bacon, coffee, and sugar. Johnson ordered two companies of cavalry to take over the guard duty that night. Then he sent the two Sioux scouts into the Cheyenne camp to look for weapons. One of them, Two Lance, had a daughter and two grandchildren among Morning Star's band. The Sioux were promised any arms they saw or captured.

Next morning the captain surrounded the Cheyennes with his command. Johnson told the Cheyenne leaders that he had come for their arms and horses and that he was prepared to take them. Twice the Cheyenne head men refused to turn them over and left the captain. Finally, they returned and agreed to hand them over. Old Crow put down his rifle first. Wild Hog had no gun, but he laid down his bow and quiver. Blacksmith surrendered a muzzle-loader. Thirteen guns, four revolvers, and about twenty bows with arrows were piled on the ground. Nine of the rifles were muzzle-loaders, and one of the pistols was an old muzzle-loading dragoon model. The people were permitted to keep their knives. The soldiers did not search the men's blankets, nor did they touch the women. Consequently, some women were able to hide rifles and pistols under their blankets and in their clothing. Black Bear's wife had a carbine captured by her husband at the Little Big Horn hanging down her back.

The people were counted at this time. They were 149 in all: 46 warriors, 61 women and 42 children. The Cheyennes surrendered their horses reluctantly, handing most of them over to the Sioux army scouts and to Larrabee, an interpreter, in the hope that they could get back some of the ponies later. They kept some

217

of their horses concealed in the tall weeds. Johnson demanded these, too, and the Cheyennes finally turned them over to the soldiers. One pony was left for Old Sitting Man, whose broken leg had not yet healed.

The disarmament and the seizure of these last horses caused even greater uneasiness among Morning Star's people. Roman Nose drew his bow and arrow on a soldier who was leading a horse from the camp. When the cavalry officers saw him, they quickly moved in to restrain their men. At the same time, Morning Star, Hog, and the other headmen moved among the people, quieting the warriors who wanted to attack the soldiers.

In all, the people surrendered 131 horses and 9 mules. Johnson ordered Second Lieutenant George Chase, Third Cavalry, to drive the ponies ahead to Camp Robinson, some twenty-five miles away.

About 4:00 P.M. Major Carlton rode into camp. When he heard Captain Johnson's report, he ordered him to tie the hands of the Cheyenne men behind them and march them off to Camp Robinson. However, the captain responded that there would be trouble if that order were carried out. He added that he did not believe the Cheyennes were totally disarmed, and thought that there would be fighting if the major insisted on such action so late in the day. Then Carlton ordered Johnson to take two companies and bring in Morning Star and his men. Again Johnson replied that it would be easier for the entire command to do so next day, thereby preventing any Cheyenne escapes. Finally the major agreed to this suggestion.

On the morning of October 25, Major Carlton dispatched Long Joe Larrabee, his mixed-blood interpreter, to the Cheyenne camp. Larrabee was instructed to tell the people that they must leave camp, and make ready to move in wagons to Camp Robinson. The soldier chief said that the wagons would be moved in close to the thicket, and that the Cheyennes could load them with their belongings.

During these talks, there was no Cheyenne interpreter with the soldiers. Tangle Hair or Big Head was a Sioux who had ridden

218

south with the people in 1876. He also was a Dog Soldier chief. In the south, he had become homesick for his country, so he came north with the Cheyennes. Now he served as interpreter, since he spoke both tribal languages. In Sioux, Tangle Hair would tell Larrabee what the Cheyennes had said. Larrabee then translated the Sioux into English for the soldiers.[4]

When the people heard they must go to Robinson, there was great excitement in the camp. Morning Star, Wild Hog, and the headmen discussed the matter once more. They had decided to go into Spotted Tail Agency, and from there had hoped to move on to Red Cloud Agency. Now they were being told that they must go to Robinson, the very same place from which they had been sent south the first time. They would never go south again; they sent in word that they would not move.

Larrabee reported this to Carlton, advising the major to walk over to the camp and council with the Cheyennes himself. For over three hours, Carlton and the Cheyennes discussed the matter. The Cheyennes insisted that they would not go south. They must talk to their friends the Sioux, they said. Finally Carlton agreed to go with them to Camp Sheridan, believing that this was the only way to get them out of the thicket. His plan was to accompany the Cheyennes to Spotted Tail Agency. Then, next day, he planned to start back to Camp Robinson with them. The trip was a fairly short one, and could be made with no great difficulty.

However, even when they heard this, the people would not move from the thicket. They still did not trust the soldiers. Drumming began in the camp, with dancing and the singing of war songs. Some of the people declared that they would die right there rather than return to the south. Joe Larrabee became so frightened that he would not re-enter the camp to quiet the people. He reported that the Cheyennes were getting suspicious and had said that once the soldier chief got them out of the thicket he would shoot them down. Some Cheyennes began to dig rifle

[4] Tangle Hair is invariably called Big Head in the "Proceedings . . . ."

pits; and the watching soldiers reported that they saw arms among the people.

By this time it was too late to reach either Camp Sheridan or Camp Robinson that day. Carlton ordered Joe Larrabee to tell the Cheyennes that he had given them their choice of Camp Robinson or Camp Sheridan. They had refused both. Now, when they came out of the thicket, they would be moved to Robinson. Carlton said that he did not wish to hurt them, and to prove this he would camp close to the thicket on open ground and in plain view. However, he added that he would not feed the Cheyennes until he got them to Robinson.

Then the soldiers moved into camp around the Cheyennes. The people watched where each soldier company was camping. Then the men cut down trees and used them to erect breastworks opposite each soldier camp.

There were more sounds to upset the Cheyennes throughout the night. After dark, two companies of the Seventh Cavalry rode in from the direction of Spotted Tail Agency, dragging a howitzer with them. Lieutenant Chase, who had taken the captured horses to Robinson, also returned, with Company A of the Third Cavalry. They brought along a Napoleon gun. The two fieldpieces were moved into positions commanding the bend of the river where the Cheyennes remained camped in the thicket.

Carlton ordered Lone Bear and Two Lance, the Sioux army scouts, to sleep in the Cheyenne camp that night. About 3:00 A.M. Lone Bear reported to Carlton that the Cheyennes finally were ready to go to Spotted Tail Agency in the morning. Carlton made no reply.

Next morning, October 26, the major ordered the cavalry horses moved out of range of the Cheyennes. The soldiers were instructed to pick up all their baggage and to dig breastworks if firing broke out. When the soldier preparations ended, Carlton sent for the Cheyenne leaders. Morning Star, Hog, and the others came quickly. Then the major delivered his ultimatum: they must tell their people to pack and be ready to move to Robinson in an hour. The Cheyennes still were fearful of what would happen to them there. They kept asking what was to be done with them. Carlton replied that he had nothing to do with that, and that he could promise them nothing further than Robinson.

The Cheyennes were in pitiful condition. Many were suffering from frostbite. They were both dirty and ragged from the terrible hardships of the flight north. Their moccasins were poor. Some wore quilts instead of blankets. Others were wrapped in thin sheeting that offered little protection against the cold and snow. Nevertheless, the people were not cowed. They insisted to Carlton that they would die rather than return south. They would never return south again, they said.

While this conversation continued, a Sioux courier from the new Pine Ridge Agency entered the tent. He spoke to the Cheyennes, telling them that there were no rations except beef at Red Cloud's new agency. They would be better off to go to Camp Robinson, where they would be fed until the Great Father decided what to do with them, he added. The Cheyennes had little choice after they heard that. Major Carlton quickly promised that he would not fire the big guns at the people, for there were too many women and children in the camp. However, he repeated that he would not feed them again until they agreed to move.

The women and children finally climbed into the wagons. As they did so, Two Lance rode off with his daughter and grandchildren. It was about noon when they started through the deep snow and bitter cold to Camp Robinson. The men trudged behind and along either side of the slow-moving wagons. Soldiers rode before and behind the wagon train. Suddenly Wild Hog jumped up onto the tail of a wagon. He spoke to the warriors, encouraging them to be brave and to die like men. Some of the warriors began singing strong-heart songs. When Captain Johnson heard the songs, he sent for another company of cavalry. The soldiers quickly rode in among the men, separating them from each other and from the wagons with the women.

While the wagons creaked on through the cold, Sergeant Hunter, Third Cavalry, searched a wagon that had been left behind with a broken tongue. Inside it he found some engraved silver napkin rings and a little girl's white apron. Near the edge of the apron were one or two spots of blood—one spot about the size of a silver dollar. Other soldiers reported that they had found a white boy's saddle and women's linen drawers in one of the rifle pits. An embroidered kerchief, quilts, and white people's clothing were discovered in a bank near the Cheyenne rifle pits.[5]

When the wagon train reached old Red Cloud Agency, now abandoned, the wagons crossed a snow-filled creek. As they were crossing, some Sioux army scouts rode up, crowding their horses in between the wagons and the soldiers. The snow was deep, and this prevented the soldiers from crossing close to the wagons. They swung out on either side of the Cheyennes. By this time, the men had been allowed to join the women in the wagons. Big Beaver was sitting on a wagon tail. As he watched, he saw Leaf, Bull Hump's wife, roll herself up into a ball. As they crossed the creek, she threw herself out into the deep snow. The Sioux scouts immediately surrounded her, covering her as she made her escape. Then the Sioux rode off to one side of the trail, allowing the soldiers following the wagons to pass. Leaf visited the people next day. By that time she was dressed as one of the Sioux scouts.

The exhausted Cheyennes reached Camp Robinson between ten and eleven o'clock that night. They were taken from the wagons with their belongings, and were moved into an empty set of company quarters. There they were fed. Then Lieutenant Chase, Company A, Third Cavalry, and half his company were stationed in and around the building for the night. This guard was replaced by another guard the next day.

There was no interpreter who spoke Cheyenne at Robinson, so Tangle Hair told the post interpreter in Sioux what the Cheyennes said, and the interpreter translated this into English for the officers.

[5] Testimony of First Lieutenant J. C. Thompson, "Proceedings . . . , loc. cit., 60.
Red Feather and The Enemy, both women, later testified that the warriors who brought the white people's clothing to the women had escaped with Little Wolf.
Sandoz, Cheyenne Autumn, 146, states that Bear Shield, one of the prisoners at Fort Marion, had sent the napkin rings to his family. The rings had been given to him by a white woman.

The day after their arrival, the Cheyennes again were ordered to hand over their weapons. This time they gave up six rifles and two or three pistols. On October 28, Lieutenant Chase insisted upon searching both the building and the Cheyennes' own bundles of belongings. He found some lead, powder, caps, bows, and arrows—but no more firearms. These items were removed and Chase ordered his sentinels to keep close watch on the people. A short time later, the sergeant in charge of the Indian kitchen reported that he had seen a pistol drop from the person of one of the women, Young Medicine Man's wife. Chase reported this to Morning Star, and the Chief asked for the pistol. The woman handed it over to Chase, telling him that it had belonged to her husband. He had been killed during the journey north, and she had kept it as a memento of him.

Chase also found bedspreads, children's dresses, aprons, and underclothing. A child's parasol was found in Morning Star's possession. A number of fancy pictures also were discovered in the bundles. However, there was no real proof that all of these had been taken in the Kansas fighting. Articles of white-man clothing had been issued to the Cheyennes while they were in the south, quilts, shirts, pants, coats, shoes, stockings, and shawls among them.[6] They did not find the canvas-covered ledger book in which Little Finger Nail, Roached Mane, and Elk recorded their war deeds, many of them battles with the soldiers.

Chase tightened the security around the building, placing a twenty-four hour guard both within and without. However, after midnight of October 29, two warriors from Little Wolf's band slipped into a tipi above the post. One of them was Little Wolf's son. Little Big Man and Fire Coal, both Sioux army scouts, were in the lodge. Little Big Man managed to capture one of the Cheyenne scouts, but Little Wolf's son escaped. The prisoner was taken before Major Carlton that night. Next morning, Carlton sent a command out with the prisoner. The soldiers found three strongly fortified camps in the bluffs near Robinson. However,

6 Testimony of Cheyenne Woman, "Proceedings . . . , *loc. cit.,* 13.

Little Wolf's son had warned the people in time, and they had escaped.

For a time, all remained peaceful. Lieutenant Chase continued to occupy a room in the same barrack with the people until about November 20. Morning Star, Hog, and the headmen met with the officers continually, and they repeated over and over again that they preferred death in the north to any return to the south.

However, the older men now had little control over the younger men such as Little Finger Nail and Roman Nose. The whites continued to recognize Morning Star, Hog, and the older men as the Cheyenne leaders; but with Little Wolf gone, there was nobody strong enough to control them.

Tangle Hair later testified:

> The reason the young men had all the say was that Little Wolf, who was leader of the whole band when it left the south, had left this portion without a head. Dull Knife, though formerly a chief, had not been considered so for a long time, except by the whites.[7]

Now it was the younger warriors who brought greater pressure to bear on the people as a whole. The young men gathered in a room that controlled the entrance to the barrack. Their talks were guarded from the older men, the women, and the children. The young men also had been able to conceal some guns beneath the floor boards. The older men had advised them to surrender these weapons, but they had refused.

Eventually, the Cheyennes were given the freedom of the post. They were allowed to wander, as long as they were back for supper each night. Some of the older people walked down to the stream to gather red willow bark for kinnikinnick. They also brought back sacred white sage, to purify themselves and the sacred objects they still possessed for what lay ahead. Old Crow was permitted to scout with young Lieutenant Hugh Scott of the Seventh Cavalry, and Tangle Hair covered the country looking for the trail of any passing people. The soldier search for Little Wolf's people continued throughout the country.

[7] Big Head, testimony before the Board of Officers, *ibid.*, 11–12.

Lieutenant Chase was kind to the people. He asked them what they liked to eat, and they told him they liked soup. When he heard this, Chase got beef bones from the butcher to make it for them. He also purchased cornmeal, so they could have the mush of which they had grown fond. Periodically, he would ask the Cheyennes if they liked their food. Their answer was that they did, but they also said that their beef ration was not enough for them. They told the lieutenant that they would do anything they were asked, except go to the south. After his earlier inspection of their bundles, Chase had searched many of the men again. They willingly threw off their blankets and came to him for inspection. While he was searching them, they told him that if he would let them go, they would leave their belongings behind, and they would go naked to Red Cloud Agency. They asked the lieutenant to tell General Crook of their wishes in this matter, and he promised them that he would. Again they repeated that they would rather die at Robinson than to be starved to death in the south. This was their country, and they wanted to live here with Red Cloud's people and at peace with the whites.[8]

The quiet time continued for several weeks. The Cheyennes often sat around in small groups, the men playing cards and the women making beadwork or playing the hand game. Dances were held in the soldier barracks. The soldiers continued to treat the people with kindness, buying them food and giving gifts of money to the girls they danced with, so that they could buy beads and personal decorations.

During this period no one died from disease, but the terrible malarial fever remained from the hard months in the south. One girl was so wracked by it that she became hysterical. Some people shook with the chills throughout their entire stay at Robinson. Assistant Surgeon (First Lieutenant) Moseley went through the barrack each morning, treating all those who asked for medical aid. He also cared for Old Sitting Man's wounded leg.

Elsewhere, however, pressure was mounting for their removal

[8] Lieutenant George F. Chase testimony, *ibid.*, 27–28.

to Indian Territory again. As early as October 29, General Sheridan had wired the adjutant general of the army, expressing his belief that the Cheyennes had been encouraged to come north. He claimed that the whole reservation system would be endangered unless the people were returned south and forced to remain there. He also recommended that the Cheyenne leaders be sent to Florida—as Medicine Water, Gray Beard, and the others had been sent to Fort Marion in 1875.[9]

On October 31, Major Carlton telegraphed General Crook, the commanding officer of the Military Department of the Platte, stating that if the prisoners were to go south, it would be necessary to tie and to haul them. He recommended that they not be told about the matter at present, or they would give trouble, and he had few soldiers to spare to guard them.[10]

At this point, Red Cloud rode down from his new agency to visit the Cheyennes. He listened to them repeat that they would never return to the south, and he advised the soldiers to take the knives away from the Cheyennes, because the people would kill themselves, if necessary, to stop such a return. Red Cloud also reported that the warriors active in the Kansas killings had escaped north, while the people at Robinson had avoided committing any outrages.[11]

On November 11, the governor of Kansas called upon the secretary of war to surrender the Cheyennes responsible for the killings and alleged rapes in Kansas. He requested that Dull Knife, Old Crow, Hog, Little Wolf, and any others who could be connected with these killings be turned over to the civil authorities of his state. Then he also asked that additional troops be stationed at Forts Sill and Reno.[12]

On November 22, the fears of Morning Star's people were realized, although they did not know it at the time. On that day the commissioner of Indian affairs recommended that the Chey-

[9] Brief 8987. Military Division of the Missouri.
[10] Brief 9079. Military Division of the Missouri.
[11] Brief 9095. Military Division of the Missouri.
[12] Brief 9421. Military Division of the Missouri.

enne prisoners be taken to Fort Wallace, or another post in Kansas. There identifications would be made of the warriors who were involved in the Kansas fighting and they would be held for trial by the civil authorities. The rest of the Cheyennes were to be returned to Indian Territory.[13]

A copy of this communication was sent confidentially to General Crook on December 16, with directions to send the prisoners, under guard, by rail to Fort Leavenworth.

However, before this telegram reached Crook he had telegraphed the adjutant general's office on December 20, stating that the Cheyennes were greatly in need of clothing. He asked that the Indian Bureau issue the needed items from the annuity goods at Red Cloud or Spotted Tail agencies. The clothing was to be charged to the appropriation for the support of the Cheyennes in Indian Territory.[14]

On December 24, Crook acknowledged receipt of the communication ordering the removal of the Cheyennes to Fort Leavenworth. He stated that it would be inhuman to move them, since the mercury at Fort Robinson had stood at below zero for several days. He also said that it would take some time to arrange transportation for their removal. Then he added that the men would have to be handcuffed. He again requested a response to his telegram concerning the need for clothing for the people. General Sheridan's response was that he wished the Cheyennes to be "moved as soon as it was right and proper to do so."[15]

Finally, on December 26, Crook decided to assume responsibility for clothing the people. He ordered Captain Henry W. Wessells to issue such clothing as could be made available to the Cheyennes from the Quartermaster Department. However, this was soldier clothing, which still left the women and children uncared for. Wessells telegraphed Crook on two occasions, stating that he was ready to move whenever suitable clothing arrived.[16]

[13] Brief 9983. Military Division of the Missouri.
[14] Brief 10209. Military Division of the Missouri.
[15] Brief 10315. Military Division of the Missouri.
[16] General Crook to the Adjutant General, Military Division of the Missouri, January 22, 1879.

Not until January 4, 1879, did the secretary of the Interior see fit to issue permission for the "purchase in open market [of] such clothing as may be needed for said Indians to an amount not exceeding $500.00."[17]

By that time, it was too late anyway.

One day toward the end of December the cook discovered an extra cup after the people had been fed. This meant that someone was missing. When the soldiers checked, they discovered that it was Bull Hump. His wife had ridden off with the Sioux scouts from Pine Ridge, and, lonely for her, he had gone to find her. The cook did not report Bull Hump's absence until three meals had been eaten. Then the soldier chiefs counted the people once more. They ordered them inside the barrack, and the doors were locked behind them. Now the people were forced to remain in one room all day long. Outside, sentries guarded the building again. Bull Hump was brought in two or three days later. Nonetheless, what freedom the people had was gone now.

The people had no privacy—none from each other and none from Wessells and the other soldier officers who came by to see that no one had escaped. None of the men or boys were allowed to leave the barrack, but were forced to use the one indoor water closet and sink. The women and children were herded out, ten or fifteen at a time, by the guards. Their comfort station was the land beyond the stables. Then they were marched back. When they were inside once more, there was nothing for them to do.[18]

On December 17, Captain Henry W. Wessells, Jr., Third Cavalry, replaced Major Carlton as the commanding officer. Now life became even less pleasant. The weather had turned much colder, but most of the Cheyennes still wore the thin and ragged clothing in which they had surrendered. The women had managed to make some moccasins; and their Oglala friends and relatives had sent them over a hundred pairs as gifts. Doctor Moseley, the Post

[17] Secretary of the Interior to the Secretary of War, January 4, 1879.
[18] Captain Henry W. Wessells testimony, "Proceedings . . . ," *loc. cit.*, 78–79. John Stands in Timber stated that Bull Hump's wife was the real cause of the Cheyennes' bad luck at Fort Robinson.

228

Surgeon, advised exercise for the women, so Wessells put them to work policing the area near the barrack. They picked up trash and paper, and shoveled up frozen horse droppings. The women had no gloves, and they often suffered from the cold. An old woman who was walking around a corner where they were working was struck with a gun by one of the soldiers. However, he did not hurt her. Ten or fifteen of the women were ordered to unload grain from the soldier wagons. While they were doing this work, they were able to hide some of the corn beneath their blankets and clothing.[19]

Later in December, Red Cloud, American Horse, Red Dog, and No Flesh rode down from Pine Ridge for one last council with the people. They met in the barrack room. Wessells was present, as well as the lesser soldier chiefs. The Cheyennes were gathered in a closely packed circle. The soldier officers took seats near the center of the room, and the Lakota chiefs sat cross-legged on the floor beside them. The Cheyenne men stood crowded behind them, with the women and children standing quietly at the rear.

Red Cloud spoke for the Lakotas. He said that the Sioux were sorry for the Cheyennes, and he remembered that many of the Lakotas had fallen beside the Cheyenne fighting men. This filled the Sioux with sorrow. However, there was nothing that the Oglalas could do to help. The Great Father was more powerful, and the whites outnumbered them, so the Cheyennes would have to do what the Great Father said. The Oglalas had asked Washington to allow the Cheyennes to live with them. They hoped that the people would be allowed to come with them. Whatever the Oglalas had, they would share with the people. However, whatever the Great Father said, the Cheyennes would have to do.

Red Cloud continued to say that the Oglalas could no longer help the people. The snow was deep, and their horses were thin. Game was scarce. The Cheyennes could not resist. Neither could the Oglalas. "Do what the Great Father tells you without complaining," the Oglala concluded.[20]

[19] Testimony of Red Feather and The Enemy, "Proceedings . . . ," *loc. cit.*, 14–16; A Woman, testimony, 14.
[20] Bronson, *op. cit.*, 167–68.

229

After that, Morning Star slowly moved out into the center of the circle. He was wrapped in a ragged threadbare blanket, and his moccasins were worn. On his breast hung the beaded lizard that represented the Maiyun who had offered him help years before. He spoke to Red Cloud and the other Sioux leaders first:

> We know you for our friends, whose words we may believe. We thank you for asking us to share your lands. We hope that the Great Father will let us come to you. All we ask is to be allowed to live, and to live in peace. I do not seek war with anyone. I am an old man, and my fighting days are done. We bowed to the will of the Great Father and went far into the south where he told us to go. There we found that a Cheyenne cannot live. Sickness came among us that made mourning in every lodge. Then the treaty promises were broken, and our rations were short. Those not worn by disease were wasted by hunger. To stay there meant that all of us would die. Our petitions to the great Father were unheeded. We thought that it was better to die fighting to regain our old home than to die of sickness. Then our march began. The rest you know.

Then Morning Star looked at Captain Wessells and his officers:

> Tell the Great Father that Dull Knife and his people ask only to end their days here in the north where they were born. Tell him that we want no more war. We cannot live in the south; there is no game. Here, when rations are short we can hunt. Tell him if he lets us stay here Dull Knife's people will hurt no one. Tell him if he tries to send us back we will butcher each other with our own knives. I have spoken.[21]

Most of the Cheyennes sat in silence while the council continued. However, Bull Hump, Morning Star's elder son, soon was on his feet. Wrapped in an old strip of canvas, he paced back and forth across the room, his face showing the anger, indignation, and hatred that he felt for the whites.[22]

James Rowland, the son of William Rowland and his Cheyenne wife, translated Morning Star's words into English. James had

21 *Ibid.*, 168f.
22 *Ibid.*, 170.

been living with his father at Pine Ridge, and he had recently come down to Camp Robinson to serve as interpreter for the soldiers.

Wessells's response to Morning Star was short. He said that Dull Knife's words would go to the Great Father. Rowland translated this into Cheyenne. Then the council broke up, and the Cheyennes were locked in their room again.

The formal orders to move the people arrived about December 24. General Crook took no pleasure in issuing them; and he ordered Wessells to "provide everything possible for the comfort of the Indians on their journey."[23] The Cheyennes had grown slightly in numbers since their surrender at Robinson. A few separated people such as Porcupine had straggled in during the days that followed. By this time they numbered forty-nine men, fifty-one women, and forty-eight children.

It was not until January 3 that Wessells told Morning Star, Hog, and Tangle Hair that the people must pack up and move south. He gave them one day in which to think about the matter. Next day, Hog gave Wessells their reply. The Cheyennes would not move. They would do anything else; but they would not go south, he said.

Morning Star, Tangle Hair, and Hog held fast. They said that this was their land, and that the Cheyennes had lived here. Their children had been born here. The southern agency was not healthy. Fifty-eight of the people had died there while they were in the south. Even the horses got sick there. There was not enough to eat. Even the children did not want to go back. They would die rather than return, the Cheyennes told Wessells.

Wessells replied that the Great Father had ordered this, and that it had to be done. He was merely a subordinate, and he had to obey orders. He added that he hoped the Cheyennes would not give the soldiers any trouble.

The people still refused to move. So, on the same day, January 4, Wessells ordered all food and fuel cut off from them.[24]

---

[23] General Crook to the Adjutant General, January 22, 1879.
[24] Wessells testimony, "Proceedings . . . ," *loc. cit.*, 75–76. Wessells said that

Outside, the bitter cold of January numbed the land. The barracks windows had been covered with thick frost for days, and the top of the snow was hard frozen. Wessells waited four days for the Cheyennes to give in. Then he cut off their water, too. Snow had fallen on the window ledges; but this was soon scraped away by the thirsty people. Some of the children tried to slip by the guards to get water or snow, but they were caught and turned back.

Still the people endured. Some of the women had saved some corn and a little beef tallow. For fuel, there was some of the horse manure that Wessells had ordered the women to shovel, and the wooden barrack benches were broken up for kindling when the chips had disappeared.

The weather dropped to zero at night. Wessells still waited, intending to starve the Cheyennes until they agreed to go south, or until General Crook ordered them fed.[25] The captain pitied the children, however. Each morning he instructed James Rowland to tell the people that they could send out their children to be fed. Some of the older men were willing to do this for the sake of the little ones, but the younger warriors would not hear of it. Morning Star himself spoke to the young men, asking them to allow the children to be fed, but they refused. If one Cheyenne starved, all starved, was their reply.[26]

There were other signs of trouble. Henry Clifford lived between Robinson and the old Red Cloud Agency. He also served as a part-time interpreter at the camp. Late in the afternoon of January 8, he rode near the rear of the prison barrack. A young man called out to him in Sioux, "Hold on my friend. I want to tell you something. We are all going to die tomorrow. You will not

---

food and fuel were cut off on January 4; water on January 8. Others give varying dates. Some Cheyennes told Grinnell they had no food or water for eight days; others that they had no food for five days and no water for three days.
   Cf. Grinnell, *Fighting Cheyennes*, 419.
   [25] Wessells testimony, "Proceedings . . . ," *loc. cit.*, 78.
   [26] Testimony of a woman captured in the final engagement, *ibid.*, 3; testimony of Blacksmith and testimony of a woman who surrendered after the outbreak, *ibid.*, 12–14.

see me again." When Clifford asked why, the young man answered, "They say we must all go south and we are going to die here."[27]

That night, Second Lieutenant F. H. Hardie was on duty as officer of the day. He happened to look into the little room at one end of the prison barrack. There was an Indian sitting over the stove, which had a fire burning in it. Hardie put his head in the door and said to him in Sioux, "Pretty cold." The Cheyenne beckoned to Hardie. Then he called Tangle Hair, who put his hand through a broken pane in the window. Tangle Hair shook hands with the soldier chief. Then he told Hardie in Sioux that he wanted to leave the Cheyennes and go to Red Cloud. He would rather die right here than go south again, he added. Then he asked Hardie for some tobacco.[28]

Captain Wessells made another move to break down the resistance of the people. Wild Hog was the strongest of the older leaders after Little Wolf left. Wessells now planned to seize him. He instructed James Rowland to bring Hog to the adjutant's office around midday, January 9.

When Rowland arrived with Wessells's message, Hog hesitated. He knew that no one Chief could speak for the people, especially not without witnesses to support him. Then Old Crow said he would go, too. However, the younger men, Little Finger Nail, Roman Nose, and others, suspected a trap. They still did not trust Old Crow, because he had ridden against the people with Mackenzie's soldiers. Now some cried out against Hog's going. Some of them threatened to kill Old Crow if he left.[29]

Despite this opposition, the two older warriors moved through the door and out into the snow. When they reached the adjutant's office, they found the room crowded. Six or seven soldiers were there on guard duty. First Lieutenant James F. Simpson, Second Lieutenant J. F. Cummings and the sergeant major also were on hand.

[27] Henry Clifford testimony, *ibid.*, 164.
[28] Second Lieutenant F. H. Hardie testimony, *ibid.*, 132–33.
[29] Old Crow testimony, *ibid.*, 5.

Captain Wessells asked Wild Hog if the Cheyennes were ready to go south. Hog replied that they would die first. When Wessells heard this, he ordered Hog and Old Crow seized. The soldiers moved in with handcuffs. Old Crow offered no resistance, but Hog drew his knife and attempted to kill himself. The soldiers grappled with him, and he wounded one private. Lieutenant Cummings received a cut on the hand during the struggle.[30]

Hog shouted for help, but the other warriors were too far away to hear him. However, a Cheyenne woman was standing outside the adjutant's office, talking to her brother from Red Cloud Agency. She saw the attack on Hog, and she carried news of his capture to the others. Hog's wife had come out to see him, and she rushed back inside with the news.

When the people heard what had happened, an uproar broke out in the barrack. Two or three warriors rushed the doors at the west end of the prison room, but they were driven back by the soldiers. Young Hog came to the door, his sheet pulled up over his head. He called to Lieutenant Simpson and to some other soldiers who were at the corner of the adjutant's office, warning them to get out of the way, because he was coming. Ten or twelve soldiers armed with carbines were stationed near the barrack door. They quickly slipped cartridges into their rifles. After that, the door was shut, and none of the Cheyennes attempted to leave for a time.

Wild Hog watched the soldiers drive the people back into the room, his son among them. Then Hog told Wessells that if they would take off the irons he would return to the barrack and tell the others to give up and move south. Wessells dismissed this offer as a ruse.[31]

Soon afterward, Strong Left Hand, who received his name

[30] Hog, testimony, *ibid.*, 7. Two more knives were found on Hog. He told Wessells that the people would have surrendered their knives if they had been asked to do so.
  Cf. Wessells testimony, *ibid.*, 64; First Lieutenant James F. Simpson, *ibid.*, 94–95; Second Lieutenant J. F. Cummings, *ibid.*, 172–73.
  [31] Hog, testimony, *ibid.*, 7; First Lieutenant James Simpson testimony, *ibid.*, 96; Second Lieutenant J. F. Cummings testimony, *ibid.*, 173.

from his power to kill an antelope or buffalo with a thrown rock, came out of the barrack. He had decided to surrender with his friend Hog. The soldiers immediately handcuffed him. A short time later, all three Cheyennes were moved to the cavalry camp, about a mile from the post.

The young men declared war after that. Thenceforth, they had no good answer for anyone who spoke to them. The Council Chiefs were pushed aside, just as the Southern Cheyenne warriors had pushed aside their Council Chiefs during the 1874–75 fighting. The influence of Little Finger Nail and Roman Nose had grown during the weeks at Robinson. Younger men like Black Bear, Little Shield, Bull Hump, and Pug Nose, a southerner, wished to die fighting. So did the younger sons of the Chiefs, Little Hump and Young Hog.

After so many days of suffering and starvation, many of the people were ready for death. During the imprisonment, some had acted as if they were drunk. One young man said, "I want to jump out now and be killed." Others said that they might as well be killed outside as to starve to death inside the barrack. Many of the women seemed as ready to die as the young men.

They warned James Rowland not to come in and not to let anyone else come in, because they would kill whoever entered. One of the Cheyennes from Pine Ridge was attacked when he came on a visit, and he was saved only through the help of a friend. Some of the men spoke to Rowland through the window, telling him that they expected to die there and that they were hoping they would die soon.[32]

Once an officer called to Tangle Hair, the Dog Soldier Chief, telling him to come out. The Dog Soldier membership included both Cheyennes and Sioux, and Tangle Hair was a Sioux, so the officer offered to send him and his family to Pine Ridge.

During the flight north, Tangle Hair had always led the march while the young men scattered over the countryside. Now they threatened to kill him if he tried to leave. Little Shield said to the others, "This man cannot go out. He owns us, and he can do what

[32] Grinnell, *Fighting Cheyennes*, 419–20.

235

he likes with us." Because he was the Dog Soldier Chief, in the same way that the Sacred Arrow Keeper held the entire Cheyenne tribe in his palm, Tangle Hair was entrusted with the care of his own society. He stayed behind in the barrack.[33]

After Hog was put in irons, the young men prepared to break out. They covered the windows with blankets. Then they ripped up the floor boards and some of the men made war clubs from the lumber. One warrior came to the window and showed the sentries a club made from a piece of board with six or eight spikes driven into the end of it. Others brandished similar weapons. The windows on the north side of the prison room were covered with broken pieces of flooring, kettles, and other objects from the post store. Breastworks were thrown up, and rifle pits were dug for protection from a soldier charge. The people were singing strong-heart songs as they made these preparations to die.

Outside, while Hog, Left Hand, and Old Crow were being taken to the lower camp, two companies of armed troopers were moved in close to the barrack. The companies were divided into four reliefs, with an officer in charge of each. At about 4:00 P.M., Captain Wessells sent six more men to act as sentries. Now there were seven guards on duty around the building; three at the east end, one at the front, one at the rear, and two at the west end, next to the adjutant's office.

A short time after Hog was handcuffed, Wessells had called to Morning Star. The Chief came to the door of the prison room, but no farther. Wessells shook hands with him, and he told Morning Star that he wanted him to visit Hog. He promised the Chief that he would be returned to the people unharmed. Morning Star refused to go, and turned back toward the prison room. One of the young men pulled him in, and the door was shut behind him.

Just before dark, Wild Hog and Old Crow came up from the lower camp to get their families. Guards were standing near as Hog spoke to the people through the holes in the log chinking. Inside, there was much angry talk and noise, especially from the young men. Finally they ordered the wives of Hog and Old Crow

[33] *Ibid.*, 425–26.

out of the room, with their children and some old women. However, Young Hog, Wild Hog's son, stayed behind. His brother and his oldest sister, called Hog's Daughter, stayed also. She would not leave her brothers.

Wessells told Wild Hog to tell the people that those who were willing to go south were to come out. He said that they would not be harmed, and that they would be fed. The Cheyennes made no reply to the soldier chief's offer, because they could see that Hog's hands were still manacled.

During the time that Hog was near the barrack, Lieutenant Chase reported to Captain Wessells that Wild Hog had said that the Cheyennes planned to break out that night. Some fifty men were within hearing distance of the lieutenant as he said this. Yet Wessells apparently paid no attention to the warning.[34]

Wessells also called to Morning Star, asking him why he did not come out. He promised the Chief plenty to eat. Morning Star answered through some chinks in the logs that he wanted to come out, but that the others would not let him.[35] Wessells and other officers never understood that a Chief belonged to the people; and that Morning Star's actions must be in accord with the needs and wishes of the people, even when those wishes differed from his own personal feelings.

About 5:00 P.M., soldiers move in to board up the door opening from the cook room into the prison room. Three heavy planks were nailed across the outside of the door. At about 8:00 P.M., the Cheyennes, who were just on the other side, heard the clank of chains and the noise of hammering as the blacksmith stapled three heavy chains across the boards. The soldiers already had fastened both front doors of the barrack securely, using an iron bar to hold one of them tightly in place. Outside, a chain guard of sentries watched the building. The beats of these men crossed

---

[34] Private Arthur Ross testimony, "Proceedings . . . ," *loc. cit.*, Private Louis Young testimony, *ibid.*, 17-18; First Lieutenant C. A. Johnson testimony, *ibid.*, 142.

[35] Testimony of James Roland (Rowland), *ibid.*, 149f.; Wessells testimony, *ibid.*, 80–81; Simpson testimony, *ibid.*, 100.

each other, each soldier's beat overlapping the beats of the two soldiers on either side of him.

There was no peaceful escape for the people now.

That afternoon, Little Shield, the Elk chief, had said to the others, "Now dress up and put on your best clothing. We will all die together." The people had been thinking about death, and talking about it to each other. Some of them said, "It is true that we must die, but we will not die here shut up like dogs. We will die on the prairie. We will die fighting." Then they carefully painted their faces, many of them rubbing on the old red, the life color. They put on their best clothing and the new moccasins that remained among them. The people were looking for death, hence they took few precautions against the bitter cold that waited outside the barrack.

The few guns the people still retained had been lifted out of hiding when they ripped up the floor boards. Most of these had been concealed in the floor beneath the heating stove. There were at least twelve guns and three revolvers, with a little ammunition. Black Bear assembled the carbine he had captured in the fight with Long Hair's men. Singing Wolf carried his Sharps rifle, the most powerful gun among them. The people had hidden these arms well. The rifle barrels and stock and the six-shooter frames had been carried beneath the women's clothing and blankets. Almost every child had been wearing some small weapon part as a personal ornament. A trigger had been hanging around the neck of one, while another wore a spring tied to his scalplock. Other small parts were tied to the wrists or elsewhere on the bodies of the children. The soldiers had seen these things, but had thought nothing about them.[36]

[36] The Court of Inquiry listed the Cheyenne weapons as:
5 Springfield carbines, 45 calibre, 1873 model (Only one of these was a Cheyenne gun. The others were captured from the sentries).
7 Springfield carbines, B.L. Rifle Muskets, 50 calibre
3 Sharps carbines, 50 calibre
1 Sharps rifle
3 revolvers
The Court also noted that some of the arms captured could not be found in the command. The above was a list of those presented for inspection. *Ibid.*, 3–4.

By the time the sun had set, the preparations were almost completed. The people had finished putting on their best clothing. They tied on their blankets, so that their hands would be free. Those who had two blankets tied one around their necks, the other around the waist. Then they moved about in the bitterly cold room, embracing one another for the last time.

Most of the Elks had followed Little Wolf. Now Little Shield, the Elk chief, was given the old place of bravery, because his was the lesser society here. He was to lead the flight through the window at his end of the barrack. He was to be the first to strike down the sentry outside, with the hope of capturing his rifle. Little Finger Nail was to lead the people on the opposite side of the room. Tangle Hair and his Dog Soldiers were to guard the rear, as they had done so often in the past, holding back the soldiers while the other men helped the women and children to flee.

Some horse catchers were to run ahead to Bronson's ranch on Dead Man's Creek to the southwest. This was the closest pony herd, and they would need as many horses as possible.

Outside, the mercury stood at zero. Five or six inches of hard-crusted snow covered the prairie. The moon was shining so brightly that it truly was the Sun of the Night that the Cheyennes venerated in the ceremonies. Now, more than ever, Box Elder's Ox'zem was needed to draw the dark clouds across the face of the moon, concealing the people as they fled. However, the Sacred Wheel Lance still hung far away in the south, near the Sacred Arrows and Buffalo Hat.

Great Eyes took out the ancient shield that Oak, his grandfather, had carried before him. Its cover bore the sacred symbols of the Sun and the Moon, with great grizzly claws to mark the four directions. Four rows of eagle feathers trailed below, mounted on a leather streamer. Great Eyes was sixty years old. He placed the shield on the slender back of Red Bird, his thirteen-year-old nephew. The few old sacred objects that remained must be saved, and there was far more hope of a boy escaping than of an older warrior.

There were 130 people left. Forty-four were men, but this included the young boys. They piled saddles, parfleches, and the other heavier possessions under the windows, so the people could climb out more easily. Then, after dark, a young man was stationed at each window along the west and north sides of the building. Little Shield sat in the north window. Other warriors waited at the remaining windows, ready to shoot the guards when Little Shield gave the signal. The older men and women gathered at the windows along the east end. There were a few men who had no guns, but carried children instead. They were fast runners, men who could get the youngsters away. A few strong women, such as the wives of White Antelope and She Bear, were to flee with them. They were to rear the children in the Cheyenne way, so that the people here would not all be wiped out. As was usually the case, the older men like Morning Star and Blacksmith, neither of whom had a gun, were to move with the women to help them. Two young warriors would come last of all, to see that all the people got out and running.

Now they were prepared to flee.

7. Morning Star's People Are Killed

Suddenly, at about ten o'clock, the long wait ended. Little Shield threw up his rifle and fired at the sentry outside his window. The soldier fell. As he went down, Little Shield knocked out the window sash. Then the warriors at the other windows opened fire.

Little Finger Nail's bullets killed the sentinels at the southwest corner. Two other guards fell, one at the west and one at the east. A bullet brought down the corporal of the guard, who, hearing the crash of window glass, ran from the guardroom at the northwest corner. Two other soldiers in the guardroom also were brought down. As the warriors ran by, they paused to capture four of the soldiers' guns.[1]

The people were spilling out the windows. Not all the women had known of the plans to escape, and some of them were in bed when the first shots were fired. When Red Feather and The Enemy, both women, heard the first shot, they thought that one of the Cheyennes had opened the door, that a soldier had fired at him, and that the warrior had returned the shot. Red Feather and The Enemy had not packed their bundles. They left their belongings behind in the rush as they followed the first group fleeing the barrack.

The young men had planned to make for the steep bluff rising west of the post. "That is where our bodies will be," some of them had said.

Wessells had believed that once the uproar over handcuffing Hog had ceased, all would remain quiet. Believing the Cheyennes to be disarmed, he had no idea that the people could fight their way past the sentinels. Thus he had kept no troops prepared for pursuit. The men in the barracks some fifty yards northeast of the prison had been warned by their captain to be ready for an emergency. At the first alarm, they turned out, half-dressed. Soldiers ran from other barracks, some of them in their underwear. They opened fire on the Dog Soldiers, who formed the rear guard for the fleeing people.

Some of the Cheyennes were wounded before they even escaped the barrack. A few of the women held back, and the young men had to push them out. Then the people raced toward the river, the men attempting to hold the women and children together as they hurried toward the bridge across White River. Some of them were carrying the saddles, lariats, and bridles needed for capturing horses at the Bronson ranch.

Tangle Hair had been the first to jump through his window. He and four other Dog Soldiers made their stand below the

[1] First Lieutenant James F. Simpson testimony, "Proceedings . . . ," *loc. cit.,* 110, reported one private killed. One noncommissioned officer and four privates were wounded. One was mortally wounded and died later.

stables. They were firing carbines, covering the people in their flight, as the Dog Men were vowed to do. Their very position caused the death of some Cheyennes, because many of the shots fired at Tangle Hair's men missed, and brought down the people beyond as they ran toward the steep bluffs to the west. Finally all five Dog Soldiers lay shot on the snow. Tangle Hair himself was badly wounded. However, he dragged himself to some soldier quarters. The soldiers treated him well, and they sent for a doctor to care for his wounds. Soon afterward, the bleeding women and children began to be carried in.[2]

Old Sitting Man was among the first to fall. He had hung back, not wanting to slow down the others with his wounded leg. As he struck the ground, the leg broke again, and he sat there in the snow, singing his death song. He did not have to wait long. A soldier soon rushed up, put the muzzle of his rifle against the wounded man's head, and pulled the trigger, blowing off the top of the head. Sitting Man was seen lying there later. The top of his skull lay beside him, while his brains splattered the snow in another spot.[3]

Nine men were killed and twice as many wounded before the people reached the river. As the men dropped, their weapons were seized by the women and boys, who used them as best they could.

The survivors fled on toward the bridge over White River, a few hundred yards from their barrack. When they reached the water, most of them threw themselves down to ease the long thirst of the past days. The soldier bullets were flying thick and fast. Many of the Cheyennes drank too much and could hardly continue to run. They crossed the bridge and turned up the south side, heading toward the sawmill on the second bottom. The foot soldiers continued to press them.

A few Cheyennes stopped by the sawmill to make a stand. However, by this time Captain P. D. Vroom's Third Cavalry was charging in, replacing the soldiers on foot. Soon all of this little group were shot down.

---

[2] Grinnell, *Fighting Cheyennes*, 426.
[3] *Ibid.*, 422.

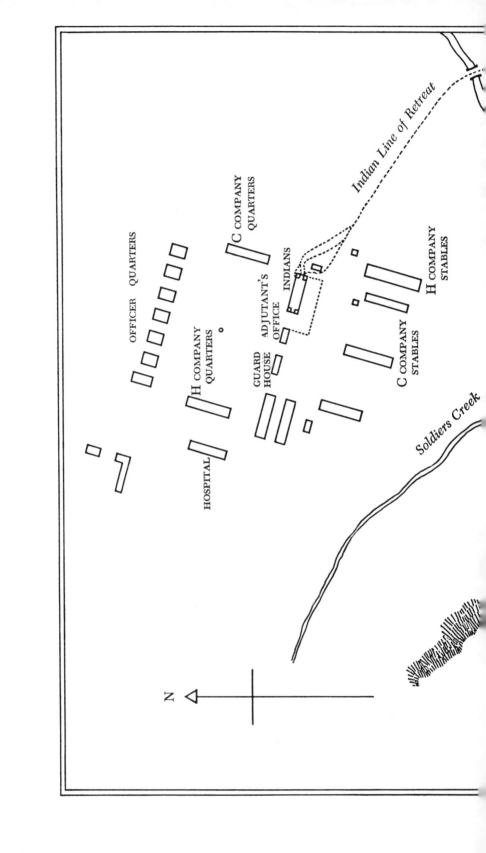

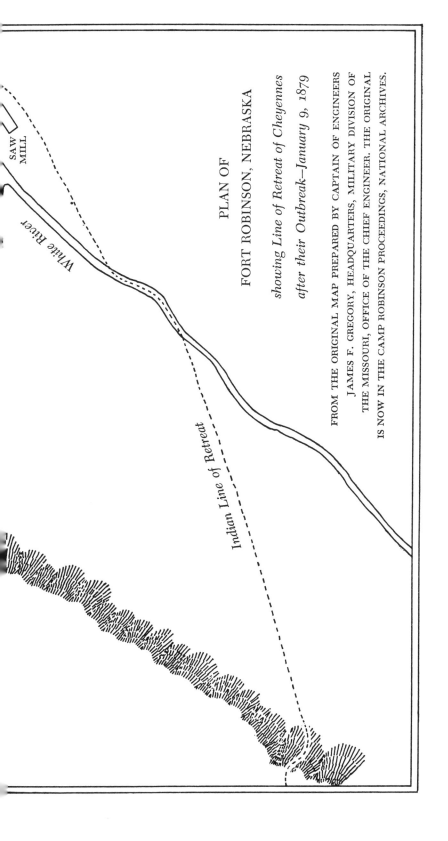

SAW MILL

White River

Indian Line of Retreat

PLAN OF
FORT ROBINSON, NEBRASKA

*showing Line of Retreat of Cheyennes
after their Outbreak—January 9, 1879*

FROM THE ORIGINAL MAP PREPARED BY CAPTAIN OF ENGINEERS
JAMES F. GREGORY, HEADQUARTERS, MILITARY DIVISION OF
THE MISSOURI, OFFICE OF THE CHIEF ENGINEER. THE ORIGINAL
IS NOW IN THE CAMP ROBINSON PROCEEDINGS, NATIONAL ARCHIVES.

The first Cheyenne movement had been southwestward, toward Bronson's ranch, where horses might be captured. However, the soldiers were moving in too quickly. The people dropped their horse equipment and turned toward the river again. Racing up the valley, they cut across the bends of the creek and started to cross it on the ice. The ice was too thin, and many of them fell into the water, getting soaked through. There was no wind, but the night was bitter cold, and their clothing was frozen hard against their bodies as they ran on.

Then they began to scatter. Some were falling, short of breath and exhausted by the long starvation. Many of these were carrying babies. Behind them, the soldier fire never stopped. The slowness of the women and children held the men back. They might have escaped alone; but many families were determined to die together, and the men protected their women and children to the end. Half the fighting men were cut down in the first half-mile.

Those who still had strength to run hurried on toward the steep bluffs on the north. A few of the weaker ones hid in the tangled brush and grass close to White River.

The soldiers could not tell men from women in the darkness. Lieutenant Cummings rode into a washout near the sawmill, nearly landing on two Cheyennes who were hiding there. They charged him with knives, and he shot them with his pistol. Then he found that both were women.[4]

Lieutenant Chase and his men were riding along the bank of White River when they came upon a Cheyenne who had hidden in the brush. The man refused to surrender and Chase's men shot him down.

Dull Knife, Bull Hump, and their families started off in a group. Great Eyes and Red Bird fled with them. One of Morning Star's daughters had been hurt, and she was left behind as the others struggled on. Bull Hump fell back to attempt a delaying stand for this sister. Another sister stayed with him until the soldiers were close. Then she picked up a child whose parent already lay

[4] Bronson, *op. cit.*, 178. Cummings does not mention this in his testimony.

on the snow and ran toward the sheltering bluffs carrying the little one.[5]

Later that night, rancher Bronson and a companion rode into Robinson. When they reached the timber lining Soldier Creek, they could see a broad dark line across the snow ahead of them. It was the trail of the fleeing Cheyennes and the pursuing soldiers —the line of the people's flight toward the bluffs. The wounded lay there, "so thick for a long way that one could leap from one body to another," Bronson wrote. The wounded Cheyennes were lean and gaunt from starvation, lying there in ragged half-nakedness in the midst of a bitter cold night.

As the ranchers crossed the trail, Bronson recognized a warrior lying on his back, his arms extended. It was Little Hump. His only weapon was a small knife held in his right hand—a knife so worn down that its blade was no more than a quarter-inch wide at the hilt. Suddenly, Little Hump rose to a sitting position and aimed a slashing blow at Bronson's leg. Bronson instinctively spurred his horse out of reach, and pulled out his pistol. But before the rancher could fire, Little Hump fell back dead.[6]

Elsewhere it was almost impossible to tell men from women in the darkness. A woman whose body bore six wounds later was identified by Captain Wessells as having been killed by a volley near the sawmill. She was standing behind a stump when the soldiers shot her down, believing that she was a warrior. At another spot, a sergeant and several men were chasing a man and woman who had been cut off from the others. Suddenly the two turned and charged their pursuers. The man had only a knife; the woman carried a piece of iron stove. They were shot down.

The running fight continued nearly a mile. Then the foot troops, many of them already badly frozen, were turned back to the garrison to get clothing and horses. Cavalrymen already had ridden out to replace them.

There were others who followed the trail of dead and wounded

---

[5] Sandoz, *Cheyenne Autumn*, 205.
[6] Bronson, *op. cit.*, 181–82.

Cheyennes that night. While Second Lieutenant J. F. Cummings was returning to the post with the wounded and prisoners, he met about a dozen civilians with guns in their hands. One was J. W. Dear, a trader. Just before he met this group, Lieutenant Cummings heard two shots fired. After meeting them, he found no more Cheyennes alive. "As there were no soldiers there, I was convinced that these citizens were killing wounded Indians," he later testified.[7]

The people were exhausted when they reached the scattered pines and rocks marking the lower area of the bluffs. They could see the flash of the soldier rifles and hear the crack of carbine fire across the still night air as the soldiers overtook those who had fallen first.

White Antelope and his wife were among those in a small group that dropped beside a tree to rest. The wife was already wounded, and White Antelope was carrying their baby. When the soldiers were close, he rushed out against them, his knife drawn. He fought for a little while, but soon their bullets brought him down. Then the soldiers moved in closer. They killed two women there. Another they shot in the back and in the side of the head. Then they knocked her senseless.

But the soldier bullet had only caught White Antelope in the thigh. His wife ran toward him and was cut down by rifle fire. When the soldiers moved on, White Antelope crawled to where she lay wounded. He saw that the baby was dead. He spoke to his wife, saying that they should die together. Then he stabbed her and turned the knife on himself. They lived barely long enough to be carried in blankets into Robinson.[8]

Most of the Cheyennes had been struggling toward a high bluff two or three miles west of Robinson. By horseback it was more

7 Second Lieutenant J. F. Cummings testimony, "Proceedings . . . ," loc. cit., 169.
  Cf. First Lieutenant Emmett Crawford testimony, ibid., 147; Second Lieutenant F. H. Hardie testimony, ibid., 132–33.
8 Grinnell, Fighting Cheyennes, 422.
  First Lieutenant C. A. Johnson testimony, "Proceedings . . . ," loc. cit., 143. (Johnson called him Big Antelope.)

than six miles to the summit. However, hidden in an angle of the cliff was a slope that the fleeing people could climb on foot.

Just below this slope, Captain P. D. Vroom and his company of Third Cavalry caught up with them. Vroom dismounted his men, forming them into a line of skirmishers. Then they moved up the hill toward the steep and rugged bluffs along the left bank of White River.

Second Lieutenant George F. Chase rode up with his men. Vroom directed Chase to send his own company back to Robinson, then Chase dismounted and advanced with the left side of Vroom's skirmish line. The left line was moving along the crest of the hill, with the right of the line extending down its slope. These soldiers had advanced only a short way when they found some Cheyennes. Chase called to the people to surrender. They refused, and he ordered them shot.

On this slope Dull Knife's youngest daughter—The Princess— was killed. After the soldiers had moved on, a man who had followed them from Robinson found her. She was with four other women lying under some pine trees—the trees the people had longed for in the south. All were dead except Morning Star's daughter. She sat with her back against a tree, too far gone to speak aloud. Another woman's child was on her back, and the little one also was shot. Two or three other children lay dead beside the women, who had run with the little ones until they were exhausted. They had paused here to catch their breath, and the soldiers had come up and immediately opened fire on the women and children, shooting them as they sat there.[9]

Meanwhile, Lieutenant Chase moved on, leaving the Cheyenne dead and wounded behind. He advanced with four men to within a few yards of a perpendicular rock some seventy-five feet high. There was an opening in the rock, and the soldier chief could see the people passing through. Again he ordered his men to open fire.

[9] Grinnell, *Fighting Cheyennes,* 422.
Bronson, *op. cit.,* 184, says The Princess fell fighting in the ranks of the Cheyenne rear guard.

Some of the Cheyennes had already reached the top of the rock. From there they fired down upon the soldiers, and they succeeded in stopping Chase and his men. Chase placed his soldiers under cover and hurried back to check with Vroom. Vroom returned with him, but as soon as they showed themselves, the Cheyennes fired down a volley of shots.

Vroom pulled back in a hurry, moving back about five hundred yards. As Chase moved back down, he discovered a number of women and children hiding behind rocks or huddled beneath the trees. Some were wounded. All were made prisoners.

At this point Captain Wessells rode up and assumed command. He directed Chase, with a company of men, to take charge of the women and children, to care for them, and to accompany them back to Robinson.

Wessells sent Captain Vroom and a company of cavalry up through the valley to the Hat Creek road. The soldiers were directed to cut off the Cheyennes if they attempted to flee east to Red Cloud. Then he sent the greater part of another company to scout the right bank of White River, between the river and the bluffs.

Taking seven men with him, Wessells himself followed the bluffs north of the Laramie road, attempting to find a place to get the soldiers over the bluffs. When he gained the top of the ridge, he found many moccasin tracks. He followed the tracks and soon encountered three Cheyennes. The Cheyennes charged him; and the recruit who held the horses was so badly frightened that he allowed the horses to escape. The soldiers shot down two of the people as they charged, while the third managed to escape into the rocks and brush. With their horses gone, Wessells and his men were forced to walk back several miles to the post. The soldier chief slept an hour and a half. Then he was after the people again.

By the time daylight came, the soldiers had brought both captives and wounded back to the post. Morning Star's daughter was among the wounded. Those not wounded were once more placed in the old prison barrack or in the guardhouse.

Most of the injured were women and children. The surgeon

noted their wounds. Short Woman was shot in the right hand, head, chest, and back, and her thigh was fractured as well. Buffalo Girl, a child of five, suffered from a bad gunshot wound in the thigh. Another five-year-old girl had been shot through the shoulder. She lived only twelve hours. Medicine Woman's right eye had been destroyed by a bullet, and she was wounded in the head besides. A six-months-old baby girl cried from the pain of a fractured left thigh. She was dead within two days. A year-old baby girl did not last that long. Both her thighs had been fractured. She was gone an hour after a soldier carried her in. Tangle Hair, the only grown man among them, had taken a bullet in his thigh. Stub Foot, a sixteen-year-old, was wounded twice in the arm as well as in the thigh. White Antelope and his wife died from their stab wounds an hour after they were brought in. Lame Girl, an orphan of about six, had been hit in the foot during the first fight after the people started north. Now she was wounded again, this time from a bullet that pierced her left lung.

And so the list of wounded ran on. There were about twenty Cheyennes carried into the post hospital during the first day of fighting. Now it was Surgeon Moseley, the soldier doctor, who cared for the people; Bridge, the old Ree doctor who once guarded the sacred ear of corn, was among those who lay dead in the snow outside.[10]

On the morning of January 10, Second Lieutenant J. F. Cummings, the post adjutant, requested Captain Wessells's permission to take the guardhouse prisoners and three wagons to scout out further survivors and to bring in the dead.

They followed the main Cheyenne trail up the bluffs, passing blankets, lariats, moccasins, and pools of frozen blood as they moved along. Finally Lieutenant Cummings dispatched a corporal with one man down a steep ravine to follow a trail. The lieutenant specifically instructed the corporal not to shoot or to frighten the Indians unless it was necessary to save his own life. In about fifteen minutes he heard a shout, followed by four

10 "List of Indians Wounded," "Proceedings . . . ," *loc. cit.*, 139-40.

shots. The lieutenant hurried down, calling out, "Don't kill them unless you have to." He found a trail leading directly to the face of the cliff. Just outside a cave, a woman of about forty was sitting on a rock. It was Tangle Hair's wife. A young man, a girl of about fifteen and a little child stood nearby. The bodies of two warriors lay on the ground, both shot through the head.

When the corporal first discovered them he had called out, "How! How! Waste! Waste!" However, the warriors were Dog Soldiers, men who were vowed never to surrender or retreat. Tangle Hair's wife had been crying and she began to climb from the cave, but one of the Dog Men pulled her inside again. He immediately loaded a carbine, captured on the way north, and his companion raised an old-time pistol, one that used paper cartridges. The corporal and his companion opened fire, and the warrior with the pistol fell over dead. The warrior with the carbine dodged. He raised his head again to fire at the soldiers, and this time the corporal's bullet hit him, killing him instantly. The young man had a knife, but he finally threw it down in the snow in surrender.[11]

Just before daylight, Lieutenants Emmett Crawford, James F. Simpson, and F. H. Hardie had ridden through the battle area hunting for wounded. They found three women. Two were wounded, and they were carried in blankets back to the post. The officers also examined the dead. No bodies had been disturbed by the troops. Some of the dead were covered with blankets. While the officers were engaged in this duty they saw three civilians with a buckboard. One civilian remained with the horses, while the other two searched the Cheyenne bodies. These men were recognized as Henry Clifford, a part-time interpreter at Robinson, William E. Cook, division superintendent of the Sidney and Black Hills Stage Line, and an unidentified man. The soldiers were close enough to hear their conversation. One man

---

[11] Lieutenant Cummings said the young man was about eighteen. Sandoz, *Cheyenne Autumn*, 219, says he was Little Bear, Tangle Hair's thirteen-year-old. The "List of Indians Wounded," "Proceedings . . . ," *loc. cit.*, 139, gives Little Bear's age as ten.
Cf. Cummings testimony, "Proceedings . . . ," *loc. cit.*, 170–72.

said that he had a pipe, and that was what he had been looking for. The man at the buckboard called to the others to bring him blankets from the dead Cheyennes. Lieutenant Crawford heard the unidentified man say that he got there a little too late, but he was in time to kill a squaw.[12]

When Lieutenant Cummings and his burial detail arrived near the bluffs, they also noticed two civilians riding among the bodies. Again, one of them was Henry Clifford. He shouted to Cummings, and the lieutenant rode to him. There he discovered that Clifford was holding a pistol on The Sioux, an elderly man who had not been wounded. He carried a little girl strapped to his back. Clifford spoke Lakota, so Cummings asked him to interpret for him. The Sioux pointed to a washout and said he thought there was a boy hidden there. Then the old man walked to the edge of the bank and shouted. Soon a woman and three children slowly came out, crying, and frightened by the sight of the soldiers. The Sioux continued to call, but no one else appeared.

Shortly thereafter, the lieutenant and his men began the work of collecting the dead. At one spot they discovered that fifteen to eighteen of the bodies were freshly scalped—one of them in two places. The women's bodies had been mutilated and were indecently exposed, with their dresses pulled up over their heads. Clifford and his companion had left by this time. However, Cummings had seen them moving about the area where the bodies were discovered. "It is most decidedly my opinion that these two citizens were the men who exposed and mutilated the bodies," the lieutenant later testified.[13]

Other mutilations were noted too. One man had been shot in the face, the side of the face blown away. This had happened at least several hours after his death. Others, too, apparently had been shot after they were dead.[14]

When the bodies in the bluffs had been collected, the lieutenant

[12] Crawford testimony, *ibid.*, 147; First Lieutenant James F. Simpson testimony, *ibid.*, 112–13; Hardie testimony, *ibid.*, 132–33.
[13] Cummings testimony, *ibid.*, 167–69. Clifford denied this, saying that he, too, had seen the scalped and exposed bodies. Clifford testimony, *ibid.*, 161–65.
[14] Testimony of Lieutenant Edward Moseley, assistant surgeon, *ibid.*, 135.

ordered them covered. Then he sent the burial detail back to Robinson with a request for a detail of soldiers to help him continue the search for wounded and dead. While the lieutenant awaited their arrival, two more civilians rode up. They waited for the officer to move on, but he refused to go, and they finally left the area.[15]

There were acts of kindness, too. The night of the outbreak a Cheyenne baby was found by a soldier who turned the little one over to First Lieutenant C. A. Johnson. Johnson sent it to his wife, with the request that she feed the child. The little one was dressed in doll's clothing with tatting ornamentation.

Captain Wessells himself carried a child less than two years old for a hundred yards to a place of safety.

Lieutenant Cummings reported fourteen men and seven women and children killed the night of January 9 and early in the morning of January 10. Four women and children died of wounds at the post the morning of the 10th. Later that day four more men and another woman would be shot down by the soldiers.[16]

When the wagons reached the fort, the guardhouse prisoners unloaded the bodies. They climbed into the wagons, which were piled high with dead, and stood upon the bodies. Then they lifted the frozen corpses by the hands and feet and threw them out upon the ground. When a wagon was partially empty, the soldiers stood behind it. Then they grabbed the dead Cheyennes by their heads or feet, slid them out, and allowed them to fall to the ground. The bodies were arranged in rows by the roadside near the sawmill. The men lay in one row, the women and children in another. They were buried in a common trench.[17]

Later that morning, Wessells telegraphed General Crook that about thirty Cheyennes had been killed. Thirty-five had been

[15] Cummings testimony, *ibid.*, 169.

[16] James Rowland, in his testimony, *ibid.*, 150–51, stated that he counted fourteen men, nine women, and three children dead. Two women and a child died later.

Grinnell, *Fighting Cheyennes*, 423, says the burial detail found about fifty dead.

[17] Grinnell, *ibid.*

recaptured, making a total of fifty-three prisoners including Hog, Crow, and Left Hand. "We will have many more before dark as the trailing is good and five companies are out," Wessells confidently concluded.[18]

The day the bodies were carried in, Captain Wessells visited the prison barrack. He looked at the people scattered about on the floor, and asked, "Now will you go south?" One of the young women had been badly shot in the foot. When she heard that, she pulled herself up to a standing position. Then she looked straight at Wessells. "No. We will not go back. We will die instead. You have killed most of us. Why do you not go ahead and finish the work?" she asked.[19]

The people's spirit remained unbroken. They were still "all Cheyenne."

By daylight, the Cheyenne wolves watching from the bluffs signaled the presence of soldiers all around the people. Wessells had ordered L Company of the Third Cavalry to ride up Hat Creek road. A Company rode up the Sidney road and through the bluffs behind Robinson. Company C was to follow one of the Cheyenne trails the soldiers had already discovered. Company H rode out in the direction of Crow Butte, following the right bank of the river. Then they cut through the bluffs to the country of the Running Water and White rivers. E Company rode up White River. To the fleeing Cheyennes, there seemed to be soldiers everywhere.

Wessells rode up Hat Creek road with Captain Vroom and L Company. This was the road the people must cross if they were ever to get to Red Cloud. The soldiers found signs of flight for about ten miles along the summit of the divide between White River and Soldier Creek. The Cheyennes had been fleeing westward. Then they had moved down into the valley of Soldier Creek. Now it was easy to see their trail as Woman's Dress, the

---

[18] Letters Received by the Office of the Adjutant General, Roll 449. General Crook to the Adjutant General's Office, January 10, 1879.
[19] Grinnell, *Fighting Cheyennes*, 424.

255

Sioux scout, led the cavalry in pursuit. There were drops of blood in the snow, and occasionally a little hollow where someone had paused briefly to rest.

The signs indicated that for nearly eighteen miles the Cheyennes had made no halt. Finally their trail wound around the foot of a high, steep hill covered with timber. The soldiers rode single file to pass it and to follow the trail that led through the snow over another hill still farther ahead. The people had moved over the crest of the second hill, then they had made a wide swing towards the north, moving back to take cover in a patch of fallen timber lying on the crest of the first hill. When the soldiers were below this timber, the Cheyennes opened fire, seriously wounding one trooper, and shooting several horses. The soldiers made a rush for the brush ahead and back of the hill, and fired back at the people from there. The Cheyennes kept the soldiers pinned down until Lieutenant Chase and his Company A rode up.

Chase dismounted, and he and Wessells attempted to circle around the Cheyennes. They moved to within 150 yards of the people before they were discovered. Then the people spotted the soldier chiefs and opened fire on them. Shooting back and forth continued for over an hour. Finally, Wessells ordered the soldiers back to Robinson. He had counted on catching the people early, and had carried no rations and blankets. Now he reasoned that the people could travel only slowly through the snow, therefore the soldiers could catch them later. Vroom moved out first, taking the wounded soldier with him. Chase and his men ate dinner within two hundred yards of the hungry people. Then, after dark, they returned to Robinson.

Earlier in the day, as Chase and his men searched along the bluffs they discovered the trail of half a dozen of the escapees. Chase detailed a corporal and five men to kill or capture them. Next morning the corporal reported that he had found four women, and had brought them as prisoners to Robinson.

Now, as Chase, Wessells, and the others turned back to Robinson, the Cheyenne wolves reported the soldiers gone. Some of the people moved down to butcher the dead horses, the first food they had eaten since Wessells's order six days before. The skins were taken, too. They could be used for moccasins during the flight ahead.

However, the killing was not over. Four more Cheyennes died together in the bluffs. They had been among the first of the escaping people. The soldiers had charged in, cutting them off from the people behind. The troops rode on by without firing a shot. Suddenly the soldiers made a sweeping circle, stopping right in front of these Cheyennes. The troopers jumped from their horses, firing on the people as they dropped to the snow. Some of the Cheyennes were cut down right there. However, the soldiers were standing ten or twelve feet apart, and five young men managed to run through their lines.

The young men had hurried on until they reached the sandstone bluffs, a hundred yards or so away. There were holes in the bluffs, and they hid themselves there. In the distance they could hear the sounds of women and children crying and the crack of rifle fire. These sounds finally stopped, and then there were other noises—the creaking of wagons and the shrill crying of women as they were loaded into them. Later the young men heard more wagons coming, and they heard them leave, this time with the frozen bodies of the dead.

Next morning when they looked out from the bluffs they saw soldiers riding in pursuit of some of the people who had fled past them. This group of Cheyennes were about a mile away. When the soldiers reached them, the young men heard the sounds of rifles and shouting, continuing until sundown.

At sundown, the soldiers rode into the bluffs again. The five young men had one gun and one pistol among them. Soon the soldiers found them and opened fire. The soldiers kept shooting until all the young men were dead except Pumpkin Seed's son, a boy of thirteen or fourteen. As the firing stopped, he looked around, hestitating. He decided that it was better to die than to remain there. He wrapped himself in the blood-soaked blanket of his cousin Charging Bear. Then he climbed down and walked toward the soldiers. An officer rode out, carrying his saber ready for action, but instead of striking down the boy, he stretched out his hand. They shook hands. Then Pumpkin Seed's son was helped up behind a trooper, and he rode with the soldiers back to the post.[20]

During the early afternoon of January 10, smoke was reported within a mile of Bronson's ranch. Second Lieutenant George Baxter and fifteen men had been scouting east of Robinson, looking for trails leading into the bluffs. When they saw the fire, they assumed that only a large band of warriors would risk building a fire so near the post. Baxter dispatched a courier to Robinson, announcing his discovery. Then he dismounted his men and they moved toward the fire in skirmish order.

The fire was deserted, but the tracks of a single man led into the nearby washout. There was no sign of the warrior, and no tracks showing that he had left. After searching the area, Lieutenant Baxter left two troopers near the fire. Then the officer and his men rode up the bluff to look for the Cheyenne trail.

Down below, the two troopers began to ride back and forth, trying to keep warm. In the course of this activity they neared a shallow washout that some of the soldiers had looked into from about twenty feet away. Suddenly they spotted a Cheyenne lying at the bottom, his body wrapped in a strip of dirty canvas the color of the gray clay soil around him. One of the soldiers dismounted and walked toward the man, calling to him to come out. When the old warrior heard the soldier he threw back his canvas blanket and fired two shots with a carbine. The shots caught the soldier in the stomach, and he went over in the snow.

Just then Lieutenant Baxter's detail was reinforced by the arrival of Joseph Lawson and his troop. The soldiers opened fire, and Lawson's men dismounted to charge the old man on foot. It was one man against nearly sixty, but the warrior kept returning the soldier fire. Toward the end, his right hand was hanging useless and he fired his carbine with his left hand, resting the barrel on the edge of the washout. When he finally dropped, the soldiers

[20] *Ibid.*, 423-24.
The son of Pumpkin Seed testimony, "Proceedings . . . ," *loc. cit.*, 10.

258

found he had received four bullets before the fatal shot entered his head.

It was clear that the old man had been heading for Bronson's horse herds, for he still carried a bridle and lariat wrapped around him. His feet had become so badly frozen during the bitter night that he could go no farther. So he built a fire to be warm, and he did it in the open, so that he would not have to wait long to die bravely.

An ambulance had come with Lawson's troop, and the warrior's body was thrown into the boot of it. However, somewhere along the four miles to Robinson the body fell out. A detail of soldiers was sent to recover it, but no one ever found where the brave man finally lay.[21]

Yet some of the people lived. Earlier in the day, Captain Joseph Lawson's cavalry was patrolling twelve miles up White River. They had passed several dead Cheyennes, and they had been passed by two mounted civilians going in the other direction. Afterward Lawson's men had ridden past a wagon gathering up the dead and the captain, also, had seen the ragged wounds in the heads of those who had been scalped.

Finally the soldiers discovered the trails of two Cheyennes. They never located one of them, but the tracks of the other led up the ice that covered the river. Lawson sent in a man to see where the moccasin prints ended. The trooper found a little girl, seven or eight years old. She was sitting all alone in the snow, playing with a deck of cards. A soldier lifted her gently, and Lawson and his men escorted her back to the post. There she survived to carry on the Cheyenne way.

Soon after Lawson returned from this mission, he received Lieutenant Baxter's message of fire on the bluff south of the river. Lawson rode out at top speed to where the fire was burning, and his men joined in shooting down the one old man who fought as bravely as a bear.

It was a day of both death and unexpected life for the people.

[21] Second Lieutenant George Baxter testimony, *ibid.*, 130–31. Bronson, *op. cit.*, 187–92.

The morning of January 11, the Cheyennes saw the black shadows of men and horses moving across the white sweep of snow-covered prairie as the troops approached the bluffs. The people still needed horses, and wolves had slipped away to scout the most likely places to get them. There was a herd at Bluff Station, west on the trail running from Laramie to Deadwood. There was also the chance that some white travelers might be riding the Hat Creek road to the north. The Bluff Station road was more dangerous, because the soldiers guarded it.

The day brought little more than shooting back and forth. Captain Lawson arrived with his men first. He ordered a non-commissioned officer and six men to the right of the bluff, and sent another party of seven men to the left, to locate the Cheyenne trail in case the people had escaped. The Cheyennes were very much still there. They opened fire on one party, bringing down a soldier horse. Lawson quickly moved his men to the bluffs on the west. There he exchanged shots with the people until Wessells arrived.

When Wessells dismounted he took an interpreter with him and the two men crawled to within easy hearing distance of the people. The interpreter shouted the soldier chief's offer; if the Cheyennes would send out their women and children, they would be well cared for.

The people's answer was a carbine shot.

Wessells moved his men beyond Lawson's troopers. However, the distance was too great for bullets to have any effect. One of Lawson's men was mortally wounded by accident. A sergeant was slipping his carbine into the boot of his saddle when the gun went off, the bullet hitting the other soldier.

One of the Cheyennes managed to bring down Captain Vroom's horse, but the people received no comfort from that. When night came, Wessells ordered Lawson to return to Robinson; but before he left, Lawson ordered a detail of men to burn the horse to cinders, so the Cheyennes would not be able to eat the animal.

Back at Robinson, Lieutenant Cummings noted that another Cheyenne man was killed that day.

That night the people moved on toward Pine Ridge, traveling as far as their weakened legs could carry them during the dark hours. They still had no horses, and their march was in the direction of Hat Creek road. Next day a party of four or five warriors scouting for horses paused to build a fire at the bottom of a ravine. An advance guard from Lieutenant Chase's company discovered them, and the soldiers opened fire. The wolves retreated down the ravine, taking cover in the rifle pits they had dug to protect the back trail of the fleeing people.

Chase ordered Corporal Ore and four soldiers to circle the ravine, hoping to surprise the Cheyenne wolves from the rear. The scouts saw these soldiers and brought down the corporal. Lieutenants Chase and Simpson moved on after the main body of the people, leaving behind a sergeant and a dozen men to keep the scouts pinned down in their rifle pits. That night the soldiers recovered the corporal's body and his carbine, so the people did not even capture one more rifle to protect them in their flight.

Meanwhile, Lieutenants Chase and Simpson pushed on after the main body of Cheyennes. The trail was easy to follow, although the soldiers lost it for a time beneath the hoofprints of a herd of cattle. Finally they discovered the imprint of a hole made by the stick that a lame Cheyenne was using to support him. When Chase and Simpson saw this, they sent Sergeant Taggart and four men to scout the opposite side of the creek. Chase pushed on in advance. The soldiers followed the people across a ravine and up onto a level stretch of prairie. Another ravine lay ahead of them.

As the soldiers neared the second ravine, the Cheyennes abruptly appeared above its crest and opened fire on Chase's men. The troops dismounted, and most of them found cover in a gulch. However, the Cheyennes succeeded in wounding a trooper and three horses. Chase dispatched a courier to Robinson for reinforcements, and Captain Vroom and his company arrived about 1:00 A.M. About 10:00 A.M. on January 13, Captain Wessells brought up a Napoleon gun.

Wessells ordered his men to surround the people. Then the Napoleon gun was moved into position so that it pointed at the Cheyenne rifle pits at the bottom of the ravine. Lieutenant Chase fired twelve or fifteen shells into the pits, and the shells burst immediately over them. The soldiers moved down afterward and found the pits filled with iron and shell fragments, but no Cheyennes were killed. The Cheyenne scouts had quietly withdrawn, joining the others in rifle pits near the crest of the ravine. Finally, after they had fired forty or more shells at the people, the soldiers ran out of ammunition.[22]

That night, Wessells ordered the troopers to camp on the spot. He later testified that he thought it would be wise to allow the Cheyennes to move out of the hills and onto the prairie, where the cavalry could overtake them.

The Cheyennes did move that night. Hidden by the darkness, they hurried out onto the plain. Then they headed for the rugged bluffs again, and moved farther back into the protecting walls of rock where the soldiers never had been able to reach them.

Next morning, Wessells found that the people had escaped again. He also found that he was out of food, because his supply train had overturned on the icy slopes of the road. Again he ordered the soldiers back to Robinson.

So the flight northwest continued, with the soldiers driving the people farther and farther away from Pine Ridge Agency. The Cheyennes kept close to the bluffs along Hat Creek. When night fell, they climbed down to the open prairie, moving fast, killing what beef or game they could find. When daylight came, they climbed back into the bluffs. From there they could look out over

[22] Chase testimony, "Proceedings . . . ," *loc. cit.*, 36–37; Second Lieutenant George Baxter testimony, *ibid.*, 131.

Bronson, *op. cit.*, 194, says that Captain Wessells and Lieutenants Crawford and Hardie crept near the rifle pits with an interpreter. They called to the Cheyennes to bring out their women and children, promising them shelter and protection. The Cheyennes' answer was a feeble volley.

the country, and they could fire what little ammunition they had left whenever the soldiers came too close.

All was quiet for them on January 15 and 16. The soldiers were still on their trail, but the people managed to keep ahead of their pursuers.

On January 16, Wessells sent Woman's Dress and the mixed-blood John Shangreau to ride in front of the soldiers. These were dangerous men, men who knew the people far better than did the soldier chiefs. Nineteen men remained among the fleeing Cheyennes; nineteen men including the boys. There were fifteen women and children, Hog's Daughter, Singing Cloud, and Brave One among them. Little Wolf's scouts had lost contact with them. Morning Star had disappeared in the snow along White River the first night. Bridge, the old Ree doctor, was dead. Hog was in irons. There remained only the young men such as Little Finger Nail, Roman Nose, Young Magpie, Young Medicine Man, Pug Nose the southerner, and Bear.

Next day the soldiers rode out along the base of the bluffs, but some distance out from the cliffs. Woman's Dress and Shangreau were ahead when they spotted the Cheyennes. The people were waiting for the soldiers near a high chimney of rock, one of the strongest positions they had been able to find yet.

When the scouts and soldiers were in close, the Cheyennes opened fire. The army horses reared and plunged, and one private was killed. This time the Cheyennes were able to capture the soldier's arms. Pug Nose was killed, too. Shangreau shot him down when he moved out to parley with the soldier scouts. Small Woman, also, was hit by a bullet. In the past she had often helped by carrying some wounded child through the darkness. Now she and Pug Nose were buried near each other in the rocks.[23]

That night the people moved farther into the bluffs. There was no time to pause for mourning.

[23] Sandoz, *Cheyenne Autumn*, 229.
Lieutenant Cummings reported one man and one woman killed in the Indian stronghold that day.

In the soldier camps, a report came to Wessells that there was a large herd of horses at Bluff Station, about twelve miles away on the Fort Laramie and Black Hills road. Wessells dispatched Captain Lawson to ride there with his company and gather up all the horses roaming in the vicinity, so the Cheyennes could not capture any of the stage stock.

The soldiers kept on pursuing, kept on driving the people before them. Elsewhere there had been official and public dissatisfaction with Wessells for his slowness in recapturing the Cheyennes. As a consequence, Major A. W. Evans started up from Fort Laramie to assume command. Two fresh companies of the Third Cavalry rode ahead of him. They joined Wessells's command the afternoon of January 18. Later that day, Wessells and his men rode up to Bluff Station. There he reported to Major Evans, who assumed command of the entire expedition.

Then the soldiers made ready for the kill.

On January 19, the Cheyennes were reported to have crossed the stage road. Captain Lawson and his company rode out to reconnoiter along the bluffs. They covered about twelve miles, but could find no way to cross the wall of rock.

The next day Captains Wessells and Lawson led their companies along the base of the bluffs, heading in the direction of Hat Creek. A wagon train followed them. They continued for some twenty miles, searching the low ground for the people's moccasin prints. Wessells and Lawson went into camp about 5:00 P.M., about eleven miles from Bluff Station. Soon after dark, Lieutenant Chase and his command rode in. They had ridden out from Robinson at a fast pace.

Elsewhere, Major Evans had led the companies from Laramie along the crest of the line of bluffs. They, also, were heading in the direction of Hat Creek crossing. Shangreau again located the Cheyennes, this time on a high point of rocks. There was some firing back and forth, the Cheyenne shots few compared to those of the soldiers, since the people were nearly out of ammunition. Evans immediately dispatched a messenger to Wessells, sending word of what had happened.

That evening, some of the Cheyennes were able to slip by the soldiers and kill a beef. The people made preparations for the final run through the encircling soldiers. Then, in the darkness, they slipped down from the bluffs and fled up the valley.

By this time the cold that had brought them such suffering at Robinson had turned into warmer weather. There was new misery now. The snow was melting and the prairie was wet and soggy underfoot. The warriors flanked the women and children as they hurried along, just as they had done in earlier, prouder marches. The women and children were carrying what dry meat they had been able to prepare in the midst of the constant flight. Some of the men carried clubs, and there were some knives, as well as a few guns—the soldier weapon captured three days before among them. However, cartridges were too scarce for the guns to be of any real protection.

Soon after daybreak on January 21 the soldiers scattered, searching along the foot of the bluffs for the Cheyenne trail. Wessells turned both companies over to Lieutenant Chase and rode back to check on the wagon train. Woman's Dress and Shangreau rode off to examine the prairie beneath the bluff the people had held the day before. For a while the soldiers thought the people might still be there. Then the scouts found where the Cheyennes had climbed down from the bluffs. Soon Shangreau and Woman's Dress announced that they could not follow the trail any longer, because the people had scattered across the prairie where the snow had melted. Chase believed the Cheyennes might still be in the bluff, and he continued to scout that general area.

After Woman's Dress and Shangreau announced that they had lost the Cheyenne trail, Lieutenant Chase decided to deploy two companies of men in two skirmish lines, five to seven yards apart. The soldiers moved out some four miles, carefully examining the country as they went. During this advance, a sergeant and a corporal discovered a trail in a sandy ravine that ran toward the south. Then, shortly before the companies reassembled, Chase found the beef the Cheyennes had killed the night before.

Chase deployed a corporal and four men to move down a ravine leading to the right. Another corporal and four men of Chase's own company were sent to the left to search for any signs of the people. After these soldiers had left, a courier arrived from Wessells, telling Chase to hold his position until Wessells arrived in person.

When Wessells arrived, he ordered the soldiers to march in columns of twos toward a hilltop about two and a half miles away. Woman's dress had dismounted there to scout the country, but when the soldiers rode up, he reported no sign of the trail.

Wessells advanced two or three miles in the direction that Chase supposed the earlier-discovered trail led, then decided to return to camp with his wagon train on Hat Creek road.

However, just before Chase had deployed the two skirmish lines, a courier had arrived to say that Major Evans ordered Wessells to camp his command around the bluff in order to cut off any attempted Cheyenne escape. Evans, of course, did not realize that the people already had left the area. Now Chase repeated this order to Wessells. When Wessells heard it, he ordered a detail of twenty men formed from each of the three companies. With Wessells in command, accompanied by Lieutenants Baxter and Chase, the three companies rode out to surround the bluff.

While they were moving into position, Wessells saw a campfire in a ravine about a mile to the rear. Some of the soldiers investigated and found a detachment from Wessells's own company. Chase had sent them out to scout the previous afternoon. They had lost their way in the dark and had not been able to locate Wessells's camp.

These soldiers reported that they had discovered moccasin tracks crossing a prairie-dog town. The tracks led in the general direction that Chase's skirmish lines had ridden, and they were about ten miles from the soldier wagon train. At just that point, Wessells spied the reflection of a campfire at exactly the place where the Cheyennes ought to be according to this description.

Wessells ordered his command down from the bluff. Then he

left instructions for the soldiers to be ready to move out as early as possible in the morning carrying all the rations they could manage on horseback.

By daylight on January 22 the Cheyennes had reached the north side of a deep dry creek. Here they took refuge in a washout, one that was gouged out near the edge of the bluffs. They were thirty-five or forty miles from Robinson now, and the soldiers had been pursuing them for thirteen days.

Their refuge was a hole about fifty feet long, twelve feet wide, and five feet deep. The women dug into the frozen sides with their knives, enlarging their hiding places a bit. The men threw up rough breastworks, piling sod before them so that the defenses blended into the winter grass and brush around them. In spite of this shelter, the people still were open to attack from three sides. Here they waited for the soldiers.

The moccasin tracks across the prairie-dog village pointed the soldiers squarely in the direction of the people's hiding place. The cavalry started out at 7:00 A.M. Again, Shangreau and Woman's Dress, with two soldiers, rode in advance. The Cheyennes could hear them coming and they prepared to die as bravely as they could. Now they looked at each other for the last time, remembering each other's faces. A woman stroked the cheek of a frightened but silent child. Then the young men moved quietly to the edge of the washout. The women strong enough to help stood behind them. The older people and the children were huddled in a deep spot at the middle of the washout. No soldier fire could reach them unless the bullet was fired down from the very edge of the incline. Then the people began softly singing the old strong-heart songs, the songs that other brave ones before them had sung when they looked death in the face.

The four soldier scouts continued their advance along the little creek. When it appeared that they were surely discovered, the Cheyennes opened fire. Woman's Dress was hit, the bullet knocking him down. The horse of a soldier with him was killed, and a Cheyenne bullet wounded the trooper as he ran for cover.

267

Shangreau and the others pulled back quickly. Wessells ordered Sergeant Taggart and a few men of Lieutenant Chase's company to dismount and cover the scouts' retreat.

At the same time, Wessells ordered Chase and his company to charge the people on horseback. Some five hundred yards separated the Cheyennes from the soldiers at this point. Soon Wessells ordered Chase to dismount his men and hold the ground they occupied.

Wessells dismounted his other three companies and divided them so that all the exposed sides of the washout could be fired upon. For nearly three hours the soldiers remained at these positions, pouring bullets in on the Cheyennes. The people returned the fire sporadically.

Finally Wessells ordered Chase to prepare to charge the washout with him. While Chase was moving into position, a Cheyenne bullet killed Sergeant Taggart. When Chase was finally in position, he found that his men were open to fire on three sides. He decided not to wait for Wessells's arrival, and ordered an immediate advance on the Cheyennes.

The people waited until Chase's men were only a dozen yards away. Then they opened fire. As Chase's men reached the crest of the washout, some of the warriors raised themselves up. Volleys were exchanged simultaneously, and another soldier was killed. A third was killed soon afterward.

Chase's company moved to within five yards of the washout. Then the soldiers fired two or three volleys into it. When Captain Wessells saw this action, he moved his own company up at double time. Within five or ten minutes, the people were surrounded.

Twice Wessells ordered the soldier firing to cease while he called to the Cheyennes to surrender and come out. Their only answer was a few shots.

For nearly three-quarters of an hour this close fighting continued. The Cheyennes had to jump up above the breastworks in order to see where to aim. Most of them were firing blindly, reaching up a hand to shoot the rifle or pistol over the edge of the washout. The Cheyenne men fell, one after another, as the soldier fire continued. As one dropped, another grabbed his gun. The women helped with the reloading as best they could, as long as there was any lead left to fire.

Finally even the sporadic shots from the washout stopped. When it seemed that the people really were finished, Chase and Wessells ordered their men to follow them to the crest of the washout. The soldiers held back, and Chase finally had to call out the names of men he could trust. Wessells did the same. Then the two officers moved up to the very edge of the pit, their pistols cocked. As they approached, a warrior raised his head above the dead bodies lying around him. He fired at the soldiers, and they returned his shot at the same time. Wessells staggered, caught in the head by the Cheyenne bullet. Chase caught him, and ran back with him about fifteen yards.

Then Chase shouted for a foot charge from all sides. The soldiers ran right to the edge of the washout, firing some two hundred shots into it. They retreated six or eight yards to reload, and then they charged again. For nearly fifteen minutes after Wessells was wounded this deadly charging, firing, and retreating continued. Rising above the crack of the rifles, the high, thin death songs of the people cut the air until they, too, were gone. Finally the soldiers pulled back from the stinking, blinding powder smoke that filled the washout, covering the crumpled Cheyenne bodies like a black blanket.

There was quiet for a few moments. Then all at once three dirt-covered and blood-stained Cheyennes jumped out. Their only arms were an empty pistol and two knives, but they charged the hundred troopers surrounding them. Soldier bullets riddled them, and the three brave men lay sprawled on the winter ground near the dry stream.[24]

When the air had cleared and they were sure the three young men were dead, the troops approached the washout. They stood there on the edge, gazing down at the bloody bodies that covered

[24] Chase's testimony says two men charged the soldiers. Bronson, *op. cit.*, 196, says three. Sandoz, *Cheyenne Autumn*, 236–37, identifies them as Little Finger Nail, Roman Nose, and Bear.

the bottom. Captain Lawson was among the first to look into the pit. He saw a little girl, her eyes turned imploringly up at him. He leaped in on the Cheyenne bodies, took the child by the hand, and gently helped her out. Then he also took an older woman's hand, assisting her to rise up from among the dead. He called on his men to help out those who were wounded and still alive.

All the young men died there. There were seventeen in all, and one mortally wounded, who died the next day. Surgeon C. V. Pettys bandaged his bullet-shattered leg. The soldier doctor asked, through the interpreter, if he could do anything more for him. The wounded man answered that he only wanted to die; he only wanted to be thrown into the pit where the others had died.[25]

Four women and two little children were dead too, Brave One and Singing Cloud among them. Seven women and children were carried from the pit alive. Some were wounded, one of them mortally. Hog's once-lovely daughter was among them; shot in the neck, she was bloody and wild-eyed now.

After the dead were removed from the washout, the soldiers laid them side by side and counted them. As Little Finger Nail's body was being moved, they noticed something on his back. It was the ledger book filled with paintings of soldiers and warriors moving against each other in battle. The right side of the book was torn, shredded by the bullets that had passed through it into Little Finger Nail's own body.

Lieutenant Cummings counted the bodies stretched out on the earth. Then he added their number to his list of the people who died in the flight from Robinson. The final line read:

Total killed and died of wounds: 39 men and 22 women and children.[26]

The next day a detachment of soldiers buried these last Cheyennes who chose death back home in the north country.

[25] Acting Assistant Surgeon C. V. Pettys testimony, "Proceedings . . . ," *loc. cit.*, 138.
[26] The summary of the Proceedings gives the Cheyenne deaths as sixty-four. Seventy-eight were captured and in confinement. Seven—Morning Star and his family—were unaccounted for. Eleven soldiers were killed or died from wounds. Wessells and nine enlisted men were wounded.

But the matter did not end with the burial of the dead. General Crook immediately ordered Major Andrew Evans, Third Cavalry, Captain John M. Hamilton, Fifth Cavalry, and First Lieutenant Walter S. Schuyler, Crook's aide-de-camp, to ascertain both the facts of the outbreak and the causes that led to it. The hearings began at Robinson on January 25, three days after the last of the fighting on the Warbonnet.

The Cheyennes were questioned first—those who would speak about it. A woman captured in the final fighting told of the flight north, and of how they survived after food was denied them. She also stated that at the time Major Evans's soldiers attacked, the men had decided to send the women back. The women were to flee toward Red Cloud, while the warriors stayed out. They had planned to separate the evening of the day of that last battle on the Warbonnet.

The soldier chiefs then asked her about a little girl who was found with a knife wound in her neck. The woman replied that the child had been stabbed by her own mother during that last fighting. Then the mother had stabbed herself.

Old Crow spoke, and he repeated that none of the Cheyennes would return south because of the starvation and sickness there. Then Hog and Left Hand were examined together. They spoke of the terrible conditions in the south, and, briefly, of the flight north. Hog said that he and some young men had come to a white man's house. Hog had kept the young men quiet, and the white man had fed them. The young men had obtained clothing somewhere and had brought it to the women. But he could not always control the young men, Hog added.

The following day, January 26, Blacksmith quietly spoke of the trip north and the flight from the barrack. Captain Wessells had told the Cheyennes to go south. They thought that if they went south they would all die; so they might as well die here, he told the soldier chiefs.

Pumpkin Seed's thirteen-year-old boy also spoke. Then a woman and her two children, who surrendered at Robinson two weeks after the outbreak, told how they survived on a little tallow and corn. Her husband had thrown her away in the south, so she came north because "people were starving and dying off." Red Feather and The Enemy, two more women, were examined together. Each had lost a child while the people were in the south.

The wounded Tangle Hair (Big Head) appeared before the soldier chiefs only briefly. He ended by saying,

> Now you have killed nearly all the Cheyennes and these few women and children are all that are left, we beg you to have mercy on us and spare this remnant.[27]

The Cheyenne testimony ended in two days, and the Board of Officers began to call the soldiers, officers, and civilians.

The proceedings finally adjourned on February 7. The board pointed out that certain errors had been committed. However,

> Beyond that [the Board] attaches no blame to anyone in the Military Service, and in view of all the circumstances of this unfortunate business, of the manifest fact that collision with these Indians and consequent loss of life was unavoidable; of the evident desire of everyone concerned to carry out the orders of the Government in the most effective and yet most humane manner; and of the probability that no one else—of equal experience or judgment—could have done any better, respectfully recommends that no action be taken . . . .[28]

Crook forwarded the record of the proceedings to the assistant adjutant general. He had nothing to add to them, and approved them, he wrote.

After the terrible struggle to reach Pine Ridge, some of the people finally were permitted to go there. Of the men, only a handful remained alive. Wild Hog, Old Crow, Left Hand, and Porcupine had been handcuffed in the prison tent when the others broke from the barrack. Tangle Hair, Noisy Walker or Old Man, Blacksmith, The Sioux, and Young Stub Foot were the men who

[27] Big Head testimony, *ibid.*, 27.
[28] *Ibid.*, 215.

had survived the fighting without fatal wounds or mutilations. On January 31, 1879, the crippled remnant climbed into the five canvas-covered wagons that would carry them to Pine Ridge, sixty-five miles away. Red Cloud had asked for the survivors, and Crook had agreed to his request. There were forty-eight women and children and a few old ones—about fifty-eight people in all. They were covered with wounds and still gaunt from hunger.

All was going quietly until the wagons reached the lower camp. Here Wild Hog, Old Crow, Left Hand, and the other men— fifteen in all—still were held in irons. Lieutenant G. W. Dodd, who was in charge of the Indian scouts, was waiting to add the remaining women and children with relatives among the Sioux. Suddenly the Cheyenne women who had to remain behind began to weep and to gesticulate. Wild Hog's wife, with half a dozen others, stood screaming and weeping on a small hill behind the camp. Her ragged clothing flapped in the wind as she waved her lean and shriveled arms in mourning and despair.

Lieutenant Dodd ordered their lodges searched. No Flesh, the Sioux soldier scout, was asked to disarm Hog's wife. When he approached her, she began striking her breast violently with both hands. Then it was discovered that she was clutching half of a sharp-pointed pair of scissors in one hand. With the other, she was stabbing herself with a broken fork. Only the middle prong remained, but it was sharpened like a stiletto. When Hog's wife was finally disarmed, she was taken to a nearby tent. There it was found that she had tried to kill one of her own children and that she had stamped on all the others, crying that she would kill every child there.

After the soldiers took care of her, someone looked in on Wild Hog himself. He was lying on the floor of his tent, unconscious and covered with blood. Surgeon Pettys, who was in the midst of his testimony before the Board of Officers at Robinson, was called to attend to him. He found Wild Hog suffering from several wounds near the sternum and below the heart. In spite of being manacled, he had managed to stab himself four times, apparently with the other half of the sharp broken scissors his wife had used

273

on herself. He had hoped that if he killed himself, his wife and children would be sent to Pine Ridge with the others.

That evening about ten o'clock, Lieutenant Dodd and a reporter from the *Chicago Tribune* visited Wild Hog's flimsy prison tent. Hog was breathing heavily and moaning with pain, even though Dr. Pettys had administered morphia to him. Corporal Lewis gave the wounded man another pill, and he spoke kindly to him.

Hog's wife, wild and terrified still, was sitting at the doorway. Her face slashed by a wound beneath the right eye, she stared out the opening.

Hog's daughter lay slumped in exhausted sleep, her face near the burning wood fire. Her neck was gashed by the raw bullet wound she had received in the last fighting. She lay there head to head with her father. Suddenly she awoke with a shrill cry of pain. Seeing the soldiers through the smoke of the fire, she began to scream hysterically, thrashing about as if she again felt the rain of bullets that cut down the people inside the pit on the Warbonnet. Finally she quieted down again, and the *Tribune* correspondent withdrew.[29] Despite their pitiful condition, all three survived their wounds.

In February, more wagons left Robinson. This group was headed for Sidney, Nebraska, and a special railroad car that was to carry seven of the men to Leavenworth. There they were to face trial for their part in the fighting along the Beaver and Sappa. Wild Hog, Tangle Hair, Left Hand, Old Crow, Porcupine, Blacksmith, and Noisy Walker all climbed stiffly aboard. Some fourteen women and children were with them. The men still wore manacles.

But the wind was shifting to a better direction. Much public sentiment had been aroused in favor of the people after the shootings at Robinson. In Kansas, attorneys came forward to

[29] *Chicago Tribune*, February 6, 1879, 11; and February 11, 1879, 6.
Pettys testimony, "Proceedings . . . ," *loc. cit.*, 137. Hog and the others arrived in Omaha on February 10.

defend the Cheyennes without charge. By autumn of 1879, Wild Hog's irons had been removed and he and the other men freed for want of evidence. They were taken south for a time, but eventually were allowed to return to Pine Ridge. There, about the end of 1889, Hog sickened with pneumonia. This time he did not win his battle.[30]

Morning Star finally reached Pine Ridge, too. The night of the outbreak he had hurried through the snow with his daughters and Pawnee Woman, his wife. Bull Hump followed with his own wife and child and Great Eyes, his father-in-law. Red Bird kept up with them as best he could. He had been wounded in the knee during the rush from the barrack, but he still carried Great Eyes' sacred shield on his back. Calf, Morning Star's grandson, and two other young warriors were with them, also.

Near White River, one of Morning Star's daughters had been hit. She urged the others to go on. Little Hump and his sister had dropped back then, and they had died between White River and the bluffs.

North of the river, Morning Star and the others had turned away from the path most of the Cheyennes followed. They had climbed up a gully into the bluffs. Once the soldiers almost discovered their trail. Then Great Eyes dropped back, holding off the soldiers until one of their bullets killed him. The others escaped in the darkness.

Finally Morning Star led them to a huge hole in the rocks. They hid there for ten days, almost starving to death. Then they started for Pine Ridge.

Red Bird's wound was too bad for him to move as quickly as

[30] Sandoz, *Cheyenne Autumn, 270,* says he returned north with Little Chief's people. However, Hog's name does not appear on the list of Little Chief's band transferred to Pine Ridge Agency in October, 1881. Tangle Hair's name is there. It is possible that Hog was among the group of about eighty people who quietly joined Little Chief's band on the way north. Or, it is possible he came north with Standing Elk's band, who followed Little Chief's band to Pine Ridge several months later. Wild Hog died between the census of Northern Cheyennes at Pine Ridge in June, 1889, and the same census dated July 1, 1890.

the others must travel in order to cross the open country ahead, so the boy remained in the cave alone, with only the power of the sacred shield to protect him. He managed to cut two sticks for crutches, and many days later he hobbled into the house of John Shettler, a mile and a half below Robinson. He was nearly starved, but he still bore the sacred shield on his back. Afterward, he was sent to Pine Ridge.[31]

Meanwhile, Morning Star and the others were moving northeast. For eighteen days they traveled at night, eating what few roots they could find and some sinew that one of the women had hidden. Finally they ate their own moccasin tops, chewing the leather for what little sustenance was left in it. Finally they stumbled into Gus Craven's place. Craven was married to a Sioux woman, and the Cheyennes had known him when he was around old Red Cloud Agency. Craven and his wife fed Morning Star and his family, and they rested for a while. The next night they were taken to the house of William Rowland, now the interpreter at Pine Ridge. Rowland saw to it that they were quietly slipped in among Red Cloud's people.

A lodge was erected for Morning Star under a little bluff on Wounded Knee Creek. Meat, blankets, and wood were carried there for him. When he had rested for two days, he asked what had happened at Robinson. Then he was finally told how few of the people remained alive. His wounded daughter was brought to him, and one of the women who was lifted from the blood-soaked washout on the Warbonnet spoke to him of that last fighting.

Afterward, Morning Star sat for hours on the crest of the bluff near his lodge.[32]

Finally, at the request of General Miles himself, Morning Star was allowed to return home. The old Chief led his crippled, orphaned band back to the valley of the Rosebud. Sorrowing and embittered, he lived on there until 1883. Then the people carried

[31] Grinnell, *The Cheyenne Indians*, I, 194.
[32] Grinnell, *The Fighting Cheyennes*, 426. Sandoz, *Cheyenne Autumn*, 244–47. Bronson, *op. cit.*, 196.

his body to a high butte towering above the pine-blanketed hills near the Rosebud.[33]

[33] Later George Bird Grinnell had the bodies of both Morning Star and Little Wolf reinterred. They now lie side by side in Lame Deer cemetery.

18. Is'siwun Comes North

While the people of Little Wolf
and Morning Star were dying in the south, the Cheyennes at
Fort Keogh remained contented. White Bull and Brave Wolf had
become the first scouts to enlist with Miles, and they fought
against Lame Deer and his Minniconjou Sioux band in May,
1877. Then in September about thirty scouts, Cheyennes and a
few Sioux, left Fort Keogh to help the soldiers fight Chief Joseph's
fleeing Nez Percés. Two Moon, Brave Wolf, Bob Tailed Horse,
Shot in the Head (White Wolf), and Magpie Eagle were among
these scouts.

Meanwhile, in spite of Miles's promise that all the Cheyennes
who surrendered to him could remain in the north, Washington

had other plans. Some forty lodges of the people were allowed to remain near Fort Keogh.[1] Most of them were army scouts and their families. Two Moon and White Bull were the principal men. However, in autumn of 1877, Little Chief and his followers were ordered to move to the south.

They reached Fort Abraham Lincoln, Dakota, in December, 1877. There they remained as prisoners of war until July 24, 1878. Then, escorted by two companies of the Seventh Cavalry, they began to ride westward toward Bear Butte. Ben Clark, who had been Custer's chief of scouts at the Washita, rode with them. He had a Cheyenne wife and spoke the language well.[2]

At Bear Butte, other companies of the Seventh were in cantonment immediately north of the mountain. A pause was made here, and some of the Cheyennes climbed to the summit of the Sacred Mountain, where they left offerings. Others fasted and prayed, gaining power for the hard, new days that lay ahead. Then the Cheyennes began the march south to Sidney Barracks, Nebraska. Troopers of the Seventh Cavalry continued to escort them.[3]

The trip was quiet until they neared old Red Cloud Agency. There Black Wolf and Iron Shirt declared that they would go no farther; that they wished to remain at Red Cloud. However, the commanding officer refused their request, and the Cheyennes moved on south. They reached Sidney Barracks about September 14, 1878. By that time, the people of Little Wolf and Morning Star were fighting their way northward, but the two bands never met.[4]

On October 20, Little Chief's band rode out of Sidney Barracks, with Captain Mauck and four troops of the Fourth Cavalry escorting them. They reached the Cheyenne and Arapaho Agency in Indian Territory on December 9.

[1] George Bent to Hyde, October 16, 1906, Coe Collection.
[2] The documents relating to this move are printed in Dennis Collins, *The Indians' Last Fight or the Dull Knife Raid*, 312–15.
Cf. Hugh Scott, *Some Memories of a Soldier*, 88–90; and Hugh Scott, "A Report to the Secretary of the Interior," September 5, 1919, MS., Hugh Scott Papers, National Anthropological Archives, Smithsonian Institution.
[3] Scott, "A Report," *loc. cit.*
[4] Sandoz, *Cheyenne Autumn*, 114–15, records a meeting between two men of Little Chief's band and Little Wolf's people.

It was not long before they discovered that they, too, found it impossible to endure life in the hot south country. Jonathan Miles, the agent for the Cheyennes and Arapahoes, feared an outbreak, and in May, 1879, Little Chief and five other representatives were allowed to travel to Washington. Agent Miles and Ben Clark went with them. The Cheyennes presented their grievances to Secretary of the Interior Carl Schurz, and to E. A. Hayt, the commissioner of Indian affairs. Little Chief insisted that Miles and his officers had told them that they would be allowed to return north if they were not happy in Indian Territory.

Commissioner Hayt wrote of that meeting:

> Little Chief was very earnest in the presentation of his case, and was sustained by the other members of the delegation. For some time it appeared doubtful whether they would voluntarily consent to go back to the Indian Territory, but by perseveringly following their arguments and making plain the requirements of the law in their case, their full consent was finally obtained, and they went back to their homes cheerfully and with the evident intention of remaining there quietly and peacefully; which they have so far done.[5]

This quotation alone indicates a bit of Hayt's naïveté when it came to dealing with the Northern Cheyennes. However, Jonathan Miles had a better understanding of the fact that Little Chief's people would not relinquish their longing for the north country. Agent Miles wrote in 1879:

> The discontent of Little Chief's band became so apparent during early spring as to threaten another Dull Knife affair, unless something could be done to satisfy them of the good intentions of the government . . .
>
> It was promised Little Chief, while in Washington, that the balance of the Northern Cheyennes remaining north should be sent south, and it is due that this promise should be carried out at the proper time, or that he should be permitted to return north himself. Divided as they are, there will be always an excuse for

[5] *Annual Report of the Commissioner of Indian Affairs to the Secretary of the Interior*, 1879, xviii.

passing back and forth, and so long as one Northern Cheyenne is permitted to remain north, there will be discontent among those here, and as a result, an obstruction to their progress here.[6]

A year later, Agent Miles wrote that a number of the Northern Cheyennes were clinging to the belief that they would be allowed to return north, "This belief is the outgrowth of absolute promises made to them by unauthorized parties," he added, making an oblique reference to Colonel Miles's pledge when the Cheyennes surrendered at Tongue River.[7]

By this time, Little Wolf's band and the remnant of Morning Star's people had been permitted to settle near Fort Keogh. Indeed, Dull Knife had been allowed to settle there at the request of Miles himself. This was all the proof that Little Chief's followers needed to keep alive the hope that they would also return north. With this hope in mind, Little Chief refused to place his children in school. Such a course would have been "a virtual abandonment of his plans and purposes—to accept no home as permanent, except in Powder river or vacinity [sic]," Agent Miles wrote in 1880.[8]

So Little Chief's people waited. While they did, they still looked forward to the return of the buffalo. By this time the southern herd had been all but wiped out. Even so, for the Cheyennes it still seemed incomprehensible that the great herds could be gone forever, especially when Is'siwun's buffalo power lived on among the people. Therefore, in July, 1881, Little Chief, Little Robe, Bob Tail, Jake, and Wild Horse led some of the Cheyennes to the north fork of Red River. There the Kiowas were gathering for the Sun Dance. The Kiowa village was alive with expectation, for Buffalo Coming Out, a Kiowa medicine man, had vowed to bring back the buffalo.[9]

The Kiowas succeeded in killing a buffalo bull and cow before

[6] *Ibid.*, 59.
[7] *Annual Report of the Commissioner of Indian Affairs* . . . , 1880, 67–68.
[8] *Ibid.*, 39.
[9] Alice Marriott, *The Ten Grandmothers*, 142–54; Mooney, *Calendar History*, 219, 349–50. On page 219, Mooney says the buffalo disappeared from the Kiowa country in 1879.

the Sun Dance ceremonies began. This was a good omen in itself, because the buffalo had disappeared from this country. Then the cottonwood tree was felled for the center pole of the Sun Dance lodge. The Kiowas had tied the buffalo bull head to the center pole with great joy, and the people's offerings had been fastened to the head. However, Little Chief's people finally left the Kiowa village in disgust. In spite of all the favorable signs, Buffalo Coming Out's power failed to bring back the buffalo.[10]

The Cheyennes left the camp on August 15, 1881. Later that month, Little Chief and another delegation again were summoned to Washington, where a new administration was in office. In Washington the Cheyennes met with several Sioux delegations. This time Little Chief returned with better news; he was given permission to settle his people among Red Cloud's Oglalas at Pine Ridge.

In Washington, Little Chief's delegation had asked that all the Northern Cheyennes be allowed to return home. That request was refused. However, the promise was made that in the future the request would be made to Congress on behalf of all the Northern Cheyennes remaining in the south. The commissioner of Indian affairs said that for the time being only Little Chief's people would be allowed to go north. Later, the Commissioner gave his reasons for this decision:

> While some of the Cheyennes have been insubordinate and disposed to give trouble, Little Chief, whose influence has been great, has always counseled patience, refusing to sanction any movement looking to the return of the Cheyennes to the north without the consent of the government.
>
> ... When, in the autumn of 1880, some of his young men armed themselves and prepared to go to the agency to unite with other Cheyennes in precipitating a disturbance, Little Chief armed himself and directed his followers to remain in their camp, threatening to kill anyone who should attempt to leave ...
>
> As these Northern Cheyennes have always lived in the North

[10] E. L. Clark to Colonel P. B. Hunt, July 14, 1881; E. L. Clark to J. D. Miles, July 22, July 26, and August 15, 1881, Cheyenne and Arapaho Files, Oklahoma Historical Society.

among the Sioux, and will advance more rapidly than if compelled to remain in Indian Territory, I respectfully recommend that provision be made to permit them to rejoin their relatives.[11]

On October 6, 1881, Little Chief's band started toward Pine Ridge. There were 235 people in all. Among the prominent men were American Horse, White Shield, Iron Shirt, and Young Little Wolf. Elk River, the old and respected horse catcher, also was with them. He was one of the few who could recall the day Mahuts were captured by the Pawnees.[12]

Chief Black Wolf and his Suhtai band rode with Little Chief's followers. Coal Bear was leading the Suhtai people, his wife bearing the Sacred Buffalo Hat upon her back. Box Elder rode in their midst, the sacred wheel lance cradled in his arms as the horses slowly moved northward.

Charles Sitting Man was among the young men of Black Wolf's band. Three years before, his family had started north with Little Wolf and Morning Star. His father, Holy or Doll Man, had been sick then, and had not been able to stand the trip, so the family turned back. Now Doll Man and his family were heading north again. This time the journey was a peaceful one. Years later, Charles Sitting Man would recall it:

> I remember when we started north. A troop of soldiers came with us. Also a doctor. They had many wagons to move our belongings. Though the Indians were early risers, the soldiers were already moving, tearing down the camp before daylight.
>
> As usual, the Sacred Hat Woman carried the sacred bundle on her back. In the morning, Coal Bear, holding the horse, would have it saddled. The Woman would walk as far as she could, carrying the Hat on her back. When she got tired, she got on the horse. Coal Bear led the horse, riding his own horse. They did that all the way.
>
> As a rule, when camp was ready to move, everybody waited for Coal Bear. No one dared to move until he did.

[11] *Annual Report of the Commissioner of Indian Affairs* . . . , 1881, l–lii.
[12] "List of people enrolled with Little Chief to be transferred to Pine Ridge Agency, Dakota," Cheyenne and Arapaho files, Volume 3, Indian Archives, Oklahoma Historical Society.

I remember one time, when we were half way there, we had excitement. Someone reported that they had seen Utes, who were enemies of the Cheyennes. All the young men got on their ponies, put on their sacred objects, to go fight. They came out, but they could not find anything. They lost track of the Utes. They could be mistaken. Maybe they saw a bunch of antelopes and thought they were Indians. Or the Utes could have seen the army and the Cheyennes, and escaped.

The Cheyennes did not find much difficulty on the way north. The army had many wagons, loaded with supplies: sugar, coffee, other stuff, and a big herd of cattle. They butchered whenever the meat got short. Some of the families who did not have horses rode in the army wagons. Those who had horses rode their own. We had a good time all the way to the end of the trip.

When we got to Fort Robinson, where Dull Knife's people were killed, over the ridge to the east we stopped and put up a camp. We butchered the last beef there. They must have figured just right—how long the beef would last from Oklahoma to that place.

Next morning the camp moved over to the fort. There was excitement there. A man by the name of Red Cherries, a brave man, attacked a soldier, hitting him and forcing him out of the way. But the soldiers did not do anything.

From that camp, people all walked over to the barracks where the Cheyennes were put in prison. We found many bullet holes in the logs. Windows were smashed and the glass was lying still along the edge of the house. They didn't kill all who came out of those barracks. Some were wounded and pulled through and lived a long time.

We also saw a place where the dead were buried. They dug a long hole and loaded the dead in that great pit—men, women, and children. There was snow on the ground when these were killed; so they reloaded dirt in the hole. But the wounded got good care; they saved them.

Those that were killed at Fort Robinson: there is only one alive today. That is Little Coyote's wife. She is the only survivor.[13]

Little Chief's band reached Pine Ridge in December, 1881. When they were enrolled there, it was discovered that eighty-two

[13] To the author, August, 1960.

extra people had joined them along the way, secretly and without permission. The Cheyennes received a cold reception at their new agency, because Valentine T. McGillycuddy, the agent, had no time for Indians who held fast to the old ways. Little Chief's people were determined to remain Cheyenne, and McGillycuddy failed to appreciate such independence. He and the Cheyennes would clash on many occasions in the days ahead. Among the more moderate statements that he made about Little Chief's people were these written to Washington in October, 1882:

> The transfer of the Northern Cheyennes to this agency, as I predicted in my last annual report, has in no way assisted our people toward civilization or progress. They are an insubordinate, uncontrollable, and migratory lot of aborigines. They have done nothing in the way of house building or farming, and spend most of the time in finding fault, loafing and dancing.
>
> I should presume that their former agent in the South has every reason to congratulate himself on having lost this portion of his population . . . .[14]

However, McGillycuddy's fulminations made little impression upon the Cheyennes. Now the people were near the swift flowing waters of the Yellowstone and the scoria-red valley of the Rosebud. For years they had longed for the north country, and here they were almost within reach of it. Suddenly, on September 23, 1882, two hundred Cheyennes bolted Pine Ridge. Most of them were members of Black Wolf's band.[15]

Coal Bear and his wife rode before them, for now Is'siwun, the Sacred Buffalo Hat, was leading the Suhtaio back to the Yellowstone country.

[14] *Annual Report of the Commissioner of Indian Affairs . . .* , 1882, 35.
[15] *Ibid.*

PART TWO

New Battles to be Fought:
Episodes from the 1880–1965 Era

19. Coal Bear's People, 1883–1896

Little Wolf's great work was done. He had brought his people home. Now he was a prisoner of war, and in no position to refuse the requests of his captors. So when Miles asked Little Wolf and his young men to scout against Sitting Bull's Sioux, the Chief finally yielded.[1] However, this fighting against former friends was a poor substitute for the old Elk Society victories won against enemy tribes. More and more, Little Wolf felt the boredom of life at a white man's army post.

Finally, on December 13, 1880, he got some whiskey and downed it.[2] Then he walked unsteadily over to where Pretty

[1] Grinnell, *The Fighting Cheyennes*, 413.
[2] Letter from Whistler, commanding Fort Keogh, to Assistant Adjutant

Walker, his daughter, was playing cards. Starving Elk, now a corporal of scouts, was among those who stood by looking on. Twenty years before, Little Wolf had warned Starving Elk to stay away from his wife. The bad feeling had remained after that. During the flight from the south, the old trouble had flared up again when Starving Elk had become too attentive to Pretty Walker and to the Chief's wives.

Little Wolf had choked back his anger for a long time. He was the Sweet Medicine Chief, the one who carried Sweet Root's bundle with him always. When he first accepted the Chief's position, he and the other Forty-four knew that now they must never show anger; now they must avoid personal irritation. Only after a Chief had been wronged four times by the same person was he free to act in retaliation. Even then, the ideal Chief remained the one who grabbed his pipe and smoked it during some crisis that would have infuriated a lesser man.[3] Therefore, through all these years Little Wolf had held back his anger at Starving Elk's attentions to his women.

Now the Chief was slightly drunk. When he saw Starving Elk standing nearby, watching Pretty Walker as she gambled for candy, the old anger finally overcame him. He attempted to stop the card game and he ordered his daughter to go home. The other players ignored him. Such arbitrary meddling was unbecoming the dignity of a Chief, and Little Wolf was drunk anyway. Little Wolf lost his temper completely after that. He left to get a rifle. When he returned, he shot down Starving Elk.

The dreadfulness of that action sobered him quickly. He returned to his tipi and told his two wives what he had done.

General, Department of Dakota, St. Paul. Dated December 13, 1880. See also Llwellyn and Hobel, *op. cit.*, 83–86 and cf. Marquis *Warrior Who Fought Custer*, 330–33 and 346–47.

Cf. also Sandoz, *Cheyenne Autumn*, 271–72; Stands in Timber, Liberty and Utley, *Op. cit.*, 47, 54–55.

[3] Llwellyn and Hoebel, *op. cit.*, 78; and Grinnell, *Cheyenne Indians*, I, 344. The former adds that no Cheyenne within present memory was ever so provoked.

Contemporary Cheyennes still recall examples of Chiefs under grave pressure who grabbed their pipes and smoked until they regained control of themselves. Cf. Stands in Timber, Liberty and Utley, *op. cit.*, 45–47; Grinnell, *The Cheyenne Indians*, I, 155.

"I am going to that hill by the bend of the creek," he announced. "If anybody wants me, I'll be there." Little Wolf sat there two days, waiting for anyone who wanted to take revenge on him, or who wished to pass sentence on him. He was fasting the entire time. Meanwhile, Starving Elk's relatives slashed Little Wolf's tipi and chopped the tongue of the new wagon the soldiers had given him, but the other Cheyennes stopped them from doing anything more violent than that.

Finally, William Rowland persuaded Little Wolf to take refuge at Fort Keogh. Public pressure was put on Starving Elk's relatives to agree not to attack the Chief if he was released from the fort. They finally agreed to it; partly because they admitted that he had reason for the grudge, and partly because Little Wolf did the killing while he was drunk. As a result, after several months in confinement the Chief was set free.

There was no formal banishment, because the Council of the Forty-four could no longer convene to pass sentence. The Sacred Arrows were far to the south, so it was impossible to hold the renewing ceremonies immediately. However, Little Wolf knew his obligations. He immediately went into self-imposed exile with his family. They slowly moved along the Tongue until they were opposite Muddy Creek. Then they cut across country and followed Muddy almost to its forks some fourteen miles southwest of present Lame Deer. Here Little Wolf finally halted, near the homestead that William Rowland and his wife had taken.[4] Other families joined him in exile, since Little Wolf still was the Sweet Medicine Chief. Most of these people were Suhtaio.

Immediately after the killing, Little Wolf had smashed his long-stemmed pipe, the symbol of the Chief's office. He was permitted to smoke one of the short pipes made from the leg bone of a deer, but he denied himself even this. Smoking was basically sacred work, so he never smoked again. Nor did he ever sit with the other Cheyenne men when they were smoking together. He

[4] William Rowland and his Southern Cheyenne wife had settled on Muddy Creek prior to this, becoming the first persons to live on what is now the Northern Cheyenne Reservation.

gave away all his horses, and went everywhere on foot. From that time on, he stayed apart from the people; he followed a life of self-humiliation. And soon some of the younger Cheyennes began to call him by the name Putrified Flesh, saying that he carried the smell of death with him.[5]

Even so, Little Wolf remained a Chief. He still had possession of Sweet Medicine's bundle until the reorganization of the Council again could be held. That would not happen until 1892.[6]

[5] Rufus Wallowing stated that he and his boyhood companions called the Chief by this name rather than by the name Little Wolf. It is the common appellation for a murderer.

The author's informants were mixed in their judgment of Little Wolf. The Kit Foxes, John Stands in Timber among them, strongly condemned him for murder, because it brought blood to the Arrows and the smell of death to the Chiefs' bundle. However, Elk Society men stressed Little Wolf's greatness in bringing the people back home.

An objective evaluation of contemporary Cheyenne thought on the matter is needed. Such an evaluation should include a comparison of Suhtai and Tsistsistas, Elk and Kit Fox, opinion.

Wooden Leg stated: "Even the nearest relatives of Starving Elk never kept bad hearts against Little Wolf. At different times I have heard talk of him from Bald Eagle, a brother of the young man he killed. Bald Eagle said: 'Little Wolf did not kill my brother. It was the white man whiskey that did.'" Marquis, *Warrior Who Fought Custer,* 347.

[6] On two occasions, John Stands in Timber and the author examined and photographed the contents of the Chiefs' bundle.

Frank Waters, Keeper of the bundle from 1940 until his death in 1962, stated, "It is true that Little Wolf murdered another Cheyenne. This was considered a bad sin. However, the Sacred Hat bundle had the same kind of medicine as that in the sacred bundle Little Wolf carried. It was considered that the Sacred Hat priest would return this medicine to the Chiefs. Little Wolf's was buried; for the smell of death was on it. But both Little Wolf and the Sacred Hat had the same medicine from Sweet Root Standing." To the author, 1958.

Hoebel states that the Chiefs' bundle was passed on to Grasshopper at the 1892 reorganization of the Chiefs. Whistling Elk added these details in 1958. He said that he had heard them from Brady, his father: "There was trouble again [after the 1892 reorganization], and in 1900 the Chiefs reorganized again. The bundle was given to American Horse. He had two wives [*sic*]. When the Chiefs reorganized in 1940, the bundle was given to Frank Waters, son of Braided Locks. In 1950, Waters kept the bundle . . . .

"Murder, or the shedding of blood, can be removed by renewing the Arrows. The Sacred Arrows purify the Chiefs' bundle and everything else. The Chiefs' bundle came from Mahuts, rather than [from] Is'siwun. The Cheyennes are strict about the Chiefs' medicine because no human made that medicine. The Ones Above made it through Sweet Medicine."

The statement attributed to Frank Waters in the footnote on page 48 of Stands in Timber, Liberty, and Utley, *Cheyenne Memories,* appears to be an inaccurate quoting of the above statement. Cf. Llewellyn and Hoebel, *op. cit.,* 84–88.

292

Miles had promised Two Moons that he and his people could locate their own reservation once the fighting days were over. When the wars did end, he finally allowed Two Moon and some of his followers to begin looking for a permanent home. About 1881, they had met Little Wolf and some of his people at the mouth of Lame Deer Creek. There Little Wolf had described the land along the Muddy, near the Rowland place. Two Moon and his people rode over to see the country. They found that the hunting was good and the water was plentiful. So were the wood and grass for the horses. Two Moon's people were satisfied. This was where they wanted to stay, they told the army officers who were with them.[7]

So the Cheyennes began to move again. This time it was the bands of Two Moon and White Bull that were moving south, but only as far as the Rosebud and Tongue River country. There they joined Little Wolf's followers in filling up the lands that ultimately became their reservation. Finally, on November 26, 1884, President Chester A. Arthur set aside a tract adjoining the east side of the Crow Reservation and the southern forty-mile limit of the Northern Pacific Railway grant, for the use of the Northern Cheyennes. The people were described as "parties captured by the military in 1877 and 'hostiles' from the Pine Ridge Agency who have been permitted to settle in the vicinity of the Tongue and Rosebud rivers."[8] Some 371,200 acres were set aside, much of the land high, rolling hills, forested with pine.[9]

Frank Waters died on July 2, 1962. Prior to that, the Chiefs had decided to reorganize, and the date had been set for July 4, 1962. Father Powell was asked to keep the Chiefs' bundle in the interim. John Stands in Timber, John Woodenlegs, Verne Dusenberry, and Father Powell were inducted into the Chiefs' Society on July 4. Then the question of caring for the bundle arose. It was decided to place it with Willis Medicine Bull. After a time, Medicine Bull decided that the responsibility was too great, and the bundle passed to Eugene Little Coyote, son of the former Keeper of the Hat. From him, the bundle passed to Albert Tall Bull. As of August, 1969, the bundle remained with Tall Bull.

[7] Rufus Wallowing and John Stands in Timber to the author, 1958.

[8] *Annual Report of the Commissioner of Indian Affairs* . . . , 1885.

[9] A later Executive Order of March 19, 1900, expanded the reservation lands to 460,000 acres. Charles J. Kappler (ed.), *Indian Affairs, Lands and Treaties*, I, 860.

Now this was all that remained of the Cheyenne north country, but at least it was Cheyenne land once more.

When Coal Bear first reached the present reservation lands, about 1883, the Sacred Hat tipi was erected near the forks of the Muddy. Many of the other Suhtai members of Black Wolf's band pitched their own lodges nearby. Then, about 1895, the Keeper moved over to the forks of the Lame Deer. Glad Traveler, his favorite wife, carried Is'siwun on her back during the move. Her sons, Head Swift and Sand Crane, rode nearby, and so did White Woman, the Keeper's second wife. Altogether, the two women had borne eleven children.

There were other Suhtai families who rode behind the Keeper and his immediate family. Among them were the families of Bull Thigh, Black Horse, Wrapped Hair, American Horse, Short Sioux, Elk Shoulder, and Hoarse Voice. They were often called "Coal Bear's People"; and they are still called by that name today.[10]

Life in Is'siwun's lodge remained quiet, as Erect Horns had told the Suhtaio it must be. The Hat Keeper rose at sunrise. He lit the pipe and offered it to Maheo, to the Earth, to the Sacred Persons, and finally to Is'siwun herself.[11] Next, one of the wives took the stick that lay near the lodge pole to the right (southeast) of the doorway. She struck the pole four times, announcing that Is'siwun's home was open to visitors.

The Sacred Hat was suspended at the head of Coal Bear's bed, resting against the Turner. On a bright day the Keeper, or one of his wives, carried Is'siwun outdoors. There the bundle was tied

[10] The description of Coal Bear's People is from John Stands in Timber. Details of life in the sacred tipi during Coal Bear's later years are from Sitting Man, Little Coyote, Rufus Wallowing, Wesley Little White Man, and John Stands in Timber. Details concerning Coal Bear's wives are from Buffalo White Cow, the daughter of Coal Bear's sister.

[11] Grinnell, "Great Mysteries . . . ," loc. cit., 563, states that the pipe is first offered to the pole which the Keeper's wife strikes each morning and night. He states that this pole represents the Hat. However, the male informants cited in the note above insisted that the pipe is offered to Maheo, to the Sacred Persons, and to Is'siwun herself.

above the doorway. In the free times, the Suhtaio had carried rich gifts to the Hat; beautifully tanned and painted robes, fine blankets, the tail feathers of an eagle, or even a long-haired enemy scalp. Now the offerings usually were varicolored strips of calico. Even these poorer offerings received Is'siwun's blessing, sending that blessing on to the person who gave the present.

Then Coal Bear would carry Nimhoyoh from the lodge. The Turner was lashed to a pole and raised above the tipi. Breezes often caused its fringe of buffalo tails to dance as the Turner's sacred power continued to turn away sickness and trouble from the Suhtaio.

Occasionally a sick man came to the sacred tipi, his pipe extended to Coal Bear in supplication. The Keeper would untie Nimhoyoh and place the Turner on the earth just inside the doorway of the lodge. The sick man would lie down on Nimhoyoh and slowly roll over the surface of the Turner, receiving a share of the healing power of the sacred object. After that, Coal Bear would shake Nimhoyoh, just as a buffalo cow shakes when she rises from the ground. Then the Keeper would again suspend the Turner from the forks of the tripod near the head of his bed.

There were rules to be observed in Is'siwun's home. No moisture could fall there, or a rainstorm would come. Therefore, spilling water, spitting, or blowing the nose with the thumb was forbidden. A person was not permitted to scratch there, so many visitors carried a small stick for special use within the sacred tipi. Anyone who broke this rule would find an itching rash on the skin where the fingernails had been used.

A great storm would arise if anyone blew directly upon the fire. Therefore, the coals were kept glowing by Coal Bear or one of his wives exhaling through the "blower," a tube of red catlinite. Sacred designs were carved upon its surface. When the blower was not in use, customarily it was kept in the Hat bundle.

A man bearing an offering for Is'siwun entered her lodge quietly. He stood there with his head uncovered, remaining on his feet only long enough to present the gift. Then the Keeper motioned him to a seat at the side of the lodge. The man moved there directly and silently. Any conversation was carried on in low and respectful tones.

The Suhtaio frequently carried special meals to Coal Bear, thus honoring his sacred position. Glad Traveler would take five pieces of meat from the dinner. Then she would call the donor to her and place the portions of meat in his outstretched palm. The man would leave the tipi. Outside, he offered a piece of meat to each of the Maheyuno at the four directions. Then he placed a piece of meat upon the earth at each direction. When he re-entered the lodge, he moved over before Is'siwun. There he left the fifth portion of meat on the ground beneath the Sacred Hat bundle. Now the Sacred Persons were fed and the food blessed. Now the Maheyuno would be eating with the Keeper, his family, and his guest. The food would bless them, bringing them health and strength from the Sacred Persons.

A child who entered the sacred lodge for the first time, was instructed in the holiness of Is'siwun's home. He or she was warned not to be noisy. Then the child was prayed over by Coal Bear. The Keeper would take one of the offering cloths that covered the Hat bundle, or he himself would touch the bundle. Then he would run the offering cloth or his bare hand over the little one's body, blessing the child with the blessing of Is'siwun herself.

Children were not permitted to play near the Sacred Hat tipi. No one was permitted to run in front of the lodge, or to ride a horse there. Even when riding at a distance the Suhtaio passed by slowly, respectfully. If one of the military societies was parading, the leaders guided their ponies past the rear of Is'siwun's home.

If someone accidentally threw a stick or stone against the sacred tipi, he was brought inside. There Coal Bear, or one of the Buffalo priests, would pray for him, asking Is'siwun and the Powers to forgive him. The Keeper or priest touched the earth. Then he passed his hands over the person's body, making the sacred purifying motions and thus removing the effects of the misdeed.

Each year, early in the spring, Coal Bear's nieces entered Is'siwun's lodge. There the women offered their own flesh, begging the blessing of the Sacred Powers upon themselves and upon all the people as they did so. The Keeper cut a piece of skin about the size of the fingertip from the arm of each woman. He offered the flesh to Maheo, to the Sacred Persons, and to Is'siwun. One niece made this sacrifice almost fifty times.[12]

Throughout his life, Coal Bear remained a priest of great force and character. He had shared the sufferings of his people almost from the day he took charge of the sacred tipi. He had lived through Ho'ko's sacrilege and the sorrows of the wars with the whites. The Suhtaio never had been a large people; and their numbers were further decimated by the final battles with the soldiers. Through it all, Coal Bear carried out his responsibilities with dignity and strength.[13]

Old Wolf Tooth once remarked about this to John Stands in Timber, his step-grandson. The two of them often visited the Keeper when Wolf Tooth was traveling from Birney to the agency at Lame Deer. Wolf Tooth said that,

> Coal Bear, the Keeper of Is'siwun, was careful about his actions and talk. The ceremonies were done quietly and carefully by him. If he did anything hastily, things would go wrong for the Suhtaio. The people imitated the Keeper of the Hat. If the Keeper was sloppy; so were the lives of the people.[14]

Old contemporary Suhtaio recall that the people's lives rarely, if ever, were sloppy while Coal Bear guarded Is'siwun.

So the quiet life continued at the forks of the Lame Deer. It was there, in 1896, that Coal Bear died. He was barely seventy years old, a young age for the passing of the Keeper of Is'siwun. Some people said that his early death was due to the fact that

---

[12] Wesley Little White Man to the author. The niece who made this offering almost fifty times was his mother.

[13] Coal Bear had his own personal sorrows, too. Llewellyn and Hoebel, *op. cit.*, 227, notes that for three generations the Keeper's family had suffered from kleptomania. Coal Bear's children were well known as being thieves. Even when they were whipped, they kept right on stealing. It got to the point that people simply covered their belongings when they saw the Keeper's children coming. Unfortunately, the author could uncover no further details as to which of the children were involved.

[14] To the author, 1958.

devotion to the Hat was not as strong as it had been in former years. Others recalled that the effects of Ho'ko's deed still were being felt by the people.

At Coal Bear's death, the Suhtaio carried the Keeper's body to a hill, because, like the Sacred Mountain itself, the pine hills possess a special closeness to Maheo and the Powers. There Coal Bear was placed upon the earth, and his body was covered with a pile of stones.

The great bison herds long since had disappeared from the valleys of the Rosebud, the Tongue, and the Yellowstone. Nevertheless, buffalo skulls still were placed at each corner of the Keeper's grave. Their empty eye sockets faced each of the four directions, the home of the Sacred Persons. It was believed that if this respect was not shown Is'siwun's Keeper, the buffalo would return to the north and the prairie would be empty. However, if this was done, there would always be plenty of buffalo. Coal Bear's People again prayed that the buffalo would return from their ancient home in the north, their herds blackening the prairies as they did when they first followed Erect Horns, the bringer of Is'siwun.[15]

15 Grinnell, "Great Mysteries . . . ," loc. cit., 567.

20. The Sun Dance Is Forbidden, 1897

The Cheyennes call the white
man Veho or Wihio. The name means "spider." It first was applied
to the Spider trickster who figures in many of the Cheyenne fun
stories, the stories recited for the children's amusement.[1] Spider
was a creature of unusual powers, therefore the Cheyennes gave
his name to the white man, whose inventions were so numerous
and so amazing.

[1] The trickster is a famous figure in American Indian mythology. As such, he
appears under various names and guises. The Sioux know him as Inktomi, the
Kiowas as Saynday, and so on. In Cheyenne tradition, Spider is the trickster.
Cf. The Wihio tales in Grinnell, *Cheyenne Campfires*, 281–305; Paul Radin,
The Trickster: A Study in American Indian Mythology; Stands in Timber, Liberty,
and Utley, *op. cit.*, 24–26.

However, the old word for spider has a much more subtle connotation when it means white man. Here "Veho" implies intricacy, trickery, or a trap. The white man's mind is deceitful; the white man's thoughts are all too often focused upon tricking the Cheyennes and upon destroying the Cheyenne way of life.[2]

These white traits were revealed in the Veho attitude toward the Cheyenne sacred ceremonies. White persons rarely have understood, much less respected, the old Cheyenne concept of sacrifice. Nor have most whites perceived the sacredness of male and female sacrifice within the context of the sacred ceremonies. Most early white observers used the term "barbaric" to describe the Cheyenne offering of one's own flesh to the Powers. Few whites realized that a Cheyenne seeks to offer his or her own very best to Maheo and to the Sacred Powers; and for the Cheyennes, the best sacrifice a man or woman could offer was his or her own body. Army officers, Indian agents, Christian missionaries—all were united in arguing that the so-called Sun Dance torture proved that the entire Sun Dance ceremony should be abolished by this "civilized" nation. Some white observers made the error of describing the sacrifice in the Medicine Lodge as the primitive testing of a man's endurance or the public proving of a warrior's strength. Only a handful of whites realized the intensely sacred character of a Cheyenne man's vow to sacrifice his body on the

---

[2] Grinnell, *Cheyenne Indians*, II, 88f., states, "Wihio . . . means spider and white man, and appears to embody the idea of mental ability of an order higher than common—superior intelligence. To the Indian the white man appears superior in intelligence to other men . . . . On account of his ability, they call him wihio. The spider spins a web, and goes up and down, seemingly walking on nothing. It is more able than other insects . . . ."

Doctor Petter's personal copy of Grinnell's above work is now in the possession of James King, Lame Deer, Montana. Beside the above quotation from Grinnell, Rodolphe Petter added this comment in his own handwriting: "Here veho and veko are confounded. On medicine rattles the web of the spider is represented, the center of a system. It (veho) also implies intricacy, then trickery, trap, etc. It refers not to web neither to wisdom in no way."

The author's Northern Cheyenne informants were unanimous in stating that the word "veho," when applied to a white person, implies intelligence used in a tricky fashion, such as tricking the Cheyennes away from following their own traditions.

crest of a hill, during the lesser sacred ceremonies or in the Sun Dance lodge itself.

Solitary fasting and sacrificing in the hills was the older, more common form of male sacrifice.[3] Swinging from the center pole of the Sun Dance lodge or dragging buffalo skulls tied to wooden skewers piercing the flesh were not part of the older Sun Dance ceremonies. However, the Medicine Lodge was a fitting place in which to fulfill a vow to the Sacred Powers. All the Cheyennes were gathered together at that time. Thus, the pledger could fulfill his spiritual obligations in the presence of the entire tribe. He could publicly thank Maheo for hearing his plea during a time of personal need or trouble. A man could gain the pity of the Sacred Powers by his willingness to suffer in the Medicine Lodge. Then he would receive a full share in the new life that flows from the ceremonies in the Sun Dance Lodge, the Sacred Lodge of Renewing.

Cheyenne sacrifice follows a definite procedure. First a vow is made; a promise is given that one will offer his or her body to the Sacred Powers. The sacrifice may be pledged to avert misfortune, or it may be made to fulfill an earlier vow. It may be offered as a petition for Maheo's blessing upon one's relatives who are in trouble, or who are experiencing misfortune of any kind.

Sometimes a Maiyun appears in a dream or vision and instructs a person to offer sacrifice. A man who fears thunder can vow to stand on a hilltop with his chest pierced by skewers. Through the sacrifice of his body he can gain Thunder's pity and sometimes even a share in Thunder's supernatural power.

During a time of great danger, a man might vow to swing from the center pole during the next Sun Dance. Or he might promise to drag buffalo skulls as a thank offering for delivery from some peril. The skulls might be tied to his chest, back, legs, arms, or

[3] John Stands in Timber, Little Coyote, Fire Wolf, et al. Cf. George Bird Grinnell, "The Cheyenne Medicine Lodge," *American Anthropologist*, N.S. Vol. XVI, No. 2 (April–June, 1914), 245ff., 250, 256; Dorsey, *The Cheyenne*, II, 175ff.; George Bent to Hyde, May 10, 1906, Coe Collection, Yale.

even below his eyes. A man or woman might offer small bits of flesh, cut from his or her arms or legs, as a sacrifice to the Powers. A Cheyenne also might pledge an offering of his flesh as his personal sharing in the suffering of a friend who was offering a similar sacrifice. Such a sacrifice proved the depth of one man's loyalty to another.[4]

Some husbands pledged years of sexual abstinence in order to bring blessings to the child who would be conceived at the end of that period of sacrifice. A man of strong character might vow, at the birth of his first child, not to have another child for either seven or fourteen years. Then all the father's growth powers would be concentrated on the growth of this one child, rather than being dissipated among other youngsters. This sacrifice was comparable to a man's offering of his body in the Sun Dance lodge or staking himself on a hilltop. Maheo would abundantly bless the child as a reward for the father's fulfillment of this vow of sexual abstinence. The Cheyennes, in turn, honored such a father with their high esteem.[5]

A Cheyenne who seeks great spiritual power pledges the Crossing of the Four Ridges. He vows to make four sacrifices—to offer four of the sacred ceremonies. There is no special order in which the ceremonies must be offered, nor do the ceremonies need to be the same. A man who has pledged the Sun Dance has crossed one ridge. The pledging of the Sacred Arrow ceremonies takes him across another. The offering of flesh to the Sacred Buffalo Hat fulfills a third. To cross the final ridge, a man might fast and sacrifice his body on a hilltop. Under any circumstances, the Cheyennes believe that Maheo is especially pleased with a man

[4] George Brady, John Stands in Timber, William Tall Bull, and Henry Tall Bull to the author.

Cf. Grinnell, *Cheyenne Indians,* I, 79ff.; II, 195ff., 213ff.; Grinnell, "The Cheyenne Medicine Lodge," *loc. cit.,* 245ff.; and also Petter, *Dictionary,* s.v., "torture," 1061 f.

[5] Hoebel, *The Cheyennes,* 84, fully develops this theme. Llewellyn and Hoebel, *The Cheyenne Way,* 262f., states that it is not clearly established whether intercourse with a second wife was allowed during that time. There are indications that it was.

The earliest known photograph of the Sacred Hat tipi, ca. 1882. This picture was taken by Stanley J. Morrow, evidently at about the time Coal Bear returned to the north. The original, in the W. H. Over Dakota Museum, Vermillion, South Dakota, is merely labeled, "Cheyenne Medicine Lodge on the Yellowstone." However, the presence of Nimhoyoh and the painting of the buffalo head identify it as Is'siwun's lodge.

Photograph courtesy of the W. H. Over Dakota Museum, University of South Dakota, Vermillion.

Issiwun's missing horn was kept in this lodge, the tipi of Dragging Otter. The horn rests in the pouch suspended above the doorway. Dragging Otter also kept a replica of Nimhoyoh the Turner, and it is the replica that flies above the tipi here. This is one of a series of photographs taken by James Mooney ca. 1906, among the Southern Cheyennes living in the area of Darlington and Cantonment, Oklahoma.

Photograph courtesy of the Smithsonian Institution, National Anthropological Archives, Bureau of American Ethnology Collection.

Dragging Otter. The Suhtai priest who cared for Is'siwun's missing horn after the death of his wife, who was Ho'ko's sister. Dragging Otter also felt the effects of the sacrilege; most of his family died after he assumed custody of the horn.

Photograph by James Mooney, 1906. Courtesy of the Smithsonian Institution, National Anthropological Archives, Bureau of American Ethnology Collection.

White men in Is'siwun's tipi, 1930. Wolf Chief's arm appears at the left, while Black Bird sits pensively looking ahead. Congressman Scott Leavitt is behind the Keeper, with General Hugh Scott to the right. Black Bird went through the purifying ceremonies after Is'siwun was exposed to white men on this occasion.

Photograph courtesy of the Smithsonian Institution, National Anthropological Archives, Bureau of American Ethnology Collection.

Is'siwun is opened, 1959. Fred Last Bull places the pipe beside the Sacred Hat. John Woodenlegs, chairman of the Northern Cheyenne Tribal Council at that time, sits in the middle. John Stands in Timber is to the right.

Photograph by the author.

The contents of the Sacred Hat bundle, 1959. The scalps rest to the left of Is'siwun. The "old animal hide" and lesser objects from the buffalo hide sack rest behind the Hat. The piece of sacred sweet root rests on the Earth drawing directly in front of Is'siwun.

Photograph by the author.

Bearing Is'siwun to the Sun Dance camp, 1961. Eugene Little Coyote places the Sacred Hat bundle on the shoulders of his father, the Keeper. A leather thong holds the bundle in place.

Photograph by the author.

John Woodenlegs bears Is'siwun's bundle into the Sacred Hat tipi.
Sun Dance, 1961.

Photograph by the author.

After the Sun Dance, July 1961. The Keeper sits beside Is'siwun's bundle, which rests against Nimhoyoh, the Turner. Elsewhere, the sacred tipi is being dismantled.

Photograph by the author.

Nimhoyoh is carried to a waiting automobile by John Woodenlegs. Wesley White Man looks on, following the Sun Dance, 1961.

Photograph by the author.

John Woodenlegs places Is'siwun upon Little Coyote's shoulders, as the Keeper prepares to return to Ashland, Montana, with the sacred bundle, 1961.

Photograph by the author.

Erecting the Sacred Hat lodge. Little Coyote looks on as the military erect the framework of Is'siwun's home. The site is Little Coyote's allotment, near Ashland, Montana, 1961.

Photograph by the author.

Sand Crane. Coal Bear's son, he became Keeper of Is'siwun about 1934. It was Sand Crane who instructed many of the young men who are Northern Cheyenne Sun Dance priests today.

Head Swift. He succeeded his brother Sand Crane as Keeper. At Head Swift's death, his daughter, Josie Limpy, watched over the sacred tipi from 1952 until the beginning of 1958. These photographs of her uncle and father appear through her kindness.

316

Weasel Woman, Little Coyote and John Stands in Timber. 1959. They are examining an old-time painted canvas, bearing drawings of the Custer fight and of the Sun Dance that preceded it.

Photograph by the author.

Little Coyote and Weasel Woman seated before Is'siwun, 1961. When the author finished taking this photograph, Little Coyote said that he and Weasel Woman would remain there before Is'siwun, praying for the people, until the Morning Star appeared.

Photograph by the author.

who vows and who fulfills the Crossing of the Four Ridges during his lifetime.[6]
Finally, whatever the nature of a man's personal vow, he also begs Maheo and the Powers to bless his relatives and all the Cheyennes through his sacrifice.

However, as mentioned above, few whites had any understanding of or respect for these Cheyenne religious concepts. During the early reservation years both government and missionary sentiment were aimed at destroying the old sacred ceremonies —especially the Sun Dance. In 1884, Doctor T. V. McGillycuddy, the doughty agent at Pine Ridge, did ban the Sun Dance ceremonies for Little Chief's Northern Cheyennes, who were living among the Oglalas there. However, on Tongue River reservation, the Sun Dance continued to be offered until about 1897.

John Stands in Timber recalled the events leading to the ban on the ceremony at that time:

At the beginning, the men sacrificed themselves up in the hills, away from the Sun Dance. White, Stemper White's father, set up a poplar tree that was standing in the ground. He stood there fasting, facing the Sun to the east. He kept following the Sun, facing it all the time. As it started going down, he kept on facing it. There is a bed of sage on which the faster stands, and the sagebrush is arranged in a circle. He walks on this all night. Then, as sunrise approaches, he walks to the East. White did this walking for three days, without torturing himself.

Towards the end of the Sun Dance, the last four songs are sung. During that time, the instructors use their spiritual power and sacred objects to show the watchers what power they have. White Bull was the Instructor this Sun Dance. He had a "man power" mirror. Its handle was wrapped in snake skin; which seemed to come alive as he offered the mirror towards the Sun Dance pole.

The last four songs were beginning to be sung. Then the faster [White] walked down from the hill with his instructor. They walked into the Sun Dance Lodge, and took a position near the

[6] Fire Wolf, James Medicine Elk, Ralph White Tail, John Stands in Timber, and Rufus Wallowing to the author.

319

buffalo skull, to the left [south] of it. When the rest of the dancers started raising their pipes and images toward the center pole, White used a rawhide rope, offering it toward the pole.

When there was one more song left, they spread sage on the ground. White lay down, with his head toward the center pole. The instructor got a sharp-pointed knife. He cut the flesh on each side of White's chest, and placed in the sharp-pointed skewers. They were three or four inches long. A rawhide rope was tied to these pins. White stood up; and the end of the rope was tied to the center pole. Then the fourth song began.

Every time there was a change in the beat of the drums and singing, White stepped back. The fourth time he pulled hard, the skin stretching out from his chest. Sometimes the skin breaks and the men fall hard. Then they are covered with a buffalo robe. Finally they laid the faster [White] down; and they cut away the strings of flesh, leaving a clean wound.

The next Sun Dance, one more man offered his flesh in the Lodge. The year after that, three more offered their bodies. Then the Government banned the Sun Dance. This happened about 1897.[7]

[7] To the author, 1963.
White was born about 1857, according to the 1891 Tongue River census. John Stands in Timber witnessed this event as a boy of about thirteen.
Northern Cheyenne memories are hazy as to the exact date. A study of the Tongue River Agency records in the National Archives did not reveal an exact date for the ban, either. Fire Wolf stated that he first pledged the Sun Dance in 1896. The most generally accepted date among the author's informants was 1897, with the ban lifted ten years later, in 1907.

21. Wounded Eye, ca. 1901–1920

After Coal Bear's death, there was
a period during which Is'siwun had no male Keeper. Finally,
about 1901, Coal Bear's wife, White Woman, entered the tipi of
Wounded Eye. The Keeper's wife was entitled to a respect of her
own, and it is recalled that it was White Woman herself, rather
than the Chiefs and military society leaders, who first asked
Wounded Eye if he would guard Is'siwun.[1]

[1] This is a disputed point. Fire Wolf said categorically, "When Coal Bear
died, his wife, White Woman, went and talked to Wounded Eye about taking
Is'siwun. The military didn't take the bundle to Wounded Eye."

Davis Wounded Eye was away from home, attending government school,
when his father was elected Keeper. He said, "I don't recall when Wounded Eye
got the Hat. We lived at the forks of the Lame Deer. Coal Bear had the Hat. Then
the military chose Wounded Eye."

The probable answer is that both parties had a hand in the choice. White

Wounded Eye had been a member of Little Chief's band, the Cheyennes who were detained at Pine Ridge until 1890. When he returned home, he had settled near Coal Bear's people, who were camped near the forks of the Lame Deer.[2]

Is'siwun's new Keeper was a man about fifty-five years old at this time. He was another warrior who had seen Box Elder's power displayed during Mackenzie's attack. In the midst of that fight, the new Keeper had been charging in close to the soldiers when a bullet hit him near the eye. The wound was severe, but the eye was undamaged. Friends carried him to safety, and then Box Elder was led to him. The blind holy man doctored the wound, and his power caused the bleeding to stop. From that time on, the Cheyennes called the warrior by a new name, Wounded Eye.

Wounded Eye had been a restless man, one who moved about often, building a house at each stopping place. But now he moved into the Sacred Hat tipi, because Is'siwun is not allowed to hang in a white man's type of home. Nor, at that time, was the Sacred Hat allowed to be carried on a white man wagon.

Woman, the Sacred Hat Woman, asked Wounded Eye to be Keeper. He agreed. Word of this informal agreement was carried to the military societies, and then the Chiefs and the military societies made the formal request of Wounded Eye. He formally accepted, and the Chiefs and military societies formally announced their choice. In characteristic Cheyenne fashion, all parties concerned would be satisfied, and their formal role in ceremonial matters would be maintained.

Davis Wounded Eye also stated that there was a definite time lapse between Coal Bear's death and Wounded Eye's election as Keeper. In the interim, White Woman would have had charge of Is'siwun—a hard responsibility, especially in those days. Older Cheyennes recall that Coal Bear had two wives, White Woman and Glad Traveler. Glad Traveler was considered Coal Bear's favorite, and thus probably knew the Sacred Hat Woman's duties better than White Woman. It is not clear whether or not Glad Traveler was dead at this time. If she was, this would explain why White Woman rather than Glad Traveler approached Wounded Eye.

A situation requiring that a woman assume temporary care of Is'siwun would be repeated in the years between Head Swift's death and the appointment of Ernest American Horse as Keeper.

[2] Wounded Eye was born between 1842 (1906 Tongue River census) and 1846 (1891 and 1896 censuses). His son, Davis Wounded Eye, stated that he became Keeper sometime between 1901 and 1904—the years in which Davis was away at school.

Davis Wounded Eye is the principal informant for this chapter.

However, the wandering habit died hard for Wounded Eye. During the summer of 1906 he left Is'siwun's lodge for a time. A storm arose, and the wind blew down the sacred tipi. No one in the village knew what to do. There the Buffalo Hat lay on the ground, exposed to the elements. Finally one of the men picked up Is'siwun. As he lifted the Hat, he offered many prayers, begging Maheo and the Powers for forgiveness if he was doing anything wrong.[3] When Wounded Eye finally returned, he prayed over the man and cleansed him by rubbing his entire body with sacred white "man" sage.

The Keeper predicted that this fall of the Sacred Hat tipi would bring on a heavy windstorm. The prediction came true about two weeks later. This is how the event was recalled by Davis Wounded Eye, the Keeper's son:

> It was a heavy storm, with hail; one that knocked down trees and other things. When the storm was over, all the other tipis were on the ground, but the Sacred tipi was left standing. The cover was gone from it; but the poles were still there. Is'siwun was not touched. She was hanging there as she always does.
>
> When it was discovered what happened, the Kit Foxes got together right away. They went after another cover for the sacred tipi right away.
>
> After that, when my father went on a visit some place, I stayed right there at the tipi, to care for it.[4]

Gradually, the old disciplines surrounding the Hat Keeper's position became fewer. Wounded Eye did not follow the rule that Is'siwun's guardian never left the sacred tipi. Even after the storm he accepted an occasional invitation to visit a friend or to sit in the lodge when one of the military societies gathered. In 1911, during the last Massaum ceremony in the north, Wounded Eye was present in the Animal Dance lodge. However, when he left home, his son Davis remained behind to guard Is'siwun. Again, the son recalled those days:

> Keepers are not supposed to leave the tipi to go on pleasure

[3] Grinnell, "Great Mysteries . . . ," loc. cit., 568.
[4] To the author, 1960.

trips. My father used to tell me: "In case I am gone overnight, you must build a fire before sunrise, you must do the same in the evening. Take the pipe and smoke it; but do not offer it to the four directions."[5]

On one occasion a trip away from Is'siwun's lodge brought Wounded Eye near to death. John Stands in Timber described that close call:

> About 1910, the Sheridan water system was being built. We helped haul materials to the mountains. There was a ditch that was quite high on the other side; [one that had a high bank of dirt beside it]. Wounded Eye was hauling two huge pipes with a team and wagon. They weighed about a ton and a half, I guess. Wounded Eye came along, got almost to the top of the bank and stopped. They put a block under the rear wheel. They were going to hitch extra horses to the wagon. One of the huge iron pipes came loose and fell to the ground. It just missed Wounded Eye by a few inches.
>
> Wounded Eye was there a few days. I heard remarks that he should be home minding the tipi.[6]

Nevertheless, Wounded Eye held fast to his position as a leader in the sacred ceremonies. In September, 1906, he and his wife assumed the chief roles in the Buffalo ceremony, the Suhtaio healing ceremony whose power is linked to Is'siwun and the Buffalo People. This ceremony had been pledged for the curing of Squint Eye's daughter. The little girl was eight or ten years old, and she was suffering from tuberculosis.

The sweat house used in the Buffalo ceremony is "Vonhaom," the ceremonial sweat lodge, rather than the ordinary sweat house, "emaom." Like the Sun Dance, the Buffalo ceremony brings the pledger and worshippers a share in the Sun's life-renewing power. During the final ceremonies, the instructor sprinkles the hot stones with water. Through the actual sweat rite, the worshippers are cleansed, both inwardly and outwardly. Thus they are purified to receive a share in the Sun's new life power. At this time, also,

[5] *Ibid.*
[6] To the author, 1960.

healing is brought to persons such as the little girl for whom the ceremony was pledged in 1906.[7]

On this occasion, Wounded Eye, his wife, and the sick child represented the Buffalo Family; the bull, the cow, and the Yellow Calf. This is the holy buffalo family who traditionally figure in the old account of the Great Race. It was the winning of this race that first gave the Suhtaio power over the buffalo. The ceremonial sweat lodge was erected in the Rosebud River bottom, near the place where Is'siwun's tipi was standing. Wolf Chief was the Instructor. American Horse, Old Bull, Bull Thigh, and Three Fingers assisted him. All four priests were Suhtaio.[8]

Squint Eye's daughter lived for nearly three years after the offering of the Buffalo Ceremony, but the tuberculosis finally killed her. Before she died she asked that her little dog and saddle pony go with her. They were killed at her grave, so that they might journey with her up the Milky Way to Se'han, the Place of the Dead.[9]

[7] The Buffalo Ceremony demonstrates the same theme of life renewal and much of the same symbolism that we find in the Sun Dance. The Buffalo Ceremony is principally a healing ceremony. The chief male and female participants represent the Buffalo Bull and Cow, with their offspring, the Yellow Calf. The sweat lodge represents the world. The principal pole in the lodge runs east and west, representing the Sun's path. Outside, to the east, sits a buffalo skull, symbol of Is'siwun's female generative power. There is a hole in the ground at the center of the lodge. Leading from the buffalo skull to this hole is a trail of white "man" sage, the male generative symbol. The fire burning outside represents the Sun's heat, the force that makes living things grow. The Buffalo sweat lodge ceremony brings the Sun's power for new life, symbolized by the male procreative organ, to the worshippers inside the sweat lodge. Therefore, the Buffalo priests were noted for their power as doctors.

Fine insight into the nature of the Sun Dance Ceremonies and the Buffalo Ceremonies is found in Petter, *Dictionary*, s.v. "sun," 1029, and s.v. "sweat," 1034f. Compare Petter's interpretations with the ceremonies as described in Grinnell, "A Buffalo Sweat Lodge," *American Anthropologist*, N.S. Vol. XXI, No. 4 (October–December, 1919), and "The Cheyenne Medicine Lodge," *loc. cit.*, and Robert Anderson, "The Buffalo Men, A Cheyenne Ceremony of Petition Deriving From the Sutaio," *Southwestern Journal of Anthropology*, Vol. XII, No. 1 (Spring, 1956).

The author discussed the meaning of the Buffalo Ceremony with Fire Wolf, Albert Tall Bull, John Stands in Timber, Josie Head Swift, and others. These informants substantiated Petter's interpretation of the ceremonies.

[8] Grinnell, "A Buffalo Sweat Lodge," *loc. cit.*, 363. Cf. "The Great Race," Chapter 34, Vol. II of this book.

[9] *Ibid.*, 361.

Shortly after the Buffalo Ceremony ended, the Sacred Hat
bundle was opened. Fire Wolf was present, and in 1959 he recalled the occasion:

During Wounded Eye's days as Keeper, it was decided that
Is'siwun should be exposed. Word was sent to the priests of the
Buffalo Ceremony and to the warrior societies. When they had
gathered in the Sacred Hat tipi, Wounded Eye, the Buffalo priests
and the others who were assisting, first touched the earth. In that
way they received the blessing of Grandmother Earth and the
Maiyun who live in her. Then the Keeper and the priests made the
purifying motions over themselves, preparing their bodies for the
work ahead.[10]

Hershey Wolf Chief was a noted Suhtai Buffalo and Massaum
priest. He was the one who restored Is'siwun's missing horn after
Wounded Eye carried the horn home from Oklahoma in 1908.
Now Wolf Chief was chosen to open the Sacred Hat bundle. First,
he made the four forward motions that are made before touching
any holy object. He removed the offering cloths that were tied
around the Hat bundle. Again he made the four motions with his
hands. Then he lifted Is'siwun's bundle down from the tripod, and
placed the bundle upon the earth.

Nimhoyoh, the Turner, also was placed on the ground, in front
of the Hat bundle. The two "old skin animal hides" were taken
from the buffalo hide sack. These were laid upon the Turner. Then
the five scalps were counted, to be certain all were there. Finally,
Is'siwun was placed on top of the scalps. Now the Hat could be
seen by everyone in the lodge.

Wounded Eye, the Buffalo priests and the military prayed
silently for a time. Then Wolf Chief again made the four forward
motions. He raised Is'siwun slowly. Then he placed the Hat back
in the buffalo hide sack, with the Hat's beaded brow band facing
upward. The laces were tied. Then Wolf Chief prayed in Suhtai:

"We have opened the sacred object which represents our Sacred
Powers. We beg you Powers: give us strength! Give good lives to
every person, so that we will be strong and live longer. The military societies are looking at you. Bless all of them! Not only do

[10] This 1906 ceremony is the only recorded occasion upon which Is'siwun
was opened prior to Hugh Scott's visit to the Hat in 1930.

those of us here ask for these blessings. We also ask that the whole Suhtai tribe may receive benefits from you, so that everything may be carried out in a good way on behalf of the people."

After the prayer, Is'siwun's bundle again was suspended from the tripod at the head of Wounded Eye's bed. After darkness came, Young Bird was chosen to speak with the Maiyun in the Spirit Lodge ceremonies.

On another occasion, Wounded Eye assisted Little White Man in fulfilling a sacrifice to the Sacred Powers. Little White Man was a young man then, and his first child, a little baby, was very ill. The father determined to offer a sacrifice to save the child's life. While he was pondering what form the sacrifice should take, the answer came to him in his sleep. In his dreams he saw persons standing up and swinging from the pole.

Little White Man was convinced that this was the sacrifice he should make. He still hesitated before making up his mind to act, but he kept thinking that he saw a person swinging from a pole, and he continued to see this vision even when he was awake. Finally, another dream led him to make his decision. The Maiyun who appeared to him in the dream told him that if he made this sacrifice his child would be healed.

Little White Man carried a pipe to Wounded Eye and Black Whetstone. He told them what he had seen and he begged their help in carrying out his sacrifice. They accepted the pipe, promising their assistance.

Then the Keeper and priest helped Little White Man prepare the cottonwood pole to which he would be tied. They readied the braided rawhide ropes, rubbing their hands over the ropes four times, and incensing them in sweet grass smoke. Two deerskin strings were tied to the end of each rope. Later these would be tied to the skewers in Little White Man's chest. Just before daybreak, Wounded Eye and Black Whetstone painted the Pledger's body with white clay. Then they had him sit down. One priest filled a pipe. He offered it to the Pledger four times, and each time Little White Man smoked. While he was smoking, the priest held the pipe, so the Pledger did not touch it with his hands.

When the smoking ended, Wounded Eye and Black Whetstone told Little White Man that this sacrifice was the greatest favor he could receive. Now he would have the privilege of standing on a hill where all the Sacred Powers could look at him. He could stand by a pole in the Sun's road, and there the Sun could look down and see him. It would be a hard trial, but he must not give up, they told Little White Man. When the Sun rose he should keep gazing at the Sun until Sun reached the zenith of the heavens. Then Little White Man should continue to watch the Sun until that Maiyun disappeared.

Now the two priests pierced Little White Man's chest. They inserted the two wooden skewers, tied the strings to them, and raised the Pledger to his feet. They pulled four times on his breast, to straighten out the ropes. Then they started him walking along the trail of sage. All day the Pledger walked back and forth, constantly trying to break loose. His skin stretched, but never broke. Finally, at sundown, Wounded Eye and Black Whetstone returned. They cut him loose, offered the flesh to the Sacred Powers, and led him back to camp. There, the Pledger entered the sweat house for the first of four sweats and four wipings with sage brush. On each of the next four days he took a sweat. After the fourth sweat, his body again belonged to him.

Little White Man gave Wounded Eye and Black Whetstone a horse, a gun, a suit of deerskin clothing, moccasins, and blankets as payment for their assistance.

The next morning his child recovered.[11]

Meanwhile, Wounded Eye's wife carried on the Sacred Hat Woman's tasks.[12] People constantly visited Is'siwun's lodge, so she worked hard to keep it clean. Early in the morning she arose and struck the tipi pole just to the south of the doorway four times, announcing that Is'siwun's home was open for the day.

When she cooked meals, she used soup to settle the dust on the ground. If water was spilled in Is'siwun's lodge, a storm would

---

[11] Grinnell, "The Cheyenne Medicine Lodge," *loc. cit.*, 251–55.
[12] The following information is from Davis Wounded Eye to the author, 1960.

arise, but soup was food, and no wind would come up if it was sprinkled over the floor. Since no one was allowed to scratch in the presence of the Hat, Wounded Eye's wife provided sticks for the people who visited the Hat Keeper. Since no one was allowed to blow upon the fire with his mouth, she saw to it that a pipestem rested close to the fire.

The last thing in the evening she again struck the door pole four times. Thus she announced that Is'siwun's home was closed for another day. Then everyone in camp slept.

There were other rules observed by those who visited Is'siwun. The Hat's power was that of the female buffalo, yet Cheyenne and Suhtai women were bound by strict rules within her presence. Davis Wounded Eye described them as they were observed in his father's day:

Women could come in, but the Hat bundle was covered. A woman could not see Is'siwun: that was strictly against the rules. Men are allowed to bring offerings; but if a woman vowed an offering cloth she must find a man to represent her in bringing the offerings to the priest.[13]

All the people—men, women and children—came to purify themselves in the sacred tipi, after the cloths were offered. The man who brought the cloth went outside the tipi. He stood facing the sunrise. Then the people knew what was coming. They stood in a single file, off to one side. Then, when the man had offered the cloth [to the Sacred Hat], the people would file in and touch themselves with the cloth [thus receiving a blessing].

There is the same rule with both the Arrows and Hat: all women have a season when they bleed. It is strictly against our religion to spill blood in the sacred tipi. That is why no woman was allowed to carry in offering cloths.

[13] Grinnell states that on certain occasions, when the Arrows were renewed, the Hat was exposed to the women of the tribe. Cf. "Cheyenne Medicine Arrows," MS. 70, Southwest Museum Library, and Grinnell, "Great Mysteries . . . ," *loc. cit.*, 563.

However, Fire Wolf, Davis Wounded Eye, Henry Little Coyote, and Josephine Head Swift Limpy all denied that the Hat was exposed to women for the reasons given here. In 1959, Fred Last Bull was criticized for allowing women to gaze at Is'siwun at the time of the opening of the Hat bundle. Misfortune was predicted for him because of this action.

Wounded Eye's role in the Buffalo Ceremony underlined the traditional identification of the Keeper and his family with the Buffalo People. Davis Wounded Eye described that relationship:

You have the Keeper of the Sacred Hat. His family are considered Is'siwun. They are the Buffalo family. If the Keeper has sisters, he is not ashamed to talk with them because the buffalo mingle with their sisters.

Even today I have Buffalo power. If you truly believe in it, even in grief you will receive a blessing and power. If you truly believe in it![14]

Thus life passed quietly for Wounded Eye and his family—the Buffalo Family who guarded Is'siwun. In later years, however, the Keeper's old bullet wound again became infected. Box Elder was long since gone, and no one was left who possessed his great healing power. So it was that, about 1920, Wounded Eye died in the valley of the Rosebud.[15]

[14] To the author, 1960. Verified by Josie Head Swift Limpy. John Stands in Timber stated that the Tsistsistas often criticized the Suhtaio for this "loose" attitude toward their sisters.
[15] Davis Wounded Eye to the author, 1960. The date of Wounded Eye's death is from the Tongue River Agency probate records.

22. Standing Against the Thunder, 1909

There long have been Cheyennes who fear Thunder, the terrible Maiyun who takes the form of a great bird or a rider on a white horse. Thunder appears to such a man in a dream or vision, telling him that he must become Hohnuhk'e, a Contrary.

The name "Contrary" was derived from the sacred obligation to speak and to act in reverse. A Contrary lived alone, apart from the rest of the people. Ask him to do one thing, and he would do another. He might never sit or lie on a bed. Whatever he did in social relationships, he did backward.[1]

[1] Cf. Grinnell, *Cheyenne Indians*, I, 187, 231–33; II, 80–85, 120; Grinnell, *Fighting Cheyennes*, 1915, 43; Dorsey, *The Cheyenne Indians*, I, 24f.; George Bent to Hyde, December 31, 1906, Colorado State Historical Society.

A Contrary never married. If he did, he must give up Hohnu-kawo', the sacred Contrary Bow from which he derived his power. The Contrary Bow was actually a lance, shaped like a bow, strung with two strings, with a stone or metal head lashed to one end. The skin of a sacred tanager, and the feathers of an owl, hawk, and eagle, were fastened to the lance shaft. The sacred bow was repaired and renewed at the same time that the renewing ceremonies were held for Mahuts.

The Contrary Bow was not actually a weapon. It was carried into battle, but was used only for counting coup—not for killing an enemy. When its bearer shifted the Bow to his right hand, he could never retreat. However, armed with that sacred lance, a Contrary warrior was the bravest of a brave people. During a battle, he charged the enemy alone, since he had to ride along the flank of the other fighting men. A Contrary could court death with recklessness, because the power of the Contrary Bow would protect him.

The Contraries never were a warrior society. There were no Contrary chiefs or officers, since these men fought and acted alone. Yet, they were always prepared for battle, their bodies and their Contrary Bows covered with sacred red paint. Their reputation for bravery was such that they were often sought out as leaders for war parties. For instance, it was a Contrary warrior who led the Elks when they charged the soldiers at the Platte River bridge in July, 1865.[2]

The possession of a Contrary Bow committed a man to tremendous spiritual obligations. The point of the Bow must never be allowed to touch the earth, because the Earth is the bearer of life for the Cheyennes. She brings forth the living plants and vegetation that sustain the people and the game upon which they depend. Thus, like the power of the Buffalo Hat, Earth's power is the power of woman. Symbolically, the Thunder Bow suggested male reproductive power tied and restrained in order that the Contrary warrior might use all his strength for the protection of the people.

[2] George Bent to Hyde, 1907.

Therefore, when a Cheyenne dreamed that he must become a Contrary, he awakened to a fearsome and terrible responsibility. His would be an almost unbearable burden. Indeed, the duties were so demanding that there were only three or four Contraries among the Cheyennes at the period prior to the Mackenzie fight. In recompense, the willingness to assume these awful obligations give a Contrary power over the great Maiyun whose noise and lightning once had filled him with terror. Armed with the supernatural strength of the Contrary Bow, a Cheyenne warrior no longer feared the Thunder.

Charles Whistling Elk was born in 1876, too late to carry a Contrary Bow.[3] However, he feared the Thunder. When the lightning flashed and Thunder's sound rolled across the prairie, Whistling Elk ran from his lodge, nearly blind with fear. It was even affecting his health.

One day, he and Buffalo Wallow, his younger brother, had ridden to Lame Deer Agency. A storm was coming, and the dark clouds were gathering overhead. When the brothers reached the hill above Lame Deer Creek, they looked around them. It seemed that the rain surely would catch them, and the two men whipped their horses into a gallop. Whistling Elk warned Buffalo Wallow not to ride near him, and the younger man followed at a distance. They galloped along the lone trail at the top of the divide. Whistling Elk's fear became so great that he was zigzagging his horse back and forth across the road. Buffalo Wallow raced along behind, keeping his pony on a straight path down the trail.

As they reached the road along Muddy Creek, the storm clouds split in two. Suddenly it was quiet and clear. Once it was certain that the rain would not hit them, Whistling Elk stopped. Then

[3] This account of Whistling Elk's fast is from his brother, George Brady, or Buffalo Wallow, 1964. Buffalo Wallow was born in 1881, and was respected as the instructor of a number of the Cheyennes who continue the old-time fasting and sacrificing in the hills. He died in 1968.

John Stands in Timber was interpreting for the author while Buffalo Wallow was describing his brother's sacrifice. John Stands in Timber added the details concerning the vision of Thunder, which he had heard from Whistling Elk himself.

he let his horse move ahead again, slowly. Buffalo Wallow rode up beside him, and the brothers traveled home at a slow pace.

They had been riding in silence for some time when Whistling Elk finally spoke. He told his brother that he had gone through the minor sacred ceremonies, and that he had used the pipe in other ceremonies. "All those were not as powerful as what the Powers wish me to go through," he said.

Soon afterward, Whistling Elk rode off into the pine hills nearby. He fasted there two days and two nights. After he finished, he carried the pipe to White Bull, the holy man to whom Thunder himself had appeared years before. It was Thunder's own red-and-white horned war bonnet that Ice had made to protect Roman Nose from the soldier bullets.

A year before this time, during the 1908 Sun Dance, the Cheyennes again had seen White Bull's power. Little Fish had collapsed under the pressure of heat, fasting, and exhaustion. By the fourth day, the final day of the Sun Dance, he lay on a buffalo robe, hardly able to move. The singers and drummers were beginning the final songs—the four sacred songs that are sung while the Instructor, Pledger, priests, and Sun dancers showed the fullness of their sacred power and strength. Little Fish later said that he was helpless at this point, and that he could not go on.

Then White Bull was kneeling beside him, bending over him. "My friend," Ice said, "Sit on the tail end of that buffalo robe." Little Fish did as he was directed, as White Bull moved on down to the head of the robe.

"Look me in the eye! Have your mouth open as you do!" the old priest instructed.

Suddenly cold objects were hitting Little Fish in the face and mouth. They were hailstones; the ice from which White Bull had received his second name. "I became alive!" Little Fish said afterward.

As White Bull picked up the buffalo robe, Little Fish rose from the earth of the Medicine Lodge. He continued dancing through the final sacred songs, fulfilling his pledge to Maheo and to the Powers.

334

Now White Bull smoked the pipe, accepting Whistling Elk's plea for help. Ice was growing feeble; he was an old man of well over seventy years. Therefore, he asked his "son," Medicine Bird, to assist him in preparing Whistling Elk for the sacrifice ahead.[4]

When White Bull and Medicine Bird arrived at Whistling Elk's home, he and Buffalo Wallow begin to gather the objects needed for fasting in the hills: a buffalo skull, rawhide ropes, paint, the white "man" sage, offering cloths, rawhide laces, and an eagle-wing bone whistle with which to summon the Powers. A new knife was needed for carving and sharpening the wooden skewers that would pierce the Pledger's chest.

When these objects were assembled, Whistling Elk, Buffalo Wallow, White Bull, and the other priests all rode off toward the hills by Muddy Creek. They stopped at the southwest end of the ridge dividing the north and south forks of the Muddy. There, in an open spot on top of the ridge, a half-moon circle of "man" sage was laid upon the earth around a lone cedar tree. This was the sacred pathway upon which Whistling Elk would walk during his sacrifice. As he moved upon the sage, he would draw into his own body the power that flows through the sacred plant. A buffalo skull was placed upon the earth at the opening of the half-moon circle. It opened toward the sunrise, in the direction of the Sacred Mountain. As Whistling Elk endured in offering his sacrifice, the buffalo skull would bring him a share of Is'siwun's power.

The priests then covered the faster's body, face, and limbs with yellow paint, the Sun color. The "man power" design was painted in blue across his forehead, under his eyes, on his wrists, and above his ankles.[5]

Whistling Elk dropped to his knees. Medicine Bird and Wolf Name, another priest, were kneeling on either side of him as they carried out White Bull's instructions. However, when the knife was brought for the piercing of Whistling Elk's chest, one priest could not cut the slits. The other moved around, taking his place.

[4] Medicine Bird was the son of White Bull's brother Red Head. In the Cheyenne kinship system, this would make Medicine Bird the son of White Bull, also.
[5] For a drawing of the "man power" design, see Chapter 30, Vol. II, "Maheo and the Sacred Powers."

Again, this second priest was unable to pinch the Pledger's skin and pierce it with the knife.

Ice was encouraging Whistling Elk. "Do not try to hold back. Just give yourself! Let your faith loose, so the sacred work can be done easily!" White Bull said.

Still the knife was not piercing the skin. Then the priests called to Buffalo Wallow, who was standing off to one side. Buffalo Wallow took the knife, and he slit his brother's flesh easily. Then he inserted the wooden skewers through the loops of skin.

The priests raised Whistling Elk to his feet. An eagle-wing bone whistle was placed around his neck. The two rawhide ropes had been thrown over the top branch of the lone cedar tree that grew straight from the earth at the center of the half-moon of sage. The ends of the ropes then were lashed to the wooden skewers that pierced the Pledger's chest.

Whistling Elk stood there for a minute, facing the buffalo skull. Then he fainted, falling right on top of the skull. Buffalo Wallow helped him to his feet. "Try to make a stand!" he urged his brother.

Medicine Bird caught Whistling Elk by the shoulders. The priest pulled the Pledger back three times. Then, on the sacred fourth time, he pushed Whistling Elk ahead. The Pledger began his journey upon the half-moon trail of sage. The rawhide ropes pulled taut as he threw himself back against them, the skin protruding under that pressure. The buffalo skull, Is'siwun's symbol, looked on as he offered his sacrifice.

The others watched for a few minutes as Whistling Elk strained against the ropes. Then they walked down the hill. Throughout the night, they could hear the sound of the eagle-wing bone whistle, calling the Powers to come and to look down upon the Pledger.

Black clouds moved in during the night, covering the face of the moon. Rain came pouring down, and lightning cut the darkness. White Bull had encouraged Whistling Elk before he left him alone on the hill. "Do not be afraid! Do not fear any danger!" he had said. Yet the Pledger knew that he would be afraid.

336

Suddenly a white horse and rider appeared, charging through the rain clouds. The Maiyun was riding bareback, and an offering cloth was tied around his head. The rider was Thunder himself. He waved a war club as he charged down through the storm, attacking Whistling Elk. But the Pledger stood firm.

Throughout the night, Whistling Elk continued his journey back and forth across the pathway of sage. His whistle blew constantly, summoning the Sacred Powers. Dawn came, and the offering of Whistling Elk's sacrifice continued through the day. Then darkness came once more.

Again Thunder appeared, the offering cloth tied around his head. Once more the Maiyun charged his white horse down through the sky, attacking Whistling Elk. Again Whistling Elk stood fast, his eagle-wing bone whistle sounding in defiance as his feet continued to move along the pathway of sacred sage.

At last Thunder's voice rolled through the darkness, telling Whistling Elk that he had saved his own life by not being afraid.

At daybreak, White Bull and the others climbed the hill. Ice announced that Whistling Elk's sacrifice was completed. One of the priests cut away the flesh surrounding the wooden skewers. The skin was placed upon the earth before the buffalo skull, as an offering to Maheo and the Sacred Powers.

After that, the old fear was gone. Whistling Elk had won his battle against the Thunder.

23. Fighting for the Sun Dance, 1907–1934

By 1907 the Cheyennes knew how to deal effectively with the "Government Men," as the representatives of Washington were designated. That year, the four Old Man Chiefs, Two Moon, American Horse, Crazy Head, and Brave Bear, paid a formal call on the superintendent at Lame Deer. Young Bird went with them, along with many other leaders in the sacred ceremonies, because the Cheyennes were protesting the abolition of the Sun Dance.

The Chiefs designated Little Sun as their spokesman, and he did his work well. He began by telling Superintendent J. C. Eddy that the Grandfather in Washington had permitted the Cheyennes freedom to worship in any way they wished. Then the government had banned the Sun Dance because of the public sacrificing of the men's bodies in the Medicine Lodge. However, this tying of a man to the center pole was not part of the ancient ceremonies. Since it was a new ceremony, the Cheyennes were willing to omit it. The Chiefs now requested permission for a "Willow Dance," a ceremony receiving its name from the custom of draping the dancers with willow wreaths and garlands.

Little Sun warned Eddy:

> We aren't doing anything that isn't religious. We are using our original ceremonies. This Willow Dance is for anyone who believes it. Indian, White Man, Black Man—we all have the same right. I think it is wrong when they cut off Indians from this law [meaning freedom of worship]. My talk, and the talk of others, will reach Washington![1]

The superintendent's reply was that Little Sun had spoken wisely, and no one would be prevented from exercising his religion. "I will permit you and your people to have a Willow Dance. But keep this in mind: there will be no torture!" Eddy stated.

"This a Willow Dance. There is no torture in it," the Chiefs replied.

So it was that the offering of the Sun Dance was permitted once more, under the new name of "Willow Dance."

Clubfoot pledged the ceremony. Then he offered the pipe to Young Bird, who smoked it, agreeing to be the Instructor. The Medicine Lodge was erected during the Fourth of July weekend, the only summer holiday long enough for a four-day ceremony.[2]

---

[1] John Stands in Timber was present at this meeting and is the source of the quotation.

Eugene Fisher was interpreting on this occasion. Fisher was born c. 1878, the son of Little Wolf's eldest daughter and a white man. He came to Lame Deer with Little Chief's band in 1891. After four years at Carlisle, he entered Montana State University in 1904, with the intention of studying law. However, his eyes were injured playing football there, and on doctor's advice he withdrew from the university. Eugene Fisher was president of the Northern Cheyenne Tribal Council for five terms. He died c. 1956.

John Stands in Timber's opinion was that Fisher advised Little Sun to use this argument of freedom of worship.

[2] Since the early 1900's, the Fourth of July weekend has been the usual time for holding the Sun Dance ceremonies.

For three years the offering of the Willow Dance continued. However, by November, 1911, Washington's ban was renewed— not only against the Willow Dance but also against other dances of a ceremonial nature. The Indian Bureau's tone was firm but paternal, the principal argument being that the ceremonies kept the Cheyennes away from their ranches for too long a time:

> Now that you are seriously engaged in the work of making your-selves self-supporting, it is improper for you to devote any con-siderable amount of time to ceremonial dancing, and it is my desire that the so-called Willow dance, and the animal dance, which you have in recent years celebrated annually, be hereafter discontinued . . . .
>
> You cannot continue your Willow dance and animal dance without doing great injury to your health and various indus-tries . . . .[3]

The Cheyennes disagreed, and a stream of letters flowed back and forth between Lame Deer and Washington. In 1915, Medi-cine Top, Box Elder's son, explained the harmless nature of the Willow Dance to John Buntin, the new superintendent at Lame Deer. He said that the ceremony received its name

> from the fact that the Indians have a custom which is many years old, of having a dance sometime after the willows are out . . . It is the custom of the Indians to largely dress themselves with willows. Everyone should have a large willow hat . . . made of willows and small willow branches platted and fastened about their person . . . .[4]

Medicine Top added that none of the features of the Sun Dance were connected with the Willow Dance. Also, that the dance would not be held for more than two days, after the crops had matured.

[3] F. H. Abbott, assistant commissioner of Indian affairs, to Thaddeus Red Water, Willis Rowland, Charles Lone Elk, Samuel Little Sun, Big Head Man, and Jacob Tall Bull. November 4, 1911. Tongue River Agency records, National Archives.

[4] John A. Buntin to the Commissioner of Indian Affairs, April 16, 1915.

Buntin listened. Then he offered the Cheyennes an alternative, a fair where they could exhibit their prize crops.[5] The people responded to that suggestion by slipping off to the privacy of the hills. Maheo still heard their prayers, and the men still quietly offered their flesh as sacrifices. The Buffalo Ceremony continued to be pledged, and sweat lodges still stood near many cabins. Government eyes were not so far-seeing as to observe the Cheyennes slipping, one or two at a time, into the Sacred Hat tipi. Offering cloths of linen and calico were carried to Is'siwun's Keeper, who, in turn, tied them to the sacred bundle.

The Cheyennes knew how to fight, and they also knew how to endure. A few white friends were willing to come to their aid. James Mooney offered his assistance, and so did his superior, F. W. Hodge, chief of the Bureau of American Ethnology.[6] Hodge wrote the commissioner of Indian affairs, arguing that

> such harmless rites [as the Sun Dance] have a tendency in a psychological way, to promote moral uplift. I shall be glad . . . to detail Mr. Mooney to proceed to Montana in order to make observations of a ceremony that will soon be entirely extinct . . . .[7]

The assistant commissioner's reply was that the Indian Bureau disapproved of the Willow Dance, which was a modified form of the Sun Dance. The ceremony was detrimental to the welfare of the Indians, and a step backward in their civilization. Therefore every effort was being made to discourage the repetition of the Sun Dances where they were still being held.[8] However, the Cheyennes had no thought of allowing the Sun Dance to become extinct. Each year they petitioned the commissioner of Indian affairs for permission to hold the ceremonies. Each year the commissioner refused. In 1917, the Cheyennes went so far as to say they would permit the superintendent and

[5] Ibid.
[6] J. White Elk, Medicine Top, Old Bull, and Frank Lightning to James Mooney, July 14, 1916.
[7] F. W. Hodge to Cato Sells, commissioner of Indian affairs, July 29, 1916.
[8] E. B. Merritt, assistant commissioner of Indian affairs, to F. W. Hodge, August 8, 1916.

other government employees to be present at the Willow Dance. "If anything is seen wrong and our attention is called to it, we are ready to cut out that part of it," they added.[9]

Commissioner Cato Sells again refused permission, and again he urged the Cheyennes to attend their annual fair.[10]

Thus the years dragged by and 1919 began like any of the other years which held little meaning without the Sun Dance. Some of the Cheyennes began the new year by worshipping in the Mennonite Mission Church at the northern edge of Lame Deer. The pastor was Doctor Rodolphe Petter. Both in Oklahoma and in Montana the people listened with respect to this Veho speaking their language so fluently that he was named "Cheyenne Talker." Rodolphe Petter, in turn, understood and respected much of the old spirituality of the Cheyennes, especially the Sacred Arrow ceremonies. However, that is not to say that he agreed with all the forms that Cheyenne spirituality assumed!

Doctor Petter had announced a new series of homilies for the year 1919. The title of the series was "The Kingdom of Satan." The pastor's message was soon made clear to the people; the Kingdom of Satan lay in the practice of the Cheyenne sacred ways.[11]

Robert Yellowfox and George Enemy Captive were among the younger men who heard Doctor Petter's sermons. Five years before, Enemy Captive had sought membership in the Buffalo Society. Now the pastor's words, plus a touch of jealousy, brought him to the Mennonite parsonage. His testimony to Doctor Petter sparked off the final struggle for the survival of the Cheyenne sacred ways.[12]

Enemy Captive confessed that secretly the people were pre-

[9] Hugh White Frog, Charles Spotted Elk, et al. to Commissioner of Indian Affairs, June 13, 1917.
[10] Cato Sells to the Commissioner of Indian Affairs, June 26, 1917.
[11] Mrs. Rodolphe Petter to the author, August, 1958.
[12] The name George Enemy Captive is fictitious, because the actual person involved is still living. "Testimony of 'George Enemy Captive,' age 33 years . . ." January 3, 1919. Tongue River Agency records, National Archives.

paring to hold a Sun Dance. The ceremonies possibly would be offered near Ashland, Montana, or off the reservation itself.

Enemy Captive continued to relate that, in 1914, he had sought instructions in becoming a Buffalo doctor, a medicine man.[13] Following his initial instructions in the healing ceremonies, a feast was given. About midnight, Charles Teeth, one of the doctors, gave him further counsel.[14] The older priest warned Enemy Captive "not to get cold feet." He told the younger man that he must leave his wife, Emma, with Fred Iron Shirt, a senior priest of the Buffalo Society.[15] Then Iron Shirt had used her as the sacred woman was used in the Suhtai ceremonies.[16]

When Enemy Captive's wife returned, she bore a piece of sacred herb in her mouth. She placed the plant in her husband's mouth. The herb tasted sweet, but Enemy Captive spit it out, fearing that it might be poisoned.[17]

A sweat bath followed the next morning. At the end of the sweat, Enemy Captive's initiation was completed, but he was far from satisfied. The ceremony cost him ten horses, over a hundred dollars in money, plus supplies and sustenance. He also com-

---

[13] These instructions were sought in the Buffalo society, the Suhtaio society whose priests were closely linked to the Sacred Hat. The Buffalo ceremony may be pledged to bring healing to an individual or to his or her loved ones. Originally, the ceremony was offered to insure the abundance of buffalo. Therefore, the woman was used in her role as the renewer of life.

Cf. Robert Anderson, "The Buffalo Men," *loc. cit.* Anderson's informant unfortunately did not mention the use of the woman. Undoubtedly this was still too touchy a subject to discuss with a non-Cheyenne after the disturbances recorded in this chapter.

Fire Wolf, Rufus Wallowing, John Stands in Timber, Charles Sitting Man, Sr., Albert Tall Bull—all verified the use of the sacred woman in both the Sun Dance and the Buffalo ceremony.

[14] Teeth was later the keeper of the Ox'zem bundle and the straight pipe formerly owned by Box Elder.

[15] The wife's Cheyenne name was Haseoveo. She was Rufus Wallowing's sister.

[16] Iron Shirt was the old warrior-priest who attempted to take the fringed shirt from the soldier during the Custer fight, *q.v.*

[17] This was probably the sacred sweet root used to transmit power in the Sun Dance, the Arrow renewing, and other ceremonies.

plained to Petter that Iron Shirt's use of his wife had left him a jealous man.

Enemy Captive stated that a majority of the Cheyenne men over thirty years of age were doctors (that is, medicine men or priests) of some kind. The younger men were frightened into these beliefs, and were afraid to oppose them, he testified to Doctor Petter.[18]

Robert Yellowfox was also touched by the pastor's eloquence. As a boy, Yellowfox had danced in the Ghost Dance ceremonies. He had sacrificed bits of flesh to the Powers, thus fulfilling a pledge made by his imprisoned father. He had fasted four days and nights, seeking healing for a relative's daughter—but she had died, nevertheless. Yellowfox had also offered sacred cloths to the Maiyun, seeking their blessing. On twelve occasions, he had offered the sacrifice of his body on a hilltop. In later years, he had joined in the Peyote religion. Now Yellowfox had decided to become a Mennonite.

In his testimony, the new convert gave his impression of the Cheyenne sacred ways:

.... [Men] who have sacrificed the honor of their wives in certain religious worship, they are honored .... In their religion they pray to the sun, the moon, the stars, sacred bull and many others. They also consider different kinds of beasts to have supernatural power. They pray to water, springs, trees, rocks, mountains and to demons under the earth. Some even worship each other! I count 183 medicine men and women among my tribe here. These people are leaders in all the doings.

The medicine men or religious men are all connected with doings with women; that belongs to their system and they cannot refuse .... In the Sun Dance and Crazy Dance the women are also given over to the use of the ceremonial teachers. All this is kept from the knowledge of white men who come to attend such ceremonials .... White men who have not lived a long time with us and have to use interpreters to find out things can never know

[18] "Testimony of 'George Enemy Captive' ...," *loc. cit.*

what is going on among my people, can they call good what is bad? . . . How can they defend a religion that breeds immorality and disease?[19]

Doctor Petter forwarded the Yellowfox testimonies to Washington. There, Commissioner Burke reiterated the Indian Bureau's policy of discouraging the Cheyennes in their practice of the old sacred ways, which "retard their moral and intellectual advancement . . . and their self-supporting activities."[20]

Back at Lame Deer, affairs were in a turmoil. Not the least of latter-day Cheyenne difficulties had been the rapid turnover in superintendents for Tongue River Agency. John Buntin was the superintendent at that time. Prior to his appointment, the longest superintendency had lasted two years, and the next longest a year and a half. In 1919, Buntin had been in charge for about five years.[21] As late as the 1960's, older Northern Cheyennes recall with respect his fairness and his steady, quiet manner. Characteristically, in the midst of the uproar involving Tongue River Agency, Washington, and the Mennonites, Buntin acted with courage and dispatch.

The Cheyenne priests and doctors were summoned to Lame Deer, where the testimonies of Enemy Captive and Yellowfox were read to them. The priests and doctors were then asked to appoint a man to answer these charges. Jacob Tall Bull was their choice as spokesman.

Tall Bull denied that the doctors terrorized anyone. He also stated that a man did not have to be married to be a Cheyenne doctor, nor was it necessary for him to have a woman to represent a wife in the ceremonies. He also denied that the giving of the woman was a regular part of the ceremonies. "If the Indian doctors in general had known of it [the use of the woman] they

[19] "Robert Yellowfox Testimony," in a letter from Rodolphe Petter to George Bird Grinnell, February 15, 1922. This testimony was originally given in 1919. Superintendent Buntin notes it in a letter dated January 20, 1919.
[20] Commissioner Burke to Rodolphe Petter, March 18, 1922.
[21] "Report on the Cheyenne Indians No. 1 to the Commissioner of Indian Affairs," September 5, 1919, Hugh Scott Papers.

would not tolerate it at all . . . They will not stand for anything that is immoral," Tall Bull declared.[22]

However, it is not recorded, or recalled, whether he added that what the whites might consider immoral was not necessarily so in the sacred concepts of the People.

Enemy Captive's testimony to Petter referred to events five years prior to this time. Buntin stated that since these events were past, no efforts would be made to punish the priests and doctors. However, the Cheyennes present were made to understand that the commissioner's office would not tolerate the conduct described by Enemy Captive and others. If such events occurred again, and were proved to be true, punishment would follow.

Buntin then wrote the commissioner:

> The leading medicine men assured me that such ceremonies would not be repeated; at the same time they denied such ceremonies had been conducted . . . .
>
> . . . I think a bold stand against it taken in the presence of the medicine men will have at least a very intimidating effect and have a strong tendency to stamp out such proceedings . . . .[23]

Even Buntin did not understand Cheyenne devotion to the old sacred ways.

News moves quickly in an Indian community, where the "moccasin telegraph" moves with uncanny speed. Long before the superintendent's report reached Washington, the Cheyennes knew what had occurred.

Threats were made against Enemy Captive and his wife, against the Mennonite converts, and even against Doctor and Mrs. Petter. Dissension was rising among the Cheyennes who were nominal Mennonites. Mrs. Petter wrote:

> While all our Christians claim to have nothing more to do with the ceremonial life of the Cheyennes, it was soon evident that we

[22] "Statement of Jacob Tall Bull," sworn to on January 29, 1919, at Lame Deer. Correspondence dated February 7, 1919, Tongue River Agency records, National Archives.
[23] Buntin to Commissioner of Indian Affairs, January 20, 1919, Tongue River Agency Records, National Archives.

had one Daniel and a few of his friends. Vohokass [Eugene Standing Elk] is a born leader.[24] At one . . . [prayer] meeting, when he touched many forms of the ceremonial life, it created such a stir that several women arose from their seats, muttering and sputtering, and left the room . . . .[25]

Conflict was mounting between the Cheyenne Mennonites who kept their sympathy for the old sacred ways and those who favored a clean break with the past. The Petters decided to temporarily discontinue the Sunday evening prayer meetings normally held in the church. Instead, smaller gatherings met in the parsonage, gatherings which included Enemy Captive, Yellowfox, and the other converts who were advocating a clean rejection of the older ways.[26]

Washington had been busy too. In March, 1919, Superintendent Buntin again summoned the priests and doctors to his office. About thirty Cheyennes appeared this time. The air was tense around Lame Deer; some of the warriors were singing their death songs, awaiting the reprisals they were certain lay ahead.[27]

The meeting lasted almost six hours. Buntin took the precaution of placing a pistol in his desk drawer. The room was ringed with Indian agency policemen, under Vohokass, Eugene Standing Elk.[28]

Buntin began by explaining the nature of disease, and how germs could be spread. He elaborated on how dangerous the Cheyenne healing ceremonies could be, with the doctor blowing on his patients, spitting sacred herbs on them, and then sucking out the malady. The superintendent added that one of the medicine men present recently had been accused of manslaughter in the case of the death of a child he had treated. The same medicine

24 Light, or Eugene Standing Elk, son of the Chief who betrayed the Cheyennes into going south in 1877. Light was chief of police at Lame Deer. He had succeeded his father as one of the Northern Council Chiefs.
25 "Disclosures at Lame Deer and What Became of Them," a mimeographed letter dated March 13, 1919. It was sent by Bertha K. (Mrs. Rodolphe) Petter to readers of *The Mennonite.*
26 *Ibid.*
27 Rufus Wallowing to the author.
28 Bertha K. Petter (Mrs. Rodolphe) to the author, 1959.

man was awaiting trial by the laws of Montana. Furthermore, the "vile practices" of the Cheyenne doctors had been disclosed to Washington by letter. The return orders informed Buntin to deal with such Indian offenses in accordance with both state and national laws.

As Buntin continued, the priests' heads were lowered and their faces darkened in anger and resentment. One after another they rose to their feet, denying that vile rites were practiced in the sacred ceremonies. Enemy Captive was called into the room, and he repeated his charges. Finally Iron Shirt arose, his frail body bent with age. The old priest-warrior fairly shook and trembled with rage as he denied the accusations. Then he demanded that the woman be called to make the charges herself.[29]

A low murmur of approval came from the priests and doctors. No woman had ever publicly revealed the sacred ways before, and they were confident she would not do so now. The priests agreed that they would accept Haseoveo's statements as truth. Iron Shirt shouted, "Send for the woman! Let her tell her charges in the faces of the priests and medicine men!"

Vohokass, the Chief of Police, slipped from the gathering to search for Haseoveo. Meanwhile, some of the Cheyenne women had gathered in an outer room of the superintendent's office. Vohokass and Haseoveo had to go through the crowd as they returned. Hissing and the taunts that sound so soft when spoken in Cheyenne rose from the waiting women when they saw Haseoveo, who was carrying her baby in her arms. As she and Standing Elk passed through their ranks, one woman slipped behind Haseoveo, following her into the council room. Haseoveo's appearance amazed the waiting priests. Their exclamations were so loud that Buntin had to rap for silence before she could even speak. Then the superintendent asked her the questions that exploded the whole affair.

Softly, Haseoveo repeated her accusations. Now there was only silence in the room. Finally, Thomas Flying arose. He ad-

[29] "Disclosures at Lame Deer . . . ," *loc. cit.*, 2f. Doctor Petter was present throughout the entire proceeding.

mitted the importance of the woman's role in the ceremonies. Then he concluded, "I am ready to take my punishment for it, and will stab myself if necessary for it!"[30]

Buntin used "fairly strong language" in addressing the priests. He commended Haseoveo and her husband, adding that a white man would have shot anyone guilty of such deeds with his wife. The superintendent then instructed Vohokass to address the gathering, since he was one of the Chiefs. "Everyone gave him [Vohokass] respectful attention because of his position in the tribe, even though they hated him with bitter hatred," Mrs. Petter wrote at the time. Vohokass denounced the priests and doctors as being liars, and reiterated his own position as a Mennonite.[31]

Buntin followed up the meeting with a list of rules aimed at limiting the power of the Cheyenne priests and doctors. Sucking or spitting on the body of a patient was forbidden. Doctors were forbidden to initiate other doctors, and they were forbidden to charge money or property for their healing services. "All ceremonies wherein the debauching of women forms a part and the collection of fees from candidates to become doctors is prohibited and is considered an Indian offense." Cheyenne doctors were forbidden to advise others against stock raising, farming, placing their children in schools, "or doing anything else which will prevent Indians from progressing and becoming self-supporting, respectable people.... No Indian was permitted to claim more than three dollars a day for assisting a sick person by providing water, cleaning the patient, or otherwise caring for him. Even the use of the rattle was forbidden, and also the singing of songs that might prevent a weak person from sleeping. All these offenses were now punishable.[32]

The Cheyennes were temporarily silenced, but certainly not beaten. Two months later, a group of older priests appealed to

[30] Bertha Petter, to the author, 1958–61. Mrs. Petter stated that Flying actually gave testimony which was directly the opposite of what he intended to say.
Cf. "Disclosures at Lame Deer . . . ," loc. cit., 3.
Cf. Buntin to the commissioner of Indian affairs, March 17, 1919.
[31] Ibid.
[32] Buntin to commissioner of Indian affairs, March 17, 1919.

Commissioner Cato Sells for permission to continue doctoring. The appeal was refused. Sells repeated the ban against the older medicine men initiating younger men, and the younger men making payment for initiation.[33]

Again the Northern Cheyennes withdrew to the isolation of the pine hills, offering there the solitary acts of fasting and sacrificing that Buntin and Washington did not notice. Offering cloths were still borne to the Sacred Hat. Men journeyed to Oklahoma in order to join in the Sacred Arrow ceremonies. Riders traveling among the hills occasionally stumbled across a whitened buffalo skull and a lone tree with rope burns scarring its upper branches.

However, Doctor Petter knew the Cheyennes too well to believe that mere government orders would wipe out the sacred ways. Even George Bird Grinnell had failed to note—or, at least, to record—the use of the Sacred Woman in the ceremonies. At the height of the controversy, Petter wrote the noted historian of the Cheyennes:

> The well-meaning Government is under the impression that with the passing of the old men all 'medicine practice' will be discarded! What a fallacy! There are here on this reservation between one hundred sixty and one hundred eighty initiated medicine men, and of these not thirty are really old men. Younger men are constantly recruited, yes even returned students, men who speak well English, become medicine men . . . .[34]

The Mennonites continued to press for enforcement of the regulations against doctoring and the use of the Sacred Woman. Esevona, Mrs. Scalpcane, described to Mrs. Petter how Mosa, or Calf, a Buffalo priest, gave her to Teeth during one of the cere-

[33] The letter, dated May 23, 1919, was addressed to John Two Moon, David Little White Man, Samuel Little Sun, Pius Shoulderblade, and Milton Little White Man.

[34] Rodolphe Petter to George Bird Grinnell, February 15, 1922.

Cf. later statement of Exovona (Mrs. Frank Little Wolf), who said, "George Bird Grinnell was present during the four days ceremonial but failed to know what was done at night." Letter from Assistant Commissioner E. B. Merritt to Mrs. Petter, August 28, 1923.

Cf., also, letter from Doctor Petter to Charles Burke, commissioner of Indian affairs, May 4, 1926.

monies. Esevona was a widow, and the ceremony had been pledged to bring health to her and to her children, especially to one son. However, the very child for whom it was pledged, died afterward.

Esevona also stated that since Enemy Captive's confession many Cheyennes had been unable to fulfill their vows to offer the ceremonies. During the influenza epidemic, many such pledges had been made.

> I have heard Indians say there are over forty [vows] still not carried out. I hear them talk how they have written to Washington and now expect permission to be allowed all their ceremonies as [are] the Oklahoma Cheyennes . . . . I know very well how scientists who have come to study the ceremonies were deceived, and went away thinking they were innocent . . . .[35]

The conflict continued. The Cheyennes watched, waited, and slipped off into the hills until more effective results could be obtained.

> *My friends,*
> *Nothing lives long,*
> *Except the rocks!*

The words of the old Kit Fox song had new meaning as the people sought out the only place of sanctuary remaining to them.

However, the wind on the buffalo grass was shifting. By May, 1926, Doctor Petter was deploring the current revival of the old sacred ways. One of the Cheyenne tribal delegates, then in Washington, had written that the ceremonies, including Peyote, would again be permitted by the government.

> A great wave of relief and rejoicing is now going through the circles of Shamans and all improgressive Indians . . . . The Indians tell me Mr. Grinnell is helping them and declared he had attended the Crazy Ceremony or Buffalo Dance and saw nothing wrong in it.

[35] Superintendent Boggis of Tongue River Agency to commissioner of Indian affairs, May 15, 1922. Esevona's statement to Mrs. Petter is included in this report.

However, he like some ethnologists excuse such immoral doings on the ground they are part of the religious worship which should not be judged with our moral standards. This rests only on fallacy for the Cheyenne tell me that long before any school or Church teaching came to them, the immoral parts of these ceremonies were not approved by all, only the fear of the Shamans kept many from remonstrating and a few individuals opposed the obscene rites, even in the long ago.

About 30 years ago the then 80 years old Left Hand Bull assured me that Sun Dance, Crazy Dance and Sweatlodge ceremony were comparatively recent innovations coming to them from other tribes. He himself deplored the fact that the Cheyenne had introduced "bad things" to their former ceremonies. There is here in Montana a Cheyenne organization (called Offering Men) which will have nothing to do with the obscene rites. Then at times the very woman given for those rites would run away. And all such Indians felt so before school and church came among them . . . .[36]

Referring to Grinnell's recording of the Massaum ceremony, Petter continued:

The last Buffalo Dance, which Mr. Grinnell attended, was made by Frank Little Wolf . . . . He tells me with a smile, "Mr. Grinnell attended our dance but he heard nothing except what the Indians choose to let him hear through interpreters. Then some parts of the ceremony were kept from his eyes and presence" [so] says Frank who himself is initiated and "offered" his wife.[37]

While the white men argued, John Clubfoot carried the pipe to old Wolf Chief. Clubfoot was thanking Maheo for the recovery of his sick son, and he had prayed that he might express his gratitude in the Sun Dance lodge itself, even though the ceremony was still forbidden.[38]

The Cheyennes say that Maheo frequently blesses a man as soon as he vows the Sun Dance. Clubfoot was one Pledger who

[36] Rodolphe Petter to Charles Burke, commissioner of Indian affairs, May 4, 1926.
[37] Ibid.
[38] Firewolf and John Stands in Timber to the author.

saw his prayers quickly answered. By the following September, 1927, he was fulfilling his vow within the Medicine Lodge itself. Wolf Chief was the Instructor, and Clubfoot's wife proudly sat on the Sacred Woman's bed at the rear of the lodge. However, once again charges were raised concerning the use of the Woman. This time, the protester was Milton Little White Man, another Mennonite convert. He carried his cause to the commissioner of Indian affairs himself.

Little White Man wrote Washington that during the 1927 Sun Dance, the Woman had indeed been offered. However, this time, Pledger and Instructor planned in advance not to make her offering a public affair, as it was in earlier times. Instead, the Sacred Woman's sacrifice was to be completed when the public Sun Dance ceremonies were over and the tribe as a whole had scattered home. "All indications and information point to the fact that they did give up their wives to the instructors for immoral purposes which completed the offering at the time of the Willow Dance . . . ." Little White Man stated.[39]

Charges and countercharges followed. C. B. Lohmiller, the superintendent at Lame Deer, denied White Man's allegations:

> . . . Nothing immoral transpired at said "Willow Dance"; nor have I at this late date been able to detect anyone in paying off—through immorality—any so-called obligation that may have been incurred by participants at said dance. To corroborate the statement I detailed Mr. Espy G. Cate, teacher at Birney Day School, to represent me at all time at said dance . . . . Also, I detailed three policemen, one of the three on duty all the time, day and night. In addition, the Mennonite missionary—Mr. Habegger—had three members of his church detailed, one of whom was on duty at all times.
>
> . . . It is true that occasionally the instructors spit on their hands. It is also true that the three women were disrobed down to the waist when they were being painted, but I cannot conceive any-

[39] Milton Little White Man to commissioner of Indian affairs, December 14, 1927. This lengthy correspondence begins June 14, 1927, and extends to February 16, 1928. Cf. especially, correspondence of August 26, 1927, through December 14, 1927.

thing immoral in this. Art galleries, statues in public places, ac-
tresses on the stage, bathers at seaside resorts are less [sic] scantily
clad . . . .[40]

Nevertheless, there is abundant evidence that again the Cheyennes had outwitted the whites, and that the Sacred Woman's
sacrifice was indeed offered with that of her husband. There is
also ample evidence that, to this day, the use of the Woman in
this sacred context continues, away from the hostile and inquisi-
tive eyes of the whites.[41]

Freedom of religion did not become a reality for the Cheyennes
until the passage of the Indian Reorganization Act in 1934. During that year, a white resident of Birney, Montana, attempted to
induce the Cheyennes to hold the Sun Dance off the reservation.
William Zimmerman, the assistant commissioner of Indian affairs,
was consulted by W. R. Centerwall, the superintendent at Lame
Deer. Mr. Zimmerman's instructions were to urge the Cheyennes
not to leave Tongue River Reservation:

> Of course, if the Indians desire to hold their dance off the
> reservation we cannot interfere, but we do not favor this plan and
> believe it would be to their interest to hold it on the reserva-
> tion . . . . Point out to them the disadvantage of holding the dance
> off the reservation, not only because it is evidently a scheme on the
> part of the [Birney] merchant to commercialize it, but because of
> the fact that adequate protection cannot be given the Indians
> while they are away from the reservation . . . .[42]

After much debate, the Northern Cheyennes agreed to abide
by Mr. Zimmerman's request. W. R. Centerwall notified Washington of this decision. Then he added:

> I am very pleased to state the outcome of this meeting and I am
> happy because the Indians realized that we [the B.I.A.] were en-

[40] C. B. Lohmiller to commissioner of Indian affairs, February 16, 1928. Cf.
correspondence of June 15, 1927, through February 16, 1928.
[41] Cf. Chapter 31, "Like the Morning Star."
[42] William Zimmerman, assistant commissioner of Indian affairs, to W. R.
Centerwall, May 25, 1934.

deavoring to help them in their dance, rather than interfering with their religious ceremonies . . . .[43]

Superintendent Centerwall's statement was quite a contrast to the statement of a Northern Cheyenne superintendent fifty years earlier. In 1884, V. T. McGillycuddy, the agent at Pine Ridge, also wrote his report to Washington. He stated:

THE SUN DANCE

which for the first time in the history of the Ogalalla Sioux and Northern Cheyennes was not held. The abandonment of such a barbarous and demoralizing ceremony, antagonistic to civilization and progress, as it has been proved, is a bright and promising event in the tribes struggle toward advancement in the white man's ways, and for this credit and thanks are due to the younger element of the tribe, having encountered in so doing the opposition of the old and non-progressive Indians. It is to be hoped that a firm stand on the part of the Government in the future will prevent the reappearance of the Sun Dance.[44]

Half a century earlier, Little Chief's followers silently received that edict. Then they and the other Northern Cheyenne bands began a new form of warfare against the Vehos. Thus the early reservation years were filled with this hardest of all fighting, this struggle to keep alive the sacred ceremonies, the very soul of Cheyenne identity as the People. After fifty years of steady but quiet warfare, Maheo's People had triumphed at last.[45]

[43] W. R. Centerwall to commissioner of Indian affairs, June 30, 1934.
[44] Annual Report of the Commissioner of Indian Affairs, 1884, 37.
[45] It is interesting to note the later history of the men whose "revelations" caused the government-Mennonite attempt to end the sacred ceremonies. The author's Northern Cheyenne informants state that Yellowfox again became a strong Peyote man in his later years. "Enemy Captive" has been active as a Sun Dance priest during the years the author has known the Northern Cheyennes.

24. White Men in Is'siwun's Tipi, ca. 1920–1930

Rock Roads, a Crazy Dog Society
man, succeeded Wounded Eye as Keeper of Is'siwun. Most of his
fighting days had been spent in Lieutenant Edward W. Casey's
Cheyenne Scouts, during the Ghost Dance troubles of 1890–91.[1]

[1] The time of Rock Roads's succession has been debated. Frank Waters stated
that Rock Roads succeeded Wounded Eye as Keeper. Henry Little Coyote also
stated that he (Little Coyote) was a Kit Fox leader when Rock Roads died, and
that Black Bird was chosen to succeed him. A letter from C. B. Lohmiller, superintendent of Tongue River Agency, to Hugh Scott, dated November 12, 1924,
says that James Rock Roads was keeping the sacred tipi on the upper Rosebud at
that time. Hugh Scott Papers, National Anthropological Archives, Smithsonian
Institution.

However, John Stands in Timber stated to the author that, following Wounded
Eye's death, the Hat went to Black Bird about 1920. Then Rock Roads succeeded

In later years, Rock Roads had continued strong in the sacred ways. He was a member of the Contrary Lodge. He also pledged the Sun Dance four times, thus gaining power to be an Instructor. "Rock Roads was sincere. He was devout in the sacred ways of the people," older Cheyennes recalled.[2]

Wolf Name and Spotted Elk had been chosen to carry Is'siwun to Rock Roads's lodge. However, the new Keeper did not guard the Hat for long. The effects of Ho'ko's mutilation of Is'siwun still were being felt. Even with the horn restored, the old gift of long lives had not returned to the Keepers. Rock Roads died about 1927. He was about sixty-two years old, and he had guarded Is'siwun barely seven years.

When the Cheyennes gathered for the Sun Dance about 1927, camp was pitched along the flats near Lame Deer, not far from the agency itself. This was a favorite Sun Dance spot, especially in later years. There were far more tents than tipis now. However, the canvas lodges still were pitched in the half-moon circle, its opening toward the Sacred Mountain and the East.

On this occasion, only the Elks and Kit Foxes gathered to decide on a successor to Rock Roads. The usual procedure was for the Crazy Dogs to be present also, for now the military societies had an equal share in choosing Is'siwun's Keepers.[3] Any Suhtai man could be considered. When a man's name was suggested, the military discussed him in the light of the qualifications that Erect

as Keeper, followed by Sand Crane. Cf. Stands in Timber, Liberty, and Utley, *op. cit.*, 74.

The 1890 Tongue River census gives Rock Roads's age as twenty-five, indicating that he was born in 1865.

For Rock Roads's role in the events surrounding Lieutenant Casey's death, see Maurice Frink with Casey Barthelmess, *Photographer on an Army Mule*, 97, 107, 177. Cf. Marquis, *Warrior Who Fought Custer*, 336.

[2] Rufus Wallowing to the author. Similar comments were made by John Stands in Timber and Henry Little Coyote.

[3] With the decline in power of the Council of the Forty-four, the military societies have become the major decision-making body in matters regarding the Sacred Hat. At the death of a Keeper, it is the military who assume the initiative in choosing a new Keeper. However, they continue to act in consultation with the Chiefs' Society.

These details are from Henry Little Coyote to the author, 1964. Verified by John Stands in Timber.

Horns had laid down for his successors: Was the man quiet, reliable, a peacemaker? Was he generous? Did he put the good of the people before his own good? Finally the Elks and Kit Foxes decided on Black Bird. His father, Spotted Hawk, was brother to White Shield, who had counted coup on Is'siwun's new lodge after the Rosebud fight. Spotted Hawk had named his son Black Bird, honoring the boy with the name his uncle had borne before the fight with Crook's soldiers. Black Bird met Erect Horns's qualifications. He is still recalled as being "a generous, good-natured man. One who talked slowly and kindly to everyone."[4]

Henry Little Coyote, who himself became Keeper of Is'siwun in 1959, was one of the two Kit Fox Doorkeepers at this time. He remembered the moving of the Sacred Hat to Black Bird's lodge:

There were two societies who joined to move the Sacred Hat from the Rosebud. The two bands went up together to get the Hat and carry it to Black Bird. A man by the name of Yellow Man, an Elk, was the one who carried the Hat in its bundle on his back.

There was a gathering of the camps at Lame Deer. Then the Elks and Foxes met to decide who was qualified to keep Is'siwun. It was decided to give the Hat to Black Bird, who was a Fox. This meant the Fox society was in charge of [moving] that tipi.

When we moved the Hat, we all went into the sacred tipi. There is a certain medicine that is used [sweet root]. One man takes that medicine. A man is chosen to pick up the Hat and carry it. This medicine is spit on the man's hands. He purifies himself, carries out the bundle, and hangs it on a pole in front while the lodge is taken down.

Then, praying as they marched along, the Foxes carried Is'siwun and the lodge frame to where the new Keeper lived. The Foxes didn't have to put up the original tipi, for Black Bird had a

---

[4] Black Bird was born in 1863 (1928 Census, Tongue River Reservation). He died c. 1934–35.
Cora Young Bear recalled that the Hat came to Black Bird, her step-father, in 1927, at the Sun Dance camp. Henry Little Coyote recalled the event as occurring at the Sun Dance gathering "about 1927." There is a reference to Black Bird's presence at the 1929 Sun Dance on page 1, second section, *The Billings Gazette*, May 1, 1932.

tipi there. A man took the bundle from the carrier's back, and hung it above the door of the tipi in which Black Bird was living. A religious priest [a Buffalo priest] talked to Black Bird in a good way. Then we all prayed. Black Bird said, "I will accept! I will sit down in the tipi!" Then all the military said, "Ha ho!" After Black Bird accepted, all the Cheyenne felt the same way. All were filled with gratitude. Every man and woman felt good. They knew the Keeper would receive blessings and carry on in a good way. Now the people would be blessed and the tribe made better.[5]

With the Sun Dance permitted once more, some of the old-time harmony returned to Northern Cheyenne life. Is'siwun again was carried into the Sun Dance circle with dignity and reverence. Black Bird was married to Does Flying Woman at this time. She often called upon Cora Young Bear, her daughter, to assist her in the sacred lodge. Cora Young Bear remembered one such moving of Is'siwun to the Sun Dance camp. The time was the late 1920's, and Black Bird was camped on the Rosebud, about three miles from Busby. Cora Young Bear recalled:

At Sun Dance time, the leaders of one of the military societies would gather in Is'siwun's tipi. Black Bird spit sweet root upon the palms of the warrior who was to carry the Hat from the lodge. The warrior made the purifying motions. Then he carried Nim-hoyoh and Is'siwun outside. First he hung the Turner on a forked stick that had been pushed into the earth. Then the Hat bundle was hung there, resting against the Turner. The military society members moved in to take down the tipi. Then they loaded the poles, lodge cover, and household furnishings into a wagon that was waiting. A horse was saddled for the Woman.[6]

As they rode along, they sometimes met someone on horseback or in a wagon. The man on horseback turned off to avoid the Hat. Then he got off his horse and stood there quietly. When they came to the Sun Dance camp there were many tipis already standing.

[5] Little Coyote to the author, 1964.
[6] This work usually was performed by one society, chosen to do the work on this occasion. In earlier times, such work was the special duty of the Elks. During later years, the Kit Foxes seem to have assumed the responsibility more frequently. Certainly this was true of the 1959–65 era.

Everybody stood still as the Hat bundle was brought into the village.

The Hat tipi was put up at the left side of the camp circle.[7] Then the military men walked over to Does Flying Woman, and they took the bundle from her. A forked stick had been set up in the ground. The Hat bundle was hung on it. Then Does Flying Woman got off the horse.

She called me [Cora] to come to her. Then she told me to put my hands together, palms up. She blew on the palms of my hands. Then I touched my four limbs and head. Now I could touch any property connected with the Sacred tipi.

After the tipi was completely set up with beds and everything, two of the military men walked over to Is'siwun. One man held the Hat. The other man untied the strings, took the Hat off the stick and carried the bundle inside. The other man helped him. Inside, one man held the Hat. The other tied Is'siwun to the tripod. When that was done, Black Bird took over.

Then the military men gathered. Some people provided food for them, and the feast had been cooked before this for both the military and their families. Pots of food were carried into the sacred tipi. The military went in. They left their hats outside and went in there bareheaded.[8]

From the time they started to tear down the tipi up by Busby, during the trip down, during the unloading and during the feast, they were careful not to do anything quickly. They mustn't drop anything. When you are inside the Hat tipi, you must remember not to scratch your body or your head with your fingers. Corn cobs were provided by the Keeper, so anyone could scratch himself. If there wasn't a cob, you could use a stick. Also, they didn't use just any piece of wood for a toothpick. A whole sinew lay on the ground there. They could take out a string—pull it apart —and use it for a toothpick.

Black Bird, the Keeper, was careful what he said. He talked slowly and kindly to everyone. He didn't talk too loud and he walked slowly. Everything had to go smoothly. If he did this, the

[7] The Northeast side—the present-day location for the tipi. The sacred lodge sits in front of the innermost circle of tents.

[8] John Stands in Timber attributed this custom of removing hats inside the Sacred Hat tipi to the missionary influence that stressed removing hats in church.

day would turn out well, with no wind. Then all the people would act the same way. If they do, nothing will happen to them. I have seen the military men sitting in the Hat tipi. They all seemed to be happy; and every family was supposed to be that way. They should not be sad in the presence of the Hat.

Once the tipi was set up, the Criers were not permitted to cry through the camp anymore. Now the Crier must come in and receive a blessing. He must receive the Hat Keeper's permission. Then he can make announcements. The Crier came into the tipi, bringing a gift as an offering. He handed the gift to Black Bird. Then the Crier put his hands together, palms up. Black Bird blew on the palms.

During Sun Dance, any Chief who wanted to make an announcement went into the Sacred Hat tipi.[9] He offered the pipe, smoked, and prayed there before Is'siwun. Then he could cry through the camp. Only the Chiefs had this privilege. Otherwise, the Old Man Crier, appointed in the Lone Tipi, was the only one who could cry during Sun Dance. However, he also should go to Is'siwun's tipi to receive a blessing first.

In the camp, anyone on horseback had to go slowly. He must stay away from the front of the Hat tipi. Everybody knew they must not walk too near the tipi. If you lived close to the Hat tipi, you had to walk behind it. Sometimes there was a parade in the camp. The parade stopped before it came to the tipi. Then the marchers walked their horses at a slow pace behind the tipi. When they were on the other side, they could trot and shoot. People were allowed to have a good time, and make a lot of noise. But they couldn't do anything for fun near the Sacred tipi. Young men used to shout in the darkness. They used to mock each other. But they did this only when the Hat tipi wasn't there. If a dance was to be held, or if someone wished to make noise, it could be done only if the Hat Keeper approved. These rules applied whenever the Hat was in the village.

Old men and young men came into the tipi to smoke. They did this continuously. At meal times, the military often assisted. Sometimes they carried in food, especially when many men were smoking inside the tipi. People in the camp collected food, which they

[9] This paragraph is from John Stands in Timber and Marion Mexican Cheyenne, 1959. Cora Young Bear's narrative begins again with the next paragraph.

gave to Does Flying Woman. Others cooked the food beforehand; and they brought it to the military men who were helping. Everything was provided for the Keeper and his wife.

At morning, Does Flying Woman tapped the tipi pole at the right of the door four times. Then she called her grandchildren. While she sat on the bed, they both walked over to her. She blew on their hands, and touched them. Then they touched themselves all over as a blessing. They held out their hands, palms up. She blew on their palms at the four directions and in the middle. They rubbed their hands together. Then they rubbed their faces and all four limbs, touching their entire bodies in blessing.

When the people came in to smoke or pray, they knew to go to the left [south] of the tipi. They must leave by the same way. No one crossed to the other side. No one peeked out. They just got out and left without hesitating. The tipi was kept clean. If it got dusty, soup was taken from the kettle and sprinkled around the fire. That kept the dust settled.

After the first meal was eaten, the dishes were put away. Then Does Flying Woman and Black Bird began to comb each other's hair. They painted their faces, hands and the tops of their heads with red earthpaint. They just touched their faces with red paint —it didn't have to be smeared all over.

There might be excitement in the camp—a dance or something. But the Keeper and his wife don't go over. They stay right in the tipi. They never left at anytime, except to go short distances. They would never go from Busby to Lame Deer without the Hat.

Black Bird and Does Flying Woman had land above Busby, where they had a house. The Hat tipi sat a little way in front of the house, so the Hat wouldn't be bothered too much. Sometimes my Mother and Father sent word for me to come there. I was living at a distance—east of Lame Deer. When I got there, both would say, "We're going to move. The tribe will move. We're going to move from this spot. Everything's bad. May be there's sickness. We're going to leave it behind."

Then they would start to move to a good, new camp ground. They would say, "We're going to camp in a good place, where there may be no sickness and nothing bad. We'll leave everything behind."

During that time there were quite a few other Cheyennes who

lived in houses during the winter, but in tipis and tents during the summer. They often moved from district to district during the summer. The Sacred Hat tipi never sat in one spot all summer. It changed places many times during the summer.

So Black Bird and Does Flying Woman carried the power and blessings of Is'siwun to every part of the Tongue River reservation.

In September, 1930, Black Bird was camped near the Rosebud, a short distance above Lame Deer village. One day, several automobiles appeared, driving from the direction of the agency. The cars stopped at a distance from the Sacred Hat tipi. Two white men and some Cheyennes climbed out of the cars. The whites were General Hugh Scott and Congressman Scott Leavitt of Montana.

Hugh Scott was no stranger to the Cheyennes. In 1877 he was a newly commissioned lieutenant in the Seventh Cavalry. He first met Little Chief's band that year, shortly after they had surrendered to Miles. In spite of Miles's promises to keep them in the north, orders had come to escort the Cheyennes south. Little Chief's band spent the winter at old Fort Abraham Lincoln, Dakota Territory. Then, in the spring of 1878, they moved to the Black Hills under escort of the Seventh Cavalry. Their camp was just north of the Sacred Mountain. Many of the Cheyennes climbed to the summit, where they left offerings to the Sacred Powers. Some of them fasted there three days and nights, preparing for the new days that lay ahead. From this camp they moved on south to Indian Territory.[10]

Later, Hugh Scott had known Dull Knife's band during their captivity at Fort Robinson. Years afterward, in 1919, he had been appointed to the Board of Indian Commissioners, a group first instituted by President Grant. It consisted of ten philanthropists,

[10] General Scott blamed this move on Secretary of the Interior Carl Schurz, whose policy was to force all Indians to live in Indian Territory. Hugh L. Scott, "Report to the Secretary of the Interior," September 5, 1919, Hugh Scott Papers, National Anthropological Archives, Smithsonian Institution.

all serving without salary. The board's function was to keep the president apprised of conditions on the reservations. The commissioners had divided the Indian country among themselves, and each man made an annual visit to the various agencies in his area.

Scott had admired the Northern Cheyennes since his first days as a young cavalry officer. Now, in 1930, he was inspecting the northern reservation agencies. Scott Leavitt, chairman of the Indian Subcommittee of the House of Representatives, was with him. They had spent some of their time interviewing the Cheyenne survivors of the Custer fight. Eugene Fisher and Willis Rowland (High Forehead) were their interpreters.[11]

When these interviews had ended, General Scott expressed his desire to see the Sacred Buffalo Hat. Fisher and Rowland said this would be difficult to accomplish. "That cap is very hard to see. No white man has ever seen it, and it will be very hard to see," they said. Scott asked where the Buffalo Hat was located, and he was told that the tipi was up the Rosebud in the care of Black Bird. Scott repeated his request, and the interpreters promised to ask Black Bird about the matter. They started driving up along the Rosebud in automobiles.

The Cheyennes left the automobiles near the Hat tipi. Some of them walked over to see the Keeper, while Scott and Leavitt watched from about a hundred yards away. General Scott told the congressman, "We are never going to see that Cap. The Cheyennes are stiffer than anybody else about their religion. I can see from here that he is angry at the bare mention of showing it to a white man." Soon the interpreters returned with the message, "Black Bird says no. No white man has ever seen that Cap and no white man is going to see it as long as I have it!"

Spotted Elk, an old Crazy Dog warrior, was standing nearby when this message was given to Scott.[12] He and Wolf Name had assisted in carrying Is'siwun to Rock Roads's lodge. Spotted Elk had taken the part of the Yellow Wolf during four offerings of

11 This account of the opening of Is'siwun is from "The Sacred Buffalo Hat," MS., Hugh Scott Papers, National Anthropological Archives, Smithsonian Institution.
12 This is Charles Spotted Elk, who was born c. 1863.

the Massaum ceremony. He was also an old friend of Hugh Scott. Now Spotted Elk said, "Huh! I'll go talk to him." He marched over to where Black Bird was standing. There, he beat himself on the breast several times and said,

> I am Spotted Elk and I want you to look at me. I have brought my friend here to see that Hat, and we are not going to take him back without showing it to him. You are nothing but the Keeper. You get out that Hat!

The Hat Keeper is a man of peace. Black Bird finally gave in, and Scott's party entered the sacred tipi. Hershey Wolf Chief, the old Buffalo priest who restored Is'siwun's missing horn, was chosen to open the bundle. He carefully made the purifying gestures. Then he exposed Is'siwun upon a bed of sage. At Scott's insistence the first photograph of the Sacred Hat was taken.[13]

Afterward, Black Bird entered the sweat lodge to purify himself. There, he also asked Maheo and the Powers to forgive him for exposing Is'siwun to the eyes of a white man.[14]

[13] The photograph is reproduced in Powell, "Is'siwun, Sacred Buffalo Hat . . . ," loc. cit.

[14] Rufus Wallowing to the author, 1959. Verified by Charles Sitting Man, Sr., and John Stands in Timber.

25. Sacrificing in the Hills, 1947

It had been a long time since Whistling Elk had won his battle against the Thunder. But even in later years, there were men who feared the sound of that Maiyun's voice. William Tall Bull was one of them. He was born in 1921, and he is the nephew of Whistling Elk. Yet it was not until 1947 that William Tall Bull won his own victory over the Thunder.[1]

[1] The entire account is from William Tall Bull to the author, 1962. William Tall Bull is a brother of Henry Tall Bull, who figured in the return of the Sacred Buffalo Hat after the Ernest American Horse incident. Both are paternal great-grandsons of the noted Dog Soldier chief who was killed at Summit Springs. William and Henry are maternal grandsons of Arthur Brady (b., c. 1840; d. 1936). Brady was the father of Charles Whistling Elk, George Brady (Buffalo Wallow), and Alex Brady (Little Swift Hawk).

Nowah'wus, the Sacred Mountain. Here Maheo first gave Sweet Medicine Mahuts, the Sacred Arrows.

Photograph by Ken Norgard, Rapid City.

Mahuts return to the Sacred Mountain. Baldwin Twins, the Arrow
Keeper, holds the sacred bundle before the tipi erected near the base
of Bear Butte. September, 1945.

Photograph courtesy of Richard B. Williams, Sturgis, South Dakota.

The June, 1951, fast. Willis Medicine Bull leads the way up the Sacred Mountain, followed by Charles White Dirt and Albert Tall Bull. Bert Two Moon also fasted, making the sacred number four.

Photograph author's collection. From John Stands in Timber.

369

Willis Medicine Bull (right, with back to camera) gives instructions before the fasters move up the mountain. August, 1965.

Photograph by Ken Norgard, Rapid City.

August, 1965. Albert Tall Bull smokes the pipe that never fails to bring a blessing.

Photograph by Ken Norgard, Rapid City.

371

August, 1965. Medicine Bull turns the buffalo skull, symbol of Is'siwun's presence, so that the head faces where the fasters will rest during their ordeal. James Medicine Elk, Keeper of the Sacred Arrows, stands to the right.

Photograph by Ken Norgard, Rapid City.

August, 1965. The fasters return from their ordeal. Alex Brady leads, followed by Charles White Dirt. Albert Tall Bull and Willis Medicine Bull bring up the rear.

Photograph by Ken Norgard, Rapid City.

August, 1965. Bertha Little Coyote (left) and Jennie Medicine Elk, the Arrow Keeper's sister-in-law and wife, prepare the first food after the fast.

Photograph by Ken Norgard, Rapid City.

In his own words, he tells the story of that victory:

As a child, I feared Thunder. You know, the Indians understand nature so well, being so close to Maheo. The Cheyennes knew that Thunder was one of the rulers of the universe. They knew how to control nature through the ceremonies. I heard that when Whistling Elk was young, he had this phobia about thunder. He called on another man to rid him of this. I told Whistling Elk that I had suffered with this for ten or eleven years. It was the type of thing that grows and develops. I was too young to realize all that goes with it.

Whistling Elk was on horseback one day, and I saw him from a hillside. I told him that I was troubled. He got down from his horse and sat down. I was afraid to approach him with my problem; but he knew I was serious. He turned his horse loose. Then I told him what I wanted to do; how I feared thunder. I had thought about it so much that I could explain it fully. Whistling Elk knew that you come to a point where you do something about it. I had thought of going to somewhere else where there is no thunder—if there is such a place. Whistling Elk realized that I was serious, and he said that the president had just told the country that prayer was needed.

Whistling Elk said, "There are some things you need to do." I already had talked to my mother, and she knew what had to be done. I said, "All right, I'll do them." Before he got back on his horse he said, "How soon can you get these things done?" I said, "Soon. I have some of the things already." He said, "Let's wait 'till pay day—about three weeks away."

I came home, and I think I had one more rawhide rope that I had to make. Other than that, I was ready. I had a horse. We had already moved camp to Charles Kills Night's camp—east of the ice well, up the divide. Things were beginning to take place there. At that time, my mother had migraine headaches. She wasn't well. She said, "I'll go up with you." At that time, I didn't know the procedures [for sacrificing in the hills].

Usually you go up on the hill about two hours before sunset.

There has to be preparation of the path of sage. You have to take a buffalo head up there. Before you go up, you prepare the things you'll need for the sweat lodge. You prepare the pins. You go out into your own camp and get a seasoned tent peg, one that has the grain running straight. The pegs are made of ash or choke-cherry. Then you begin to make two pins, the size of a regular pencil, or bigger. These are pointed on both ends.

Then Whistling Elk brought out a whistle he had. You could hold it in your teeth. You blew it in one breath, holding it in your teeth, where a straight line is marked on it. Then you could turn it clockwise, to where there was a wavy line. There you blew it in beeps. If you feel no one is hearing you, you can turn it back to where you blow the long whistle.

You have chosen a tree already. You go to it and sit down. You lay your head down, and prepare a pipe for the altar. Then you say, "We have to hurry now. The sun is going down."

Whistling Elk got ready to sing. He had said, "When I start the song, raise the rawhide (rope) and point it to the four direc-tions. At the end of the songs, throw it. If it slides back down, run and grab it before it falls to the ground." Then someone said, "How many knots do you want?" (You can take any num-ber: one, three, seven. But the more knots, the heavier the rope will be.) I said, "Give me three knots." Then George Brady evened up the rope, so the ends were even.

Then Whistling Elk began to sing.

Now you are ready to call someone over to hold your skin, while they run a knife through it. They (the priests) deaden the skin a bit by pinching it hard. The knife is run through. Then a piece of buckskin is looped over the two ends of the pins. You have been on your knees all this time. Now you get to your feet quickly, and you pull as hard as you can on the rope, throwing yourself back.

You have your pipe and buffalo head ready. Then Whistling Elk handed me a pipe and a cane of green chokecherry wood with leaves attached. He also had a white plume feather, with a long piece of buckskin attached. You hold the feather in the

376

same hand as the cane. If it starts to get windy, and the wind blows your tree back and forth, you sit down. Then you pull the feather closer to your hand, and that will stop the wind.

Whistling Elk started me out. He got hold of my shoulders. Then he pulled me back four times. On the fifth time, I started walking (along the half moon circle of white sage). Whistling Elk sat down and cried. I suppose all those things in the past had come back to him.

It was a terrible night ahead of me. When I felt that Whistling Elk had given me all the power he had, I felt no pain, no discomfort. I was ready to hang there no matter what happened. I began to whistle the beeps. It wasn't long before the wind got curious. "Who dares to call the rulers of the universe," I felt he said. I was alone. Then, of course, came darkness and thunder. Just at that point, I think I came face to face with my Maker. He was part of the thing that was going to happen. I sat down. I took the pipe. "At least they can hear my prayer," I thought.

I forgot to mention that my mother stood under the tree. Her back was to the tree, but not touching it. She held one branch with her left hand kind of above her. She could feel the movement of the tree as I pulled. As I pulled, the tree swayed. Each time I made the half circle (on the sage), I hooked branches with the rawhide rope. Then I would keep going, and the rope would slip off and snap. I hit those three branches each time. I'll never forget it.

I sat down and smoked the pipe. I said a prayer—not a long one. I felt I might be missing out on something if I didn't get on my feet. I thought of my mother first. I wanted to spare her in any way that I could.

It seemed like here was a thing I had to go on with. I couldn't give up. I had gone this far; and I was going through with it. I said a few of these words in my prayer: that I respected the ceremony given to Whistling Elk, a ceremony which is to help a person. Also, [I prayed] that we had made no mistakes in the ceremonies. If we had, they were not intended. Here was Maheo's own teaching. I prayed: "Know me! Hear my prayer.

You have given this teaching to the great teachers. Look upon it. Look upon it with respect!"

The turmoil within me died down. The thunder rolled on and died away. The clouds scattered. Then I began to hear noises. I became curious about the Spirits I could hear. There was a forest, real thick with trees, south of the hill where I was. I heard something come through the timber, breaking the trees right and left. I couldn't look back until I came around the circle.

Then the moon came up, clear as could be. Out of the trees came many horses. There was a glade where I was, and they stopped at the edge of it—about thirty head. When I looked at them, they ran towards me. Then they separated to the left and right.

After it rained, there was a noise behind me. I couldn't look back. But behind me was green brush, with a lot of leaves; about knee high. When I'd get to the south end of the circle, I would hear a little whirlwind back there. As I went east and then north, this whirlwind stayed with me, following me to the end of the half circle, and then back. It followed me back and forth until daybreak. Then it disappeared. My mother said it was a movement of grass. She could see it. But I thought it was a little whirlwind.

Whistling Elk had said: "Everything will hinder your movements. You'll find obstacles. But they're [the Maiyun] testing you to see how strong you are!" I finally sat down and offered a little prayer to the thing behind me, a prayer for my mother and myself. I thought of my people, my relatives, the Cheyenne people in general.

Every time I looked at the moon, I began to be conscious of how tired I was, how thirsty I was. I became conscious that the knots were getting heavy, and the branches were holding me longer. Even little sticks on the ground would get caught on my moccasins. Things began to hinder me. But I kept going and tried harder.

I wasn't in pain. As far as pulling back on the thongs, I wasn't in pain. The tiredest part of me was the small of my back. I wasn't used to this position. But you put one foot backward, one foot forward, and pull. That way you don't slip over backward.

I began to see daylight coming. But the moon didn't move. It didn't go across the sky. It came up and just stood in one place, not moving. It was like someone peeking over at you. Then you begin to notice the creatures; the animals. You hear them, but you don't see them. They are making their presence known.

Then I thought, "I'll have another smoke. It's about daylight." My prayers were getting longer. I wouldn't smoke all my tobacco. I just puffed long enough to get it started. It takes time to clean the tobacco out and get it ready again.

In summer, daylight comes quickly. It came, and I could see someone coming. It was Alex Brady. He had brought his knife along. We sat down and smoked together. He must have been instructed by Whistling Elk—both in the prayers to be said and the things done. Alex was very efficient, and this gave me a good feeling. He said, "Here's where we offer another prayer. Then I'll take the bits of skin off." And he did. He cut the bottom part off, and then the top. You kneel down and lean back. Then he does the same [cutting] on the other side. Then he said, "Stand up." I did stand and he started to walk backwards. I couldn't make myself go forward. I had been in the position all night and couldn't go forward.

Finally I knelt. Alex was still offering the bits of skin to the four directions. This was a prayer for me and my mother. When the prayer was over, he took my mother's hand from the branch she held all night. She came and sat down. Other men were coming for a smoke. Charles Kills Night and George Brady came up. Whistling Elk had arthritis and couldn't make it. But he had left instructions.

We exchanged small talk—how this was a real good thing. I was just as happy as could be. When you talk of something of such joy, you spoil it. That's the way I felt that day. So we smoked. Then someone took the rawhide rope. Someone took the buckskin; someone the skewers. These are used in many ways. The sticks are used in case of a wind storm. You stick them in the ground. If the wind is from the north, you stick the sticks to the north of your house. That helps to calm the wind. The buckskins are used when your limbs are swelling. You tie the strip on loosely, and the swelling goes down.

In one of my hands I had carried seven pieces of cloth. You have to include black and white cloths. The others may be any color. The black is for the Spirits of the Night, and the White for the Spirits of the Day. My mother took the black scarf to tie around her head if the headaches came back.

After I left, I was tired. But I was walking on air. I was as happy as could be. I wanted to touch everything. It was all so good. People saw how happy I was and they became happy—my family especially. My children were too young to realize what went on.

I had to go in the sweat lodge. You go in the lodge four times —but at different places. You can do it over a period of weeks. You have to have four complete sweats.

Charles Kills Night was also one who had hung himself up. So had George Brady. And there were others.[2] We went into the sweat lodge together. Special songs were sung there. After the sweat there was a smoke. Then we prepared for a feast. Food is offered to the four directions again. Then the feast begins. Everyone eats.

They had to go to Lame Deer after the feast. I rode on horseback, following Whistling Elk's wagon. I had to return some things. Then I came home. I felt so good that I wasn't tired at all.

All the time before, I'd been conscious of thunder. I watched the clouds. Now I began to think, "What's going to happen?" Before I got home, I began to hear thunder. I'd always been conscious of it. Now I heard it—loud! It was just a noise as far as I was concerned. My heart didn't skip at all.

I came home; but I thought I wouldn't say anything to anyone.

[2] In 1962, William Tall Bull gave the author the names of six contemporary Northern Cheyennes who had offered the sacrifice of their own bodies in the hills. At least one is younger than William.

Now I had an understanding with Thunder, and he had an understanding with me. But in my heart I was happy. I was free of this thing.

Later, I found that old man Thunder is ruler of the universe. He sits at the head of the lodge. He pities nobody. He hasn't any pity in his heart. Yet, out of respect for this ceremony, he must have reconsidered.

Fifteen years after these events, William Tall Bull's voice still was hushed, still was filled with wonder as he spoke of that night on the hilltop.

26. Coal Bear's Family Guards
Is'siwun Again, 1934–1958

Thirty-eight years after the death of Coal Bear, the Sacred Hat was restored to his family. It was about 1934 that the military societies escorted Is'siwun to Birney village, the most isolated of the Northern Cheyenne communities. There the tipi was erected near the home of Sand Crane, Coal Bear's younger son by Glad Traveler, his favorite wife. Now the old father-son succession of Keepers had been restored.[1]

[1] Buffalo White Cow Woman (born c. 1876) was Coal Bear's sister's daughter. She stated that Coal Bear had two wives when he came north in 1881. The wives were White Woman and Glad Traveler. Glad Traveler was the first, or favorite, wife. She bore the Keeper two sons, Head Swift and Sand Crane, and two daughters, Iron Tooth and Sacrificing Woman (Offering Woman). White Woman, the second wife, bore him seven children: Red Fox, Hairy Hand, Ugly

At first, Sand Crane's own wife objected to her husband's willingness to guard Is'siwun. She was an Arapaho woman, and did not have the proper respect for the Sacred Hat. When she heard that the military societies were on their way, she said: "I don't want the military men to bring the bundle here! If they do, I'll take that bundle. I'll hit one of those military men, and I'll knock him on the ground!" Fortunately, she was more talk than action. When she saw Is'siwun coming, she merely left in a huff. A day or so later, after the sacred tipi had been set up, she finally returned.[2]

Sand Crane was born about 1873. He is remembered as being a quiet, devout man. He had offered his body on top of a great hill near the forks of the Lame Deer. There he fasted four days and four nights, his body tied to a poplar tree with rawhide ropes, and his chest pierced with wooden skewers.[3]

In 1911, Sand Crane assisted in the last Northern Massaum ceremonies. Then, in 1937, he led a group of young men up into the pine hills near Lame Deer. By that time the Sun Dance had been restored, and the Keeper was determined that younger priests would carry on the ceremonies. For a day and a night Sand Crane taught them the Suhtai version of the Sun Dance. He was a good teacher, because the survivors of that group remain the most noted instructors among the Northern Cheyennes today. Albert Tall Bull, Ernest American Horse, Frank Red Woman, James Kingfisher, Willy Rising Sun, Charles Crazy Mule, Aaron White Man, Alex Brady, Charles Brady, Buster White Wolf, and Thomas Rock Roads all were taught by Sand Crane on that occasion.[4]

Face, Chubby, Teeth Woman (girl), Big Leggings, and Come Together (girl). To the author, 1959.
The Tongue River 1910 Probate Records list Sand Crane's mother as Morning Star or Rabbit Woman.
[2] Charles Sitting Man, Sr., 1960. Verified by Henry Little Coyote and John Stands in Timber. All three denied that Sand Crane refused to accept the care of Is'siwun until lightning struck his house.
Cf. Llewellyn and Hoebel, *Cheyenne Way*, 157.
[3] John Stands in Timber, 1962.
[4] Albert Tall Bull, 1962.
Davis Wounded Eye also stated that Sand Crane was the first Keeper to allow

Then World War II came, and the Cheyennes prepared for the new battles that had to be won. Many of the young men stopped by to visit the Hat Keeper before they left home for the army. Whistling Elk and Buffalo Wallow went with one such group of Cheyenne recruits. Sand Crane took them into the sacred tipi and prayed before Is'siwun for their safe return. Each recruit left an offering cloth before the Sacred Hat.[5]

By 1944, Sand Crane's health was beginning to fail. He was about seventy-one years old then, and blindness was overtaking him. However, the Keeper continued to pray for the people from his bed. He begged the Sacred Powers to make the Cheyenne soldiers brave, to make the people think right, and to save the Cheyennes from vanishing. Sand Crane's good disposition remained with him even during this long illness. It was still with him when he died in March, 1950.

A jeep carried the Hat Keeper's body to the Roman Catholic chapel at Birney and on to the cemetery nearby. When the prayers of the church had ended, Sand Crane's daughter, her son, and a nephew arranged the Keeper's tent, blanket, and suitcase upon his grave. Then, as the Suhtaio had done for generations, they placed a buffalo skull at each of the four directions around the grave.

Spring was coming. The weather was mild, with the sun casting a soft light upon the snow-covered pine hills. Most of the mourners soon scattered. A small cottonwood fire was burning beside the grave, and several of the women remained beside it still, keening for the dead Keeper. Sand Crane's dog remained, also, his great body stretched across his master's grave.[6]

Again the Chiefs and leaders of the military societies gathered. Their decision was to carry the Sacred Hat to Thomas

peyote to be placed within the sacred Hat bundle. However, when Is'siwun was opened in 1959, there was no sign of peyote.

[5] Henry Tall Bull, 1962. Tall Bull was present on this occasion.

[6] Details from a letter from Wilbert B. Harvey, then teacher at Birney Day School, to Mari Sandoz, March 15, 1950. Mr. Harvey assisted with Sand Crane's funeral.

Rock Roads, son of the former Keeper. However, when they got there, he refused the Keeper's position. They could find a better man, he said. So Is'siwun was carried back to Birney village and placed in the care of Head Swift, Sand Crane's older brother.

Head Swift was born about 1867. He was only a boy at the time of the Custer fight. During the parade of the Suicide fighters, he, William Yellow Robe, and Wandering Medicine had gone down to the Big Horn River for a swim. They were splashing around when someone shouted, "The camp is attacked by soldiers!" The boys jumped out of the water and headed back to their family tipis. Head Swift's family already had hurried toward the hills to the west of the camp, but a brother came back looking for him. They ran for quite a distance before they caught the brother's horse. Then they both jumped on the horse and rode to the place where the women and children were watching the fight with the soldiers.[7]

Like his father and brother, Head Swift had held fast to the Suhtai ways. He had worn the gray wolf skin in the Massaum ceremony. On one occasion, he fasted in the middle of Tongue River for a day and a night. His eyes were fastened on the Sun throughout the entire day. The river was lapping at his chin, and the Sun's heat was burning his head as he stood there, but his lips never touched the water that was flowing all around him.

On another occasion, Head Swift fasted on top of a pine hill near Birney village. There was a great thunderstorm that evening. Nevertheless, Head Swift stood fast, walking back and forth along the half-moon bed of sage as the rain pelted his body throughout the entire night.[8]

Head Swift guarded Is'siwun from 1950 to 1952. The Korean War had come, and the Cheyenne soldiers again carried offering cloths to the Sacred Hat. Once more the blessing of Is'siwun went with them. During the Korean fighting, two soldiers came home on leave. The Northern Cheyenne War Mothers sponsored a feast and a gathering for the Flag ceremony. Nimhoyoh, the

7 John Stands in Timber and Henry Little Coyote, 1959.
8 Wesley White Man, 1961.

Turner, was carried from the sacred tipi and once more was tied to a long pole which was thrust into the earth. Nimhoyoh hung there blessing the soldiers and the people who were gathered for the celebration below.[9]

About the spring of 1952, Head Swift summoned Whistling Elk, George Brady (Buffalo Wallow), Davis Wounded Eye, and Henry Little Coyote to Is'siwun's tipi. These men were leaders in the Crazy Dog and Kit Fox societies. The Keeper's health was failing, and he was thinking about a successor. The men smoked together, and then Head Swift spoke to them about the Sacred Hat. When he had finished, the Keeper sent for his daughter, Josie Head Swift Limpy, or Stands Near the Fire. When she arrived in the sacred tipi, the Keeper again addressed the four men:

> The reason I sent word for you to come is because I have had plans in my mind for some time. Now I want you to listen to me; to hear what I have to say to my daughter.
>
> Daughter, I want you to remember what I say. It is the law that a woman has the right to assist the Keeper of the sacred tipi. You have been watching me. You see how I smoke the pipe in the morning and evening. This is not merely smoking. It is more important than anything else done in the tipi. It is a ceremony which includes prayer, and the asking of blessings for the family and all the people.
>
> Some day I will die. You are not going to leave the tipi. Do not say anything to the soldier bands. They know that they may want a man to care for the tipi as I did; and they may decide to come over and take away the tipi.
>
> When they come, talk nicely to them. After they take the tipi away, a new man and his wife may not know exactly what to do. If they come and ask you, speak to them in a good way and tell them what needs to be done.
>
> Hineh ha! That's all![10]

[9] John Stands in Timber, 1959.
[10] Josie Head Swift Limpy, 1959. Verified by John Stands in Timber, who heard the story from George Brady. Cora Young Bear and Henry Little Coyote stated they heard the same details from the men who were present on that occasion.

386

Then Head Swift said that no one had any power to stop the moving of the sacred tipi to a new Keeper. The soldier societies were the only ones who would take charge of moving the tipi. They were the ones to look for a qualified man to care for Is'si-wun's lodge. Then Head Swift said:

> Now you have listened to me. I have talked to my daughter; so everything will be all right. You military leaders have the power to give Is'siwun to someone. You will come, take down the tipi, and carry it according to the rules.
> Don't forget what I have said![11]

Head Swift was nearly eighty-five years old when he died in July, 1952. His family had no team or automobile with which to carry his body into the hills for burial. In the hills, the Keeper's remains would have been placed on the earth or in a hole in the rocks. Then his family would have covered his casket with stones or pieces of timber. There the body would return to the elements from which Maheo first made man.

Instead, Head Swift's body was carried to Birney cemetery, close to the grave of his brother Sand Crane. A hole had been dug. Head Swift's body was lowered into it, and the prairie soil was replaced on top of the casket. Then the Keeper's family carried four bleached buffalo skulls to the graveside. They placed one of the sacred symbols of Is'siwun at each corner of Head Swift's grave. The buffalo heads sat there facing the four directions, the homes of the Sacred Persons.

In the years that have followed, Stands Near the Fire has continued to visit her father's grave. She lights a cigarette when she arrives there. Then she offers the cigarette as she would a pipe: first to the Persons at the four directions, then to Maheo, and finally to Grandmother Earth. She smokes quietly for a while, and leaves the ashes and remains of the cigarette at the head of her father's grave. Then she prays.[12]

[11] John Stands in Timber to Josie Limpy, in the presence of the author.
[12] Josie Limpy, 1960.

After Head Swift's death, the Chiefs and the leaders of the military societies gathered again. They carried Is'siwun and her tipi from Birney village over to the Rosebud. They offered the Sacred Hat to John Teeth, but he refused, saying that he did not know enough about the sacred ways. The Chiefs and military men swung back to Birney, and there they left Is'siwun's tipi in the care of Josie Head Swift Limpy.[13]

What was to have been temporary custody lasted from 1952 until the beginning of 1958. Stands Near the Fire had been well instructed by her uncle and father. During World War II she had vowed the Buffalo Ceremony on behalf of the Cheyenne soldiers. As she offered it, she begged Maheo to protect the men, to bring them home safely through the power this ceremony brings from Is'siwun.

Throughout all this time Stands Near the Fire kept Is'siwun's home in order. When she rose each morning, she struck the four blows upon the pole to the southeast of the tipi door. On bright days, she carried the Hat bundle outside and tied it above the doorway of the lodge. Then she went back inside, where she prayed for the people and for their needs. Next she swept the floor with buck brush, since a white man's broom is not allowed to be used inside Is'siwun's lodge. At sundown, she carried the Hat bundle back inside, fastening it to the tripod behind the Keeper's willow back-rest. Then she again offered the prayers. After sundown she struck the southeast lodge pole four times, closing Is'siwun's home for the night.

The Sacred Hat tipi continued to stand at the edge of the cluster of log houses that was Birney village. At intervals the military societies came by to assist in moving the tipi, although they did not come by as often as they had in Sand Crane's days. When the lodge cover was renewed with new white canvas, the old canvas covering again was spread upon the earth. There were still a few Suhtaio who came to walk across it, receiving blessings through the cover that had protected Is'siwun from the elements.[14]

[13] Rufus Wallowing, 1959.   [14] Josie Head Swift Limpy, 1959.

In 1957, Whistling Elk called a meeting of Crazy Dog and Kit Fox leaders. He repeated what Head Swift had told his daughter about giving the tipi to the military men whenever they asked for it. The Foxes and Crazy Dogs decided to call a general meeting of all the military societies. They also decided that before the next gathering they would collect money and gifts for the new Keeper who would be chosen at that time.

However, before such a meeting could be held, Ernest American Horse sent word to Charles White Dirt, the Elk Society head man, that he wished to be Keeper. White Dirt told this to the other leaders of the military societies. They called another meeting, and there it was decided to give the Hat to American Horse.[15]

On January 11, 1958, the leaders of the military societies again rode into Birney. This time they came in automobiles rather than on horseback. Whistling Elk and his brother George Brady (Buffalo Wallow) reminded Stands Near the Fire of her father's words. She responded quietly and in a kindly way—as her father had told her to do. Whistling Elk traveled back to Lame Deer. There he found Davis Wounded Eye, the son of the former Keeper, and they returned to Birney together. Then Is'siwun was carried from the sacred tipi. Davis Wounded Eye knelt, and the bundle was placed upon his shoulders in the old fashion. Wounded Eye climbed into the back seat of one of the automobiles. The car pulled out onto the rocky road that led from Birney to Lame Deer, and the other automobiles followed, with the Chiefs and military society men riding inside them.[16]

The cars rolled slowly along the road, just as the horsemen protecting Is'siwun had ridden slowly in times past. At Lame Deer the procession turned west, heading in the direction of Busby village, near the Rosebud River. At Busby, the automobiles finally stopped. The military erected the sacred tipi beside the home of Ernest American Horse, and Davis Wounded Eye carried Is'siwun inside. Then Ernest American Horse sat down in the Keeper's seat beside the sacred bundle.

15 John Stands in Timber and Cora Young Bear, joint interview, 1959.
16 Davis Wounded Eye, 1959.

27. The Sacred Arrows Come North, 1956–1957

Mahuts remained in the south for nearly seventy years. It was not until 1945 that the Arrows again returned to the north and to the Sacred Mountain.

World War II was reaching its climax in June, 1945. At that time David Deafy, Bert Two Moon, Albert Tall Bull, and Mike Little Wolf left Lame Deer for the Sacred Mountain. Whistling Elk rode along to instruct them. About twenty-one persons in all made the pilgrimage. The four men climbed the side of Nowah'wus. There they fasted four days, praying for peace.

In September, shortly after the end of the fighting with Japan, a smaller party of Cheyenne pilgrims returned to the Sacred Mountain. They came to thank Maheo for hearing the people's prayers for peace. Frank Limpy, Albert Magpie, Albert Monothy, and John Stands in Timber were among the Northerners who made the journey. Two visitors from the south rode with them, Baldwin Twins or Scabby, and his wife. Twins was the Keeper of the Sacred Arrows. Now he was carrying Mahuts back to their ancient home.

The Arrow tipi was erected near the base of Nowah'wus. Mahuts were exposed upon a bed of white sage and offering cloths. The Keeper offered prayers before the Arrows, thanking Maheo and the Powers for the peace that had come to the Cheyennes and to their country again. Then Twins left the Arrows exposed for a time, in order that the whole world might be blessed by the power flowing from Mahuts; just as the whole world was blessed on that day when Sweet Medicine first carried the Arrows from the Sacred Mountain.[1]

Twins returned with the Arrows again in 1948. This time the tipi was erected on the old camping grounds south of the Sacred Mountain. Again, the ceremonies were held inside.

The Sacred Arrow ceremonies were offered in the north in 1953. In 1956, Baldwin Twins again returned to Lame Deer. This time he was bringing Mahuts north for a different purpose. Shortly after he arrived, the Keeper sought out John Stands in Timber. They visited together in the shade beneath the eaves of the old Stands in Timber cabin near Lame Deer Creek. Soon the Arrow Keeper's conversation came around to his reason for returning north. Twins inquired about the Sacred Hat. How did the Northern people feel toward Is'siwun? Did they still respect the Hat and her Keepers?

John Stands in Timber recited the problems of these later years. He told how, at Sand Crane's death, the Chiefs and military societies had accompanied the Hat to the home of Rock Roads's son, and how the younger Rock Roads had refused to accept the Keeper's position. He had said that they could find a

[1] John Stands in Timber and Baldwin Twins, 1960.
The party left Lame Deer on August 27, 1945. Twins's wife was with them. Cf. Sturgis, South Dakota, *Tribune*, August 30, 1945 and September 13, 1945.

better man. So the Hat was carried back to Birney and placed in the care of Head Swift. Head Swift had lived for only a couple of years after that. Then, when Is'siwun was carried to John Teeth, he had refused to care for the bundle. Now Josie Head Swift Limpy was guarding the sacred tipi until a permanent Keeper could be chosen. She was having problems, too, because the military societies did not come by to help her move the Hat tipi to new, fresh ground often enough. The tipi cover was not being renewed with clean, white canvas as often as it had been renewed in times past. "Seems like people are losing respect for Is'siwun," John Stands in Timber had concluded.[2]

Twins was thoughtful after he heard that. The next day he returned, and his talk again was of the Sacred Arrows. John Stands in Timber remembered that the Arrow Keeper said,

> The Southerners are losing their old ways. Forty or fifty years ago, all the families moved in for the Arrow renewing. Little tipis were set up for the absent ones. Now only a few people come. Now I am all by myself. My wife is dead; so there is no woman to serve in the sacred tipi.
>
> Last year, when the camp broke after the renewing, no one moved my tipi for me.[3] Finally Ben Buffalo moved my tipi home. That day I made up my mind to take the Arrows north.
>
> However, since you have told me of the trouble in finding a Keeper for the Sacred Hat, I am going to take the Arrows back.

There the matter rested for a time.

However, a few days later, Fred Last Bull met Twins in Lame Deer. Fred was the son of old Last Bull, who had brought about the destruction of Morning Star's village. The Kit Foxes had tired of their Chief's meanness and finally deposed him. Last Bull had moved over with the Crows. His son Fred had grown up speaking Crow. However, Fred eventually moved back among the Cheyennes. There he had acquired a "can't live with him, can't live without him" reputation. He was a Sun Dance and Buffalo priest. In 1945, he had publicly pierced his flesh in

[2] John Stands in Timber to the author, 1957.
[3] The old mark of respect for the Arrow Keeper.

the Sun Dance lodge. However, the people did not quite trust him. "He's like his father," was the description that many Cheyennes used in describing Fred Last Bull.[4] During the course of this conversation in Lame Deer, Last Bull invited Twins to visit him at Busby, and to instruct him in the Sun Dance songs. Soon after that, Last Bull invited all the Northern Cheyenne Chiefs to Busby for a feast. When the feast ended, Baldwin Twins made a speech about the Sacred Arrows. He said that he had decided to bring them back to the north. Then he announced that he had given Mahuts to Fred Last Bull, who had vowed to renew the Arrows that summer. The Chiefs were happy about this news at the time. Later they felt different.[5]

Mahuts are the supremely sacred possession of the entire Cheyenne tribe, both Northern and Southern. No individual—not even the Arrow Keeper—can pass on their care without the permission of the Chiefs and the leaders of the military societies, both in Montana and in Oklahoma. Therefore, when the news that Twins had left Mahuts in the north was known in Oklahoma, a council was called. The Southerners appointed Jay Black Kettle and Ralph White Tail to meet with the Northern leaders. Both men were priests of the Arrow lodge.

On May 7, 1957, the two Southern delegates met with the Northern Chiefs and military society leaders at Lame Deer. The Chiefs conducted the meeting by military rule instead of appointing a chairman.[6] George American Horse, one of the Old Man Chiefs, was the leader of the meeting. John Stands in Timber kept the minutes. The meeting opened with Stands in Timber reading the minutes of the special meeting of the Southern

4 Some of this mistrust came from the fact that Last Bull was another man who complained to the Mennonites when the instructor used his wife in the Buffalo ceremonies. After that, the government had ordered the Buffalo sweat lodges burned. Last Bull's wife died shortly afterward. "The Cheyennes claim that if you do something wrong, harm will come to a person near you," John Stands in Timber remarked when telling about the deed. To the author, 1960.

5 John Stands in Timber obtained these details from Medicine Top, one of the Chiefs present. To the author, 1960.

6 *Ibid.* The written minutes of this meeting are in the author's keeping.

Chiefs and military men which had met in Seiling, Oklahoma, during November, 1956. The Southern leaders had stated that the Arrows had been given away by an individual; not by the decision of all the Chiefs and military society leaders.

Then Ralph White Tail and Jay Black Kettle spoke to the Northern Cheyenne leaders. They explained the most sacred parts of the Arrow ceremony, and how only the Arrow priests were authorized to perform them. "No one in the north knows how to perform these ceremonies," they explained.

When they had finished speaking, John Stands in Timber stood up. He stated that only the combined Northern and Southern Chiefs and military society leaders could authorize the transfer of Mahuts. The Northern Chiefs and military men immediately voiced their approval of this statement.

Hearing this, Fred Last Bull was on his feet immediately. He said that John Stands in Timber had no right to talk about the matter. "And if you don't stop talking about it, I'll put you behind bars," he threatened. Stands in Timber answered that the Northern and Southern Chiefs and military leaders had said that it was necessary for the leaders of both tribal divisions to approve the transfer of Mahuts. "Since this is true, maybe you could be the one behind bars," he retorted to Last Bull.[7]

Then Last Bull backed down. There was more discussion, and Last Bull rose again. "Let me go through the Arrow ceremony here in Montana. On the day I finish the ceremony, the Southerners can take the Arrows from here," he pleaded.

It is not permitted to express disapproval in the presence of Mahuts, so Frank Waters, the Sweet Medicine Chief, stood up and spoke in favor of Last Bull's request. George American Horse and Pat Spotted Wolf, both Chiefs, also agreed. Finally the matter was put to a vote. All the men stood up, so Last Bull's request was approved. Last Bull stood up and shook hands with the Doorkeeper. Then he shook hands all around.

In June, 1957, Baldwin Twins returned north to instruct Fred Last Bull in the Sacred Arrow ceremonies. Mahuts were exposed

[7] Ralph White Tail and John Stands in Timber to the author, 1960.

394

for worship. However, the actual renewing of their feathers and sinew was not carried out.[8]

That fall, the Southern Cheyenne delegation arrived to escort Mahuts home to Oklahoma. Jay Black Kettle and Ben Woods, both Arrow lodge priests, were members of the delegation. Laird Cometsevah, one of the Southern headmen, rode along. So did Sam Buffalo, a member of the Southern Cheyenne Tribal Council. Sam was the son of Ben Buffalo and Black Woman, upon whose allotment the Arrow ceremonies and Sun Dance often were held.[9]

The transfer of Mahuts went smoothly enough. Everyone expected another outburst from Fred Last Bull, but all he said was, "I want a peyote outfit. That would take the place of the Arrows I have been handling and praying to every day. Without it, I would be lonely and not feeling good!" Then Eugene Little Coyote, one of the Kit Fox headmen, left the meeting for a short time. When he returned, he handed a peyote box and its sacred contents to Last Bull. Last Bull prayed "in a fine way—the best words he could say." Then he took the Arrows down from their pole and placed the bundle on the earth before his seat. Ben Woods made the purifying motions. Then he picked up Mahuts. It was he who carried the Arrows all the way back to Oklahoma.[10]

The Southern Cheyenne delegation telegraphed ahead that all was well, and that they were returning with Mahuts. When they reached home, Jay Black Kettle carefully hung Mahuts in the house on his allotment near Canton. The house was cleaned and swept. Then they went outside and erected a tipi for the Sacred Arrows.

Word was sent out to all the Southern Cheyenne districts that a meeting was to be held at Jay Black Kettle's house. When the day arrived, many people came early. The house was soon filled; there was not room for another man inside. Outside, men sat all around the house, listening.

[8] John Stands in Timber and Rufus Wallowing to the author, 1957. Jay Black Kettle and Ralph White Tail to the author, 1960.
[9] Jay Black Kettle and Ralph White Tail, 1960.
[10] Jay Black Kettle, 1960.

Jay Black Kettle reported on the meeting in Montana. When he finished his report, he urged the Chiefs and military leaders not to wait. "The Keeper of the Sacred Arrows must be chosen at this time!" he said.

The first man chosen was Ben Woods. When his name was announced, he rose to his feet and said,

> I thank everyone for honoring me as a good man, one qualified to care for the Arrows. But the Keeper must be a full-blooded Cheyenne. I am half Cheyenne, half 'Rapaho. So let us follow our law exactly.

Ralph White Tail was the second choice. He was pleased at being chosen, but he, also, refused the honor.

Then Jay Black Kettle's name was mentioned. His father and mother both were related to Arrow Keepers. His father had pledged the renewing of Mahuts, and had become a member of the Arrow lodge. Jay Black Kettle finally accepted. Then he said to the men gathered around him:

> I do not know all the rules from the beginning. I do not know how to handle the Arrows and carry out the ceremonies. All I know how to do is to act in a good way, and to use all the good ways of the Arrows. I will start out and learn the ceremonies from the beginning. You don't expect to get to the top first. You start at the beginning and go higher and higher in knowing the sacred ceremonies.[11]

When the Arrow priests heard Jay Black Kettle say this, they all promised that they would use their combined knowledge to help the new Keeper. Then all would go smoothly, all would go well in the Sacred Arrow lodge.

So Jay Black Kettle carried his pipe into the Arrow tipi. There, this modest and good-natured descendant of Chief Black Kettle sat down in Sweet Medicine's old seat beside the Sacred Arrow bundle.

[11] Jay Black Kettle, in the presence of John Stands in Timber and the author, 1960.

28. Is'siwun Is Opened, July, 1959

Even in the free days, Is'siwun rarely was opened. But whenever the Arrows were renewed, the Hat might also be taken to the center of the village. There, five buffalo chips were placed in a line and Is'siwun was placed upon the middle one. While the men were praying before the Arrows on their pole, the procession of women passed by the Sacred Hat. They paused before Is'siwun to beg blessings for themselves and for the people, as well as good health for the children.[1]

[1] Grinnell, "Cheyenne Medicine Arrows," MS #70, Southwest Museum Library, 3. Present-day Suhtai priests insist that no woman should see the Sacred Hat. Fred Last Bull was criticized for allowing women to see it on the occasion described here.

During the reservation years, the Hat had been opened on even fewer occasions. In 1906, Hershey Wolf Chief had exposed Is'siwun in the presence of Wounded Eye and the Buffalo priests. In 1908, the Hat had been opened in order to restore the missing horn. Again, in 1930, it was Wolf Chief who exposed Is'siwun in the presence of Hugh Scott and Scott Leavitt. Then, about 1948, Sand Crane had renewed the buffalo hide sack in which Is'siwun is kept. Hollow Breast assisted the Keeper on that occasion. The Turner was placed upon the floor of the lodge. Sand Crane sang one of Is'siwun's songs. A prayer followed. Then, after making the four motions, the Keeper untied the Hat bundle. He slowly pulled Is'siwun from the sack. Again with the four motions, he placed the Hat upon the Turner. When the two priests finished renewing the buffalo hide bag, they replaced Is'siwun inside it. The lesser objects in the bundle were placed on top of the Hat. Only Sand Crane and Hollow Breast were present during this exposure of Is'siwun.[2]

After the 1959 Sun Dance at Lame Deer, many Cheyennes believed that the time surely had come to open the sacred bundle again.[3]

There had been some recent stirrings in that direction. A short time before Head Swift's death, the military societies had decided to have one of the Buffalo priests expose Is'siwun. They had asked Dan Old Bull, a respected Buffalo man, to discuss the matter with the Keeper. Head Swift answered that the Hat Keeper had no authority to order Is'siwun opened. The order must come from the military societies, he said. However, the military had taken no further action.

More recently, representatives of the military societies had ridden to Birney to talk over the situation with Josie Head Swift Limpy. They asked if ever her father had said they could open the Hat without first appointing a Keeper. She replied, "Don't do it! First have the Keeper appointed; then open the Hat!"[4]

2 John Stands in Timber to the author, 1959.

3 Except where otherwise noted, the entire chapter is from the author's 1959 field notes, covering the period June 29 through August 17, 1959. John Stands in Timber was the interpreter and, also, was a joint informant on many occasions.

There the matter had rested until Ernest American Horse's attempt to carry Is'siwun to Sheridan, Wyoming, in April, 1959. For weeks afterward there was great excitement in Lame Deer. Rumors were flying. One story said that American Horse was planning to sell the Hat to a museum, and that already he had sold some of the scalps from the bundle. Then the sacred "blower" of red catlinite appeared in Frank Cady's store in Lame Deer. One of the pipes from the Hat bundle was with it. Cady understood the blower's value, and had attached a $100.00 price tag to it. It seemed clear that Is'siwun's bundle indeed had been rifled.

The last week in June, the people began to gather for the Sun Dance. Camp was pitched near Lame Deer Creek, at the old Sun Dance site. On June 30, a meeting was held at the home of Little Coyote, the Hat Keeper. The old problem of which priests were eligible to open Is'siwun had arisen. Five men, all of them Buffalo priests, were named as being qualified. The military societies said they were in favor of opening the Hat. However, no decision as to when this would be done was reached that day. The military dismantled the sacred tipi, loading it onto the back of a truck. They started off to Lame Deer, with Little Coyote following in a car driven by his son, Eugene. The Keeper was carrying Is'siwun's bundle on his back.

The next day, during the afternoon, the military and the priests gathered in the Sun Dance camp. Again they discussed the opening of Is'siwun. Some believed that the ceremony should be vowed, in the same way as the Arrow ceremonies or the Sun Dance. Several of the older men visited the tribal office to see whether funds were available with which to pay the officiating priests. The sum of seventy-five dollars was put aside to be used for this purpose whenever the sacred bundle actually was opened.

John Fire Wolf was the Suhtai priest whose name was most frequently mentioned. He was a venerable priest of both the Sun Dance and the Buffalo ceremonies. However, Fire Wolf said that the Hat bundle should not be disturbed until the

4 Little Coyote and John Stands in Timber, July 2, 1959.

399

Sacred Arrow ceremonies, which had been pledged that year, were completed. He was holding fast to the old rule that says no other ceremonies should be held before the Arrow rites are completed in a given year. Ralph White Tail, who had represented the Southern Cheyennes when the return of the Arrows was discussed in 1957, again had come north. White Tail agreed to sing the opening songs for the Sun Dance. However, he hesitated to take any part in opening Is'siwun's bundle. He was a Sun Dance and Arrow lodge priest, not a Buffalo priest, he said.

Abraham Spotted Elk and Frank Red Cherries both had pledged the Sun Dance ceremonies. Albert Tall Bull was to be the Instructor. That evening at dusk, the three men entered the Sacred Hat tipi. White Tail and the other Sun Dance priests were present, along with Little Coyote and Weasel Woman, his wife. Outside, the military directed the children away from the area near the sacred tipi. Then the ceremony began inside.

One of the priests offered a prayer asking Maheo and the Sacred Powers to bless the Pledgers. Then he recited the old Northern Suhtai origin account of the coming of the Sacred Hat.[5] He reminded the Pledgers of their vow to offer the Sun Dance for the good of all the Cheyenne and Suhtai people, for their families, and for everyone—both Indian and non-Indian.

On July 2, the Lone Tipi was erected and the formal Sun Dance ceremonies began.

On the morning of July 2, representatives of the military societies again gathered in Is'siwun's lodge. Little Coyote told them to finish the Sun Dance ceremonies. Afterward, the military could arrange for Is'siwun to be opened. Little Coyote also told them that he needed a new cover for the tipi. He added that he wanted to see Fire Wolf first, because Fire Wolf remembered how the contents of the sacred bundle were handled. Fire Wolf was the oldest living Buffalo priest, and he had not yet arrived in the Sun Dance camp.

Later that morning, Little Coyote and Davis Wounded Eye discussed the matter further. The Hat Keeper said, "We don't

[5] This origin account is given in Appendix VI.

400

know all the ceremonies. It is all right if the military want to have Is'siwun opened. But Fire Wolf must be here. So we must put it off until after the Sun Dance." Wounded Eye agreed.

The next day, at Busby, Fire Wolf himself was approached on the subject. He said that he did know how to open the sacred bundle. "There are two ways to do it. You don't have to wait for the Keeper to vow the ceremony. If he doesn't make the vow, the military can order the Hat opened. Now the military societies have ordered Is'siwun opened. The priests will discuss how to get back the lost articles. Then donations must be collected for the priest who opens the bundle," Fire Wolf stated.[6]

On the morning of July 5, the final day of the Sun Dance, Albert Tall Bull, Abraham Spotted Elk, and Frank Red Cherries entered the Sacred Hat tipi. There, Little Coyote was to hand them the scalps that are kept in Is'siwun's bundle. The Pledgers would carry these scalps during the dances of the final day. One of the scalps would be tied to the end of the peeled cane carried by the priest who leads the dancers in their final running to the four directions. Then the Sun Dance would end.

However, when Little Coyote reached inside the bundle, no scalps were to be found. Here was trouble! Now people said that it must be true that American Horse had sold scalps from the bundle. Alarm for the safety of Is'siwun became widespread, and a meeting of the military societies was called for the following week at Little Coyote's home.

The great question remained: who would open Is'siwun's bundle? Hershey Wolf Chief was many years dead. Dan Old Bull had died in 1956. Only a few aged Buffalo priests remained, and they were the only men truly qualified for such sacred work. Little Coyote had been one of the Kit Fox Doorkeepers. However, he was not a priest. The Keeper expressed himself again a few days later, "As far as I am concerned, it would be all right to open the bundle as long as Fire Wolf and the others know the ceremonies for opening Is'siwun."[7]

[6] Fire Wolf to the author, July 3, 1959.
[7] To the author, July 8, 1959.

Meanwhile, John Stands in Timber and Father Peter J. Powell had arranged to redeem the sacred "blower" and pipe that Frank Cady was keeping in his store. Mrs. Margot Liberty, the teacher at Birney Day School, also had shared in the expenses, and early on the morning of July 11, the three had driven to Busby to meet Fire Wolf. He was to instruct them in the ceremonies of returning the missing objects to Is'siwun's bundle.

While the four were waiting for breakfast, Fire Wolf began singing the old song that was sung when offerings were carried to the Sacred Hat. He described how the military societies used to walk slowly down the hill to the sacred tipi. They were weeping while they carried robes as offerings to Is'siwun. As they walked they sang the song that began, "I put the blanket on God . . . ."[8] Fire Wolf added that the military societies had gathered the day before. They had sent word to him that the meeting at Little Coyote's house was changed to July 12.[9]

The four started off to Ashland district, where Little Coyote lived. A stop was made in Lame Deer, where they purchased four pieces of cloth. Fire Wolf chose the colors—red, white, yellow, and light blue—the colors now identified with the Maheyuno who live at the four directions. He said that the cloths would be "blankets given to our God."

When they reached Ashland, Father Powell stopped the car behind Little Coyote's house. Fire Wolf walked over to instruct the Keeper in his duties. When this was finished, Little Coyote slowly walked down the hill to the sacred tipi. There he took a seat outside the lodge, to the east of the doorway. The offering party drove down in the car and parked behind the lodge. Fire Wolf instructed Mrs. Liberty to take the pipes and Father Powell to hold the offering cloths.

Fire Wolf, John Stands in Timber, and the two persons bearing the offerings walked to a distance east of the lodge. Fire

[8] John Stands in Timber is translating the word here in the general sense—a supernatural being, but a Maiyun rather than Maheo the All Father Himself. Cf. Appendix III, on Maheo.

[9] To the author, July 11, 1959.

Wolf began singing the old-time song that was sung when a scalp was carried to Is'siwun:

The Spirit cries out all over.
He took pity on me.
He gave me charcoal.[10]
Therefore I rejoice.
I dance the victory dance.

The song was sung four times and four pauses were made as the offering party moved toward Is'siwun's home. After the fourth singing of the song, Fire Wolf cried:

Spirits! You have heard me sing a song which was a part of Cheyenne history. The song is a part of the Sacred Hat tipi. Whenever this song is sung, it brings good news or offerings to the Sacred Hat priest!

When they reached the Keeper, Father Powell placed the offering cloths on the earth before Little Coyote. Mrs. Liberty rested the blower and pipe upon the cloths.

Little Coyote responded:

I am the Keeper of Is'siwun. By right I can ask the Spirit to bless people. He himself received the "blankets" and the pipes. You two will receive a blessing from him. Also, I declare that both of you shall find better life and better things in the future.

Then the Keeper told the offering party to enter the tipi. He carried the pipe and blower inside, while Father Powell carried the offering cloths. Little Coyote instructed Father Powell to cover the sacred bundle with the "blankets." The priest draped these over the offering cloths already surrounding the bundle. Is'siwun was suspended on the tripod that stands at the head of the Keeper's bed of peeled willow branches. Then everyone sat down. Fire Wolf and John Stands in Timber were seated by the Keeper, whose seat was beside Is'siwun. Mrs. Liberty and Father Powell sat across the lodge, on the north side.

[10] The reference here is to the charcoal with which the face of a warrior who had taken a scalp was covered in the old days.

Little Coyote turned toward Is'siwun. Then he addressed the Sacred Hat:

Now I will talk to You. My voice will cause good health and better living, as I am instructed by one of the priests and have heard what he said. He brought two—a young man and a young woman—as they believe our faith. They have brought a pipe and a blower and cloths as blankets to cover our God.

We understand You have heard every word I have said, and what Fire Wolf said. This renewal should bring glad news to You. Bless every one of us that is here now. Lift and guide us that we may do the right thing at all times. You are the cause giving us these things. Continue to keep in our minds these things we have thought, as we expect good from You.

It is important to perform a little ceremony before any come in with us, that we trust and believe we will be living better in the future and at all times. And again I say: this young man came from a long way. He has respect for You. Be with him and guide him. Wherever he goes, he will find his family in good health. And bless this young woman and give her a better and longer life as she lives on earth.

Now my God, you have seen what these people have done. They brought back your pipes and gave You the blankets. I say: consider these two people. They are our relatives now, since I have brought them into the lodge. Bless them and protect them. Give them long lives. Be with them on their trip back to their homes. Ha ho! Ha ho! Hineh ha.

The Keeper then said to the offering party, "This is the day the military are to come. I am glad that you are the very first, and that you have shown this great honor to our God."

Fire Wolf explained to the Keeper that the meeting was to be the next day. He cautioned the Keeper, "I would leave it up to the military bands. They will not open the bundle, even if they agree to do it. They will set a date far ahead in order to get things ready." Then everyone left the sacred tipi.

The next morning, July 12, one of the Kit Fox Society leaders visited Josie Head Swift Limpy at Birney. During the Sun Dance,

404

when it was believed that the scalps had been taken from Is'si-wun's bundle, his name had been called. Thus he had been chosen to be present at the meeting where the opening of the Hat was to be discussed. The Kit Fox leader asked Josie Limpy what he should do if Is'siwun was opened. She answered that the only ones qualified to see the Hat were certain old priests, and definitely not the military. "Just walk away from there," she advised him.[11]

By noon, twenty-five or thirty men had gathered beneath the sunshade near Little Coyote's house. The Sacred Hat tipi stood below them, in the midst of the grassy bottom land near Tongue River. John Woodenlegs, chairman of the Tribal Council was among them. So was Fred Last Bull.[12] Fire Wolf was not present. No one had bothered to pick him up at his cabin in Busby.

The discussion began shortly after one o'clock. Now, in Fire Wolf's absence, Fred Last Bull immediately pushed for opening Is'siwun. The other men hesitated. Last Bull was a Buffalo priest. However, after the Sacred Arrows had been returned to Okla-homa, it was discovered that certain articles were missing from the bundle. Among them was the painted strip that showed when the sweet grass offerings were to be made during the Arrow cere-monies. Last Bull insisted that he knew what to do, and he said that he would open the bundle for nothing. (Fire Wolf had held fast to the old position that the officiating priest must receive gifts, and that some time was needed to collect such donations.) The discussion continued, with Medicine Top saying that the people must hold on to the old and sacred things. Alex Spotted Elk stated that a new tipi was needed for Is'siwun. So the talk continued for over an hour.

Last Bull continued his pressure for opening the sacred bun-dle. At a gathering such as this, matters are decided by general

[11] Father Powell–Margot Liberty, joint notes for July 12, 1959.
[12] The author wishes to correct an obvious misstatement in his "Is'siwun: Sacred Buffalo Hat . . . ," *loc. cit.*, 29. Fred Last Bull was not the son of the Tall Bull who discovered the Pawnee camp during the 1853 move of the Hat and Arrows. The names Tall Bull and Last Bull were obviously confused in this article.

agreement. All should be peaceful and harmonious in discussions pertaining to the Sacred Hat or Sacred Arrows. Therefore no one spoke against Last Bull.

Finally, at about 2:30 P.M., the decision to open Is'siwun was reached by general consent. In the brilliant heat of the July afternoon, thirteen men moved slowly down the hillside to the valley of the Tongue. Little Coyote led the way, supported by his son Eugene and by Father Powell. Fred Last Bull, the only Buffalo priest present, was close by. The representatives of the military societies brought up the rear. John Woodenlegs, president of the Tribal Council, walked with them.

When they reached the tipi, Little Coyote and Last Bull entered first, with Eugene Little Coyote following. The other men knelt outside while they went in. Then the others entered, also.

Inside, both Little Coyotes were seated by the Sacred Hat, which hung from her tripod. Last Bull and Woodenlegs sat opposite the door in the place of honor. Others present were Elmore Brady, Alex Spotted Elk, Frank Lone Bear (a Southerner), Charles Sitting Man, Jr., Charles White Dirt, Frank Yellow Hair, and August Spotted Elk. John Stands in Timber and Father Powell were seated just to the north of the place of honor.[13]

The ceremonies began with Father Powell reading from George Bird Grinnell's "Great Mysteries of the Cheyenne," an article written in 1910, when Wounded Eye was Keeper. Last Bull said, "Listen. This may be the first time we ever hear the rules that have been written way back when Coal Bear was Keeper. Without asking the military, I would say that we accept it."

Father Powell began reading, with Stands in Timber and Woodenlegs translating his words into Cheyenne as he read. At this point, Mrs. Ann Hanks and Mrs. Margot Liberty entered. Both were carrying cameras. The reading continued for a while.

---

[13] John Stands in Timber was one of the Kit Fox Door Keepers; Elmore Brady, a Crazy Dog; Alex Spotted Elk, a Kit Fox; Charles Sitting Man, Jr., an Elk; and Charles White Dirt, head man of the Elk Society.

Then Father Powell stated that there was more to the article, but that it could be read later, rather than on such a sacred occasion. Fred Last Bull said, "It's good. But we have a lot more to do. It should be read to Little Coyote. It is what he needs."

Then Last Bull asked that Eugene Little Coyote assist his father in opening the sacred bundle. They were directed to lay it on the ground before Last Bull's seat. Eugene moved over before the tripod. He made the four motions. Then he lifted the Hat bundle, which was covered with many layers of offering cloths. These "blankets" were removed and placed upon the earth, and the sacred bundle was handed to Last Bull.

Little Coyote knelt before the bundle. There he traced the circular "Earth" drawing upon the ground.[14] Last Bull instructed him to untie the piece of sacred sweet root that was fastened to Nimhoyoh, the Turner. "Hold it in your left hand and put your forefinger in to touch the medicine. Touch the tip of your tongue. Then blow that medicine on my hands no more than four times," Last Bull said. Next, Little Coyote performed the "throwing it at him" ceremony for Last Bull.

The Keeper made the purifying gestures first given to the people by Sweet Medicine. Then he spat sacred sweet root in one direction of all those within the lodge. All averted their eyes. They made the purifying gestures. This touching of the earth and touching of the limbs and body represents the Creator creating the human body and blowing life into it from the earth, Old Bull had told John Stands in Timber years before.

Little Coyote placed the piece of sweet root on the ground, in the center of the "Earth" drawing.

Last Bull raised his hand toward the east. He called upon Sweet Medicine, who had brought all these sacred things to the people. He prayed:

Look at each one in this tipi. We all expect to receive a bless-

14 The making of the "Earth" in both its Cheyenne and Suhtai variations, is repeated in both the Sun Dance and the Arrow ceremonies. Details of the symbolism of the "Earth," "throwing it at him" ceremony, and purifying gestures are given below, in the chapter describing the Sun Dance and the Sacred Arrow ceremonies.

ing. Not only ourselves: but also the people, our families, our children and our relatives that are in here with us [meaning the white people]. I beseech you and I earnestly believe that because I am one of the Buffalo ceremony priests. For this reason I have attempted to open the secrets.

When Wounded Eye was priest and Keeper of the Sacred Hat tipi, I brought blankets to put on you. When Black Bird took possession of you, I also brought blankets to cover you. I also brought offerings to the bundle when Rock Roads watched over you.

Furthermore, I vowed the Buffalo Ceremony and vowed the renewal of the Arrows. And I have taken part in the Medicine Lodge eight times. I will have the right to touch the things inside the Sacred Hat bundle.

Little Coyote untied the offering cloths and Last Bull lifted them from the bundle, aided by Woodenlegs. The Buffalo priest said to Woodenlegs: "Watch the things as I get them out, so when I put them back you can remind me in what order they go back in." Next, Last Bull tugged four times on the string closing the large skin sack. On the fifth motion, he proceeded to untie the knot.

Last Bull proceeded to remove the contents. First came a bundle of braided sweet grass, tied in a red cloth. A bundle wrapped with a blue cloth followed. The five missing scalps were inside it! They were graduated in size and laced to wooden hoops. Tradition states that they were captured from the traditional enemies of the Suhtaio: the Crows, Shoshones, Utes, Pawnees, and Apaches.[15] Last Bull looked them over carefully. Then he piled then on the ground to the south of the pile of offering cloths.

Now Last Bull prepared to open the smaller buffalo hide sack containing Is'siwun herself. Again, he made the four motions. Then he slowly withdrew the Buffalo Hat. As Is'siwun was revealed, a quiet "Ah-h-h" went up from some of the watchers. Last Bull placed the Hat upright upon a bed of white sage. Is'siwun rested there, facing east.[16]

[15] The scalp tied to the scalp cane is Assiniboine.

The "old animal hide"—probably mink or otter—was removed next. This was followed by a package of long twist tobacco— the old-time trade tobacco. Finally, Last Bull removed a bundle of fluffy white material, resembling animal fur, wrapped in a yellow checkered cloth. This material was said to be the wool of the yellow buffalo calf, the youngest member of the Buffalo Family. Now the opening of the Sacred Hat bundle was completed.

There still remained the question of how many scalps should be in the bundle. Cora Young Bear, Black Bird's step-daughter, had insisted there were seven during Black Bird's term as Keeper.[17]

Last Bull lifted the scalps. Then he said:

Here's a question. Many say there were seven scalps. I have also heard five scalps. The walking cane [scalp cane] may be missing. Somebody said he knew there were only five scalps in the bundle. If it's five; we have five here.

[16] Is'siwun's horns are split, and have a tendency to fold under. Traces of sacred red paint remain in the incised designs on the surface of the horns. The drawing in Grinnell, "Great Mysteries . . . ," *loc. cit.*, 569, is substantially correct.

The brow band design is formed by white and blue pony beads, sewn on a rawhide background. The design is the "tipi design." John Stands in Timber and Rufus Wallowing both stated that the Hat's beaded brow band was the model for the brow bands on war bonnets.

The drawing in the article by Grinnell indicates light and dark shadings. These were not visible to the author. Nor was the double parallel line Grinnell notes on page 569 of "Great Mysteries . . . ." However, the "man power" design is clearly visible on the horns. The skin of the Hat is not covered with blue beads as Grinnell states. There is only the beaded brow band with the three beaded triangles projecting from it. Grinnell stated that "no hair is to be seen." This is inaccurate. At the front of the Hat, above the brow band, the hair appeared to be red and bristly. At the back, the hair resembled otter or mink skin. This may have been the second skin that Fire Wolf recalled as being present when Hershey Wolf Chief opened the bundle in Wounded Eye's time. The beads are sewn on—not glued, as Grinnell states. There are traditions that ermine skins once were attached to the Hat.

[17] Cora Young Bear stated in April, 1959, that five of the scalps were tied to Nimhoyoh on the fourth day of the Sun Dance. Then Nimhoyoh and the scalps were suspended above the Sacred Hat tipi. The largest scalp is carried by the Pledger on the final day of the Sun Dance. One scalp was kept for an emergency. It was tied to the scalp cane which was carried by the Sacred Hat woman during the moving of Is'siwun. This is said to be the same scalp carried by the priest during the final running to the four directions at the end of the Sun Dance.

409

We are all looking at these things. This is all that is in the bag. As far as I know, these scalps have never been counted. As far as I know, there are five scalps and the one on the walking cane. Does anyone know for sure how many scalps there were? Does anyone know anything else that is missing?

All was quiet in the tipi. Then Last Bull turned to Little Coyote, saying:

My friend: you see what is in this bundle. You are to remember all these things so that you may give someone who later asks, a right answer. There's been a lot of talk about this bundle from people who seem to know what's missing. I really think that nobody knows except those that are dead. So we shall say that it's all right. We have found everything that was supposed to be here.

Little Coyote responded, "It's all right. I have seen what is in it."

Now Last Bull began to pray to the Above Powers in Cheyenne, saying:

You Powers watch me! If I have made a mistake, I want you to overlook my mistake. I do not know very much about this medicine. Overlook my mistake, if I have made one!

Then he prayed on in mixed English and Cheyenne. He wept as he called, "Jesus! Jesus! Jesus!" Then he called upon Peter, Paul, Lazarus, Moses, and the Virgin Mary. The prayer ended ". . . through Jesus Christ our Lord, Amen."

Eugene Little Coyote asked if the women and children might come in. Last Bull agreed. The doorflap was thrown open and people began to enter. First came representatives of the military societies: Alex Brady of the Crazy Dogs; James Medicine Bird, Keeper of the Elk Society bundle; John Yellow Hair, Alec Black Horse, and others. Then Fred Last Bull's wife entered, leading her little granddaughter. Elmore Brady, a Crazy Dog leader, brought three small boys with him. Other women appeared:

[18] Fred Last Bull's death, not many months later, was said by some persons to be the result of allowing women to look upon the Hat on this occasion. Cf. Grinnell, "Great Mysteries . . . ," *loc. cit.*, 563.

Mrs. Frank Yellow Hair, Mrs. Nelson Medicine Bird, Weasel Woman—the Sacred Hat Woman, and others.

They stood there quietly, praying in the presence of Is'siwun. Then they slipped out of the lodge again.[18]

Last Bull, assisted by Woodenlegs, replaced the contents of the sacred bundle. The Buffalo priest offered a final prayer, followed by a short speech of thanks for the return of the missing "blower" and pipe. The Sacred Hat bundle was tied to the tripod, the sack resting against Nimhoyoh once more.

Generations before, Erect Horns had told his successor that many men would care for Is'siwun. The Keepers would die; but the Sacred Hat never would wear out.[19] It was clear to all present that Is'siwun had not worn out. In fact, some men remarked that the Hat looked as new as the day on which Erect Horns first carried Is'siwun to the Suhtaio.

All was well. "Esh piveh! That's good!" men were exclaiming as they rose to their feet inside the sacred tipi. They slowly filed from the lodge, following the Sacred Hat Keeper up the hill to the arbor on top. There the women were waiting with a feast.

[19] In 1965, care of Is'siwun passed to James Black Wolf, for Little Coyote was feeble and far advanced in years by that time. Again, some of the people questioned the younger man's following of the older rules.

Finally, in 1969, the Hat tipi again was placed in the care of Josephine Head Swift Limpy, who watches over Is'siwun at the present time (August, 1969). See Appendix IX for recent events concerning the Sacred Hat.

29. Power for New Days

Throughout the passing years, Nowah'wus, the Sacred Mountain, has remained the heart of Cheyenne worship and life. The tipis of Mahuts and Is'siwun open in the direction of the Mountain. So does the Arrow Renewal Lodge and the Medicine Lodge at Sun Dance time. Even the doors of the new prefabricated houses springing up around Lame Deer, Busby, Birney, and Ashland face Nowah'wus and the East. Whenever power is needed for new days, the Cheyennes return to the Sacred Mountain.

Little Wolf's band had paused near Nowah'wus on their way north in 1879. It was at the end of that bitter winter, and they had left the sheltered valley near the forks of the Niobrara to head toward the Yellowstone once more. Little Wolf himself climbed the Sacred Mountain, carrying the Chiefs' bundle back to the Arrows' home. There the Sweet Medicine Chief fasted and prayed for the few Cheyennes left in his care, this remnant who must face the hard, new road ahead. Then Little Wolf and his people moved on toward the Yellowstone and surrender to White Hat Clark.[1]

Little Chief's people camped in the shadow of the Sacred Mountain during their journey to Indian Territory in 1878. Prisoners of war then, they all the more deeply needed the power that flows from Nowah'wus. Some of the people fasted there. Others left offering cloths to flutter from the branches of the stunted trees growing on the Mountain. As always, each Cheyenne who visited there left a stone behind. Then Little Chief's band turned their faces toward the humid south country. Not until the winter of 1890–91 would the hearts of Little Chief's people again be gladdened by the sight of the Sacred Mountain.[2] The bands of Little Chief and Standing Elk did not join in the Ghost Dance troubles at Pine Ridge, so Agent Royer finally granted them a pass to Fort Keogh. The Cheyennes started out in the dead of winter with nearly four hundred miles of travel ahead of them. There were 276 people in all, and the journey took them almost two months. When they finally reached Keogh, they were detained there, within a hundred miles of their relatives and friends. They had expected that the military would move them to Tongue River Agency, but their passes read to Fort Keogh, and it appeared for a time that they might have to stay there. John Tulley, the newest agent at Lame Deer, wrote many letters on their behalf. However, the government red tape

[1] Sandoz, Cheyenne Autumn, 258–59.
[2] Yellow Nose, Spotted Elk, Medicine Bird, et al are quoted as saying that all the Northern Cheyennes made the pilgrimage in 1891. This is extremely unlikely, in view of the unsettled conditions at that time. Most of Yellow Nose's party had been with Little Chief's band, and all of that band had stopped there on the way back to Keogh.
Cf. Thomas E. Odell, Mato Paha, The Story of Bear Butte, 150.

dragged on, and it was not until October 3, 1891, that the waiting ended and Little Chief's people joyfully moved on to Lame Deer. There they were finally enrolled on Tongue River reservation. Now all the Northern Cheyennes were home.[3]

The dreary reservation years followed. A long succession of agents discouraged Cheyenne roaming and the sacred ceremonies themselves. Small parties occasionally managed to slip away to the Sacred Mountain, to fast and pray there briefly. Four Cheyennes fasted there during World War I. August Spotted Tail's Sioux grandfather fasted there in 1913. But it was not until the 1930's that the return to Nowah'wus gained new impetus.

Early in the 1930's Whistling Elk received a message from the Sacred Mountain. The meaning was not clear:

The white man is going to make something that isn't big; but it is very powerful. He is going to be known for it. Once that thing goes off, all the world is going to know about it.

That was all the Maiyun said. Neither Whistling Elk nor his family understood—until the bomb was dropped on Hiroshima.[4]

Then late in September, 1939, four old Cheyennes led the first pilgrimage to the Sacred Mountain since World War I. Yellow Nose, the warrior who captured the Custer guidon, was the oldest member of the group. He and Low Dog had been the first Cheyennes to cross the Big Horn and face Custer's men. They had ridden back and forth before the soldiers, slowing down their approach. In the quieter years that followed, Yellow Nose had become respected for his healing power.[5]

[3] "Census of the Pine Ridge Northern Cheyenne Indians Transferred from Fort Keogh, Mont., to Tongue River Agency, Mont., October 3rd, 1891," Tongue River Agency papers, National Archives.

Cf. Dusenberry, *op. cit.*, 16–18.

Standing Elk's band had been transferred from Indian Territory to Pine Ridge in 1883.

[4] Whistling Elk to his nephew, Henry Tall Bull. Tall Bull to the author, 1959.

[5] John Stands in Timber to the author, 1957.

Cf. "Crayon Drawings of Cheyenne Ceremonial Customs and Implements,"

414

Three other old warriors were with him: Nelson Medicine Bird, the Keeper of the Elk Society bundle, John Black Wolf, and Charles Spotted Elk, who had told Black Bird to open Is'siwun for Hugh Scott. There were younger men, too. Most of them were members of the Northern Cheyenne Tribal Council: Eugene Fisher, the president; John Stands in Timber, then a judge of the Tribal Court; Rufus Wallowing, the chief of police at Lame Deer; Eugene Limpy, Pat Spotted Wolf, and Dallas Wolf Black, all members of the Council. Most of the men were members of the warrior societies as well. James Fisher, Eugene Fisher's son, came along also.

Eugene Fisher stated that the purpose of this pilgrimage was to assist a local committee in determining Bear Butte's history, especially as it related to the Indians who had lived there before 1876. The local committee was hoping to have Bear Butte designated a national monument.[6] However, the main purpose of the Cheyenne visit was to allow the old men to worship on the Sacred Mountain once more.[7]

A drizzling rain prevented their ascent on September 28.[8] Instead, the four older Cheyennes spent hours at the base of Nowah'wus, praying and meditating upon the holiness of the place. They smiled when they discovered, near the western base of the butte, the stone tipi rings of earlier camps. They also found an eagle pit, and they recalled the old-time ceremony of capturing the bird who is so close to Thunder himself. Near Fort Meade they located sandstone boulders scarred with deep grooves in which arrowheads and spearheads had been sharpened. One of the men used his cane to overturn several stones which marked the location of a sweat lodge.

These discoveries were greeted almost silently, for the solem-

---

Daniel Little Chief, Drawing 11, MS 2016–A, National Anthropological Archives, Smithsonian Institution.

[6] Odell, *op. cit.*, 140.

[7] John Stands in Timber and Rufus Wallowing to the author, 1958.

[8] The account of the ascent is from Odell, *op. cit.*, 141–43. Cf. *Rapid City Daily Journal*, September 29, 1939.

nity of this return filled the thoughts of all the men. Later they described Sweet Medicine's pilgrimage to the Sacred Mountain. They also said that it was from this mountain that the people had received the Buffalo Hat. Now the old Suhtai mountain in the north also had become indentified with Nowah'wus. Yellow Nose and the others hunted for the door through which Sweet Medicine had entered the lodge in the mountain, but they were unable to find it.

The old men also spoke of the Cheyenne claim to the Black Hills. They said that the Cheyennes controlled the region until about 1850. Then the Sioux started gaining control of the land through treaties with the whites, and finally the Cheyennes themselves were forced to leave the area.

On September 29, Nelson Medicine Bird climbed to the summit of the Sacred Mountain. He stood there praying, asking Maheo to bless the nation and all the people who lived in it. Then Medicine Bird left an offering cloth behind. When the Cheyennes left for Tongue River Agency they promised to return the next year.

Then World War II came. At the beginning of the war years David Deafy, a younger man, had a dream. In his dream he saw four men standing in a row, one behind the other. The men were naked, and their bodies were covered with yellow paint. They stood motionless as they prayed. Deafy was too young to have gone on the old pilgrimages to the Sacred Mountain. Therefore, he carried a pipe to Whistling Elk, asking the priest to interpret the dream.

In August, 1944, the dream was repeated. This time a voice spoke to Deafy. Deafy said nothing about this until he had carried the pipe to Whistling Elk again. Whistling Elk replied that this was the way Sweet Medicine had said it would be. The Sacred Powers wanted four men to go to Nowah'wus, because the Cheyennes were troubled and were attempting to find a way to end the war.

When Deafy heard this, he vowed that he would go to the Sacred Mountain.[9]

Even in Northern Cheyenne country, the hardship of the far-away war were being felt in new ways. John Stands in Timber wrote to the Chamber of Commerce at Sturgis, South Dakota, the city located near the Sacred Mountain. He asked for food and other help for the Cheyennes while they were camped near Bear Butte. The Chamber of Commerce promised to help, but again government red tape blocked the Cheyennes. This time the Office of Price Administration refused to give them the gasoline ration stamps needed to buy fuel for the journey. Deafy's pilgrimage was delayed another year.

Even after a year, it seemed that Deafy would have to climb the Sacred Mountain by himself. However, the day before he planned to leave the reservation, three other men volunteered to fast with him. They were Bert Two Moon, grandson of the old Chief, Albert Tall Bull, and Mike Little Wolf. Whistling Elk was their instructor. John Stands in Timber went along to interpret. Twenty-one people made the trip altogether.

The four fasters started up the Sacred Mountain the first week in June, 1945. Whistling Elk had told them to pray hard for all the boys in the armed services, for all the boys who had lost their lives, and for all the people of America. He reminded Deafy and his companions that Sweet Medicine had first brought the Sacred Arrows from this mountain, and that the Prophet had told the Cheyennes to fast there in order to receive blessings.[10]

An afternoon storm had sprung up that day. However, it had passed by the time the party of twenty-one Cheyennes left the foot of the Sacred Mountain. Halfway up, they paused on a prominent point. Bedrolls were spread for the men who would be fasting; two on the south side, two more on the southwest. Deafy and his companions stripped to their breechclouts. Then Whistling Elk painted their bodies yellow, the old Sun color. As sunset arrived, he told them to form a line—just as

[9] Sturgis *Tribune*, June 7, 1945.
[10] John Stands in Timber to the author, 1958.

417

Deafy had seen the men standing in his dream. Whistling Elk climbed to a spot just above them, and the other Cheyennes moved down below, where they stood looking at the fasters. As darkness drew on, the air became crisp. Some eight hundred feet below, blinking lights marked the automobiles on the road, and the scattered homes and ranches in the distance.

The four men stood there for over an hour, constantly praying. Then, as darkness all but hid them, the fasters moved up higher on Nowah'wus. They were wrapped in their blankets, and each man carried a pipe. Meanwhile, the other Cheyennes moved down the steep side of the butte to the camp below.

Deafy described the fast afterward. "We never rested. We prayed every minute of every hour for four days, and suffered awful without food, but especially without water."[11]

On the morning of the second day, Mike Little Wolf noticed black marks on the back of Deafy's hands. The marks were triangular, like the shape of the Sacred Mountain itself. Deafy had no idea how the marks had gotten there.

It was on the morning of the fourth day that the vision came. Deafy saw a rider on top of the Sacred Mountain. The rider was facing east. Suddenly he charged. His horse galloped past Deafy at full speed, and on down the side of the mountain. However, nothing happened to either horse or rider.

Soon the horse and rider appeared again. Once more the horse charged down toward the foot of the mountain. As they went by, Deafy noticed that there was a boy sitting behind the rider. Again, they reached the bottom safely.

When evening of the fourth day arrived, Deafy and his companions moved down to the camp below. Whistling Elk was waiting for them there. Each man took a swallow of water every fifteen minutes during the first hour, four swallows in all. Next, food was offered to the Sacred Persons and to Maheo. Then the fasters ate a little food every fifteen minutes. Thus they ate four times during the first hour after their fast ended.

Whistling Elk listened quietly as Deafy spoke of his vision.

[11] Sturgis *Tribune,* June 7, 1945.

Then the priest interpreted it. The first rider was the first nation America fought—Germany. "We have beaten them," the priest said. Two riders appeared the second time. They represented the second country that America was fighting—Japan. "When the wild strawberries get ripe; that is when we will lick the Japanese," Whistling Elk said. He also interpreted the black marks on Deafy's hands. They were the color of the old black charcoal paint used to cover the faces of victorious warriors in the old days. So they, also, showed that America would win the war.[12]

Deafy's vision came in June, 1945, a month after Germany had surrendered. In August, Japan also fell.

In September, 1945, Baldwin Twins, Keeper of Mahuts, led a pilgrimage to the Arrows' home. A tipi was erected near the base of Nowah'wus. The Arrow bundle was opened, and Mahuts were exposed upon a bed of sacred white sage and offering cloths. The Keeper offered prayers of thanksgiving for the peace that had come to the nation.[13]

The old pattern of Cheyenne worship at the Sacred Mountain had been restored.

By the fall of 1950, the Korean war was raging, and the nation once more needed prayers. So David Deafy returned to the Sacred Mountain. Thirteen Cheyennes made the trip with him, all of them piled into one old car. Among them was Deafy's son, who had vowed to fast with his father.[14]

---

[12] Details of the vision are from Henry Tall Bull and John Stands in Timber, 1958–59.

The Sturgis *Tribune* gave a different version. It stated that the black marks on Deafy's hand represented the old black color of victory. The mark on the left hand was the fainter of the two. It showed the defeat of Germany. The darker mark on the right hand showed that Japan soon would be beaten. The two appearances of the horseman were symbols of victory. The rider and child represented safety for the American people—both old and young.

[13] See chapter 27, "The Sacred Arrows Come North"; Cf. Sturgis *Tribune*, September 13, 1945.

[14] This account is from Deafy's son, to the author, during the 1961 Sun Dance.

Cf. "Lame Deer Indians Fast, Pray for Peace on South Dakota Mountain," *The Billings Gazette*, October 8, 1950.

419

Again camp was made at the foot of the Sacred Mountain. The fasters' bodies were painted yellow, and they offered the pipe to the Sacred Persons and to Maheo. Deafy and his son climbed up the mountain. They were carrying their pipes and about seventy-five offering cloths—gifts from the Cheyennes who were not able to come.

The men fasted for two days. Each morning and evening they offered their pipes to Maheo and the Sacred Persons. The cloths also were offered above and to the four directions. Then the men tied them to the stunted trees and bushes growing around them. They first tied a loose knot in each cloth, offering a prayer as they did so. After that, a second knot was tied and pulled tight. This was a prayer for long life for the person who had sent the offering cloth.

While Deafy and his son lay fasting, they were stretched out upon beds of white sage. They were permitted to lie face up or face down, but they had to keep the position all day long. At morning and at nightfall, they sat up long enough to offer the pipe to Maheo and the Maheyuno. They were praying continually; for the soldiers in Korea, for the Cheyennes in the hospital, for the boys in the penitentiary, and for all the Cheyenne people.

Once, while Deafy was praying with the pipe, a bird sat nearby. Deafy told his son that this was a Maiyun who had come to listen. Then the bird flew down into the side of Nowah'wus, into the entrance to the Sacred Mountain itself.

There was no vision this time. However, Deafy's son who was fighting in Korea returned, and so did the other Cheyenne soldiers.

In June, 1951, Whistling Elk again instructed fasters on the Sacred Mountain. Again four men came with him. Albert Tall Bull and Bert Two Moon had fasted there before. Charles White Dirt and Willis Medicine Bull had come to fast there for the first time. They were coming to fast for peace.

On June 7, the four men stripped to their breechclouts and

420

Whistling Elk painted them. Wrapped in their robes, with pipes in their hands, they climbed Nowah'wus to begin their fast. They stayed there without food or water four days. At the foot of the mountain, some forty of the people watched and prayed.

When the fasters came down, Whistling Elk again listened to their experiences. Two Moon had seen a vision of many people. White Dirt said that a blue cloud and blue flame had appeared before him. Albert Tall Bull said that while he was listening to a Maiyun's voice, his partner coughed and he missed the message. Medicine Bull did not see a vision, but he left the mountain with a good feeling. However, after he returned to Birney, he dreamed that the war talk would go on, but the war itself gradually would go away. "I did not hear a voice. But it came to my mind in a dream afterward," he said.[15]

Whistling Elk's interpretation of the fasters' experiences was that the Korean War would end before four months had passed or before the snow would fall.[16]

Throughout later years, Whistling Elk's reputation as a priest had grown among the Northern Cheyennes. It was he who instructed many of the men who offered a solitary sacrifice of their bodies in the pine hills. He was the man to whom the fasters on the Sacred Mountain first carried the pipe. He was a Sun Dance priest; and younger priests often asked his guidance during the Medicine Lodge ceremonies. He and his family were prominent Crazy Dogs. The Cheyennes also respected him for his understanding of the animals, birds, and natural forces.

Old Brady was Whistling Elk's father. During the long years of government suppression of the sacred ways, Brady often spoke longingly of Nowah'wus. "When I die, I am going to the Sacred Mountain. I am going to be a servant there," the old warrior told his family. Brady was over ninety-five years old when

---

15 Willis Medicine Bull to the author, 1961.

16 *Ibid.* Whistling Elk's prediction was announced to the United States forces in Korea via a headline in *The Stars and Stripes*. The headline said: WAR END? UGH!" Sturgis *Tribune*, July 5, 1951.

he died in 1936.[17] Whistling Elk himself died in 1958. It is said that Whistling Elk, the man who once stood against Thunder, joined his father in fulfilling that wish to return to the Sacred Mountain.

When Mike Little Wolf and George Elk Shoulder vowed to fast on Nowah'wus in 1961, they carried the pipe to Willis Medicine Bull. The long-haired Medicine Bull was a Sun Dance instructor, and, as a young man, he had taken part in the Contrary dances. He was respected as a man of good disposition, one who possessed power in the sacred ways.

Their ascent of Nowah'wus was a quiet one.[18] One of the men carried the buffalo skull, as well as sage and a pipe. They paused part way up the mountain. There Medicine Bull filled the pipe and offered it. He called upon the Sacred Powers, begging their blessings upon the two men who had vowed this fast. He asked the Maiyun to bless the families of Little Wolf and Elk Shoulder, and to give them good health. Then he prayed for all people, including the white people. "Now we beg you Powers to renew all the things that have been almost forgotten, through these men who are going to fast. Carry them through the next four days," he begged.

Medicine Bull painted the two men with the yellow paint. He told them to keep in mind the purpose of their fast, the bringing of blessings to the Cheyenne people and to their own immediate relatives. "Fill the pipe. Offer it to Maheo and to Sweet Medicine," he told Little Wolf and Elk Shoulder. Then the two men moved on up the Sacred Mountain.

Shortly after sunrise of the fourth day, Medicine Bull heard a whistling sound. He looked up and saw something coming down like a bullet. It was a swift hawk. "I told them that this was the power that they had asked for through four days and nights. Both of them felt good. After they got through the cere-

[17] Henry Tall Bull, grandson of Brady, to the author, 1961.
[18] This account is from Willis Medicine Bull to the author, 1961.

monies, they ate and drank and left for Sheridan the same day," Medicine Bull later recounted.

Four years later, in August, 1965, Cheyenne pilgrims again traveled to the Sacred Mountain. This time a new Arrow Keeper was among them. He was James Medicine Elk, a Northerner who had married among the Southern Cheyennes. As a boy he had taken part in the Massaum ceremony in Oklahoma, and the people there respected him as an Arrow Lodge priest. He had been chosen Keeper several years before.

Jay Black Kettle's eyesight had been growing bad. Finally, in 1962, he had asked the Southern Chiefs and military leaders to choose a new Keeper.[19] Again there was trouble finding a man. The Chiefs had offered the position to three persons, and each had refused it. James Medicine Elk and his family had cared for Jay Black Kettle during the past several years and Medicine Elk told the Chiefs that he would care for Mahuts until they found a permanent Keeper.

Again there had been rumors, this time that Mahuts were to be placed in a museum in Oklahoma City. This news disturbed Medicine Elk. One Sunday morning he said to his wife Jennie and to her sister, Bertha Little Coyote,

> You are women, but I will tell you this: I am taking this tipi this fine morning. I will be the Keeper. I love this sacred way, and I don't want Mahuts to be put in a museum. They were brought to us from the Sacred Mountain, and we should take care of them.
>
> I am from the north, but they belong to you Southerners. I say this: I love you all. I feel I am one of you now. I have a family here.
>
> . . . I want everybody to be happy and well, for I will be Keeper now. I will go inside [the sacred tipi], make a fire and smoke the pipe.

The women cried a little when they heard that. Their tears were part joy, part sorrow. The Arrow Keeper must stay home always—he can no longer go out to work. Now Jennie Medicine Elk was worried about how they would live. However, Bertha

[19] James Medicine Elk to the author, March 1967.

423

Little Coyote comforted her. She said to her brother-in-law, "I am happy over it. I am sure the Almighty can see that you know what you are doing, and that you will never be without food."

Medicine Elk vowed that someday he would go to the Sacred Mountain. "I will report that I look after this tipi, and I will tell our Grandfathers [the Sacred Powers] that I am Keeper," he told the women.

In June, 1965, Medicine Elk had traveled north to Lame Deer in an attempt to get his claims funds there. Jay Black guarded the Arrows while he was away. One day while Medicine Elk was in Lame Deer, Charles White Dirt called him over to Alex Brady's house. Alex was Whistling Elk's youngest brother. The two men told the Keeper that they were going to fast on No-wah'wus. Medicine Elk replied that he would be happy to go with them, so he could fulfill his promise to report to the Grandfathers there.

However, no date was set for the fast, and Medicine Elk finally returned to Oklahoma. Late in August, he received word from Sturgis that the Cheyennes were going to fast on the Sacred Mountain soon. When he heard that, the Arrow Keeper, his wife, and his sister-in-law hurried back to Lame Deer. There Mike Little Wolf told Medicine Elk what he would need in the way of preparations for the fast, and he offered to supply the Keeper with everything necessary for fulfilling his vow.

They reached the Sacred Mountain late in the afternoon of August 26. Willis Medicine Bull had been chosen the chief instructor by the Northern Cheyennes. Mike Little Wolf and George Elk Shoulder were assisting him. Albert Tall Bull had joined the Keeper, White Dirt, and Brady, making four fasters, the sacred number. Brady's nephew, Henry Tall Bull, came along to interpret. So did Sam Buffalo, the Southern Cheyenne leader who assisted in returning Mahuts to Oklahoma in 1957. There were some forty Cheyennes altogether. Most of them camped in a ravine near the foot of the butte, with the Northern and Southern people in separate camps.

Medicine Bull asked the Arrow Keeper to take the lead. As the sun lay low over the Sacred Mountain, the four fasters, their families, and the instructors started up the southern face of Nowah'wus. They stopped on a small knoll. Medicine Elk and his companions spread their robes upon beds of white "man" sage. The fasters stripped to their breechclouts, and Medicine Bull, Little Wolf, and Elk Shoulder began to paint their bodies yellow.[20] Mike Little Wolf painted the Arrow Keeper first, and took care of him throughout the preparations for the ascent. Medicine Bull painted Brady and Tall Bull. George Elk Shoulder painted White Dirt. After the yellow paint had been rubbed on, the Sun symbol was painted on each faster's chest, and the Moon symbol on each man's right shoulder blade. A dark lightning mark was traced around each faster's face, and a lizard was painted on either side of each man's nose. This design represented the Maiyun who takes the form of this tiny reptile, which has great power to resist the elements.

Medicine Bull prepared the buffalo skull, the sacred symbol of Is'siwun's presence among the people. He offered the prayers, made the four forward motions, and moved the skull so that it faced where the fasters would rest. Now Is'siwun would be watching them, and blessing them in their sacrifice.

The priests and fasters seated themselves in a half-circle around the buffalo head. A cold wind was rising, and the four men pulled their blankets around them. The pipe was filled and offered. Prayers were offered to Maheo and to the Sacred Persons at the four directions. Medicine Bull rested the pipe bowl upon the earth, while the Arrow Keeper and his three companions inhaled smoke from it four times. The fasters made the purifying gestures, covering their limbs, bodies, and heads with smoke from the pipe that never fails to bring a blessing. Then the pipe was passed around the half-circle four times.

While these ceremonies continued, the other Cheyennes stood looking on from a respectful distance. When the smoking ended,

---

[20] These details are from James Medicine Elk and Sam Buffalo to the author, 1965. Also, *Rapid City Daily Journal*, August 27, 1965; *Black Hills Press* (Sturgis), August 28, 1965; Sturgis *Tribune*, September 1, 1965.

425

the relatives returned to the camp below. A number of Sioux families had driven up from Rapid City to join their old-time allies in the prayers and waiting. White spectators also were looking on. On the side of the Sacred Mountain above them, the Arrow Keeper and his companions were beginning their fast. They were praying for peace in Vietnam, for all the Cheyenne people, and for the nation as a whole. Henry Tall Bull had said, "We all realize the seriousness of the war, and this is our way of helping."

The third night, the men had offered the pipes, smoked, and gone to bed. Medicine Elk was lying there in the darkness, thinking. It was very quiet, and he thought that he was the only one who was awake. Then a voice spoke from the head of his bed, from the north. It sounded like the voice of an older man. "You are going to get blessings," the voice said. Just then White Dirt spoke, and the Arrow Keeper did not hear any more. Then Medicine Elk sat up and loaded his pipe. He wept as he sat there praying.[21]

Shortly after sunrise of the fourth day, Willis Medicine Bull led the fasters down from the mountain. It was Sunday, August 29. They reached the bottom at about the same time astronauts Gordon Cooper and Charles Conrad came back to earth from outer space.[22] Mike Little Wolf removed the Arrow Keeper's paint with sacred sage. Medicine Bull and Elk Shoulder did the same for the other men. Each man first was given his four mouthfuls of water, with an interval between each drink. Jennie Medicine Elk and Bertha Little Coyote had prepared food for the Arrow Keeper. The relatives of the other men had done the same. Mike Little Wolf offered the first food to the Sacred Persons and to Maheo for Medicine Elk. Then the Keeper ate, and the other men broke their fast at the same time.

That afternoon a public program was held in honor of the Cheyennes. Richard B. Williams, the interpretive specialist at

[21] James Medicine Elk to the author, March 1967.
[22] This observation by Richard B. Williams, the interpretive specialist at Bear Butte State Park. He had long assisted the Cheyennes during their pilgrimages to the Sacred Mountain.

Bear Butte State Park, introduced the fasters and instructors to a crowd of both Indians and whites.

Henry Tall Bull told the crowd that the four men had related their experiences to Medicine Bull, and that it would take some time before the experiences could be properly interpreted. "They came here to pray for peace, not by guided missiles, but by guided men," he said. "The medicine man told me to withhold a prediction at this time as their dreams or visions will be explained at a later date. It takes time to interpret their meaning. . . ."[23]

For those who climb Nowah'wus, glimpses of the Cheyenne past still lie all around. A man can look out to where the horizon seems to begin. The prairie colors flow toward the four directions where the Sacred Persons dwell. In late August the greens, blues, yellows, and browns of summer are tinted by the shades of the autumn that comes early in the north country. The old Cheyenne sites lie below. The remains of the eagle-catching pit were there when Medicine Elk fasted on Nowah'wus. So was the spring from which the people once dug blue clay—the clay used to paint the old-time parfleches which, like so many other beautiful objects, perished in the fires of Morning Star's burning camp. Much of Cheyenne history still can be traced around the Sacred Mountain, if a man knows where to look.

Today there are new sights that mingle with the old. Now the Cheyennes can see the impression of a narrow trail that stretches around much of the base of the Sacred Mountain. Now, to the north, the west, and the northeast, Minuteman missiles lie hidden beneath the earth. Their wires encircle Nowah'wus, the ancient source of new life for the Cheyenne people.

Henry Tall Bull has spoken of the messages that still reach Cheyennes who have the ears to listen:

The Above Powers have sent a sign from the Sacred Mountain saying that someone must return there. There are three or four men who have the feeling they should go.

They are going to get another thing from there—something

23 Sturgis *Tribune*, September 1, 1965.

427

that will save the Cheyennes from this new destructive power the white people have developed.

Whistling Elk used to be the man who made the pilgrimages. Now he is gone. Now the people feel it is necessary for someone to go back. They feel that time is an important factor now.

Someone is being selected who has a lot of faith . . . .[24]

In their first ancient days of despair, Maheo sent his People the Sacred Arrows that, for some of them at least, remain the soul of Cheyenne tribal existence. Since then, in nearly every generation the Cheyennes have known that someone must return to Nowah'wus; someone must represent the People on the wind-blown sides of the Sacred Mountain. For power in abundance awaits the Cheyennes there; strength like the power flowing from Mahuts themselves.

Blessed by the Sacred Arrows, the Sacred Buffalo Hat, and the strength that pours from Nowah'wus, the Sacred Mountain, all will be well for Maheo's People, even in the strange new days that lie ahead.

[24] To the author, August 1959; repeated in August, 1969.